DELIVERING COLLECTIVE REDRESS:
NEW TECHNOLOGIES

This book charts the transformative shifts in techniques that seek to deliver collective redress, especially for mass consumer claims in Europe. It shows how traditional approaches of class litigation (old technology) have been eclipsed by the new technology of regulatory redress techniques and consumer ombudsmen. It describes a series of these techniques, each illustrated by leading examples taken from a 2016 pan-EU research project. It then undertakes a comparative evaluation of each technique against key criteria, such as effective outcomes, speed, and cost. The book reveals major transformations in European legal systems, shows the overriding need to view legal systems from fresh viewpoints, and to devise a new integrated model.

Volume 7 in the series Civil Justice Systems

Civil Justice Systems

Series General Editor: Christopher Hodges, Director, Swiss Re Research Programme, Centre for Socio-Legal Studies, University of Oxford

This series covers new theoretical and empirical research on the mechanisms for resolution of civil disputes, including courts, tribunals, arbitration, compensation schemes, ombudsmen, codes of practice, complaint mechanisms, mediation and various forms of Alternative Dispute Resolution. It examines frameworks for dispute resolution that comprise combinations of the above mechanisms, and the parameters and conditions for selecting certain types of techniques and procedures rather than others. It also evaluates individual techniques, against parameters such as cost, duration, accessibility, and delivery of desired outcomes, and illuminates how legal rights and obligations are operated in practice.

Volume 1: *The Costs and Funding of Civil Litigation: A Comparative Perspective*
edited by Christopher Hodges, Stefan Vogenauer and Magdalena Tulibacka

Volume 2: *Consumer ADR in Europe*
Christopher Hodges, Iris Benöhr and Naomi Creutzfeldt-Banda

Volume 3: *Law and Corporate Behaviour: Integrating Theories of Regulation, Enforcement, Compliance and Ethics*
Christopher Hodges

Volume 4: *A Comparative Examination of Multi-Party Actions*
Joanne Blennerhassett

Volume 5: *Redress Schemes for Personal Injuries*
Sonia Macleod and Christopher Hodges

Volume 6: *Ethical Business Practice and Regulation: A Behavioural and Values-Based Approach to Compliance and Enforcement*
Christopher Hodges and Ruth Steinholtz

Volume 7: *Delivering Collective Redress: New Technologies*
Christopher Hodges and Stefaan Voet

Delivering Collective Redress: New Technologies

Christopher Hodges

Professor of Justice Systems at the University of Oxford
Supernumerary Fellow, Wolfson College, Oxford
Head of the Swiss Re Research Programme on Civil Justice Systems,
Centre for Socio-Legal Studies, Oxford
Fellow of the European Law Institute
Solicitor (non-practising)

Stefaan Voet

Associate Professor of Law at KU Leuven (University of Leuven)
Visiting Professor of Law at UHasselt (University of Hasselt)
Programme Affiliate of the Swiss Re Research Programme
on Civil Justice Systems,
Centre for Socio-Legal Studies, Oxford
Substitute Justice of the Peace, Bruges

·HART·
OXFORD · LONDON · NEW YORK · NEW DELHI · SYDNEY

HART PUBLISHING

Bloomsbury Publishing Plc

Kemp House, Chawley Park, Cumnor Hill, Oxford, OX2 9PH, UK

HART PUBLISHING, the Hart/Stag logo, BLOOMSBURY and the Diana logo are
trademarks of Bloomsbury Publishing Plc

First published in Great Britain 2018

A catalogue record for this book is available from the British Library.

Library of Congress Cataloging-in-Publication data

Names: Hodges, Christopher J. S., author. | Voet, Stefaan, author.

Title: Delivering collective redress : new technologies / Christopher Hodges, Professor of Justice Systems
at the University of Oxford, Supernumerary Fellow, Wolfson College, Oxford, Head of the Swiss Re
Research Programme on Civil Justice Systems, Centre for Socio-Legal Studies, Oxford, Fellow of the
European Law Institute, Solicitor (non-practising) Stefaan Voet, Associate Professor of Law at
KU Leuven (University of Leuven), Visiting Professor of Law at UHasselt (University of Hasselt),
Programme Affiliate of the Swiss Re Research Programme on Civil Justice Systems,
Centre for Socio-Legal Studies, Oxford, Substitute Justice of the Peace, Bruges.

Description: Portland, Oregon : Hart Publishing, 2018. | Series: Civil justice systems ; volume 7 |
Includes bibliographical references and index.

Identifiers: LCCN 2018006875 (print) | LCCN 2018007602 (ebook) |
ISBN 9781509918560 (Epub) | ISBN 9781509918546 (hardback : alk. paper)

Subjects: LCSH: Class actions (Civil procedure)—European Union countries. | Citizen suits (Civil procedure)—
European Union countries. | Class actions (Civil procedure). | Citizen suits (Civil procedure). |
Technological innovations.

Classification: LCC KJE3846.5 (ebook) | LCC KJE3846.5 .H63 2018 (print) | DDC 347.4/053—dc23

LC record available at https://lccn.loc.gov/2018006875

ISBN: HB: 978-1-50991-854-6 (Hart)
       HB: 978-3-406-72832-7 (Beck)
       HB: 978-3-8487-5063-4 (Nomos)
       ePDF: 978-1-50991-855-3
       ePub: 978-1-50991-856-0

Typeset by Compuscript Ltd, Shannon
Printed and bound in Great Britain by CPI Group (UK) Ltd, Croydon CR0 4YY

To find out more about our authors and books visit www.hartpublishing.co.uk.
Here you will find extracts, author information, details of forthcoming events
and the option to sign up for our newsletters.

ACKNOWLEDGEMENTS

This book summarises the findings of a joint project between the Centre for Socio-Legal Studies, Oxford University and the Catholic University of Leuven aimed at evaluating different mechanisms for delivering collective redress. The editors warmly than the following colleagues who contributed to this project.

The national contributors were:

Belgium: Prof Dr Stefaan Voet and Pieter Gillaerts, KU Leuven

Bulgaria: Zsolt Okanyi and colleagues, CMS Cameron McKenna Nabarro Olswang LLP Magyarországi Fióktelepe

Finland: Johan Pråhl, HPP Attorneys Ltd

France: Dr Alexandre Biard, Erasmus University and Dr Rafael Amaro, Université Paris Descartes

Germany: Prof Dr Astrid Stadler, University of Konstanz (written report)

Italy: Daniele Vecchi, Gianni Origone Grippo Cappelli & Partners (and written report from Prof Dr Elisabetta Silvestri, University of Pavia)

Poland: Dr Magdalena Tulibacka, Emory University School of Law

Spain: Alejandro Ferreres, Uría Menéndez

Sweden: Peder Hammerskiold/Andreas Joersjo, Hammarskiold & Co

United Kingdom: Prof Dr Christopher Hodges, Oxford University; Caroline Mitchell, Financial Ombudsman Service; Matthew Vickers, Ombudsman Services

The expert commentators were:

Robert Bray, Head of the Secretariat of the Legal Affairs Committee of the European Parliament

Jacek Garstka, DG Justice, European Commission

Dr Lorenz Ködderitzsch, Assistant General Counsel, Johnson & Johnson

Augusta Maciuleviciute, BEUC

Prof Dr Hans-W Micklitz, Professor of Economic Law, European University Institute, Florence

Prof Dr Linda Mullenix, Rita and Morris Atlas Chair in Advocacy, University of Texas

Dr Rebecca Mooney, Oxford University

Robin Simpson, Consumers International

Diana Wallis, President, European Law Institute

We would like to thank most warmly all of the national reporters, and also the expert commentators, for their contributions to this project. We also thank others who have contributed further information since the conference:

Magda Bianco, Banca d'Italia

Marielle Cohen-Branche, Le Médiateur, Autorité des Marchés Financiers (AMF), France

Michele Passaro and Roberto Malaman, AEEGSI

Eline Verhage, Leiden University, the Netherlands

Dr Herbert Woopen, Germany

The names of individuals listed above who have contributed particular text to this book are listed above relevant sections.

This project would not have been possible without sponsorship by the Centre for Socio-Legal Studies, University of Oxford and the Catholic University of Leuven, and sponsorship of the conference from Swiss Re, and the Foundation for Law Society and Justice. Research funding for the Swiss Re Research Programme in Civil Justice at the Centre for Socio-Legal Studies has been from the Swiss Reinsurance Company, the European Justice Forum, and the international law firm CMS. To all of those, we are extremely grateful.

We also thank our research assistants for excellent support: Pieter Gillaerts and Harriet Harper.

TABLE OF CONTENTS

LIST OF ABBREVIATIONS

ABF	Arbitro Bancario Finanziario (Italy)
ABTA	Association of British Travel Agents
ADR	Alternative Dispute Resolution
AEEGSI	Regulatory Authority for Electricity Gas and Water (Italy)
AGCM	Autorità Garante della Concorrenza e del mercato (Italian Competition Authority)
ATM	automatic telling machine
B2C	Business to Consumer
BEUC	European Consumer Organisation
CAT	Competition Appeal Tribunal (UK)
CJEU or ECJ	Court of Justice of the European Union
CCOIC	China Chamber of International Commerce
CIVI	Commission d'indemnisation des victimes d'infractions (France)
CMC	Case Management Conference
CNL	Confédération Nationale du Logement (France)
COJEF	Consumer Justice Enforcement Forum
CPAs	Continuous payment authorities
CPC	Commission for Protection of Consumers (Bulgaria)
CPC Regulation	Regulation (EC) 2006/2004 on consumer protection cooperation, replaced by Regulation (EU) 2017/2394 on cooperation between national authorities responsible for the enforcement of consumer protection laws and repealing Regulation (EC) No 2006/2004
CMA	Competition and Markets Authority (UK)
CMC	Claims management company
CRA	Consumer Rights Act 2015 (UK)
CREG	Commission for the Regulation of Electricity and gas (Belgium)
DKK	Danish Krone
ECC-NET	The EU Network of European Consumer Centres
EU	The European Union
FCA	Financial Conduct Authority (UK)
FIN-NET	The EU Network of Financial ADR bodies
FGA	Fonds de garantie automobile (France)
FGTI	Fund for acts of terrorism committed on the French territory (France)
FOS	Financial Ombudsman Service (UK)
FSA	Food Standards Authority (UK) or (pre 2010) Financial Standards Authority
FSMA	Financial Services and Markets Authority (Belgium)
GAR	Guaranteed annuity rates

GLO	Group Litigation Order (England & Wales)
GRG	Global Restructuring Group (of RBS)
HIV	Human immunodeficiency virus
IHRPs	Interest rate hedging products
ILR	The US Chamber's Institute for Legal Reform
IVASS	Insurance Supervisory Authority (Italy)
JIHMO	Jyske Invest Hedge Markedsneutral-Obligationer (Denmark)
KapMuG	Kapitalanleger-Musterverfahrensgesetz (Germany)
LSC	Legal Services Commission (UK)
MEP	Member of the European Parliament
MMR	Measles, mumps and rubella
NCA	National Competent Authority
NAO	National Audit Office (UK)
OECD	Organisation for Economic Cooperation and Development
Ofcom	Office of Communications
Ofgem	Office of Gas and Electricity Markets
OFT	Office of Fair Trading (later replaced by the CMA)
Ofwat	Office of Water Regulation (UK)
ONIAM	Office National d'Indemnisation des Accidents Médicaux, des Affections Iatrogènes et des Infections Nosocomiales (France)
ORR	Office of Rail Regulation (UK)
OS	Ombudsman Services (UK)
QOCS	Qualified one-way cost shift
PLN	Polish złoty
PPI	Payment protection insurance
RBS	Royal Bank of Scotland
RCV	Regulated capital value
RESA	Regulatory Enforcement and Sanctions Act 2008 (UK)
SEK	Swedish Krone
SME	Small and Medium-sized Enterprise
TFEU	Treaty on the Functioning of the European Union
TPLF	Third party litigation funding
UK	The United Kingdom of Great Britain and Northern Ireland
US and USA	The United States of America
VZBV	Verbraucherzentrale Bundesverband (Germany)
WBZ	Wettbewerbszentrale (Germany)

1

Introduction: The Scope and the Criteria

I. Background and Principal Objective

This book summarises the findings of a joint project between the Centre for Socio-Legal Studies, Oxford University and the Catholic University of Leuven aimed at evaluating the empirical evidence on different mechanisms for delivering collective redress.

The project records a major paradigm shift in debates on collective redress. Traditional debates on collective redress have assumed that the only available mechanism is the court-based civil procedure mechanism of some form of collective action. That assumption has given rise to fierce political debate over the advantages and disadvantages of such civil procedure mechanisms, whether in their guise of US-style class actions or EU-style collective-actions-with-safeguards-against-abuse. The political divide can too easily be characterised, and possibly caricatured, as, on one hand, consumer advocates arguing for collective actions in order to achieve redress for multiple small claims that could otherwise not be brought (because of inherent failures in court systems and their associated funding and costs arrangements) and, on the other hand, business interests arguing against collective actions because they give rise to blackmail through unmeritorious cases with massive financial implications, brought by intermediaries who have conflicts of interest and who seek unfair personal benefit at the expense of both consumers and businesses. That sharp categorisation is subject to significant caveats on both sides, but it is not the purpose of this project to analyse such matters further.

This study is based on the realisation that new techniques other than traditional civil procedure mechanisms are available to deliver collective redress. Indeed, the authors continue to discover more examples of such techniques in more Member States. Given the availability of several options, the opportunity arises to undertake a comparative evaluation of the options. This is the principal aim of this study. We seek to answer the question: *How do the various techniques compare in terms of objective criteria as mechanisms for (effectively and efficiently) delivering collective redress?*

II. The Techniques

We identify four principal 'technologies':

— *the collective action*: a representative or non-representative action brought by a group representative acting on behalf of a group of persons who are confronted with the same or similar legal and/or factual issues;

— *civil claims piggy-backing on criminal prosecutions* (known as *parties civil* in some jurisdictions);
— *regulatory redress*: redress ordered or brought about by the intervention of public enforcers;[1]
— *consumer ombudsmen*: a specific form of alternative dispute resolution (ADR) but within the context of a dispute resolution structure that is entirely separate from the courts.

More details of these mechanisms will follow in the relevant chapters below. Almost all of the discussions on each technique have taken place in individual silos, without recognition—and usually without realisation or acknowledgement—that any of the other techniques exist. Hence, this is the first major empirical study to undertake a comprehensive evaluation of the major available techniques for collective redress, and it is intended to inform policy-making at EU and national levels.

However, it may be helpful to note here that traditional ADR is not an effective collective consumer dispute resolution mechanism. The traditional form involves mediation and/or arbitration of individual claims. That model cannot aggregate claims and resolve them together, unless it is in the context where a mass settlement is voluntarily agreed and then needs to be approved by a court to give *res judicata* binding effect, as under the Dutch system. However, although the Dutch system provides some incentives for mass settlement, there is no compulsion for the parties to enter into discussions or agree settlements. The cases that have been processed by the Dutch system are typically ones where both sides wished to achieve a *global* settlement, following on from a US class action, and needed to use a non-US jurisdiction that was amenable to approving agreements where many parties might not be locally resident.

The Consumer Ombudsman mechanism that we refer to here is a specific form of ADR body. It is the ADR form that is capable of aggregating individual cases, and data from cases, and feeding it back into regulatory and compliance systems. The Consumer Ombudsman model that we refer to here is:

(a)   an ADR entity that is independent of businesses, trade associations or consumer associations,
(b)   usually created by statute or a not-for-profit company,
(c)   whose dispute resolution process typically involves the following stages in sequence: triage, assisted negotiation between the parties (mediation), a decision that is either legally binding on the trader (but not usually the consumer) or non-legally binding but in practice having strongly persuasive effect,
(d)   free to consumers,
(e)   funded by traders either through a statutory levy or contractual fees,
(f)   satisfies all the quality requirements of Directive 2013/11/EU, articles 5–12,
(g)   publishes and feeds back data on cases to support improvements in trading and market behaviour, not identifying individual consumers.

---

[1] Regulatory redress powers may be diverse: the mechanism and a typology are at C Hodges, 'Mass Collective Redress: Consumer ADR and Regulatory Techniques' (2015) 5 *European Review of Private Law* 829.

The Consumer Ombudsman model exists in some Member States in some regulated sectors, working closely with sectoral regulators, such as a Financial Ombudsman, Energy Ombudsman, Communications Ombudsman and so on. Other forms of ADR bodies, especially ADR schemes that decide individual decisions in arbitration-like processes, do not generally have the capacity to aggregate individual claims and decide them collectively, as most Ombudsman schemes do. ADR bodies should migrate from models of individual arbitration to this ombudsman model. Thus, both sectoral legislation that requires ADR, and the generic consumer ADR legislation,[2] should specify that consumer ombudsmen models should be required, rather than other types of general ADR.

It is important to recognise different types of 'ombudsmen'. In Nordic States, the Consumer Ombudsman is the national enforcement official for consumer law, but does not act as a dispute resolution body between traders and consumer (for which there are separate Complaint Boards). In our classification, redress facilitated by a Nordic Consumer Ombudsman squarely falls into the 'regulatory redress' category. In contrast, in the UK, Ireland and Germany, ombudsmen exist to handle consumer–trader disputes (the consumer ADR function) in some individual sectors, such as financial services, pensions, energy, communications, and so on. They operate differently from public sector ombudsmen, which exist in most States to investigate citizen–State complaints. In this book, save where otherwise noted, this latter category is referred to as Consumer Ombudsmen.

It should also be noted that a further technique is not evaluated in this study, since it has been noted in related work. Various Member States process personal injury claims through 'no blame' administrative schemes, especially the Nordic states, but other leading examples are France and Poland.[3] These schemes might be viewed as another specific form of ADR. They have notable advantages in terms of the criteria noted above, as noted in the related study.

III. Description of the Project and Methodology

This project was developed from earlier work surrounding a conference held at Rüschlikon, Zurich in January 2012. The current updated project was timed to contribute to the review in 2017 of the European Commission's Recommendation relating to collective redress.[4]

The first stage of the project was to obtain national reports on a wide range of European States by colleagues in those jurisdictions. The national reports gave short summaries of the relevant legislative schemes for different mechanisms used to deliver collective redress, and various metrics, but also case studies on significant cases. The second stage was to discuss the results at an international conference in Oxford on 12–14 December 2016 attended by around 50 officials, scholars and practitioners.

---

[2] Directive 2013/11 of 21 May 2013 on Alternative Dispute Resolution for Consumer Disputes.

[3] See S Macleod and C Hodges, *Redress Schemes for Personal Injuries* (Oxford, Hart Publishing, 2017).

[4] Recommendation 2013/396 of the European Commission of 11 June 2013 on Common Principles for Injunctive and Compensatory Collective Redress Mechanisms in the Member States Concerning Violations of Rights granted under Union Law (2013 OJ (L 206) 60 (EU)).

The conference firmly succeeded in achieving these criteria. National reports were kindly submitted by colleagues across Europe, ranging from scholars, officials and lawyers. In each country, contributors were selected primarily on the basis of being known to the two organisers as experts in the field and—crucially—as being able to identify empirical evidence on the state of national mechanisms (as opposed to theoretical or legal issues) within a limited period of time. National reports were made available on the conference website of the Centre for Socio-Legal Studies, Oxford.[5] At the conference, contributors also presented abbreviated summaries of their national reports, and distinguished experts commented on the materials and conclusions.

The dataset at that stage comprised information on redress cases in around 80 class actions, four piggy-back cases, over 24 ombudsman cases, and at least 24 regulatory cases. There was a further 17 injunctions (non-damages-redress) cases, and 21 mixed cases identified by the European Consumer Organisation (BEUC) and the Consumer Justice Enforcement Forum (COJEF).[6]

The third stage of the project is to present the data in book form, together with analysis and conclusions for policy development on collective redress. In presenting in this book the different techniques and the mass of empirical evidence in a coherent fashion, the authors concluded that it would clearly be preferable for them to write a single unified text together, editing a mass of material into a consistent narrative, and to ask the contributors to check and update their contributions. The alternative of repeating the format of the conference, with a series of national reports, would be far less coherent in identifying and evaluating the basic groups of techniques that are identified here. We have sent our draft text to national reporters to check and update how we have organised the information from their contributions, and all have most kindly agreed to this method of presentation.

IV. Criteria for Evaluation of Mechanisms

Having identified a number of different mechanisms for delivering collective redress, the question arises of how they should be comparatively evaluated. Such comparative evaluation should be against a set of objective criteria.

Many may seek to evaluate collective redress systems against the sole objective of redress, ie the delivery of monetary compensation or rectification of harm. The analysis may even be restricted to the *access* or commencement of a process that has that objective, rather than

---

[5] The National Reports and conference presentations are available at https://www.law.ox.ac.uk/events/empirical-evidence-collective-redress-europe

[6] *Collective Redress. Where & how it works* (BEUC, 2012), http://www.beuc.eu/publications/2012-00308-01-e.pdf; *Guidelines for enforcement on consumer rights*, Consumer Justice Enforcement Forum, May 2013, available at http://www.cojef-project.eu/IMG/pdf/Conclusions_document_cases__FINAL_8_May.pdf; *Enforcement of Consumer Rights: Strategies and Recommendations* (COJEF II, 2016), http://www.beuc.eu/publications/beuc-x-2016-051_cojef_ii-enforcement_of_consumer_rights.pdf.

including an assessment of the critical outcome of the extent to which it is *achieved*. It is, however, well recognised that systems can fail to deliver the redress sought, to some degree or even at all. It is also recognised that systems can involve disadvantages, such as cost and delay.

We believe that contemporary society requires more than systems that perform poorly. People also expect a number of outcomes and adequate performance. Indeed, the importance of certain criteria are illuminated if we consider the viewpoints of different societal and market actors, such as consumers, traders and regulators—a multiple users' perspective.

Consumers may value an outcome in which they are repaid sums lost but, especially if that outcome involves too much cost, delay, investment of time and a modest return, the far more important objective may be that the trader who owes the money should change behaviour—stop the breach, not repeat it, and behave fairly. The same point is highly important from the market perspective. Regulators, competitors and customers would wish that traders behave well, not only in observing the norms of fair trading whilst selling, but also if responding to challenge. Honest traders who have broken rules and who understand the need to make redress should seek effective, speedy and efficient ways of achieving that outcome.

In other words, a number of outcomes and performance criteria are relevant to mechanisms of collective redress. In this study, we have adopted the following criteria:

1. *Advice.* To what extent does the mechanism enable consumers to access advice before or during the processing of their complaint? To what extent also does the system provide advice to traders, especially small traders who may not be familiar with the law or dispute resolution options or processes, so as to achieve swift, cost-effective and fair resolutions?
2. *Identification of infringement and harm.* How is it that a problem involving breach of law and/or damage has occurred is identified?
3. *Identification of people harmed and due redress.* Must individuals come forward, or can they be identified without coming forward?
4. *Access.* To what extent is the mechanism user-friendly for consumers or claimants to access?
5. *Cost to access.* What cost must a person who claims to have suffered harm pay, and fund, in order to access the process? Or is access free?
6. *Triage.* To what extent does the mechanism act as a triage to prevent unmeritorious cases or unnecessary cases proceeding further? This may include, at one extreme, preventing fraudulent claims being advanced and, at the other extreme, to swiftly resolving cases that should be resolved one way or the other?
7. *Duration.* How long does the mechanism take from start to conclusion (including possible appeal and enforcement proceedings)? How long does it take to resolve issues, from when they first arose (ie when damage occurred, before a claim was made) to final resolution?
8. *Costs.* How much are the gross transactional costs, and the standing costs of a process? Who bears the costs, both initially, and finally?
9. *Outcomes.* What is achieved? Are the outcomes the ones desired by the parties, the law, or society?

10. *Compensation for loss: making whole.* Is a person who has suffered harm fully recompensed? How much of an award is lost in transactional costs, eg of intermediaries? Are extra emotional or other costs incurred and recompensed?
11. *Changes in behaviour.* Does the mechanism directly produce changes in systemic behaviour that reduces the incidence or future risk of non-compliance with the law? To what extent does the mechanism, therefore, act as a regulatory mechanism?

These criteria are discussed further in chapter 9.

V. General Outline of this Book

Chapter 2 sets the scene on the current debates on collective redress in the EU. It notes the piecemeal nature of EU legislation on injunctions, private enforcement and ADR, all developed without a clear policy on either the status and mode of operation of private enforcement or the balance between private end public enforcement in the EU. The position is confused at EU level, with a Commission Recommendation on a model for collective actions to which no Member State adheres. Each of the different models is the result of political compromise on the difficult issue of the balance between affording effective consumer redress and of prevention of abuse by intermediaries. Chapter 2 also notes that the EU's Better Regulation rules require *all* options to be considered and evaluated. To date, this requirement does not appear to have been observed, since the Commission has only evaluated a litigation option of delivering damages.

Chapters 3 to 6 describe the evidence collected in this project from leading Member States on the four mechanisms: collective actions, civil parties piggy-backing on criminal actions, regulatory redress and consumer ombudsmen. The basic mechanisms are described, and then national reports set out how the mechanisms operate in particular Member States, both in theory and in practice, illustrated by selected case studies. Those chapters do not aim to include reports from a Member State if a particular mechanism appears to be little used. Instead, they concentrate on examples where a mechanism clearly is used. A summary of all the cases that have been identified is at Annex 1.

Chapter 7 looks at the theoretical background to the objectives of collective redress, namely delivering compensation and affecting future behaviour. It notes that the objective of affecting future behaviour is clearer than the idea of deterrence, which has a number of different meanings and is an effect that is disputed by empirical evidence. The effect of imposition of a liability to pay damages under tort law on affecting future behaviour is now strongly disputed, and the empirical evidence for the desired regulatory effect on corporations is far from clear and may be at best highly limited. If that is so, not only do other mechanisms—such as public enforcement of regulation—have to be pursued to deliver effects in future behaviour, but also this opens the possibility for re-examining the mechanisms chosen for delivery of compensation, to see if more efficient means should be prioritised over traditional litigation.

Chapter 8 summarises the findings of this project, and examines the implications for policy and for academic understanding of the changes that have occurred.

VI. Major Findings

A. Empirical Findings

The evidence presented here is clear and conclusive. Some techniques are far better at delivering collective redress than others. The two techniques that far outshine the others are regulatory redress and consumer ombudsmen, especially when they are used together. Collective actions and the piggy-back technique fall some way short of the standard set by the other leading techniques.

B. Changes in the Dispute Resolution Landscape

There have been some significant shifts in mechanisms. First, the EU rejected the US model of maximising private enforcement in favour of a more balanced (public–private) approach involving safeguards.

Second, there has been extensive experimentation by EU Member States in collective action models for damages. The current position would present a huge challenge for harmonisation. There is no coherence in national class action laws, none of which correspond to the European Commission's 2013 blueprint. Each national system is tailored to domestic need, often uninfluenced by the Commission's blueprint, and the overview is of piecemeal development, which is uncontrolled.

Third, there has been a shift in the techniques by which redress is delivered. The 'old technology' of private litigation has been superseded in some Member States by highly effective 'new technology'[7] involving regulators and consumer ombudsmen. These techniques have been approved by UNCTAD, and deserve to be widely adopted.[8]

Fourth, the empirical evidence of this project, which is the first to examine comparatively *all* of the leading mechanisms that deliver collective redress and not just the collective litigation option, clearly shows that the redress and consumer ombudsman models— especially where those two are combined—score far more highly than the collective litigation model across the criteria. The piggy-back technique is a logical development that attempts to sequence public and private enforcement so as to achieve some efficiency of process. But that first step has been eclipsed in efficiency and effectiveness by the two other techniques. Regulatory redress fuses private enforcement entirely into public enforcement. ADR in its traditional forms of arbitration or mediation can only deliver *individual* redress, absent a Dutch-style ability for a court to approve ex post a collective settlement. Consumer ombudsmen are an evolution of ADR in which the intermediary is neither a lawyer nor a judge but a new independent public or quasi-public officer, whose process is highly efficient and affords a seamless conveyor-belt for both sides (in the best models, fusing information,

---

[7] This terminology of old and new technology was first used, to our knowledge, by Derville Rowland of the Central Bank of Ireland at the Law Reform Commission's annual regulatory conference, Dublin, 2016.

[8] Draft *Manual on Consumer Protection* (UNCTAD, 2016), chs 6 and 11, http://unctad.org/en/Publications Library/webditcclp2016d1.pdf.

advice, assisted negotiation and decision). Both the ombudsman model and the regulatory model, especially where they operate in a parallel coordinated fashion, deliver significantly more functions than just dispute resolution, but also act as effective mechanisms to support fair and competitive markets.

The empirical results of this study are so clear that they clearly indicate conclusions for policy in delivering collective redress. They challenge the rationality of a policy that relies on collective actions to deliver collective redress. Other existing models have proved themselves to be effective and the preferred contemporary options. Those models should be adopted as front-line delivery mechanisms.

C. Fundamental Goals of Redress

In the light of this study, various new insights into theory and policy on redress and behaviour arise. We suggest that the fundamental objectives of redress (or payment of compensation through law) are:

1.   To deliver appropriate redress or non-monetary compensation;
2.   To affect the future behaviour of a defendant and of the market generally, and thereby ensure than an unbalanced market is rebalanced so as to be a level playing field;
3.   To achieve both of these goals in the most efficient manner, in terms of speed/duration, costs and finality.

The objective of 'affecting future behaviour' has traditionally been stated as the theory of deterrence, but research by Chris Hodges[9] has shown that: (a) the empirical evidence for deterrence as a means of regulating individual or corporate behaviour is limited; (b) the science of behavioural psychology offers far more effective insights into how to affect future behaviour, through adopting a range of approaches in which most people are supported to achieve performance, as opposed to punished for non-compliance; (c) many UK regulatory agencies have adopted supportive, responsive and often no-fault regulatory policies rather than deterrence-based enforcement policies; and (d) the ideal model appears to be to encourage consistent systemic ethical behaviour, through various approaches that support relationships built on trust (and hence co-regulatory models).[10]

If the above approach has validity, it has fundamental implications for legal systems that are based on principles of fault and deterrence. Their ability to affect future behaviour can be significantly questioned. Equally, this demonstrates why effective regulatory and ombudsmen systems are more effective in affecting behaviour than litigation-based systems. The idea that a single response to a single instance of non-compliance will result in ongoing or systemic change in behaviour, for example, as a result of the imposition of a single financial penalty, is not supported by behavioural or management science.

---

[9] C Hodges, *Law and Corporate Behaviour: Integrating Theories of Regulation and Enforcement* (Oxford, Hart Publishing, 2015).

[10] See the increasing interest and adoption of this approach by governments: C Hodges, *Ethical Business Practice: Understanding the Evidence* (Better Regulation Delivery Office, 2016); C Hodges, 'Ethical Business Regulation: Growing Empirical Evidence' (The Foundation for Law, Justice and Society, 2016) available at: http://www.fljs.org/content/ethical-business-regulation; *Striking the Balance. Upholding the Seven Principles of Public Life in Regulation* (Committee on Standards in Public Life, 2016); *Delivering better outcomes for consumers and businesses in Scotland* (Scottish Government, 2016).

D. The Objectives for Market Regulation

It follows from the above that redress is only one aspect of how markets should be safeguarded and regulated. Public policy has developed swiftly in some Member States in the past 10 years,[11] such that the role of regulators and public enforcers has broadened to move away from merely achieving safety or well-structured and priced markets, to encompass an aspiration to ensure, first, that consumers and vulnerable businesses receive redress as an integral part of a relevelled playing field and, second, that behaviour is effectively changed. Accordingly, the objectives of the most effective regulatory systems run in the following sequence:

1. Establishment of clear rules and their interpretation
2. Identification of individual and systemic problems
3. Decision on whether behaviour is illegal, unfair or acceptable
4. Cessation of illegality
5. Identification of the root cause of the problem and why it occurs
6. Identification of which actions are needed to prevent the reoccurrence of the problematic behaviour, or reduction of the risk
7. Application of the actions (a) by identified actors (b) by other actors
8. Dissemination of information to all (a) firms, (b) consumers, (c) other markets
9. Redress
10. Sanctions
11. Ongoing monitoring, oversight, amendment of the rules

In considering what mechanisms of public and/or private enforcement, either alone or in combination, can deliver these objectives, it can be seen how litigation primarily addresses item 9 alone, whereas the integrated co- and public-regulatory systems and ombudsman systems in some countries are able to address all items.

These considerations help explain why the regulatory intermediaries—regulators and ombudsmen—have emerged and are preferable to lawyers and courts as effective intermediaries. The former intermediaries simply deliver more functions than the latter. The former are all relatively new, and have developed as European markets have been subjected to regulation and harmonisation. In contrast, lawyers and courts have lengthy histories and their models were formed before the new intermediaries appeared. In an earlier age, lawyers and courts were the primary and sometimes only intermediaries, and their tools— private enforcement—therefore had to serve as best they could to provide not only private inter-personal redress but also enforcement of public norms. In contrast, the new regulatory intermediaries have the ability not only to deliver more functions to ensure fair and competitive markets, but also the ability to include redress as one of their wider outputs. It is time to recognise and make full use of the outcomes of these new technologies.

---

[11] By way of example, important milestones in the UK have been RM Macrory, *Regulatory Justice: Making Sanctions Effective* (HM Treasury, 2006); the Regulators' Code 2007 (revised 2013); the Regulatory Enforcement and Sanctions Act 2008.

2

European Policy and Mechanisms for Collective Redress

The chapter gives an overview of the recent evolution, and hence current status, of EU policy on collective redress. Several major themes emerge. First, the EU's approach to enforcement in general, and to the balance between public and private enforcement in particular, is unplanned and piecemeal. Second, collective redress has arisen as an issue in certain particular sectors—consumer protection, competition enforcement, and recently others including data protection—but no generic legislation has been passed. Third, political disagreements have coloured debates on collective redress, with the result that the European Commission has so far only been able to go as far as tabling a 2013 Recommendation on the principles for a proposed European model on collective redress.[1] Consumers argue for collective actions to be permitted, and business argues that collective actions will lead to abuse and harm the economy. Fourth, major scandals—the silicone breast implant fraud, how various airlines have treated customers, and the 'dieselgate' emissions fraud and how Volkswagen responded to it—have raised the level of annoyance by EU Commissioners and MEPs to a high level, resulting in irritation that pan-EU solutions to consumer redress are unavailable, and a desire to do something about this. Conclusions will be drawn on these points at the end of the chapter. They set the scene for the rest of this book, in that political debate has incorrectly assumed that only one mechanism is available for delivering collective redress, namely the collective action.

I. Diverse Approaches and Piecemeal Legislation

For many years, Europe struggled with taking a clear position on collective redress, and establishing a coherent legal framework.[2] Over the years, the European legislator enacted piecemeal legislation on individual issues and enforcement techniques. Debate on collective redress at EU level in the past decade has largely focused on two areas, which are

---

[1] This is how the Recommendation is referred to in the *Report from the Commission to the European Parliament, the Council and the European Economic and Social Committee on the implementation of the Commission Recommendation of 11 June 2013 on common principles for injunctive and compensatory redress mechanisms in the Member States concerning violations of rights granted under Union law* (2013/396/EU), COM(2018) 40 final p 19.

[2] For an overview see http://ec.europa.eu/consumers/redress_cons/collective_redress_en.htm.

considered further below: consumers and competition law. The debates in those two areas differ because they give rise to particular contexts, especially in two respects: first, the balance between public and private enforcement and, second, the balance in enforcement jurisdiction between EU level and the national level of different Member States. Further, Member States differ in their internal balance between public and private enforcement, and also reliance on hybrid actors, such as the extent to which trade associations or consumer associations are empowered to wield enforcement powers that might otherwise be categorised as either public or private (or administrative, or hybrid).

An example of the development away from a binary public–private categorisation is reliance on 'alternative' dispute resolution (ADR) mechanisms *as part of the market regulatory system*. Thus, regulatory legislation in various sectors—notably communications,[3] energy,[4] consumer credit,[5] payment services[6] and bus and coach passengers[7]—requires Member States to have ADR schemes, and ADR is encouraged in others—distance marketing of financial services,[8] timeshares,[9] e-commerce,[10] postal services,[11] insurance[12] and financial instruments.[13] Calls have been made by both consumer and trade representatives to improve the FIN-NET network of Financial Services Ombudsmen, including by making participation mandatory for banks.[14]

II. The Public–Private Split

It is traditional to categorise modes of legal enforcement into public or private mechanisms. Indeed, in subsequent chapters, we do just this. But one conclusion of this book is

---

[3]   Directives No 2009/136/EC and No 2009/140/EC; OJ L337, 18.12.2009, pp 11 and 37.

[4]   Directives No 2009/72/EC and No 2009/73/EC; OJ L 211, 14.8.2009, pp 55 and 94.

[5]   Directive No 2008/48/EC.

[6]   Directive No 2007/64 /EC.

[7]   Directive (EC) 2009/136 amending Directive 2002/22/EC on universal service and users' rights relating to electronic communications networks and services; Directive (EC) 2009/72 concerning common rules for the internal market in electricity and repealing Directive 2003/54/EC, [2009] OJ L211/55; and Directive (EC) 2009/73 concerning common rules for the internal market in natural gas and repealing Directive 2003/55/EC; Directive (EC) 2008/48 on credit agreements for consumers; Directive (EC) 2007/64 on payment services in the internal market amending Directives 97/7/EC, 2002/65/EC, 2005/60/EC; Regulation (EU) No 181/2011 on bus and coach passenger rights [complaints function either in house or external; also complaints and enforcement authority].

[8]   Directive 2002/65/EC concerning the distance marketing of consumer financial services, 9.10.2002, Art 14.

[9]   Directive 2008/122/EC of 14 January 2009 on the protection of consumers in respect of certain aspects of timeshare, longterm holiday product, resale and exchange contracts (Art 14(2)), OJ L 33, 3.2.2009, Art 14.

[10]   Directive (EC) 2000/31 on certain legal aspects of information society services, in particular electronic commerce, in the Internal Market (Directive on electronic commerce), [2000] OJ L 178/1.

[11]   Directive (EC) 2008/6 amending Directive 97/67/EC with regard to the full accomplishment of the internal market of Community postal services, [2008] OJ L 52, 3.

[12]   Directive 2002/92/EC on insurance mediation (Art 11(1)), OJ L 9, 15.1.2003, Art 11.

[13]   Directive (EC) 2004/39 on markets in financial instruments amending Council Directives 85/611/EEC and 93/6/EEC and Directive 2000/12/EC and repealing Council Directive 93/22/EEC, [2004] OJ L 145/1, 33.

[14]   *Summary of contributions to the Green Paper on retail financial services: Better products, more choice and greater opportunities for consumers and businesses* COM(2015) 630 final, http://ec.europa.eu/finance/consultations/2015/retail-financial-services/docs/summary-of-responses_en.pdf.

that categorisation is somewhat obsolete.[15] At the least, there is confusion, uncertainty and experimentation in relation to mechanisms and how they might be categorised.

The EU is described as a regulatory state,[16] with extensive public law rules that are primarily enforced by networks of public authorities. This balance contrasts strongly with that of the US which, until recently almost uniquely around the world, made a conscious policy choice[17] in favouring private enforcement over corporate activity and business-to-consumer (B2C) relations.[18]

In relation to public enforcement, there in a critical 'vertical' dimension in the EU architecture, namely that responsibility for public enforcement is a matter for Member States under the principle of subsidiarity. EU case law has merely developed requirements that national sanctions must be 'effective, proportionate and dissuasive'.[19] That mantra is repeated in many EU legislative texts, but it has developed on a piecemeal basis, has never been subjected to systematic research or review, and does not amount to a principled enforcement policy. Public enforcement functions at EU level are rare, examples being the role of the European Commission under competition law,[20] data protection[21] and financial services.[22]

One consequence of this situation is that the EU does not have a general policy on enforcement. Most Member States also have no formal policy on enforcement, other than the traditional idea that anyone who is found to have breached the law will be prosecuted and sanctioned.

In contrast, the United Kingdom has a policy stated by central government and repeated in customised, detailed written statements under the title 'Enforcement Policy' or similar

---

[15] C Hodges and N Creutzfeldt, 'Transformations in Public and Private Enforcement' in H-W Micklitz and A Wechsler (eds), *The Transformation of Enforcement* (Oxford, Hart Publishing, 2016).

[16] Amongst many writings, see G Majone, *Regulating Europe* (London, Routledge, 1996); F Cafaggi and H Muir Watt (eds), *The Regulatory Function of European Private Law* (Cheltenham UK, Edward Elgar, 2009).

[17] An influential analysis was H Kalven Jr and M Rosenfield, 'The Contemporary Function of the Class Suit' (1941) 8 *University of Chicago Law Review* 684–87.

[18] See BG Garth, 'Power and Legal Artifice: The Federal Class Action' 26 *Law & Society Review* (1992) 237 ('The class action is a politically empowering legal artifice'); RA Kagan, *Adversarial Legalism: The American Way of Law* (Boston MA, Harvard University Press, 2001); W Haltom, M McCann, *Distorting the Law: Politics, Media, and The Litigation Crisis* (Chicago, University of Chicago Press, 2004); WV McIntosh and CL Cates, *Multi-Party Litigation: The Strategic Context* (Vancouver, UBC Press, 2009); S Farhang, *The Litigation State. Public Regulation and Private Lawsuits in the U.S* (Princeton NJ, Princeton University Press, 2010); JC Coffee Jr, *Entrepreneurial Litigation: Its Rise, Fall, and Future* (Boston MA, Harvard University Press, 2015). CJS Hodges, 'Objectives, Mechanisms and Policy Choices in Collective Enforcement and Redress' in J Steele and W van Boom (eds), *Mass Justice* (Cheltenham UK, Edward Elgar, 2011).

[19] Case 68/88 *Commission v Greece* [1989] ECR 2965 paras 22–27; Case C-326/88 *Anklagemyndighedem v Hansen & Sons I/S* [1990] I ECR 2911; Case C-36/94 *Siesse v Director da Alfandega de Alcantara* [1995] ECR I-3573 paras 19–21; Case C-83/94 *Leifer* [1995] ECR I-3231 paras 32–41; Case C-341/94 *Allain* [1996] ECR I-4631 para 24; Case C-29/95 *Pastoors v Belgium* [1997] ECR I-285 paras 24–26.

[20] Arts 105–06 TFEU.

[21] Regulation (EU) 2016/679 of the European Parliament and of the Council of 27.4.2016 on the protection of natural persons with regard to the processing of personal data and on the free movement of such data, and repealing Directive 95/46/EC (General Data Protection Regulation), OJ L 119, 4.5.2016, 1.

[22] eg, Directive 2014/17/EU of the European Parliament and of the Council of 4.2.2014 on credit agreements for consumers relating to residential immovable property and amending Directives 2008/48/EC and 2013/36/EU and Regulation (EU) No 1093/2010, OJ L 60, 28.2.2014, 34 and Directive 2014/92/EU of the European Parliament and of the Council of 23.7.2014 on the comparability of fees related to payment accounts, payment account switching and access to payment accounts with basic features, OJ L 257, 28.8.2014, 214.

terms, issued by every regulatory authority, enforcement authority[23] and, as a standard approach to be applied by criminal courts, and the Sentencing Council.[24] The UK approach, as outlined in chapter 5 below, has left behind ideas that penalties provide deterrence, and adopts the aim of supporting actions and behaviour and culture in well-intentioned firms so as to achieve the outcome of compliance. Most authorities reserve hard sanctions for unethically-intentioned infringers, ie criminals and rogues.

In relation to private enforcement, no EU level power or function exists. Initiatives towards a goal of harmonisation of civil procedure in the internal market go back to 1994 with the Storme Report on the approximation of the laws and rules of the Member States concerning certain aspects of the procedure for civil litigation.[25] In July 2017, the European Parliament adopted a Resolution on common minimum standards of civil procedure in the European Union.[26] Such standards at Union level could

> contribute to the modernisation of national proceedings, a level playing field for businesses and increased economic growth, by making judicial systems more effective and efficient, while at the same time facilitating citizens' access to justice in the Union and helping to uphold the fundamental freedoms of the Union.[27]

The Parliament requested the Commission to submit by 30 June 2018 a concrete legislative proposal on common minimum standards of civil procedure. The question remains whether this will actually happen, in light of the obvious fault line of the existence of two broad families of civil procedure, namely those of civil law countries and those of common law countries.

There has been extensive harmonisation of Member States' substantive private law and consumer protection law. However, enforcement methods for consumer protection law vary between public and private techniques, and vary between national systems. For example, in some Member States, enforcement activities are undertaken by bodies where the public–private distinction can be said to be something of a hybrid. Much enforcement of unfair trading (unfair competition) law in Germany is undertaken by a trade association (the *Wettbewerbszentrale*: WBZ) and consumer associations (*Verbraucherzentralen*) and public authorities at neither federal nor state (*Land*) levels are particularly active, save in relation to criminal activity.[28] The UK also relies strongly on self-regulatory structures (trade association codes of conduct, and the Advertising Standards Authority, which is a private body).

---

[23] Overview in C Hodges, *Law and Corporate Behaviour: Integrating Theories of Regulation, Enforcement, Culture and Ethics* (Oxford, Hart Publishing, 2015) chs 8–16 and 20; Figure 10.1 in C Hodges and R Steinholtz, *Ethical Business Practice and Regulation: A Behavioural and Values-Based Approach to Compliance and Enforcement* (Oxford, Hart Publishing, 2017) 140–41.

[24] See a series of *Guidelines* issued under the Coroners and Justice Act 2009, s 121.

[25] M Storme, Study on the approximation of the laws and rules of the Member States concerning certain aspects of the procedure for civil litigation, Final Report, Dordrecht, 1994.

[26] European Parliament resolution of 4.7.2017 with recommendations to the Commission on common minimum standards of civil procedure in the European Union, 2015/2084(INL). The legal basis can be found in Arts 4(1), 5(1), 67(4), 81 and 114 TFEU.

[27] ibid, at I.

[28] C Hodges, I Benöhr and N Creutzfeldt-Banda, *Consumer ADR in Europe* (Oxford, Hart Publishing, 2012) 82–87.

III. Objectives and Outcomes Replace Mechanisms

It is striking how language and rhetoric has evolved in EU debate, to reflect a shift in focus from mechanisms (or a single mechanism) to the objectives of policy, namely collective redress.[29] A decade ago, the debate was all about 'class actions', influenced by the US model. It then moved to 'collective actions', to try to distinguish an EU-style procedure from the US model, since it was widely accepted that the latter gave rise to abuse because of its 'toxic cocktail' of incentives. The EU collective action 'model' (whatever it might be) was said to be different because it included a raft of safeguards that were absent from the US class action model. However, such terminology was still about mechanisms, more particularly private enforcement (litigation) mechanisms. A further shift in terminology adopted the term 'collective redress', which, in its pure form, concerns objectives and outcomes, without assuming what mechanism might achieve this. This shift reflects realisation that techniques other than private litigation were capable of delivering mass redress, and of doing so more quickly and cheaply than was possible through litigation.[30]

That shift to focus on outcomes accords also with the EU-level adoption of a Better Regulation-inspired approach to legislative policy-making. Under this approach, the EU is required to base policy on an examination of *all* the options, and on empirical evidence.[31] The European Commission has committed itself to basing policy and rule-making on evidence, and to reducing regulatory burdens.[32] Thus, a policy of proposing to deliver collective redress that only examines, and considers the costs and benefits of one or a limited number of techniques and mechanisms that deliver that objective, would be unconstitutional under the EU's rules. The essential message of the research included in this book is that options 'outside the box' provide the way forward.

IV. Consumer Enforcement

In furthering consumer protection, so as to strengthen the demand side of the internal market through enhancing the confidence of purchasers, the EU took initiatives on

---

[29] C Hodges, 'From Class Actions to Collective Redress' (2009) 28(1) *Civil Justice Quarterly* 41–66.

[30] C Hodges, *The Reform of Class and Representative Actions in European Legal Systems: A New Framework for Collective Redress in Europe* (Oxford, Hart Publishing, 2008); C Hodges, 'Collective Redress in Europe: The New Model' [2010] 7 *Civil Justice Quarterly*, 370; *Civil enforcement remedies: consultation on extending the range of remedies available to public enforcers of consumer law* (Department for Business Innovation and Skills, 5 November 2012), at http://www.bis.gov.uk/assets/biscore/consumer-issues/docs/c/12-1193-civil-enforcement-remedies-consultation-on-extending.

[31] *Commission Staff Working Document: Better Regulation Guidelines*, SWC(2017) 350, 7.7.2017, Key Question 4 ('What are the various options?' and para 2.4 ('It is important to consult widely about alternatives, think outside the box and give due consideration to all different options'); Communication from the Commission to the European Parliament, the European Council and the Council, *Better Regulation: Delivering better results for a stronger Union* (European Commission, 2016), COM(2016) 615 final, 14.9.2016.

[32] Communication from the Commission to the European Parliament, the Council, the European Economic and Social Committee and the Committee of the Regions, *Better regulation for better results: An EU agenda*, COM(2015) 215 final, 19.5.2015.

cooperation between national consumer enforcers and collective injunctive relief for consumers. We now examine these two measures.

A. The CPC Regulation

In relation to public enforcement, the 2004 Regulation on Cooperation between Member States for Consumer Protection (the CPC Regulation) established a network of national authorities, each having national investigation and enforcement powers for monitoring the application of legislation concerning consumer protection.[33] The Regulation establishes a framework for mutual assistance that covers the exchange of information, requests for enforcement measures and coordination of market surveillance and enforcement activities.

In May 2016, the European Commission proposed to reform the CPC Regulation.[34] The goal is to expand the powers of the national enforcement authorities so they can work faster and more efficiently. The Proposal was based around coordination of action between national competent authorities in cross-border cases, including 'coordinated action' cases,[35] and 'Union-wide activities' such as sweeps.[36] Competent authorities are required under national law to have specific investigation and enforcement powers.[37] They will be able to request information from domain registrars and banks to detect the identity of the responsible trader, carry out mystery shopping to check geographical discrimination or after-sales conditions, and to order the immediate take-down of websites hosting scams. The harmful practices covered will also include advertisement campaigns of short duration that may have a lasting impact, by trapping consumers in unwanted subscriptions.

The idea is also to introduce a one-stop-shop approach to consumer law where enforcement authorities will notify the businesses concerned of the issues, asking them to change their practices and, if necessary, to compensate the affected consumers. However, the Regulation is 'without prejudice to the possibility of bringing further public or private enforcement actions under national law'.[38] This reflects the unharmonised landscape of different approaches in Member States, and the overall picture remains highly confusing. In this respect, there is a curious power for a competent authority to delegate enforcement action to a private sector body.[39]

---

[33] Regulation (EC) 2006/2004 of the European Parliament and of the Council of 27 October 2004 on consumer protection cooperation, 2004 OJ L 634/1.

[34] Proposal for a Regulation of the European Parliament and of the Council on cooperation between national authorities responsible for the enforcement of consumer protection laws, COM(2016) 283 final, 25 May 2016.

[35] ibid, arts 15–25.

[36] ibid, arts 26–32.

[37] ibid, arts 9.3 and 9.4.

[38] ibid, art 1.6.

[39] ibid, art 7.1: 'A competent authority ("instructing authority") may, in accordance with its national law, instruct a designated body to gather the necessary information regarding an infringement covered by this Regulation or to take the necessary enforcement measures available to it under national law, in order to bring about the cessation or prohibition of that infringement. The instructing authority shall only instruct a designated body if, after consulting the applicant authority or the other competent authorities concerned by the infringement covered by this Regulation, both the applicant authority and requested authority, or all competent authorities concerned,

The Commission's initial proposal for the CPC Regulation included, in a new list of wide and sophisticated enforcement powers for national consumer authorities, a power to order redress.[40] Certain members of the Council objected to the inclusion of that power. That may stand as one of the great missed opportunities of the EU to deliver effective consumer redress. Amongst the Member States who objected were Germany and Italy. Germany's position was that it did not wish to undermine the effectiveness of its Civil Code, under which consumer law was enforced largely by private actors—trade associations and consumer associations, backed by the Injunctions Directive. Italy's position was ironic, given first that private enforcement through the courts takes many years and, second, that several powerful regulators already deliver effective 'regulatory redress' as noted in chapter 4 of this book.

The finally agreed reform of the CPC Regulation contained an interesting compromise, under which regulatory involvement in collective redress appears by the back door. Firms may *propose* by way of *undertaking* to make redress, and authorities may (probably) suggest or even request this. But authorities do not have power, unless under national law, spontaneously to impose redress or seek a court order for redress. The enforcement powers of competent authorities include:

a.   the power to *seek or obtain commitments* from the trader responsible for the infringement covered by this Regulation to cease that infringement;[41]
b.   the power to *receive* from the trader, on the trader's initiative, additional *remedial commitments* for the benefit of consumers that have been affected by the alleged infringement covered by this Regulation, or, where appropriate, to *seek to obtain* commitments from the trader to *offer adequate remedies to the consumers* that have been affected by that infringement;[42]
c.   where applicable, the power to *inform, by appropriate means, consumers* that claim that they have suffered harm as a consequence of an infringement covered by this Regulation about *how to seek compensation* under national law;[43]
d.   in a cross-border situation, one competent authority may request another to take necessary enforcement measures, and the requested authority shall take relevant action, and may receive from the trader, on the trader's initiative, *additional remedial commitments for the benefit of consumers that have been affected* by the alleged

---

agree that the designated body is likely to obtain the necessary information or to bring about the cessation or the prohibition of the infringement in a manner that is at least as efficient and effective as the instructing authority would have done.' A 'designated body' means a body having a legitimate interest in the cessation or prohibition of infringements of the Union laws that protect consumers' interests which is designated by a Member State and instructed by a competent authority for the purpose of gathering the necessary information and to take the necessary enforcement measures available to that body under national law in order to bring about the cessation or prohibition of the infringement, and which is acting on behalf of that competent authority; (art 3(8)).

[40]   Proposal ibid, art 8.2 (n).
[41]   Regulation (EU) 2017/2394 of the European Parliament and of the Council of 12 December 2017 on cooperation between national authorities responsible for the enforcement of consumer protection laws and repealing Regulation (EC) No 2006/2004, art 9.4(b).
[42]   ibid, art 9.4(c).
[43]   ibid, art 9.4(d).

intra-Union infringement, or, where appropriate, may seek to obtain commitments from the trader to offer *adequate remedies to consumers* that have been affected by that infringement.[44]

Interpretation of the above provisions is assisted by the recitals, which refer to:

1. Competent authorities should have the *possibility to agree with traders on commitments containing steps and measures* that a trader has to take regarding an infringement, and in particular the ceasing of an infringement.[45]
2. *Consumers should be entitled to redress for harm caused by infringements* covered by this Regulation. Depending on the case, the power of the competent authorities to receive from the trader, on the trader's initiative, *additional remedial commitments* for the benefit of consumers that have been affected by the alleged infringement covered by this Regulation, or where appropriate to seek to obtain commitments from the trader to offer adequate remedies to the consumers that have been affected by that infringement *should contribute to removing the adverse impact on consumers* caused by a cross-border infringement. Those remedies might include, inter alia, *repair, replacement, price reductions, the termination of contract or the reimbursement of the price paid* for the goods or services, as appropriate, to mitigate the negative consequences of the infringement covered by this Regulation on the affected consumer in accordance with the requirements of Union law. This should be *without prejudice to a consumer's right to seek redress through appropriate means.* Where applicable, competent authorities should *inform*, by appropriate means, consumers that claim that they have suffered harm as a consequence of an infringement covered by this Regulation about *how to seek compensation under national law.*[46]

The approach here is similar to that of the Italian Authority for Electricity Gas and Water (AEEGSI) outlined in chapter 5 below. In France, the Financial Market Authority (AMF) may contact traders, and issue recommendations for compensation inviting the latter to take into account the interests of their clients, and suggesting compensation for those of them who have been harmed.[47] It also has strong resonances with the UK regime under the Consumer Rights Act 2015, which goes further in addressing in a coordinated fashion measures addressing cessation, remediation of behaviour and redress ('enhanced consumer measures'); and prioritises the agreement of such actions between traders and authorities, enshrined in undertakings.

B. The Injunctions Directive

The 2009 Injunctions Directive aims at terminating or prohibiting infringements (regarding consumer credit, package travel, unfair terms in contracts concluded with consumers,

---

[44] ibid, art 12.
[45] ibid, recital 15.
[46] ibid, recital 17.
[47] http://www.afg.asso.fr/wp-content/uploads/2011/01/2011_01_25_consultation_AMF_rapport_indemnisation%20epargnants%20et%20investisseurs.pdf.

distance contracts and unfair commercial practices) which are contrary to the collective interests of consumers.[48] Only qualified authorities having a legitimate interest in ensuring that the collective interests of consumers are complied with (eg independent public bodies or consumer protection organisations), may bring an action. In its 2017 Review of EU Consumer law (Fitness Check), the European Commission concludes that the injunctions procedure could be further harmonised to stimulate its use and to make it more effective as an enforcement tool of EU consumer law.[49] More particularly:

> the Injunctions Directive could be made more effective. This could be achieved by, for example, expanding its scope to cover more pieces of consumer legislation and by further harmonising the injunction procedure. The possible changes would be particularly intended to: (i) facilitate access to justice and reduce the costs for the 'qualified entities' that protect collective consumers' interests; (ii) increase the deterrent effect of injunctions; and (iii) produce an even more useful impact on the affected consumers.[50]

C. Small Claims

Since consumer claims typically involve small sums, which are inherently unlikely to be cost-effective or processed swiftly enough through normal court procedures, in order to identify logical policy choices in seeking a civil procedure mechanism that can respond adequately, one either goes small or goes large—unless one looks 'outside the box' of civil procedure.

The EU Small Claims Procedure[51] has not been able to respond to individual small claims.[52] The revision in effect from 2017 seems highly unlikely to alter its extremely low usage.[53] No Member State has been able to devise a *collective small claim* procedure.

D. Consumer ADR

European policy strongly supports ADR for *individual* small claims, but there has been little realisation that *some* consumer ADR mechanisms are capable of delivering—and do currently extensively deliver—*collective* consumer redress, as discussed in chapter 6.

---

[48] Directive (EC) 2009/22 of the European Parliament and of the Council of 23 April 2009 on injunctions for the protection of consumers' interests, 2009 OJ L 110/30.

[49] Report on the Fitness check of consumer and marketing law, SWD(2017) 209 final, 23 May 2017.

[50] ibid, 86.

[51] Regulation 861/2007 of 11 July 2007 establishing a European Small Claims Procedure OJ 2007, L 199.

[52] EA Onțanu, *Cross-Border Debt Recovery in the EU. A Comparative and Empirical Study of the Use of the European Uniform Procedures* (Cambridge, Intersentia, 2017). See also *Report from the Commission of 19 November 2013 on the application of Regulation (EC) No 861/2007 of the European Parliament and of the Council establishing a European Small Claims Procedure*, COM (2013) 795 final. See also *Report from the Commission of 15 April 2014 on the application of Council Regulation (EC) No 2201/2003 concerning jurisdiction and the recognition and enforcement of judgements in matrimonial matters and the matters of parental responsibility, repealing Regulation (EC) No 1347/2000*, COM (2014) 225 final.

[53] Regulation 2015/2421 of 16 December 2015 amending Regulation (EC) No 861/2007 establishing a European Small Claims Procedure and Regulation (EC) No 1896/2006 creating a European order for payment procedure, OJ 215, L 341. See X Kramer and S Kakiuchi, 'Austerity in Civil Procedure and the Role of Simplified Procedures' (2015) 8 *Erasmus Law Review* 139.

Different types of ADR exist,[54] that have evolved over time.[55] This has led to wide confusion over terminology, techniques and architectures. Early models involved either arbitration-style consumer boards or mediation. The more modern approach is the consumer ombudsman model, using that term in the English rather than Nordic sense. Effective techniques have not always been made available efficiently in appropriate architectures: for example, in the consumer ombudsman model, mediation forms an integral component of the pathway, rather than a separate service provided by different providers.

It is the consumer ombudsman model that emerges from this study as being the most sophisticated and relevant type of ADR, and one that is capable of responding well to both large numbers of individual claims and mass claims.

V. Consumer Collective Redress: Policy Debates

European policymakers define collective redress as:

a procedural mechanism that allows, for reasons of procedural economy and/or efficiency of enforcement, many similar legal claims to be bundled into a single court action. Collective redress facilitates access to justice in particular in cases where the individual damage is so low that potential claimants would not think it worth pursuing an individual claim. It also strengthens the negotiating power of potential claimants and contributes to the efficient administration of justice, by avoiding numerous proceedings concerning claims resulting from the same infringement of law.[56]

Over the years, the European Commission ordered a series of studies on consumer collective redress.[57] The most notable one to date is the 2006 Leuven Report on alternative means of consumer redress other than redress through ordinary judicial proceedings,

---

[54] Hodges, Benöhr and Creutzfeldt-Banda (n 28); P Cortés (ed), *The New Regulatory Framework for Consumer Dispute Resolution* (Oxford, Oxford University Press, 2017).

[55] N Creutzfeldt, 'The Origins and Evolution of Consumer Dispute Resolution Systems in Europe' in C Hodges and A Stadler (eds), *Resolving Mass Disputes. ADR and Settlement of Mass Claims* (Cheltenham UK, Edward Elgar, 2013) 223.

[56] Communication from the Commission to the European Parliament, the Council, the European Economic and Social Committee and the Committee of the Regions, *Towards a European horizontal framework for collective redress*, COM(2013) 401 final, 11 June 2013, 4.

[57] Civic Consulting of the Consumer Policy Evaluation Consortium, Study regarding the problems faced by consumers in obtaining redress for infringements of consumer protection legislation, and the economic consequences of such problems. Final Report (2008), http://ec.europa.eu/consumers/redress_cons/finalreport-problemstudypart1-final.pdf (this is the so-called Problems Study); Civic Consulting (Lead)—Oxford Economics, Evaluation of the effectiveness and efficiency of collective redress mechanisms in the European Union. Final Report (2008), http://ec.europa.eu/consumers/redress_cons/finalreportevaluationstudypart1-final2008-11-26.pdf (this is the so-called Evaluation Study); Civic Consulting of the Consumer Policy Evaluation Consortium, Study on the use of Alternative Dispute Resolution in the European Union. Final Report (2009), http://ec.europa.eu/consumers/redress_cons/adr_study.pdf and tnsqual+, Consumer Redress in the European Union: Consumer Experiences, Perceptions and Choices. Aggregated Report (2009), http://ec.europa.eu/consumers/redress_cons/docs/cons_redress_EU_qual_study_report_en.pdf.

prepared by the University of Leuven in Belgium.[58] The study focuses on how in real life a consumer or business can obtain redress, other than individual redress through ordinary court procedures. The research primarily examines how alternative ways of dispute resolution work in practice for their users. By using a 'dispute resolution continuum', the study pays attention to direct negotiation, mediation and arbitration, small claims procedures, collective actions for damages and injunctive relief. Regarding class actions, the report comes to the conclusion that jurisdictions that have adopted them, sometimes in an experimental way, explicitly distance themselves from US-style class actions. Their European counterparts are embedded in the judicial systems of each Member State. Rules on 'loser pays all' and cost sharing arrangements remain strict, opt-out is used with great reluctance, and rules on standing, evidence, formalism, the role of the judge, the binding force of judgments all remain embedded in the judicial systems of the respective Member State.[59] In its EU Consumer Policy strategy 2007–13 *Empowering consumers, enhancing their welfare, effectively protecting them*,[60] the European Commission considered action on collective redress mechanisms for consumers both for infringements of consumer protection rules and for breaches of EU anti-trust rules. The first real policy document dates from November 2008 when the European Commission published a Green Paper on Consumer Collective Redress.[61] After having identified the (traditional) barriers to effective consumer redress in terms of access, effectiveness and affordability, the Paper puts forward four options for debate:

1. taking no immediate action while continuing to monitor the impact of the national and EU systems which are already in place or are about to be implemented;
2. setting up a cooperation scheme between Member States which would extend the protection of national collective redress systems to consumers from other EU countries and recommend to Member States which do not have a collective redress system to establish one;
3. putting in place a policy mix of tools which can be either non-binding or binding; the option combines promoting collective mediation or arbitration, recommending to Member States that they allow consumers to bring small mass claims under their small claims procedure, enabling consumer public authorities who are members of the EU enforcement network to require traders to compensate consumers or to skim off the profit of the traders, encouraging business to improve complaint handling schemes and raising consumers' awareness of existing means of redress;
4. proposing a non-binding or binding EU measure to ensure that a judicial collective redress procedure exists in all Member States. This would mean that every consumer

---

[58] The Study Centre for Consumer Law—Centre for European Economic Law Katholieke Universiteit Leuven, Belgium, An analysis and evaluation of alternative means of consumer redress other than redress through ordinary judicial proceedings. Final Report (2007), http://www.eurofinas.org/uploads/documents/policies/OTHER%20 POLICY%20ISSUES/comparative_report_en.pdf.

[59] ibid, 13.

[60] Communication from the Commission to the Council, the European Parliament and the European Economic and Social Committee, *EU consumer policy strategy 2007-2013 empowering consumers, enhancing their welfare, effectively protecting them*, COM(2007) 99 final, 13 March 2007.

[61] Green paper on consumer collective redress, COM(2008) 794 final, 27 November 2008.

throughout the EU would be able to obtain adequate redress in mass cases. The issues to be considered for this option include how the procedure would be financed, the conditions under which consumer organisations or public authorities could bring a mass claim to court, how unfounded claims could be prevented and whether an opt-in procedure or an opt-out procedure is chosen.

After having received numerous responses to the Green Paper,[62] and after a public hearing in May 2009,[63] the Commission adjusted the policy options in a Consultation Paper:[64]

1. no actions at all at EU level with regards to the legal framework for consumers to get adequate compensation in case of mass claims;
2. developing self-regulation; this option foresees two non-legislative measures: the development of a standard model of collective ADR and a self-regulatory measure for traders to establish an internal complaint handling system;
3. non-binding setting up of collective ADR schemes and judicial collective redress schemes in combination with additional powers under the CPC Regulation (by giving competent authorities additional powers such as a skimming-off power and a compensation order procedure for very low value cross-border claims); regarding the judicial collective redress schemes, the Commission proposes a series of benchmarks (eg, making appropriate means of financing available, prohibiting punitive damages and encouraging effective and efficient judicial case management);
4. binding setting up of collective ADR schemes and judicial collective redress schemes in combination with additional powers under the CPC Regulation; the difference between this option and option 3 is the obligation on Member States to set up collective ADR and judicial collective redress;
5. a binding EU-wide judicial collective redress mechanism including collective ADR; the latter would deal with all claims and would be open to consumers from all Member States; the binding instrument would ensure that all Member States set up a judicial collective redress mechanism with harmonised features; the mechanism chosen would be a test case procedure.

In a Joint Information Note of October 2010, the three EU Commissioners for Justice, Fundamental Rights and Citizenship; Competition and Health and Consumer Policy underlined the need for a coherent European approach to collective redress.[65] Given the diversity of existing national systems and their different levels of effectiveness, which may undermine the enjoyment of rights by citizens and businesses and give rise to uneven enforcement of those rights, the Commissioners aim to establish a coherent European framework. Such a framework should contain common principles that any potential future EU initiatives on

---

[62] See http://ec.europa.eu/consumers/redress_cons/response_GP_collective_redress_en.htm.

[63] See http://ec.europa.eu/consumers/redress_cons/docs/summary_main_trends_coll_redress_en.pdf.

[64] Consultation paper for discussion on the follow-up to the Green paper on consumer collective redress, http://ec.europa.eu/consumers/redress_cons/docs/consultation_paper2009.pdf. For the responses on the Consultation paper see http://ec.europa.eu/consumers/redress_cons/response_CP_GP_collective_redress_en.htm.

[65] Joint information note. Towards a coherent European approach to collective redress: Next Steps, SEC(2010) 1192, 5 October 2010. The note stemmed from the Commission's Work Programme 2010 Time to act (COM(2010) 135 final, 31 March 2010).

collective redress in any sector would respect. The objective is to ensure from the outset that any future proposal in this field, while serving the purpose of ensuring a more effective enforcement of EU law, fits well into the EU legal tradition and into the set of procedural remedies already available for the enforcement of EU law.

Following the Information Note, the Commission held a public consultation[66] and a public hearing on collective redress in early 2011. The purpose was to identify common legal principles on collective redress in the EU. The consultation also explored the fields in which the different forms of collective redress could have an added value for better protecting the rights of EU citizens and businesses, and for improving the enforcement of EU legislation. The following set of common core principles was identified, which could guide any possible EU initiative for collective redress: the need for effectiveness and efficiency of redress; the importance of information and of the role of representative bodies; the need to take account of collective consensual resolution as a means of alternative dispute resolution; the need for strong safeguards to avoid abusive litigation; the availability of appropriate financing mechanisms, notably for citizens and SMEs, and the importance of effective enforcement across the EU.

In February 2012, the European Parliament adopted a resolution *Towards a coherent European approach to collective redress*,[67] in which it pleads for any proposal in the field of collective redress to take the form of a horizontal framework including a common set of principles providing uniform access to justice via collective redress within the EU and specifically but not exclusively dealing with the infringement of consumers' rights and taking into account the legal traditions and legal orders of the individual Member States.[68]

VI. Commission's Recommendation on Collective Redress Mechanisms

In June 2013, the European Commission published its Recommendation on common principles for injunctive and compensatory collective redress mechanisms in the Member States concerning violations of rights granted under Union Law.[69] Together with the Recommendation, the Commission published a Communication: Towards a European horizontal framework for collective redress,[70] in which the history of the collective redress issue is

---

[66] Commission Staff Working Document. Public Consultation: Towards a coherent European approach to collective redress, SEC(2011)173 final, 4 February 2011. For the replies to the consultation see http://ec.europa.eu/dgs/health_consumer/dgs_consultations/ca/replies_collective_redress_consultation_en.htm.

[67] European Parliament resolution of 2 February 2012 on 'Towards a coherent European approach to collective redress', 2011/2089 (INI), 2 February 2012.

[68] ibid, paras 15 and 16.

[69] Recommendation (EU) 2013/396 of the European Commission of 11 June 2013 on common principles for injunctive and compensatory collective redress mechanisms in the Member States concerning violations of rights granted under Union Law, 2013 OJ L 206/60 ('Recommendation').

[70] Communication from the Commission to the European Parliament, the Council, the European Economic and Social Committee and the Committee of the Regions, Towards a European horizontal framework for collective redress, COM(2013) 401 final, 11 June 2013.

recounted and in which the Commission elucidates and justifies the enumerated common principles. The Communication concludes as follows:

> the Commission's public consultation in 2011, the European Parliament Resolution of 2 February 2012 and the Commission's own analyses have made it possible to identify particular issues to be addressed in developing a European horizontal framework for collective redress. As a principal conclusion the Commission sees the advantage of following a horizontal approach in order to avoid the risk of uncoordinated sectorial EU initiatives and to ensure the smoothest interface with national procedural rules, in the interest of the functioning of the internal market.[71]

The Commission recommends that all Member States should have collective redress mechanisms in those areas where Union law grants rights to citizens and companies: consumer protection, competition, environment protection,[72] protection of personal data, financial services legislation and investor protection. The principles set out in the Recommendation should be applied horizontally and equally in those areas but also in any other areas where collective claims for injunctions or damages in respect of violations of the rights granted under Union law would be relevant.

The goal is not to harmonise the national systems, but to list some common, non-binding, principles relating both to judicial (compensatory and injunctive) and out-of-court collective redress that Member States should take into account when crafting such mechanisms.[73] In that way, the Commission wants to facilitate access to justice, stop illegal practices and enable victims of mass cases to obtain compensation, and at the same time to provide appropriate procedural safeguards to avoid abusive litigation.[74]

At the outset, the Recommendation points out that the collective redress mechanisms it envisages are not of a regulatory nature. It is emphasised that it is a core task of public enforcement to prevent and punish the violations of rights granted under Union law. The possibility for private persons to pursue claims based on violations of such rights only supplements public enforcement.[75]

This is made concrete in the promotion of collective follow-on actions.[76] In fields of law where a public authority (ie a regulator) is empowered to adopt a decision finding that there has been a violation of Union law, collective redress actions should, as a general rule, only start after any proceedings of the public authority, which were launched before commencement of the private action, have been concluded definitively. The *ratio legis* is that the public interest and the need to avoid abuse can be presumed to have been taken into account already by the public authority as regards the finding of a violation of Union Law.[77]

If the proceedings of the public authority are launched after the commencement of the collective redress action, the court should avoid giving a decision which would conflict

---

[71] ibid, 16.

[72] See Art 9(3)–(5) Aarhus Convention.

[73] These national collective redress procedures should be fair, equitable, timely and not prohibitively expensive (Recommendation, art 2).

[74] Recommendation, art 1. See also Recommendation recitals (10) and (13).

[75] Recommendation, recital (6). See also Communication *Towards a European Horizontal Framework for Collective Redress*, 10 and 12–13.

[76] Recommendation, arts 33–34.

[77] Recommendation, recital (22).

with a decision contemplated by the public authority. To that end, the court may stay the collective redress action until the proceedings of the public authority have been concluded. In case of follow-on actions, the persons who claim to have been harmed may not be prevented from seeking compensation due to the expiry of limitation or prescription periods before the definitive conclusion of the proceedings by the public authority.

In January 2018, the European Commission published its report in which it assesses the implementation of the principles of the Collective Redress Recommendation (hereinafter the Report).[78] This will be discussed in the different subchapters below.

A. Principles Common to Injunctive and Compensatory Collective Redress

First, the Recommendation contains principles common to injunctive and compensatory collective redress. No standing is given to an individual class member. Only associational plaintiffs, as have no private cause of action or grievance against the defendant, can bring a representative action.[79] He or she is expected to possess special ability, experience or resources that would allow it to be an appropriate and adequate class representative. Besides public authorities,[80] officially designated representative entities and entities certified on an ad hoc basis by a national authority or court for a particular representative action have standing to bring a representative action.[81] The representative entities have to meet three eligibility conditions:[82]

(a) a non-profit making character;
(b) a direct relationship between the main objectives of the entity and the rights granted under Union law that are claimed to have been violated in respect of which the action is brought and;
(c) sufficient capacity in terms of financial resources, human resources, and legal expertise, to represent multiple claimants acting in their best interest.

The Report concludes that the standing principles are generally complied with, albeit with some variations in different Member States. It is underlined that more stringent rules for representative entities could potentially lead to a limitation of the right to seek collective redress and thereby of access to courts.[83]

The admissibility of any collective action should be verified, *sua sponte*, by the judge at the earliest possible stage of the litigation.[84] One of the issues that was revealed by the Call

---

[78] *Report* (n 11).
[79] A representative action is defined as an action which is brought by a representative entity, an ad hoc certified entity or a public authority on behalf and in the name of two or more natural or legal persons who claim to be exposed to the risk of suffering harm or to have been harmed in a mass harm situation whereas those persons are not parties to the proceedings (Art 3(d) Recommendation).
[80] Recommendation, art 7.
[81] Recommendation, arts 4 and 6.
[82] The designated entity will lose its status if one or more of the conditions are no longer met (Art 5 Recommendation).
[83] *Report* (n 11) 5.
[84] Recommendation, arts 8–9.

for Evidence (see below) was the reverse side of the admissibility requirement, in the sense that several replies cautioned against the use of this principle as it may make the whole procedure more lengthy and cumbersome.[85]

The class representative should be able to disseminate information about a claimed violation of rights granted under Union law and his or her intention to seek an injunction to stop it as well as about a mass harm situation and his or her intention to pursue an action for damages in the form of collective redress. The same possibilities for the representative entity, ad hoc certified entity, a public authority or for the group of claimants should be ensured as regards the information on the ongoing compensatory actions.[86] The dissemination methods should take into account the particular circumstances of the mass harm situation concerned, the freedom of expression, the right to information, and the right to protection of the reputation or the company value of a defendant before its responsibility for the alleged violation or harm is established by the final judgment of the court.[87] The dissemination methods are without prejudice to the Union rules on insider dealing and market manipulation.[88] However, the Report concludes that the principles concerning the provision of information on collective action are not appropriately reflected in the laws of the Member States, particularly at the pre-litigation stage and for injunctions.[89]

The Commission also pays attention to the funding of collective redress procedures. Besides the application of the loser pays rule,[90] the Recommendation requires the plaintiff to declare to the court at the outset of the proceedings, the origin of the funds that he or she is going to use to support the legal action.[91] Third-party litigation funding is allowed and partially regulated in the Recommendation. On the one hand, the Member States should ensure that in cases where an action for collective redress is funded by a private third party, it is prohibited for the private third party:

(a) to seek to influence procedural decisions of the claimant party, including on settlements;
(b) to provide financing for a collective action against a defendant who is a competitor of the fund provider or against a defendant on whom the fund provider is dependant; and
(c) to charge excessive interest on the funds provided.[92]

On the other hand, the court should be allowed to stay the proceedings if in the case of use of financial resources provided by a third party:

(a) there is a conflict of interest between the third party and the claimant party and its members;
(b) the third party has insufficient resources in order to meet its financial commitments to the claimant party initiating the collective redress procedure; or

---

[85] *Report* (n 11) 6.
[86] Recommendation, art 10.
[87] Recommendation, art 11.
[88] Recommendation, art 12.
[89] *Report* (n 11) 8.
[90] Recommendation, art 13. The rule is subject to the conditions provided for in the relevant national law.
[91] Recommendation, art 14.
[92] Recommendation, art 16.

(c) the claimant party has insufficient resources to meet any adverse costs should the collective redress procedure fail.[93]

According to the Report, all Member States that have collective redress mechanisms follow the loser pays rule principle.[94] With respect to the other funding and financing principles, the Report concludes that these have not been implemented in any of the Member States. For example, none of them have regulated third party funding in accordance with the Recommendation. This lack of implementation means, according to the Commission, that unregulated and uncontrolled third party financing can proliferate without legal constraints, creating potential incentives for litigation.[95] Some situations of (at least) potential conflict of interest were reported.[96]

With respect to transnational or cross-border mass harms, the Recommendation stipulates that the Member States should ensure that where a dispute concerns natural or legal persons from several Member States, a single collective action in a single forum is not prevented by national rules on admissibility or standing of the foreign groups of claimants or the representative entities originating from other national legal systems.[97] Any representative entity that has been officially designated in advance by a Member State to have standing to bring representative actions should be permitted to seize the court in the Member State having jurisdiction to consider the mass harm situation.

In other words, the Commission believes that in transnational or cross-border cases the current rules on judicial cooperation in civil matters are satisfactory to initiate a single collective action in a single forum. National rules on admissibility or standing may not prevent this. According to the Commission, the European rules on jurisdiction, recognition and enforcement of judgments in civil and commercial matters[98] and the rules on the applicable law (ie the Rome I and II Regulations[99]) are suitable and applicable in cross-border mass cases, and there is no need for specific rules.

On the one hand, the Report reveals that there are no Member States that have general obstacles to the participation of any natural or legal person from other Member States in group actions before their courts.[100] On the other hand, reference is made to the 'dieselgate' case which led to collective redress proceedings in 4 Member States, leading to possible forum shopping, risk of double compensation and conflicting decisions.[101]

---

[93] Recommendation, art 15.

[94] *Report* (n 11) 8. Lithuania is an exception. There the successful party may be awarded a procedural indemnity the amount of which is decided by a judge.

[95] ibid, at 9.

[96] ibid, at 10. It concerned the use of non-distributed damages for repayment to the fund provider, organisation of the whole action by the fund provider, institutional relations between the law firm representing claimants and the fund provider.

[97] Recommendation, art 17. See also *Communication Towards a European Horizontal Framework for Collective Redress*, 13–14.

[98] Regulation (EU) 1215/2012 of the European Parliament and of the Council of 12 December 2012 on jurisdiction and the recognition and enforcement of judgments in civil and commercial matters (recast), 2012 OJ L 351/1.

[99] Regulation (EC) 593/2008 of the European Parliament and of the Council of 17 June 2008 on the law applicable to contractual obligations (Rome I), 2008 OJ L 177/6 and Regulation (EC) 864/2007 of the European Parliament and of the Council of 11 July 2007 on the law applicable to non-contractual obligations (Rome II), 2007 OJ L 199/40.

[100] *Report* (n 11) 10.

[101] ibid, at 11.

B. Specific Principles Relating to Injunctive Collective Redress

On the one hand, courts and competent public authorities should treat claims for injunctive orders requiring cessation of or prohibiting a violation of rights granted under Union law with all due expediency, where appropriate by way of summary proceedings, in order to prevent any or further harm causing damage because of such violation.[102] On the other hand, the Member States should establish appropriate sanctions against the losing defendant with a view to ensuring effective compliance with the injunctive order, including the payments of a fixed amount for each day's delay or any other amount provided for in national legislation.[103] According to the Report, all Member States have in place penalties for non-compliance with orders made under the Injunctions Directive, including those in which non-judicial authorities are competent for injunctions. However, the question remains whether the penalties are sufficiently deterrent to discourage continued infringements.[104]

C. Specific Principles Relating to Compensatory Collective Redress

The Recommendation puts forward the opt-in principle as default. The claimant party should be formed on the basis of express consent of the natural persons claiming to have been harmed.[105] According to the European Commission, the opt-in system respects the right of a person to decide whether to participate or not. It therefore better preserves the autonomy of parties to choose whether to take part in the litigation or not. In this system the value of the collective dispute is more easily determined, since it would consist of the sum of all individual claims. The court is in a better position to assess both the merits of the case and the admissibility of the collective action. The opt-in system also guarantees that the judgment will not bind other potentially qualified claimants who did not join.[106]

Nevertheless, opt-out as exception, by law or by court order, is possible, as long as this is duly justified by reasons or sound administration of justice.[107] According to the Commission, the opt-out system gives rise to more fundamental questions as to the freedom of potential claimants to decide whether they want to litigate. The right to an effective remedy cannot be interpreted in a way that prevents people from making (informed) decisions on whether they wish to claim damages or not. In addition, an opt-out system may not be consistent with the central aim of collective redress, which is to obtain compensation for harm suffered, since such persons are not identified, and so the award will not be distributed to them.[108]

---

[102] Recommendation, art 19.
[103] Recommendation, art 20.
[104] *Report* (n 11) 12.
[105] Recommendation, art 21.
[106] *Communication Towards a European Horizontal Framework for Collective Redress*, 12.
[107] Recommendation, art 21.
[108] *Communication Towards a European Horizontal Framework for Collective Redress*, 12.

According to the Report, there are 13 Member States that exclusively apply the opt-in system, two Member States that apply the opt-out system and four Member States that apply both systems depending on the type of action or the specifics of the case.[109]

A member of the claimant party should be free to leave the claimant party at any time before the final judgment is given or the case is otherwise validly settled, subject to the same conditions that apply to withdrawal in individual actions, without being deprived of the possibility to pursue its claims in another form, if this does not undermine the sound administration of justice.[110] On the other hand, natural or legal persons claiming to have been harmed in the same mass harm situation should be able to join the claimant party at any time before the judgment is given or the case is otherwise validly settled, if this does not undermine the sound administration of justice.[111]

Particular attention is paid to collective ADR and settlements. The Member States should ensure that the parties to a dispute in a mass harm situation are encouraged to settle the dispute about compensation consensually or out-of-court, both at the pre-trial stage and during civil trial.[112] Appropriate means of collective ADR should be made available to the parties before and throughout the litigation. Use of such means should depend on the consent of the parties involved in the case.[113] Any limitation period applicable to the claims should be suspended during the period from the moment the parties agree to attempt to resolve the dispute by means of ADR until at least the moment at which one or both parties expressly withdraw from it.[114] In case a settlement is reached, its legality should be verified by the courts taking into consideration the appropriate protection of interests and rights of all parties involved.[115]

The Report concludes that 11 Member States have introduced specific provisions on collective out-of-court dispute resolution mechanisms. The Call for Evidence (see below) reveals that most cases are settled through direct settlement negotiation without the involvement of a third party.[116]

The Commission prohibits contingency fees and punitive damages. The Member States should ensure that the lawyers' remuneration and the method by which it is calculated do not create any incentive to litigation that is unnecessary from the point of view of the interest of any of the parties.[117] Contingency fees risk creating such an incentive. When contingency fees are exceptionally allowed in collective redress cases, appropriate national regulation should be provided, taking into account in particular the right to full compensation of the members of the claimant party.[118] According to the Report, nine Member

---

[109] *Report* (n 11) 13.
[110] Recommendation, art 22.
[111] Recommendation, art 23.
[112] Recommendation, art 25. This should be done in accordance with Directive (EC) 2008/52 of the European Parliament and of the Council of 21 May 2008 on certain aspects of mediation in civil and commercial matters, 2008 OJ L 136/3.
[113] Recommendation, art 26.
[114] Recommendation, art 27.
[115] Recommendation, art 28.
[116] *Report* (n 11) 15.
[117] Recommendation, art 29.
[118] Recommendation, art 30.

States allow for some form of contingency fees, although there are specific provisions on the operation of such remuneration in collective redress actions.[119] Other Member States allow for performance fees, either in the form of a success fee or a reduction in the remuneration in case certain goals are not achieved. The Report states that the latter could encourage unnecessary claims for unrealistic amounts, particularly where they are calculated as a percentage of the award. Flat rate performance fees appear less likely to create an incentive for aggressive litigation practices.[120]

The compensation awarded to natural or legal persons harmed in a mass harm situation should not exceed the compensation that would have been awarded, if the claim had been pursued by means of individual actions. In particular, punitive damages, leading to overcompensation in favour of the claimant party of the damage suffered, should be prohibited.[121] According to the Report, the majority of Member States do not award punitive damages in mass harm situations.[122]

The Member States should ensure, that, in addition to the general principles of funding, for cases of private third party funding of compensatory collective redress, it is prohibited to base remuneration given to or interest charged by the fund provider on the amount of the settlement reached or the compensation awarded unless that funding arrangement is regulated by a public authority to ensure the interests of the parties.[123]

D. Registry of Collective Redress Actions

The Recommendation wants the Member States to establish a national registry of collective redress actions, which should be available free of charge to any interested person through electronic means and otherwise. Websites publishing the registries should provide access to comprehensive and objective information on the available methods of obtaining compensation, including out-of-court methods.[124] According to the Report, this principle is by and large not followed in the collective redress schemes of the Member States.[125]

E. Supervision and 2018 Report

Although the Recommendation is of a non-binding, declaratory nature, it obliges the Member States to implement the principles set out in it in national collective redress systems by 26 July 2015 at the latest.[126] Once they have implemented them, the Member States should collect reliable annual statistics on the number of out-of-court and judicial

---

[119] *Report* (n 11) 16.
[120] ibid.
[121] Recommendation, art 31.
[122] *Report* (n 11) 17.
[123] Recommendation, art 32.
[124] Recommendation, arts 35–36.
[125] *Report* (n 11) 19.
[126] Recommendation, art 38.

collective redress procedures and information about the parties, the subject matter and outcome of the cases.[127]

In May 2016, the European Commission launched a 'Call for evidence on the operation of collective redress arrangements in the Member States of the European Union'.[128] The overall objective of the consultation is to collect information on stakeholders' practical experiences with collective actions, both injunctive and compensatory as well as on situations, where collective action could have been appropriate, but was not sought. In addition, the consultation has a number of specific objectives:

— identify collective legal actions within the scope of the Recommendation, initiated after its adoption;
— collect quantitative and qualitative data concerning these actions (subject-matter, number of people involved, harm suffered, applied remedies, obstacles, abuses, etc);
— identify situations in which collective action could have been appropriate but was not taken, identify the reasons for and effects of not taking the action;
— obtain views on the effectiveness and efficiency of collective actions.

As mentioned above, in January 2018, the Commission issued its Report assessing the implementation of the Recommendation on the basis of practical experience.[129] It evaluated its impact on access to justice, on the right to obtain compensation, on the need to prevent abusive litigation and on the functioning of the single market, on SMEs, the competitiveness of the economy of the European Union and consumer trust. The Commission also assessed whether further measures to consolidate and strengthen the horizontal approach reflected in the Recommendation should be proposed.[130]

The 2018 Report confirmed the political wish 'to strike an appropriate balance between the goal of ensuring sufficient access to justice and also the need of preventing abuses through appropriate safeguards'.[131] It noted that national collective mechanisms are mainly used in the area of consumer protection and related areas such as passenger rights or financial services.[132]

As next steps, the Commission said that it intends:

— to further promote the principles set out in the 2013 Recommendation across all areas, both in terms of availability of collective redress actions in national legislations and thus of improving access to justice, and in terms of providing the necessary safeguards against abusive litigation;
— to carry out further analysis for some aspects of the Recommendation which are key to preventing abuses and to ensuring safe use of collective redress mechanisms, such as regarding funding of collective actions, in order to get better a picture of the design and practical implementation;

---

[127] Recommendation, art 39.
[128] http://ec.europa.eu/newsroom/just/item-detail.cfm?item_id=59539. Parallel to the consultation, a study is carried out by the external contractor.
[129] *Report* (n 11).
[130] Recommendation, art 41.
[131] *Report* (n 11) 1.
[132] ibid, 4.

— to follow-up this assessment of the 2013 Recommendation in the framework of the forthcoming initiative on a 'New Deal for Consumers', as announced in the Commission Work Programme for 201854, with a particular focus on strengthening the redress and enforcement aspects of the Injunctions Directive in appropriate areas.[133]

VII. The Political and Technical Conundrum

As noted in chapter 3, although some 21 Member States have introduced at least one national mechanism for collective redress, no two models are the same, and none correspond to the Commission's model in its 2013 Recommendation. Each national model is the result of strenuous local political debate and compromises.

Taking a next step at EU level therefore poses a technical and political conundrum. The selection of a list of technical safeguards to guard against abuse has been made differently in every Member State, and differs from that of the Commission. The balance between, on the one hand, protection against abuse, so as to protect business (and hence employment and innovation), and, on the other hand, delivery of redress to multiple people who have suffered genuine losses, is not easy to make, and is politically disputed. No credible technical solution has been put forward for the basis of making such a balance. Whether the balance might prove to be too far one way or the other is entirely unpredictable. It is unclear—and arguable—whether such a single balance can be struck that would prove to be ideal in every Member State, or whether other domestic conditions, especially on funding and costs, would affect that balance.

VIII. Business Concerns on Ineffective Safeguards

In 2017, the US Chamber's Institute for Legal Reform (ILR) expressed concern that the safeguards required by the Commission were not being observed by Member States, and that the undesired outcome of abuse was, therefore, a significant risk.[134] The ILR's analysis was that:

1. *Who may file a claim.* Some Member States had little or no procedure to assess whether a representative is the appropriate entity to bring a collective claim. There have been examples of law firms or private equity/hedge funds being the true instigators and main beneficiaries of mass claims, instead of the injured parties themselves.

2. *Compensation of Representatives.* There were a number of examples of Member States having weakened or eliminated traditional rules preventing 'contingency fees', and there

---

[133] ibid, 20–21.
[134] *The Growth of Collective Redress in the EU. A Survey of Developments in 10 Member States* (US Chamber Institute for Legal Reform, 2017).

had been a 'spectacular growth' in a third party funding industry, leading to lawsuits being treated as a commodity.

3. *Loser pays principle.* The principle was said to be weakening significantly in practice across the EU.
4. *Opt-in/Opt-out.* Member States were increasingly experimenting with opt-out features.
5. *Admissibility and Certification Standards.* Some systems did not have adequate certification and admissibility procedures to filter out opportunistic claims.
6. *Jurisdictional Overreach/Forum Shopping.* There was an emerging trend allowing claimants to shop around different jurisdictions.

The ILR called for clear minimum safeguards for collective actions and for third party litigation funding (TPLF), in order to control against the risk of abuse. The ILR subsequently published a survey of 6,177 consumers in 6 Member States undertaken by research organisation WorldThinks, which found that 85% of respondents supported the introduction of safeguards for collective actions, that nearly 80% felt it was important that safeguards should be consistent across the EU, that 5% believed that TPLF would ensure that collective actions would operate in consumers' best interests, that 25% believed that TPLF should be banned entirely, and that 81% supported the introduction of safeguards for TPLF.[135] In a further paper, ILR argued that differences in the safeguard regimes applied by different Member States were matters for concern, particularly in relation to the scope for development of forum shopping between jurisdictions.[136]

IX.   Consumer Concerns from Business Scandals

Two scandals, and the attitudes of the businesses involved, had a significant effect on the political climate.[137] Volkswagen's refusal to compensate or retrofit cars fitted with 'defeat devices' aimed at producing fraudulent test results for noxious emissions, in contrast to its agreement to do so in the USA when threatened with public enforcement powers and class actions there, and also its refusal to agree a pan-EU approach with the Commission, was a source of annoyance.[138] Ryanair's cancellation of many flights just outside the period when it would be required to compensate customers, and its subsequent failure to provide adequate information or support to stranded customers, likewise annoyed authorities and politicians.[139]

---

[135] *Supporting Safeguards. EU Consumer Attitudes Towards Collective Actions and Litigation Funding* (US Chamber Institute for Legal Reform, 2017).

[136] *Collective Redress Tourism. Preventing Forum Shopping in the EU* (US Chamber Institute for Legal Reform, 2017).

[137] See Letter from M Goyens of BEUC, co-signed by 38 MEPs, to President Juncker and Commissioner Jourova, 'Time for the European Commission to legislate on collective redress', 10 October 2017.

[138] J Ewing, *Faster, Higher, Farther. The Volkswagen Scandal* (London, WW Norton & Company, 2017).

[139] Only the UK's Civil Aviation Authority used its enforcement powers to force the airline to treat customers well: this is relevant to the conclusions of this book.

X. Proposals in 2016/17

In September 2017, Mrs Vera Jourová, the EU Commissioner for Justice, Consumers and Gender Equality, announced that the 2009 Injunctions Directive opens an interesting avenue for consumers through representative actions by non-profit organisations or public authorities:

> We are assessing how to enhance the effectiveness of the Injunctions Directive in the spirit of groups acting against mass harm. The results of the Fitness Check show that the Injunctions Directive has a decisive role in protecting consumers' collective interests, enabling consumer protection organisations or public bodies to quickly stop breaches of EU consumer protection rules. However, the injunction procedure is not without flaws and not used to its full potential. It does not cover all relevant EU consumer protection legislation, and costs related to the preparation of the case and court or administrative fees in injunction proceedings are too high for underfunded consumer organisations. The length of the injunctions procedure is an issue especially in case of so-called 'short-lived' infringements like an advertisement that is only featured for a few days. There is clear scope of improving this Directive. We want a more effective procedure for stopping traders from infringing EU consumer protection rules. And we want to facilitate redress for the damages consumers suffer, in particular when they affect large numbers of people across the EU.[140]

The Inception Impact Assessment stated that four policy options would be explored:[141]

1. *The baseline scenario.* Consumers would continue benefitting from the existing EU enforcement and redress framework, and the ADR/online dispute resolution (ODR) would be improved.
2. *Non-legislative options.* This would include actions to enhance qualified entities' capacity to prepare and manage both injunction and redress actions, and to support cooperation between qualified entities from different Member States.
3. *A targeted revision of the Injunctions Directive limited to injunctive relief.* Consumers would be able to bring follow-on actions using the injunction order as proof of the breach of EU law.
4. *A targeted revision of the Injunctions Directive (option 3) + consumer collective redress.* Further procedural efficiencies could include a single procedure in which qualified entities could ask the courts and/or administrative authorities to stop the breach and ensure redress for the victims, perhaps using a redress order or inviting the trader to enter out-of-court redress negotiations. If the negotiations were unsuccessful, the court or authority would continue with redress proceedings.

We assess these proposals in chapter 8.

It should be noted that the concept of redress has become politicised. Most of the cases cited by The European Consumer Organisation (BEUC)[142] and the Consumer Justice

---

[140] Speech by Commissioner Jourova at the US Chamber Institute for Legal Reform, Brussels, 28 September 2017, at https://ec.europa.eu/commission/commissioners/2014-2019/jourova/announcements/speech-commissioner-jourova-release-us-chamber-institute-legal-reforms-consumer-public-opinion-poll_en.

[141] See https://ec.europa.eu/info/law/better-regulation/initiatives/ares-2017-5324969_en.

[142] *Collective Redress. Where & how it works* (BEUC, 2012), http://www.beuc.eu/publications/2012-00308-01-e.pdf.

Enforcement Forum (COJEF)[143] highlight failures in *public* enforcement, in which payment of money either does not arise at all or is less important than other outcomes such as changing systemic behaviour. This is a wide use of the word 'redress', which is technically incorrect and misleading. It confuses outcomes and mechanisms. Is the objective redress or changes in traders' behaviour? Is such an outcome supposed to be before problems have been identified or after? A typical situation might be unfair contract terms: the main problem there is to identify them and stop them, and it is not clear how a mass redress power would do that. Mass issues that have affected recent public debate, Volkswagen and Ryanair, relate more to companies failing to deal with consumers fairly *after* problems have been identified. We discuss these issues further in chapters 7 and 8.

The Court of Justice contributed to the debate in a case arising out of a case in Austria brought against Facebook Ireland alleging breach of individuals' data protection rights. Advocate General Bobek's opinion was that the Austrian representative claimants could not invoke claims on the same subject assigned to him by other consumers, under Regulation 44/2001, article 16(1).[144] He said:

> I do not believe that it is the role of courts, including this Court, within such a context, to attempt at creating collective redress in consumer matters at the stroke of a pen. Three reasons why such a course of action would be unwise stand out. First, it would clearly go against the wording and the logic of the regulation, thus effectively leading to its rewriting. Second, the issue is too delicate and complex. It is in need of comprehensive legislation, not an isolated judicial intervention within a related but somewhat remote legislative instrument that is clearly unfit for that purpose. That is eventually likely to cause more problems than offer systemic solutions. Third, although perhaps neither straightforward nor speedy, legislative deliberation and discussions at the EU level have been ongoing. That legislative process should not be judicially pre-empted or rendered futile.[145]

XI. Competition Damages

In parallel with the consumer redress debate just discussed, a separate debate was occurring in relation to how to deliver damages to those who suffered loss as a result of an infringement of EU competition law. The debate initially wondered if such private enforcement was preferable to, or alternative to, public enforcement, but the position remained that primary enforcement of competition law in the EU remains with public authorities (the European Commission and national competition authorities), and the role of private enforcement is as a follow-on mechanism to deliver damages rather than deterrence.

---

[143] *Guidelines for enforcement on consumer rights*, Consumer Justice Enforcement Forum, May 2013, available at http://www.cojef-project.eu/IMG/pdf/Conclusions_document_cases__FINAL_8_May.pdf; *Enforcement of Consumer Rights: Strategies and Recommendations* (COJEF II, 2016), http://www.beuc.eu/publications/beuc-x-2016-051_cojef_ii-enforcement_of_consumer_rights.pdf.

[144] Case C-498/16 *Maximilian Schrems v Facebook Ireland Limited*, Opinion of AG Bobek, 14 November 2017.

[145] ibid, para 123.

A. *Courage*

In 2001, the European Court of Justice (ECJ) issued a ground-breaking decision concerning private enforcement of competition damages. In the *Courage* case the Court stated that anyone who has been harmed by an infringement of the antitrust rules[146] must be able to claim compensation for that harm, and that national rules should ensure the effectiveness of this right.[147] The Court ruled that:

> the full effectiveness of ... the Treaty ... would be put at risk if it were not open to any individual to claim damages for loss caused to him by a contract or by conduct liable to restrict or distort competition. Indeed, the existence of such a right strengthens the working of the Community competition rules and discourages agreements or practices, which are frequently covert, which are liable to restrict or distort competition. From that point of view, actions for damages before the national courts can make a significant contribution to the maintenance of effective competition in the Community.[148]

In other words, private actions for damages also apply to breaches of EU competition law by private individuals. Since then, individual and collective actions for competition damages were catapulted up the EU agenda.[149]

In 2005 the European Commission published a Green Paper on how to facilitate actions for damages caused by violations of European competition rules.[150] Violations of these rules, in particular by price fixing cartels, can cause considerable damage to companies and consumers but numerous obstacles can hinder actions for damages by injured parties in national courts. The Green Paper identifies certain of these obstacles, such as access to evidence and the quantification of damages, and presents various options for debate for their removal, including collective actions.[151]

The Green Paper was followed in 2008 by a White Paper on Damages Actions for Breach of the EU antitrust rules.[152] The Paper presents a set of recommendations to ensure that victims of competition law infringements have access to truly effective mechanisms for claiming full compensation for the harm they have suffered: single damages leading to full compensation, collective redress for small value claims, disclosure of relevant evidence without allowing an automatic right to discovery and evidence of final decisions to avoid the time and cost of re-litigation.

B. Directive on Antitrust Damages Actions

Simultaneously with the Recommendation on collective redress mechanisms, the European Commission adopted a proposal for a Directive on certain rules governing actions for

---

[146] The rules are laid down in Arts 101 and 102 of the Treaty on the Functioning of the European Union (TFEU) (formerly Arts 81 and 82 of the EC Treaty).

[147] Case C-453/99, *Courage and Crehan* [2001] ECR I-6297. The ECJ established that private actions for damages also apply to breaches of EC competition law by private individuals. See also cases C-295/04 to C-298/04, *Manfredi and Lloyd Adriatico Assicurazioni SpA* [2006] ECR I-6619.

[148] *Courage*, ibid paras 26 and 27.

[149] For an overview see http://ec.europa.eu/competition/antitrust/actionsdamages/documents.html.

[150] Green Paper Damages actions for breach of the EC antitrust rules, COM(2005) 672 final, 19 December 2005.

[151] ibid, 9.

[152] White Paper on Damages actions for breach of the EC antitrust rules, COM(2008) 165 final, 2 April 2008.

damages under national law for infringements of the competition law provisions of the Member States and of the European Union.[153] The proposal was accompanied by an Impact Assessment Report,[154] a Communication on quantifying harm in actions for damages based on breaches of Articles 101 or 102 Treaty on the Functioning of the European Union (TFEU)[155] and a Practical Guide on quantifying harm.[156]

In 2014, the proposal became law. The Directive on Antitrust Damages Actions was published on 5 December 2014.[157] Member States had two years to implement it in their national legal systems. Although the (non-binding) Recommendation on collective redress mechanisms stipulates that the Member States should have competition collective redress mechanisms, as one of the areas where Union law grants rights to citizens and companies,[158] the (binding) Directive on Antitrust Damages Actions does 'not require Member States to introduce collective redress mechanisms for the enforcement of Articles 101 and 102 TFEU'.[159]

The core of the Directive is to remove the practical obstacles victims of infringements of the EU antitrust rules currently face when trying to get full compensation.[160] Besides some clarifications,[161] the purpose is mainly twofold: facilitating victims in obtaining evidence, and easing the causation inquiry.

The Directive aims at reversing the 2010 *Pfleiderer* decision of the Court of Justice of the European Union (CJEU).[162] In this case a German company, with a view of preparing civil actions for damages, submitted an application to the German NCA (National Competition Agency) (*Bundeskartellamt*) seeking full access to the file relating to the imposition of fines imposed on a group of manufactures of decor paper, including documents and information the manufacturers had submitted under a leniency programme. The decision of the *Bundeskartellamt* not to disclose the documents was challenged before the court, which

---

[153] Proposal for a Directive of the European Parliament and of the Council on certain rules governing actions for damages under national law for infringements of the competition law provisions of the Member States and of the European Union, COM (2013) 404 final (June 11, 2013), available at http://eur-lex.europa.eu/LexUriServ/LexUriServ.do?uri=COM:2013:0404:FIN:EN:PDF.

[154] Commission Staff Working Document. Impact Assessment Report. Damages actions for breach of the EU antitrust rules accompanying the proposal for a Directive of the European Parliament and of the Council on certain rules governing actions for damages under national law for infringements of the competition law provisions of the Member States and of the European Union, SWD(2013) 203 final, 11 June 2013.

[155] Communication from the Commission on quantifying harm in actions for damages based on breaches of Article 101 or 102 of the Treaty on the Functioning of the European Union, 2013 OJ C 167/19.

[156] Commission Staff Working Document. Practical guide quantifying harm in actions for damages based on breaches of Article 101 or 102 TFEU accompanying the Communication from the Commission on quantifying harm in actions for damages based on breaches of Article 101 or 102 TFEU, SWD(2013) 205, 11 June 2013.

[157] Directive 2014/104 (EU) of the European Parliament and of the Council of 26 November 2014 on certain rules governing actions for damages under national law for infringements of the competition law provisions of the Member States and of the European Union, 2014 OJ L 349/1.

[158] Recommendation, recital (7).

[159] Directive on Antitrust Damages Actions, recital (13).

[160] ibid, art 1.1.

[161] The Directive aims to clarify the rules on the limitation periods for bringing actions for damages (art 10), joint and several liability (art 11) and the passing-on of overcharges (arts 12–15). The Directive also reiterates that Member States have to ensure that, where national courts rule, in actions for damages, on agreements, decisions or practices which are already the subject of a final infringement decision by a national competition authority or by a review court, those courts cannot take decisions running counter to such finding of an infringement (art 9).

[162] Case C-360/09, *Pfleiderer AG and Bundeskartellamt* [2011] ECR I-05161.

referred a prejudicial question to the CJEU. The CJEU ruled that it is for the Member States to establish and apply national rules on this right of access. The national courts should determine the conditions under which such access must be permitted or refused, by weighing the interest protected by Union law, on the one hand, and the right of any individual to claim damages, on the other. In other words, the need for confidentiality of leniency statements and documents may be subordinated to the interest of civil claimants in obtaining access to such documents. The decision was seen as having a grave impact on EU cartel enforcement.

To reverse the *Pfleiderer* decision, the European legislature provided (binding) rules on the disclosure of evidence in the Directive on Antitrust Damages Actions.[163] When a plaintiff has presented a reasoned justification containing reasonably available facts and evidence sufficient to support the plausibility of his or her claim for damages, national courts are able to order the defendant or a third party to disclose relevant evidence which lies in their control.[164] National courts should limit the disclosure of evidence to that which is proportionate, which means taking into account the legitimate interests of all parties and third parties concerned.[165] They can order the disclosure of evidence containing confidential information where they consider it relevant to the action for damages.[166] Those from whom disclosure is sought have to be provided with an opportunity to be heard before a national court orders any disclosure.[167] In case of the disclosure of evidence included in the file of a NCA, the court should take into account a number of additional and specific considerations in assessing the proportionality requirement.[168] Some evidence can only be disclosed after a NCA has closed its proceedings.[169] In theory, leniency statements and settlement submissions cannot be disclosed.[170] Penalties can be imposed on parties, third parties and their legal representatives when they fail or refuse to comply with a disclosure order, when they destroy evidence, or when they fail or refuse to comply with the obligations imposed by a national court order protecting confidential information.[171]

---

[163] These rules are built on the approach adopted in Directive 2004/48 (EC) of the European Parliament and of the Council of 29 April 2004 on the enforcement of intellectual property rights, 2004 OJ L 157/45.

[164] Directive on Antitrust Damages Actions, art 5.1. The reverse is also possible. Upon request of the defendant, national courts can order the plaintiff or a third party to disclose relevant evidence (art 5.2).

[165] ibid, art 5.3. The courts shall in particular consider: '(a) the extent to which the claim or defense is supported by available facts and evidence justifying the request to disclose evidence; (b) the scope and cost of disclosure, especially for any third parties concerned, including preventing non-specific searches for information which is unlikely to be of relevance for the parties in the procedure; (c) whether the evidence the disclosure of which is sought contains confidential information, especially concerning any third parties, and what arrangements are in place for protecting such confidential information'.

[166] ibid, art 5.4.

[167] ibid, art 5.7.

[168] ibid, art 6.4: ('(a) whether the request has been formulated specifically with regard to the nature, subject matter or contents of documents submitted to a competition authority or held in the file thereof, rather than by a non-specific application concerning documents submitted to a competition authority; (b) whether the party requesting disclosure is doing so in relation to an action for damages before a national court; and (c) in relation to paragraphs 5 and 10, or upon request of a competition authority pursuant to paragraph 11, the need to safeguard the effectiveness of the public enforcement of competition law').

[169] ibid, art 6.5: ('(a) information that was prepared by a natural or legal person specifically for the proceedings of a competition authority; (b) information that the competition authority has drawn up and sent to the parties in the course of its proceedings; and (c) settlement submissions that have been withdrawn').

[170] Directive on Antitrust Damages Actions, art 6.6.

[171] ibid, art 8.

The Directive also eases the causation inquiry and the quantification of harm. The burden and standard of proof required with respect to the quantification of harm cannot be so onerous as to render the exercise of the right to damages practically impossible or excessively difficult.[172] In case of a cartel infringement, it is presumed that the infringement caused harm. The infringer has the right to rebut this presumption.[173] A notable provision is that, upon request of a national court, a NCA may assist that national court with respect to the determination of the quantum of damages where that NCA considers such assistance to be appropriate.[174] Finally, parties and courts having to estimate the amount of harm will be able to utilise the Commission's Communication on quantifying harm in actions for damages and a Practical Guide on Quantifying Harm. However, these documents are not legally binding.

To incentivise parties to settle their dispute consensually, the Directive aims at optimising the balance between out-of-court settlements and actions for damages. The proposal contains provisions regarding the suspensive effect[175] and the effect of consensual settlements on subsequent actions for damages.[176] The Directive also states that a NCA may consider compensation paid as a result of a consensual dispute settlement and prior to its decision imposing a fine to be a mitigating factor.[177]

XII. Data Protection

Finally, the new General Data Protection Regulation and Directive contains a (specific) group action-alike procedure. Data subjects have the right to mandate a not-for-profit organisation, with regard to the protection of their personal data, to lodge a complaint on his or her behalf with a supervisory authority, a controller or processor and to exercise the right to receive compensation on his or her behalf where provided for by Member State law.[178]

---

[172] ibid, art 17.1.

[173] ibid, art 17.2.

[174] ibid, art 17.3.

[175] ibid, art 18. The limitation period for bringing an action for damages must be suspended for the duration of any consensual dispute resolution process. The national courts seized of an action for damages may suspend their proceedings for up to 2 years where the parties thereto are involved in consensual dispute resolution concerning the claim covered by that action for damages.

[176] ibid, art 19. Following a consensual settlement, the claim of the settling injured party is reduced by the settling co-infringer's share of the harm that the infringement inflicted upon the injured party. Any remaining claim of the settling injured party shall be exercised only against non-settling co-infringers. Non-settling co-infringers cannot recover contribution from the settling co-infringer for the remaining claim. Only when the non-settling co-infringers are not able to pay the damages that correspond to the remaining claim can the settling co-infringer be held to pay damages to the settling injured party. This limitation of joint and several liability comes down to tort reform in the guise of procedural reform.

[177] ibid, art 18.3.

[178] Regulation (EU) 2016/679 of the European Parliament and of the Council of April 27, 2016 on the Protection of Natural Persons With Regard to the Processing of Personal Data and on the Free Movement of Such Data, and Repealing Directive 95/46/EC (General Data Protection Regulation), 2016 OJ L 119/1, art 80; and Directive (EU) 2016/680 of the European Parliament and of the Council of April 27, 2016 on the Protection of Natural Persons With Regard to the Processing of Personal Data by Competent Authorities for the Purposes of the Prevention,

XIII. Investors

The European Commission issued a public consultation in July 2017 on extending mediation as a means of resolving disputes between investors and public authorities.[179] That consultation said:

> The EU has the objective of exploiting the full potentials of amicable dispute resolution methods such as mediation while ensuring the respect of the right to an effective remedy and to a fair trial enshrined in Article 47 of the EU Charter of Fundamental Rights. Amicable resolution methods allow parties to find a consensual solution to a problem without the participation of a person with binding adjudicatory powers (such as a judge). ….

> Mediation could help to ensure a cost-effective and quick resolution of disputes between investors and public authorities. It could also prevent the existence of such disputes entirely. Another policy option which could be envisaged would be to establish a network of national contact points responsible for providing advice and information to investors about the legal environment relevant to their investment and intervening on their behalf with public authorities when complex legal or factual situations require such an intervention. ….

> Another important question to consider is the stage of the dispute at which mediation can be used. Mediation can be used when proceedings have already been brought to courts, but encouraging mediation even earlier on could be useful in preventing litigation of such disputes. In such early stages of the process, the purpose of mediation would be to fully understand the factual and legal circumstances of the case and the interests of all the parties concerned and to agree on a solution that would respect the applicable law. Such mediation procedures could even take place before a decision/act is adopted by the authority concerned. Instead of a formalised mediation process, one could also envisage an amicable intervention by a national investment contact point that would help the parties understand the national and EU legal rules applicable in their case as well as all underlying interests that need to be taken into account.[180]

XIV. Conclusions

The following broad conclusions appear from this overview of EU debates and policy. First, the EU generally favours public enforcement over private enforcement, but mechanisms at Member State level are complex, involve a number of hybrids, and are evolving. Second, the development of the balance between public and private enforcement at EU level is not

---

Investigation, Detection or Prosecution of Criminal Offences or the Execution of Criminal Penalties, and on the Free Movement of such Data, and Repealing Council Framework Decision 2008/977/JHA, 2016 OJ L 119/89, art 55.

[179] *Consultation document: Prevention and amicable resolution of disputes between investors and public authorities within the single market* (European Commission, 2017), https://ec.europa.eu/info/consultations/finance-2017-investment-protection-mediation_en.

[180] ibid.

subject to any integrated plan or vision. Individual mechanisms have been introduced and reformed piecemeal and fortuitously. Third, political proposals are made in response to sentiment and major scandals, rather than based on a convincing analysis of the root cause of the problems and identification of which mechanisms might solve them. The latest political proposals, including the ones in the Commission's Report on the implementation of the Recommendation, are opportunistic, rather than based on the available evidence.

Based on these findings, we suggest that it is imperative for the EU authorities and Council members to take a step back and evaluate all mechanisms for achieving the objectives, and then to promulgate a coherent, integrated and evidence-based plan to delivering the objectives. That plan should integrate all available mechanisms, and outline a convincing statement of the balance between all mechanisms.

Out of this process would emerge an enforcement architecture that clarifies the balance between public and private enforcement and every other kind of enforcement. We believe that the current model of enforcement that exists in Europe has at least four pillars, rather than two. Out of the public enforcement pillar has emerged self- and co-regulatory mechanisms, and out of the private enforcement-through-courts pillar has emerged a number of types of ADR, each with emerging new architectures.

Further, in this book we identify a breakdown or hybridity of the two traditional pillars. Thus, public prosecutors and regulatory agencies deliver (private) damages in addition to their core functions of supervision and public enforcement, and new bodies (ombudsmen, who have emerged from the private enforcement space, via ADR, but now occupy a hybrid public-private space) deliver both compensation and regulatory functions.

The position is illustrated in Figure 2.1. It is no longer rational to be dogmatic about 'public enforcement' or 'private enforcement'. Instead, the primary question is an empirical one of which particular mechanism, or combination of mechanisms, delivers the desired outcomes. In other words, what works?

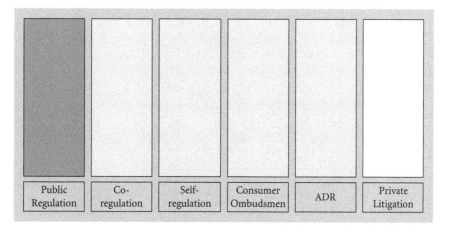

| Public Regulation | Co-regulation | Self-regulation | Consumer Ombudsmen | ADR | Private Litigation |

Figure 2.1: The Intermingling of Public and Private Pillars of Enforcement

3

Collective Actions

I. Introduction

The first technique is going to court. The (judicial) collective action is a representative or non-representative action brought by a group representative acting on behalf of a group of persons who are confronted with the same or similar legal and/or factual issues. The scope of these collective actions can be universal (in the sense that they apply to all fields of law) or sectorial (ie limited to specific fields of law; eg consumer law). The class members, on whose behalf the action is brought, can opt in or opt out. If they opt in or do not opt out, they are bound by the *res iudicata* effect of the decision. Collective actions can be used for injunctive, declaratory or monetary relief.

As mentioned in the previous chapter, the European Commission published, in June 2013, its Recommendation on common principles for injunctive and compensatory collective redress mechanisms in the Member States concerning violations of rights granted under Union Law. The Commission recommends that all Member States should have collective redress mechanisms in those areas where Union law grants rights to citizens and companies. The goal is not to harmonise the national systems, but to list some common, non-binding, principles relating both to judicial (compensatory and injunctive) and out-of-court collective redress that Member States should take into account when crafting such mechanisms. These principles relate to injunctive and compensatory collective redress mechanisms.

This chapter gives an overview of the existing collective action mechanisms in a number of Member States (Belgium, Bulgaria, England and Wales, Finland, France, Germany, Italy, Lithuania, Poland and Sweden). There is no European-model in existence on the ground. As the overview shows, there is a lot of variation in design, quality and operation. Moreover, most Member States do not adhere to the model as proposed by the European Commission in its Recommendation. Besides a brief outline of the relevant mechanism(s), each subchapter describes, in more detail, a number of case studies to illustrate the use of the collective action mechanism on the ground.

II. Belgium[1]

A. Overview

In 2014, the Belgian legislator introduced a class action system to resolve mass disputes.[2] The core idea is bringing an aggregate of individual consumer claims[3] aiming at obtaining redress before a court via one class representative meeting certain criteria in a single procedure without prior mandate. The Brussels courts have exclusive jurisdiction. The legislator centralised the class action procedures in order to develop expertise and specialisation. The class representative can freely choose to initiate legal proceedings before the court of first instance or the commercial court of Brussels.[4] On appeal, the Brussels Court of Appeals has jurisdiction.

The procedure consists of four phases: a certification phase, a mandatory negotiation phase, a potential phase on the merits and an enforcement phase.

The first phase is the certification phase. After a petition[5] is filed by the designated representative,[6] the court rules on the admissibility of the claim[7] and imposes an opt-in or opt-out system.[8] With regard to the admissibility, there are three class action prerequisites.

According to the first admissibility criterion, the cause of action must be a possible violation by the defendant (who has to be a trader) of his contractual obligations or one of the European or Belgian consumer regulations or acts which are specifically enumerated in the Code of Economic Law.[9] Thus, the claim has to be based on at least one of these regulations or acts. The listed provisions are all to be situated in the field of consumer law (C2B-disputes). Hence, the approach is sectoral. The Belgian Constitutional Court has ruled that the limited scope does not constitute a discrimination (related to (collective) access to justice).[10] In order to examine the first accessibility criterion, the court will have to engage in a difficult prima facie judgment on the merits of the case.

---

[1] This section was written by Stefaan Voet and Pieter Gillaerts.

[2] The class action was introduced by the Act of 28 March 2014 (Wet tot invoeging van titel 2 'Rechtsvordering tot collectief herstel' in boek XVII 'Bijzondere rechts procedures' van het Wetboek van economisch recht en houdende invoeging van de definities eigen aan boek XVII in boek I van het Wetboek van economisch recht), Official Belgian Gazette 29 March 2014, 35.201.

[3] Code of Economic Law (CEL), art XVII.38 states that the group of consumers represented consists of all consumers who have personally suffered a loss due to a common cause, albeit with a difference between the opt-in and the opt-out model.

[4] CEL, art XVII.35.

[5] The petition must contain evidence that the certification criteria are met, a description of the collective harm, a detailed description of the class, and the reasons for using the opt-in or opt-out system. See Art XVII.42, §1 CEL.

[6] CEL, arts XVII.42–44.

[7] CEL, art XVII.43, §1.

[8] CEL, arts XVII.38 and XVII.43, and §2, 3°.

[9] CEL, art XVII.36, 1°.

[10] Belgian Constitutional Court 17 March 2016, n° 41/2016, 27–31.

According to the second admissibility criterion, the class representative must meet the statutory requirements and must be considered as adequate by the court.[11] Only three categories of associations can act as class representative:[12]

— a limited number of consumer organisations;
— non-profit organisations meeting certain criteria (a minimum of three years of legal capacity, ministerial recognition, the activity of the organisation must overlap with its statutory aim and must be related to the collective interest concerned);
— the Consumer Mediation Service.

The Consumer Mediation Service is Belgium's residual alternative dispute resolution (ADR) entity.[13] It can only bring a class action for the purposes of reaching a collective settlement. In the absence of a settlement, the court will have to assess the merits of the case, and a consumer organisation will have to take over the procedure.[14]

Hence, the Belgian system opts for an associational plaintiff without private cause of action or grievance against the defendant. The adequacy of the representation prevents potential conflicts of interest.

According to the third admissibility criterion, the class action has to be superior to (ie more suitable than) an individual civil action.[15] The Court may take into account the following elements: the potential group size, the existence of individual damages in connection with the collective harm, the complexity and judicial efficiency of the class action mechanism, and the legal certainty for the group of consumers on whose behalf the action is brought. That way, the Court has significant discretionary powers. After notification of the certification decision, the consumers can opt in or opt out. Their decision is irrevocable.[16]

The second phase is a mandatory negotiation phase, the goal of which is to reach a collective settlement. A settlement is possible in each phase: prior to the legal proceedings,[17] during the mandatory negotiation phase[18] or during the procedure on the merits of the case.[19] If such a settlement is reached it is submitted to the court for approval (homologation).[20] If parties have reached a collective settlement before the proceedings, they can jointly request approval.[21] Their agreement must contain a minimum of information which is enumerated in the Code of Economic Law.[22] The approval is not pro forma. With the parties' consent, the court can appoint an accredited mediator to assist them.[23]

In the absence of a collective settlement, the Court will decide on the merits of the case. As a result, this third phase of deciding on the merits of the case will not always be present in each case. With regard to the extent and forms of collective redress, any collective

---

[11] CEL, art XVII.36, 2°.
[12] CEL, art XVII.39.
[13] See ch 6.
[14] CEL, art XVII.40.
[15] CEL, art XVII.36, 3°.
[16] CEL, art XVII.38, §1 in fine.
[17] CEL, art XVII.42, §2.
[18] CEL, arts XVII.45–48.
[19] CEL, art XVII.56.
[20] CEL, arts XVII.44–51.
[21] CEL, art XVII.42, §2.
[22] CEL, art XVII.45, §3, 2°–13°.
[23] CEL, art XVII.45, §2.

settlement or decision on the merits of the case must determine both the extent and forms of that collective redress. The guiding principle remains full and individual compensation and the redress can be in kind or by monetary payment.

Finally, the procedure reaches the fourth phase: the enforcement phase. In case of an approved collective settlement or a decision on the merits of the case (establishing the liability of the defendant), the Court will appoint a collective claims settler to oversee the execution of the settlement or the decision.[24] The Court can only appoint attorneys, ministerial public servants or judicial mandataries who are competent in settling claims.[25] When the settlement or the decision is fully enforced, the collective claims settler deposits a final report to the court, containing all necessary information for the Court to decide on the procedure's Closure.

In its certification decision, the Court will decide on whether the class action will follow the opt-in or opt-out model.[26] It will do so in light of the underlying facts and claims of the case, as well as the parties' motives and the nature of the collective damage. In case physical or moral damages are claimed or for class members not residing in Belgium, the opt-in model is mandatory.[27] In case a collective settlement has been reached before the procedure, the class representative and the defendant will agree on choosing the opt-in or opt-out model.[28]

There are no specific rules on funding and financing. The general rules apply so that the class action procedure is financed in the same way as individual procedures. Consequently, all will depend on the financial willingness and power of the class representative. In the absence of an exception to the loser pays rule, the class representative takes a financial risk when initiating a class action, because he can end up paying the costs and expenses. No specific rules regarding the compensation or remuneration of the class representative can be found in Code of Economic Law, apart from Article XVII.45, §3, 8°, which states that a collective settlement must contain the costs to be paid to the class representative and that these cannot exceed the actual costs borne by him. As far as the Consumer Mediation Service is concerned, its public nature implies taxpayer funding.

B. Case Studies

Table 3.1: Number of class action procedures in Belgium between 2014 and 2017

defendant	nature	number of class members	opt-in or opt-out	status
Thomas Cook Airlines Belgium	delayed airplane	183	Test-Achats asked for opt-out; the court imposed opt-in	finished (certification decision on 4 April 2016 and final judgment (settlement) in July 2017)

(continued)

---

[24] CEL, arts XVII.52–62.
[25] CEL, art XVII.57, §1.
[26] CEL, arts XVII.38 and XVII.43, §2, 3°.
[27] CEL, arts XVII.38, §1, 2° and XVII.43, §2, 3°.
[28] CEL, art XVII.42, §2.

Table 3.1: (*Continued*)

defendant	nature	number of class members	opt-in or opt-out	status
Proximus (telecom company)	misleading information about digital decoders (for watching digital TV)	±30,000 potential class members	Test-Achats asked for opt-out; the court imposed opt-out	Pending (certification decision on 4 April 2017; Proximus appealed)
Volkswagen & d'Ieteren (Belgian Volkswagen distributor)	emissions-cheating software	± 11,000 people registered, but ± 400.000 cars are involved	Test-Achats asked for opt-out; the court imposed opt-out	Pending (certification decision on 19 December 2017)
various websites reselling concert tickets	illegal reselling of concert tickets	2,650 people registered	Test-Achats asks for opt-out	Pending (introductory hearing on 4 September 2017)
Belgian Rail	compensation for delayed trains (during strikes)	44,000 people registered		case was withdrawn (most passengers were compensated and there was an agreement between Test-Achats and Belgian Rail allowing Test-Achats to help improving the existing compensation system)

Case study: Thomas Cook Airlines Belgium

The first Belgian class action case was brought by Test-Achats (Belgium's biggest consumer association) against Thomas Cook Airlines Belgium. It was a case about a delayed flight from Tenerife to Brussels on 23 March 2015. In Tenerife the plane collided with a vehicle. Thomas Cook Airlines Belgium flew in another plane from Brussels. The original flight was delayed for eight hours. Originally, Thomas Cook Airlines Belgium refused to pay the €400 compensation (for EU flights exceeding 1,500 km).

On 4 April 2016, the Brussels Court of First Instance certified the class action.[29] It imposed an opt-in system. In July 2017, the case ended with a settlement where each class member received €400 in compensation. Starting just before and ending just after the case was brought (more specifically after the certification decision), the defendant voluntarily completed the process of compensating all the passengers. Consequently, the mandatory negation phase did not deal with how to compensate the passengers. It only dealt with the costs of the procedure, including the costs and fees of the group representative.

---

[29] Brussels Court of First Instance 4 April 2016, Belgian Official Gazette 28 June 2016, 39.309.

Case study: Belgian Rail

During the winter of 2014–15, the unions at the Belgian Rail company (NMBS/SNCB) organised a series of strikes. Test-Achats decided to bring a class action because of undelivered services. 44,000 passengers registered. Test-Achats not only claimed compensation for travellers, but also a simplification of the procedure Belgian Rail uses to offer compensation in case of delays. The latter claim was successful. At one point, the class action was withdrawn because Belgian Rail offered Test-Achats the opportunity to work with them to improve the existing compensation rules about delayed trains (travellers have more time to claim compensation (30 days instead of 15 days) and it is possible to receive the compensation via wire transfer; Test-Achats was also involved in the new web design Belgian Rail offers to travellers to claim compensation online). Moreover, and similar to the Thomas Cook Airlines Belgium case, Belgian Rail compensated most of the 44,000 passengers voluntarily.

Case study: Proximus

In 2016, Proximus (a telecom company) contacted its customers three times regarding the replacement of a V3decoder that had to be used to watch Proximus TV. From February 2017 onwards, that decoder could not be used any more for technical reasons. In the letters Proximus offered a promotional deal regarding the free use of a new decoder for one year. Test-Achats claimed that the customers who accepted the offer after the first two letters received free rent only for five months and not one year. In the class action procedure Test-Achats claimed, on behalf of about 30,000 duped customers, compensation for the monetary loss they had suffered. In its decision of 4 April 2017, the (Dutch Speaking) Court of First Instance of Brussels certified the class action. The Court imposed an opt-out system. The certification decision was appealed by Proximus. The case is currently pending before the Brussels Court of Appeals.

III. Bulgaria[30]

Bulgaria introduced a collective redress mechanism in 2007.[31] The action can be brought on behalf of all persons who are harmed by the same infringement where, according to the nature of the infringement, the group of such persons cannot be defined precisely but is identifiable. The infringement can be a breach of contract or a tort, including a breach of statutory duty. All persons who claim that they are harmed by such an infringement, or any organisation responsible for the protection of injured persons or for the protection against such infringements, may bring, on behalf of all injured persons, the action. The cessation of the infringement or damages can be claimed.

Mass claims are within the jurisdiction of the district courts. The action is initiated by way of a statement of claim. It should specify the circumstances that define the group of injured persons and should contain a proposition for public announcement of the action. The goal is to inform as many people as possible. When the action is brought by an organisation representing collective interests, the plaintiff should provide evidence proving

---

[30] This section was written by Zsolt Okanyi and colleagues.
[31] Civil Procedure Act, Ch 33 (arts 379–88), State Gazette 59 20 July 2007, entering into force on 1 March 2008.

the ability of the organisation to protect the injured collective interests seriously and in good faith as well as its financial capacity to deal with such actions.

If the court allows the action to be initiated, it shall make a preliminary ruling on the adequate form of publication (including the number of announcements, the media channels and the time frame for making the announcement), the adequate time limit after the publication within which the injured persons may declare to the court that they will participate in the procedure or will pursue a remedy independently (ie an opt-in system). On the basis of this, and within the time limits as prescribed by the court, the court shall admit for participation in the procedure other injured persons, or organisations responsible for the protection of the injured persons, of the harmed collective interest or for the protection against such infringements, who or which have declared, within the time limit set, intention to participate in the procedure, or exclude the injured persons who have declared, within the time limit set, that they will pursue a remedy independently in a separate procedure.

The court should direct the parties to settlement and voluntary resolution of the dispute. If a voluntary arrangement is reached, it is subject to court approval. While the claim is pending, the court may order interim relief being that the defendant performs a specific act, refrains from a specific act, or pays a specific amount. The interim measure should be adequate to protect the injured collective interest. The court measure may be modified or revoked by the court upon change of circumstances.

The final judgment is binding on the infringer (ie the defendant), the person or persons who have brought the action, as well as on those persons who claim that they are harmed by the established infringement and who have not declared that they wish to pursue a remedy independently. The excluded persons may avail themselves of the judgment whereby the action has been granted. A list of the excluded persons is to be attached to the judgment of the court.

The judgment is subject to appeal. It can be appealed before the relevant Court of Appeal and the decision of the Court of Appeal can be challenged before the Court of Cassation.

If the judgment orders payment of compensation, the court may require that the compensation is deposited to the account of one of the persons who have brought the action, or to a special account jointly disposable by the persons who have brought the action, or to a special account jointly disposable by the injured persons.

After the judgment enters into force, the court may convene a general meeting of the injured persons by publishing an announcement in the same form as the announcement for the initiation of the action. The general meeting of the injured persons should be presided over by the judge and the requisite quorum is that at least six injured persons are present. The general meeting of the injured persons elects a committee to dispose of the assets in the special account.

The number of mass claims is not publicly known. However, according to unofficial sources mass claims in Bulgaria are very rare and this area of the law is underdeveloped. Moreover, there are only a handful of already decided cases. Most mass claims are initiated by non-profit organisations representing various sectoral interests—eg interests of consumers, interests of members of a professional group, etc. There are cases brought by the Commission for Protection of Consumers (CPC) as well. This governmental authority has standing to represent interests of consumers on the grounds of protection of a collective interest. The CPC usually brings cases for declaration of invalidity of unfair commercial clauses and practices (eg clauses in terms and conditions of public services suppliers such as electricity energy suppliers).

Decision no 86 17 August 2015 of the Court of Cassation under commercial case no 616/2015

The action was brought by the CPC against one of the major energy suppliers on the basis of the Consumer Protection Act requesting the Court to declare the nullity of some clauses in the general terms and conditions in electricity contracts. The claim was based on the argument that the clauses are unfair for consumers and in contravention of the Consumer Protection Act and hence void. The CPC also requested that the defendant be obliged to cease infringement of the collective interest of energy consumers and refrain from adopting unfair clauses. The claim was initially funded by the budget of the CPC but the expenses were finally reimbursed by the defendant. The CPC was represented by its internal legal counsel. It took about two years for the case to go through three judicial instances, and finally the Court of Cassation. The latter confirmed the decisions of the lower courts and declared the nullity of the disputed clauses.

IV. England and Wales[32]

A. Representative Action

An individual may bring an action in England and Wales[33] and Northern Ireland[34] on behalf of other parties without their consent, where the represented parties share the 'same interest'.[35] The judgment will bind such represented non-parties.[36] The 'same interest' requirement has been interpreted narrowly by the courts, requiring the individuals represented to share a 'common interest and a common grievance' and 'the relief sought was in its nature beneficial to all whom the plaintiff proposed to represent'.[37] Examples of where 'common interest' may arise are under a single statutory charter,[38] a generic contract,[39] or an audio recording involving alleged copyright infringement.[40] Recent cases have retained the strict approach,[41] and this mechanism is of little relevance to consumer claims.

B. Group Litigation Order (GLO)

During the 1990s, an ad hoc approach was developed in individual cases under the courts' inherent jurisdiction involving coordination of multiple similar claims through

---

[32]   The author of this section is Christopher Hodges.
[33]   Civil Procedure Rules 1998 (as amended) (CPR), Part 19.6.
[34]   The Rules of the Court of Judicature (NI), Order 15, Rule 12.
[35]   The Rules of the Court of Judicature (NI) Rule 12 (1); CPR Part 19.6 (1).
[36]   *Markt & Co Ltd v Knight Steamship Co Ltd* [1910] 2 KB 1021; *Prudential Assurance Co Ltd v Newman Industries Ltd* [1981] Ch 229.
[37]   *Duke of Bedford v Ellis* [1901] AC 1, 8.
[38]   ibid 9.
[39]   *Marckt & Co Ltd v Knight Steamship Co Ltd* [1910] 2 KB 1021 (CA), 1040. A successful modern case in relation to tenants of the same block of flats claiming the cost of remedial works was *Millharbour Management Limited and Others v Weston Homes Limited and Another* [2011] EWHC 661 (TCC).
[40]   *Independiente Ltd v Music Trading On-Line (HK) Ltd* [2003] EWHC 470 (Ch), para 27.
[41]   *Emerald Supplies Ltd v British Airways Plc* [2010] EWCA Civ 1284 (dismissing 'a bold attempt at keeping a procedural novelty alive'); *Breslin and others v McKevitt and others* [2011] NICA 33.

aggregation and unified case management. There has been a distinct historical pattern in the incidence of multi-party actions. There are occasional transport accidents, mass murders, holiday health or service claims. In the 1980s–1990s, the focus was on medicinal products and tobacco, many of which failed. Between 1995 and 2004 the attention shifted to abuse in child care homes, following prosecutions. In 2008 and on, the focus was on financial services.

The Group Litigation Order (GLO) was introduced under the reformed Civil Procedure Rules of 1998 (as CPR 19.III).[42] It is an opt-in procedure in which all group members are parties to the proceedings.[43] An application is made for the court to order that proceedings should be constituted and managed as a GLO, and the court must be satisfied that the claims of all group members share 'common or related issues of fact or law' (the 'GLO issues').[44] The GLO provides for the establishment of a 'group register', and identifies a particular court to manage all claims that fall within the Order. Case management may stay cases, or select test cases or generic issues to be resolved. A judgment in the GLO case is binding on all claimants in the GLO register at the time of the judgment and when the GLO was issued; the court may direct that judgment is binding on claims entered onto the register subsequent to the granting of the GLO.[45] Arrangements for funding and costs are usually complex. The normal 'loser pays costs rule' applies, but the qualified one-way cost shift (QOCS) rule applies in personal injury actions from 2013, under which claimants who lose pay their own costs and any success fee of their lawyers, but do not pay the winner's costs, and losing defendants pay the winner's base costs.[46] The QOCS rule can be altered where the claimant acts unreasonably.[47] The general position is that all parties in the register are responsible for generic costs, and they typically are required to enter into cost-sharing agreements amongst themselves.

The number of GLOs in England and Wales between 1999 and 2017 (101 in those years, an average of five a year) is shown in Table 3.2, and the number by subject matter is in Table 3.3.[48] There was a spike in actions in 2001–02, caused by a large number of claims for damages arising out of child abuse in children's homes: these cases followed police

---

[42] CPR, Part 19 III. See R Money-Kyrle, 'Collective Enforcement of Consumer Rights in the United Kingdom' in M Schmidt-Kessel, C Strünck, and M Kramme (eds), *Im Namen der Verbraucher? Kollektive Rechtsdurchsetzung in Europa*, (Schriften zu Verbraucherrecht und Verbraucherwissenschaften, Band 5 Jenaer Wissenschaftliche Verlagsgesellschaft, 2015). See also C Hodges, *Multi-Party Actions* (Oxford, Oxford University Press, 2001); C Hodges, 'Global Class Actions Project. Country Report: England and Wales' (2007), 10–20, at http://globalclassactions. stanford.edu/sites/default/files/documents/England_Country%20Report.pdf; C Hodges, *The Reform of Class and Representative Actions in European Legal Systems* (Oxford, Hart Publishing, 2008) 53–64; N Andrews, 'Multi-Party Litigation in England' in V Harsagi and CH can Rhee (eds), *Multi-Party redress Mechanisms: Squeaking Mice?* (Cambridge, Intersentia, 2014).

[43] Civil Procedure Rules 1998, Practice Direction 19B-Group Litigation para 1.

[44] CPR Part 19.10.

[45] ibid Part 19.12.

[46] For the policy on which the Rules are based see *Written Ministerial Statement: Implementation of Part 2 of the Legal Aid, Sentencing and Punishment of Offenders Act 2012: Civil Litigation Funding and Costs* (Ministry of Justice, 2012).

[47] Legal Aid, Sentencing and Punishment of Offenders Act 2012, s. 44. For implementation policy see *Written Ministerial Statement: Implementation of Part 2 of the Legal Aid, Sentencing and Punishment of Offenders Act 2012: Civil Litigation Funding and Costs* (Ministry of Justice, 2012).

[48] Data at https://www.gov.uk/guidance/group-litigation-orders. Chart prepared by Harriet Harper.

investigations and criminal cases since the 1990s. Funding of these large cases is a major issue, and third party funders have been selective in the cases they pursue.[49]

The data reveal a wide range of subject matter for cases brought under the GLO procedure or its previously developing arrangements. Different types of case have 'spiked' at different times.

Table 3.2: Number of GLOs in England and Wales between 1999 and 2017

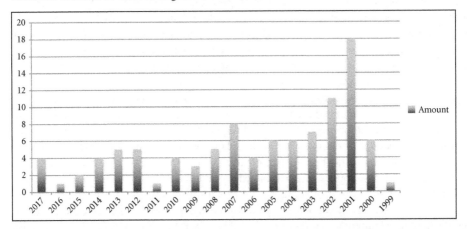

Table 3.3: Number of GLOs in England and Wales 1999–2017 by subject matter

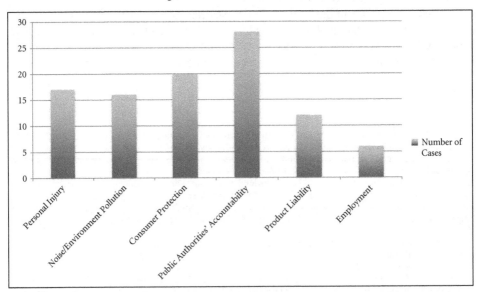

---

[49] In *Excalibur Ventures v Texas Keystone and others* [2016] EWCA Civ 1144, the third party funder put up security for the defendant's standard costs during the action, but after the action was dismissed, the trial judge's award of indemnity costs against the funder was upheld by the Court of Appeal on the principle that the funder should 'follow the fortunes of those from whom he himself hoped to derive a small fortune'.

The outcomes of these GLO cases are not known. It appears that many GLOs collapse or settle. Some cases have been criticised as not delivering access to justice, and involving huge costs.[50]

GLOs will typically take several years to resolve, whether through negotiation or judicial decision. Unlike the watershed of certification in a class action system, the fact that a GLO is made appears to have little direct effect on triggering a swift settlement. In the miners' litigation, it took two years to negotiate and put a compensation scheme in place, to deliver an estimated £4 billion compensation and £2.3 billion costs.[51] The matter took 10 years to resolve, and spawned satellite litigation on lawyers' representation and some solicitors being struck off.

A recent study of several streams of claims arising from a major explosion in an oil depot (see case study below) showed that making a GLO may be unnecessary, since judges have existing case management powers that can be sufficient.[52] In that case, managerial control of the litigation was passed between different judges as the case progressed, so that differing judicial expertise could be engaged, such as relating to general management, construction of complex commercial contracts, and costs issues.

C. Case Studies: GLO

The first four cases are illustrative of the period before the GLO was introduced, in which the judiciary developed the case management techniques that were codified in the GLO.

Case study: Benzodiazepine tranquillizers[53]

Various products have been used to treat anxiety. Opiates and hypnotics were used for some 2,000 years. Barbiturates became available in the twentieth century but were dangerous and lethal in overdose and used for suicide. Benzodiazepines produced from the 1960s were found to have a much improved risk–benefit balance. Benzodiazepines were found to be safe in overdose but after some 20 years of use, there were reports of dependency and withdrawal symptoms on cessation of therapy.

Following media publicity, legal claims were made from 1987 alleging negligence against the two manufacturers, and in some claims prescribing doctors were joined as defendants. By 1990 over 15,000 claimants had approached solicitors and intimated claims, of which 5,500 issued proceedings, represented by around 3,000 firms of solicitors.

A single judge was appointed to manage the litigation, and adopted an approach that was consistent with, although pre-dated, the case management philosophy of Lord Woolf that was

---

[50] Presentation by Carl Dray (Nabarro, Sheffield) at the Danish European Presidency Conference on Collective Actions, Copenhagen, March 2012.

[51] National Audit Office, *Coal Health Compensation Schemes. Report by the Comptroller and Auditor General, HC 608 Session 2006–2007, 18 July 2007.*

[52] N Creutzfeld and C Hodges, 'Parallel Public and Private Responses: the Buncefield Explosion' in D Hensler, C Hodges and I Tzankova (eds), *Class Actions in Context: How Economics, Politics and Culture Shape Collective Litigation* (Cheltenham, Edward Elgar, 2016).

[53] See G Hickinbottom, 'Benzodiazepine Litigation' in Hodges, *Multi-Party Actions* (n 40).

subsequently enshrined in the Civil Procedure Rules 1998. The courts held that they had inherent power to devise such rules as may be necessary to control mass litigation fairly, untrammelled by the normal adversarial system. Important techniques deployed were the voluntary transfer of cases to the appointed judge by courts around the country, the imposition of cut-off dates for claims to be brought within the coordinated management arrangements, the making of orders that cases would be struck out unless they were brought by the cut-off date, requiring pleadings to be made in the form of a Master against which individual claimants could identify in schedules which points applied to them thereby avoiding lengthy repetition, and striking out cases that were economically unviable. The judge also indicated concerns over the merits of individual cases.

Nearly all claimants were funded from state Legal Aid. The Legal Aid Board suspected that many individual claims had not been sufficiently investigated, and required legal teams to audit claims, which resulted in many discontinuing and ultimately in the withdrawal of public funding from the entire litigation. The doctors and later the manufacturers applied to the court to strike out individual claims, which the court did, on the grounds that the expert medical reports did not substantiate the injuries alleged or that the claimant had no reasonable chance of success. The remaining claims were struck out as an abuse of process, taking into account factors such as limitation defences and considerable problems in proving causation, plus the fact that delay had prejudiced the defendants' right to a fair trial.

After the case collapsed, the Legal Aid Board said that £40 million of public money had been spent on lawyers and medical experts. The defendants had presumably also spent significant sums. No claimants received any money.

Case study: MMR vaccines[54]

In February 1988 the *Lancet* published an Early Report on 12 children in eight of whom parents had linked onset of behavioural symptoms to the triple vaccine given for immunisation against measles, mumps and rubella (MMR). Dr Andrew Wakefield of the Royal Free Hospital in London, a former surgeon with an interest in adult gastroenterology who was known to be interested in whether the measles virus might have a causal role in Crohn's disease, suggested that there was a causal association between MMR and autism.

A solicitor, Richard Barr, helped facilitate the referral to Dr Wakefield of children whose parents thought the vaccine might have caused an inflammatory bowel disorder as well as autism. In August 1996 the Legal Aid Board granted £55,000 for Dr Wakefield's research on a possible link between the MMR vaccine and autism.

Considerable media publicity was given to Dr Wakefield's assertion that the MMR vaccine could cause autism, and this led to a major public health scare. Thus in broad terms the research which led to the public health scare came about because the Legal Aid Board was prepared to grant funding for exploratory scientific research to support otherwise speculative litigation.

In 1998, the first claims were issued against three pharmaceutical companies; two manufacturers, SmithKline Beecham and Merck Co Inc, and a marketing authorisation holder, Aventis Pasteur MSD. The claims were brought under Part 1 of the Consumer Protection Act (CPA), which implements the 1985 EU Product Liability Directive. The CPA came into effect in 1988, the same year as the MMR vaccination was first routinely administered to children in the UK.

---

[54] Information kindly supplied by J Meltzer of Hogan Lovells LLP and J Stuart-Smith QC at the December 2016 Oxford Conference.

The claimants in the MMR litigation were almost all children whose claims alleged that the vaccine caused autism and other disorders. It was said that the claimants were developing normally until usually their second year when they were given the MMR vaccination and within a few weeks or months they became ill and/or their development regressed leaving them with continuing serious disorders. The claimants said that this was not a coincidence but attributable to the MMR vaccine.

The group of claimants was constituted in July 1999, under a practice direction from the Lord Chief Justice. Although this was before GLOs came into effect, for all practical purposes the litigation was conducted under the GLO procedures in Part 19 of the Civil Procedure Rules. The claimants were funded by the Legal Aid Board (later known as the Legal Services Commission (LSC)).

The defendants said that there was no medical or scientific evidence that the vaccine caused such disorders in any group of children so as to render it defective within the meaning of the CPA nor was there any evidence that it had caused such a disorder in any of the claimants. It was well established that autism commonly manifested itself during the second year of an affected child's life at a time shortly after most children in this country received their routine MMR immunisation. This timing was the same prior to the introduction of MMR in 1988.

The case proceeded with eight illustrative lead cases, four chosen by the claimants and four by the defendants from a cohort of over 1,000 cases. The trial of these lead cases, which was due to have started in April 2004, was to have been restricted to the issue of whether the vaccines were defective and if so whether the defects caused the conditions complained of by the eight lead claimants.

The litigation effectively collapsed in the summer of 2003 when the LSC withdrew funding. This was a direct consequence of the LSC having assessed the experts' reports served by the parties (28 from the claimants and 32 from the defendants) from which it became apparent that the claimants' case was not supported by the scientific evidence.

One of the reasons that the litigation was so drawn out was because from an evidential point of view it was started before the claimants' lawyers were able to establish if they had a viable case. The CPA imposes a 10 year 'long stop' cut-off period for claims, which required that children immunised with vaccine put into circulation in 1988 had to bring their claims by the relevant date in 1998.

The difficulty for the claimants was that they were not really ready to proceed, having at that stage, as they admitted, inadequate evidence of causation to succeed at trial. At the first Case Management Conference in September 1999, in asking the Court for the opportunity to gather further evidence, the claimants' counsel made the somewhat unusual admission that the claimants would not succeed if there were a trial in the near future because of inadequate evidence of causation.

The search for evidence of causation, which had, as it were, been licensed by public funding, had a pervasive impact on the management of the litigation. The claimants were repeatedly given time to conduct research and carry out a range of tests on the claimants and others which they hoped would provide supportive evidence. The pursuit of such evidence was one of the main reasons for the length of the pre-trial period.

When the LSC finally withdrew funding for the litigation, which had cost it at least £15 million, it candidly acknowledged that the 10 year time limit under the CPA meant that 'it was necessary to start court proceedings before the medical research had concluded' and that 'this was the first case in which research had been funded by legal aid. In retrospect, it was not effective or appropriate for the LSC to fund research. The court is not the place to prove new medical truths'.

An example of where efficient coordination of mass individual small claims did not work was the bank charges litigation.

Case study: Bank charges

In March 2006 Which?, the consumers' association, launched a campaign that retail banks' charges were unfair in various circumstances, such as charges for overdrawn accounts when there was no overdraft facility, or for exceeding an agreed limit, or there were insufficient funds in an account to honour a cheque or other payment.[55]

Many thousands complained to the Financial Services Ombudsman, which involved no cost to the complainant. The campaign received wide publicity, and there was a significant amount of advertising by private companies offering claims management services for bringing individual court actions. Between March 2006 and August 2007 some 53,000 customers filed claims in the county courts,[56] which significantly overloaded the system. Banks usually filed standard defences and frequently settled cases shortly before the hearing.

On 26 July 2007, the Office of Fair Trading (OFT) commenced a test case in the Commercial Court against seven banks for determination of whether the Unfair Terms in Consumer Contracts Regulations applied to unauthorised overdrafts, and whether the prevalent terms were unfair under such Regulations.[57] The banks then applied in the county courts for claims there to be stayed pending the outcome of the Commercial Court process, and District Judges listed cases in blocks, so as to afford claimants an opportunity to object to a stay, with around 30% objecting.

On 27 July 2007, the Ministry of Justice took the unusual step of issuing Guidance that the Financial Ombudsman Service had put its activities on hold pending the outcome of the Commercial Court test case, that the county courts were anticipated to do the same, and that claims management companies were reminded to do the same.[58]

In October 2007, it was reported that, if the test case were to be decided against the banks, the Financial Services Authority would consider using its power[59] to order them to repay amounts unfairly charged.[60] In April 2008 the High Court decided that the banks' terms were subject to the unfair terms legislation.[61] In November 2009 the Supreme Court decided that the charges could not be assessed for fairness by the OFT or the courts. The reason was that the charges constituted 'the price or remuneration, as against the services supplied in exchange' under the Unfair Terms in Consumer Contracts Regulations 1999 regulation 6(2), and so any assessment of the overdraft fees could not be challenged.[62] Regulatory control of such charges was subsequently introduced.

---

[55] http://www.which.co.uk/reports_and_campaigns/money/campaigns/Banking%20and%20credit/Bank%20 charges/banl_charges_campaign_559_74996.jsp.

[56] See figures quoted in R Mulheron, *Reform of Collective Redress in England and Wales: A Perspective of Need* (Civil Justice Council, 2008) table 16.

[57] http://www.oft.gov.uk/advice_and_resources/resource_base/market-studies/personal2.

[58] Claims Management Services Regulation: Claims in Respect of Bank Charges: Guidance Note 2007.

[59] Financial Services and Markets Act 2000, ss 382 and 383.

[60] M Hickman, 'FSA could "force banks to return penalty charges"', *The Independent*, 20 October 2007.

[61] *The Office of Fair Trading v. Abbey National PLC and 7 others* [2008] EWHC 875.

[62] *Office of Fair Trading v Abbey National plc and Others* [2009] UKSC 6.

Case study: Equitable Life[63]

The Equitable Life Assurance Society, a highly regarded mutual assurance company, issued policies from the 1950s, including around 90,000 with guaranteed annuity rates (GAR). Subsequently, life expectancies increased and interest rates fell, and the Society consistently under-reserved sufficient funds to cover the guaranteed annuities of policy holders. After the House of Lords held that the Society could not subsequently alter the GAR agreements, its asset shortfall was critical (£1.5 billion) and it closed to new business and in 2001 cancelled interim bonuses and cut all pension policy values (£4 billion) by 16% (14% for life policies). A scheme to alter the status of GAR and non-GAR investments was approved by shareholders and the Court in 2002. In 2001, there were some one million with-profits policyholders, mostly in the UK, with around 15,000 in Germany, Ireland and other EU states.

A small number of policyholders issued proceedings in the courts: the outcomes are unclear but some later policyholders were apparently repaid in full. Of around 6,000 complaints made to the Financial Ombudsman Service (FOS), by March 2007 some 2,087 had resulted in awards of compensation. The FOS processed claims by resolving a sequence of lead cases, which were illustrative of others. Since nearly all policyholders had a grievance, the FOS commented that awards merely reduced the value of the fund available to other policyholders.

An investigation by the European Parliament[64] concluded that the Society had been chronically short of assets through the 1990s, that the UK had not correctly implemented the Third Life Directive, its 'light touch' to regulation had not been sufficient and there had been insufficient communication between regulators in different states. It noted that litigation was not a viable option for the average policyholder in view of the costs and risks, that, although the FOS was one of the more advanced ADR schemes in Europe, it was not an appropriate means of redress in the circumstances, and alternative solutions were required including strengthening of the EU's FIN-NET system. It concluded that the losses involved were relatively small for individuals but nevertheless caused real hardship, and that the UK government should assume responsibility for failures of supervision and provide compensation for all victims. It also recommended that consumers should be able to act collectively before national courts against providers or supervisory authorities.

Case study: Buncefield explosion

A massive explosion occurred at the Buncefield oil storage depot on 10 December 2005. Damage claims were made by 3,379 individuals, seven local authorities, and 754 businesses. Claims totalling around £625 million included personal injury, damage to residential or business property, and economic loss.

The two oil companies who owned and operated the area that was the source of the explosion (Total and Chevron) decided to respond pro-actively to settle claims, and in October 2006 announced they would pay all personal liability claims as if liability was not in issue. Insurers' loss adjusters worked intensively to assess and agree many claims over several years. Different groups of claimants experienced some challenges in organising legal representation in a coordinated manner. One solicitors firm applied for a GLO on 25 January 2006. The High Court summoned

---

[63] Report on the crisis of the Equitable Life Assurance Society, 2006/2026(INI), A6-0203/2007.

[64] European Parliament Resolution on the crisis of the Equitable Life Assurance Society, 2006/2026(INI), P6_TA(2006)0293.

all parties to a Case Management Conference (CMC) in March 2016, where a Master gave various directions but did not order a GLO. A series of other CMCs was held. In mid-2007, the cases were transferred to the Commercial Court, after which a single appointed judge kept up pressure on the parties' settlement negotiations of individual claims and identified that the major obstacle to resolution was interpretation of the contract between Total and Chevron over how ultimate liability should be split between them. The judge tried that issue, after which settlements continued, under the encouragement of a single judge of the Technology and Construction Court. All claimants' cases were settled by 2010, and none resolved by trial. However, arguments over legal costs continued for a further two years.

Case study: RBS shareholders

The Royal Bank of Scotland (RBS) issued a prospectus in a £12 billion rights issue in April–June 2008, a few months before it received a £45.5 billion bail-out from the UK government. In December 2013 the High Court approved a GLO alleging misrepresentation, involving over 10 thousand large and small investors with claims totalling over £4 billion.

In December 2016 RBS agreed an £800 million settlement with three of the five investor groups, without admission of liability.[65] In June 2017, nearly 9,000 investors in the RBS Shareholder Action Group agreed a settlement of 82 pence per share, totalling £200 million.

D. The Competition Damages Class Action

From 2003 to 2016, damages for losses of consumers caused by breach of competition law could be claimed in an opt-in representative claim in the Competition Appeal Tribunal (CAT) brought by the consumers' association Which?.[66] The mechanism was widely criticised and only one case was brought: *JJB Sports*, relating to overcharges for football T-shirts.[67]

The Consumer Rights Act 2015 (CRA) introduced a series of new mechanisms, including the right to bring individual and collective actions for damages in the CAT,[68] a power for the CAT to approve a collective settlement,[69] and a power for the Competition and Markets Authority (CMA) to approve a voluntary redress scheme.[70] It came into force on 1 October 2015.

---

[65] A Frankel '$1 bln U.K. RBS deal highlights globalization of securities litigation' ThompsonReuters, http://www.nera.com/content/dam/nera/publications/2016/1%20bln%20UK%20RBS%20deal%20highlights%20 globalization%20of%20securities%20litigation.pdf.

[66] Competition Act 1998, s47A and B–E. Introduced from 20 June 2003 under The Enterprise Act 2002 (Commencement No. 3, Transitional and Transitory Provisions and Savings) Order 2003 No 1397.

[67] *JJB Sports Plc v Office of Fair Trading* [2006] EWCA Civ 1318; *Umbro Holdings Ltd, Manchester Unite Plc, Allsports Ltd v Office of Fair Trading* [2005] CAT 22; *Allsports Ltd, JJB Sports Plc v Office of Fair Trading* [2004] CAT 17.

[68] Consumer Rights Act 2015, s8 and Sch 8.

[69] Competition Act 1998, s 49C, inserted by the Consumer Rights Act 2015.

[70] Competition Act 1998, s. 49C, as amended by the Consumer Rights Act 2015. This is discussed below. See generally *Guide to Proceedings* (Competition Appeal Tribunal, 2015).

The class action for damages was introduced by Schedule 8 of CRA, which modified section 47B Competition Act 1998, adding an opt-out possibility to the pre-existing opt-in model. It also provided for broader reform of the CAT's authority by giving it the power to hear standalone claims (where the group must prove violation of competition law) as well as follow-on claims for damages (following an infringement decision by the Competition and Markets Authority, the CAT, or the European Commission).

The CRA was accompanied by the publication of CAT Rules 2105 which expanded on Schedule 8's provisions, and in detail set out the procedural and substantive aspects of the new collective regime, including the operation of its collective settlement provisions.

In summary, the class action for damages arising out of breaches of competition law may only be brought by certain specified bodies or by a party who is authorised by the CAT on the basis that it 'will fairly and adequately act in the interests of class members'. It may be either:

(a)   a stand-alone claim based on an alleged infringement of competition law, or

(b)   a follow-on claim based on a finding of infringement by the CMA, or the CAT (on appeal from the CMA), or the European Commission (to the extent that although the CAT and EU can make a finding as to the infringement of a breach of competition law and fine businesses, neither can award damages to affected parties). The EU Damages Directive 2014/104 was implemented by the UK in late 2016, and included rules on recognising a final infringement decision of national competition authority or review court of any EU Member State.[71]

The CAT decides, at the stage of considering whether to make a collective proceedings order, whether the proceedings are to be opt-in or opt-out.[72] Under the opt-in procedure, class members notify the class representative of inclusion of their claim. Under the opt-out procedure, claimants domiciled in the UK who fall within the class automatically participate unless they expressly opt out, while claimants not domiciled in the UK must opt in. Businesses, individuals or trade associations (whether class members or not) directly affected by the alleged infringement can bring claims as long as the CAT deems their representation of the class 'just and reasonable'.[73] Funding of the representative is a crucial part of the CAT's determination. Claims can be considered using the collective procedure if they raise the same, similar or related issues of fact or law.[74] The Act does not allow damages-based fee arrangements[75] nor exemplary damages.[76]

Further, the CAT is now able to assess damages on an aggregated basis for the group.[77] This is a new approach—the CAT could only previously assess damages individually. If the CAT awards damages in respect of collective proceedings, it will make an award of damages for the entirety of the claim and make an order specifying how the money is to be paid to the class members. It will not assess the amount of damages to be awarded to each

---

[71]   *Competition law redress: A guide to taking action for breaches of competition law* (CMA, 2016), CMA55.
[72]   Competition Act 1998, s 47B(2)(4).
[73]   Competition Act 1998, s 47B.8.
[74]   ibid, s 47B.6.
[75]   ibid, s 47.C.8.
[76]   ibid, s 47C.1.
[77]   ibid, s47C.2.

class member—it is not clear how this aggregate calculation should be made. In opt-out proceedings, if damages are not claimed by class members by a certain time they will be paid to charity unless the CAT orders them to be paid to cover the representative's costs. Any damages awarded in opt-out proceedings that are unclaimed within a specified period will either be paid to a prescribed charity (currently Access to Justice Foundation) or towards a representative's costs as incurred in connection with the proceedings.[78]

Two cases have been decided under the 2015 opt-out regime, relating to mobility scooters and on Mastercard charges. It seems that the follow-on procedure is attractive to litigation funders and lawyers, since the risk of failing to establish liability ought to be very low, and the argument may be essentially about the assessment of damages and hence about settlement and costs. However, both those cases led to problems: the first was discontinued and the second was refused certification at first instance.

The CRA also introduced a power for the CMA to make an order approving a collective settlement agreement made by the parties, copying the successful Dutch Collective Settlements procedure,[79] irrespective of whether collective proceedings are or are not in existence. If collective proceedings are in existence, an order approving such an agreement is only possible in respect of opt-out collective proceedings. A collective settlement order will therefore be binding on all class members except those who have opted out.

E. Early Competition Damages Cases

The following cases relate to breaches of competition law. The consumers' association Which? has brought one collective damages claim, after a finding by the CAT that various companies were involved in a cartel to fix the prices of replica football T-shirts.[80] The popular perception of this case was that it involved a clear case of liability following a binding finding of infringement, and that the association was frustrated by the opt-in requirement in not being able to facilitate compensation for more consumers. On investigation, the facts and issues turn out to be more complex.[81]

Case study: Replica football shirts[82]

On 1 August 2003 the Office of Fair Trading fined nine companies for unlawfully fixing the prices of a range of replica football shirts between 2000 and 2001.[83] In the case of JJB Sports plc, the OFT based its fine on 2% of the UK turnover infringements affected,[84] which was £659 million in

---

[78] ibid, s 47.C.5.

[79] Consumer Rights Act 2015, Sch 8, adding Competition Act 1998 s 49A.

[80] http://www.which.co.uk/reports_and_campaigns/consumer_rights/campaigns/Football%20shirts/index.jsp.

[81] The above para is taken from Hodges, *The Reform of Class* (n 40)).

[82] Certain information kindly supplied by Deborah Prince of Which? and Martin Rees and Kate Vernon of DLA Piper LLP, who acted for JJB Sports plc.

[83] Oft decision dated 1 August 2003 No. CA98/06/2003; appealed as *Allsports Limited, JJB Sports plc v Office of Fair Trading* [2004] CAT 17; *Umbro Holdings Ltd, Manchester United plc, Allsports Limited v Office of Fair Trading* [2005] CAT 22; *JJB Sports plc v Office of Fair Trading* [2006] Court of Appeal EWCA Civ 1318. The fines initially totalled £18.57 million but were reduced on appeal to £15.49 million.

[84] Judgment on Penalty, 19 May 2005, para 58.

the year ended 31 January 2001.[85] The Competition Appeal Tribunal (CAT) reduced the penalty to £6.70 million, noting that it represented approximately 1% of the company's UK turnover. However, neither body identified the amount of illicit gain nor the extent of any overcharge to consumers.

After extensive publicity of the OFT action, the company had issued an offer for anyone who came to its shops with the shirts concerned to exchange them with a current England shirt and mug, with retail value £25, irrespective of whether the shirts had been bought in its shops of from other retailers. This voluntary good will offer, made in the light of adverse publicity, was advertised in football magazines and some 16,000 people availed themselves of the deal.

The UK consumers' association Which? believed that around two million consumers had purchased shirts and that prices had been inflated by £15–£20 per shirt. In March 2007 it instituted the first collective claim for damages under Schedule 4 of the Enterprise Act in the CAT[86] but, for jurisdictional reasons in relation to the date of introduction of the new powers, could only claim against one company that had been involved in the cartel, JJB Sports plc. The damages claim included a claim for exemplary damages for disregard of consumer detriment, on the basis that that head of claim had not been included in the OFT's fine.[87]

Which? faced various problems. First, the opt-in procedure meant that individual consumers had to be attracted to sign up. Which? launched a media campaign, including a page on its website that included details of how to register, but only some 130 consumers signed up and were named in the initial complaint. Second, all essential documents were required to be annexed to the claim form, and claimants faced problems in producing proof of purchase, many having no available receipt. Third, gaining access to evidence from OFT and the defendant was a considerable and expensive task. Fourth, the issue of funding lawyers was solved by holding a competition for lawyers to act on behalf of claimants on a conditional fee agreement that provided for a 100% success fee.

JJB Sports plc argued that it had not in fact been involved in any collusion, that consumers had suffered no overcharge but that the products had in fact been sold at a loss (although it was found to have broken the law). It asserted that it had pursued a publicly stated policy of holding prices of replica shirts below £40 and it was the manufacturers who had colluded to raise the price, in which JJB Sports plc had become involved merely because of communications on the issue but without intent to fix prices to consumers' detriment.

In January 2008 a settlement was reached that JJB Sports plc would pay £20 per shirt bought to those consumers who signed up to the action and could produce their shirts or other proof of purchase, and sign a statement of truth. Which? had been contacted by around 600 people (involving around 1,000 shirts), although did not have full details for all of them, so the total amount involved would be a maximum of £18,000. The company would also pay the reasonable costs of Which? but there was a dispute over whether this would include the whole of the success fee.[88] Further, anyone who had previously accepted JJB Sports's earlier exchange offer could claim a further £5, and anyone else could bring in an unmarked shirt or receipt and be paid £10, these two offers remaining open to the end of the limitation period in 2009.[89]

---

[85] Judgment, 1 October 2004, para 28.
[86] The Notice of a Claim for Damages is at http://www.catribunal.org.uk/archive/casedet.asp?id=127.
[87] See the *OFT's guidance as to the appropriate amount of a penalty*, at http://www.oft.gov.uk/shared_oft/business_leaflets/ca98_guidelines/oft423.pdf.
[88] See *The Lawyer*, 9 January 2008.
[89] Details at http://www.which.co.uk/reports_and_campaigns/consumer_rights/campaigns/Football%20shirts/index.jsp.

Case study: Private schools cartel

Many of the private schools in the UK were found to have fixed prices. If the OFT were to have imposed its normal level of fine, it would have had to have been funded by parents who had not paid the inflated prices, and many schools might have been forced into bankruptcy. The negotiated solution was that the schools would pay comparatively modest amounts into a scholarship fund for the further education of those pupils whose parents had paid inflated fees.

Case study: Milk price cartel

On 20 September 2007, the OFT issued a provisional finding of collusion between five large supermarkets and five dairy processors over the retail prices of milk and certain dairy products between 2002 and 2003. On 7 December 2007 it announced agreement with six companies, which admitted involvement and paid penalties totalling £116 million, including significant reductions for cooperation. One company received complete immunity after applying for leniency disclosure.[90] The companies denied wrongdoing and asserted that their action in raising prices had been under pressure from the government in order to assist dairy farmers.[91]

The small amounts of individual compensation and difficulties over proof led law firms to conclude that a case under the existing opt-in procedures would not be viable. This meant that consumers received no redress in relation to an estimated total cost of £270 million.[92]

Case study: Airline fuel surcharges

In August 2007 the UK and US authorities imposed fines on British Airways for infringements under a cartel with Virgin Atlantic involving fuel surcharges on flights between August 2004 and March 2006.[93] Virgin Atlantic escaped a fine as it had confessed the cartel to the OFT, and was excused under the leniency programme.[94]

A US-based law firm subsequently brought damages claims in a class action in a US Federal court, which was settled in February 2008. The surcharges involved between £5 and £60, and applied to 5.6 million passengers. The two airlines agreeing to repay a total of $200 million ($59 million to US passengers and £73.5 million to UK passengers), representing up to £20, which was around one-third of the fuel surcharge levied per long-haul ticket, and could be claimed until 2012. Around 40,000 individual travellers and 300 businesses registered via a website.[95]

Michael Hausfeld, the senior partner of Cohen Milstein Hausfeld & Toll, who brought the class action, said that 'This is the first time that there has been a trans-jurisdictional recovery on a parity basis'[96] with 'non-US citizens [being] rewarded on an equal footing to US citizens before the US courts'.[97] The firm's fees, to be approved by the Court, were expected to be around $60 million.

---

[90] OFT Press Release, http://www.oft.gov.uk/news/press/2007/170-07.

[91] J Moore, 'OFT pays Morrisons £100,000 damages over price-fixing claims', *The Independent*, 24 April 2008.

[92] N Rose, 'Class actions will make claims easier', *Gazette*, 21 February 2008.

[93] *Press release*, Office of Fair Trading, 1 August 2007. British Airways was fined £121.5 million by the British authorities, and $300 million by the US Federal Trade Commission.

[94] See *OFT's Guidance as to the appropriate amount of a penalty*, Office of Fair Trading, 2004.

[95] *Financial Times*, 23 February 2008.

[96] C Ruckin, 'Cohen Milstein lands $200m BA-Virgin settlement', *Legal Week*, 15 February 2008.

[97] D Fortson, 'UK businesses braced for class action suits after BA and Virgin pay out $200m', *The Independent*, 16 February 2008.

Case study: Airline freight charges

In 2011 law firm Hausfeld & Co LLP (Hausfeld) contacted the China Chamber of International Commerce (CCOIC), as a result of which CCOIC prepared a list of members who the Director of the Legal Counsel Office believed 'were likely to have suffered harm as a result of the airlines' cartel activities'. In fact, Hausfeld was not instructed by any of the claimants.

Hausfeld issued a claim form on 8 May 2014 in the name of Bao Xiang International Garment Centre, PRC and 64,696 other claimants, all based in China, claiming damages arising from an unlawful price-fixing cartel in relation to air freight services supplied by British Airways and other airlines to the claimants between 1999 and 2007. The claim form and statement of truth was signed by Boris Bronfentrinker, a former partner in Hausfeld. The total value of commerce claimed was £7,958,526,473.

On 19 December 2014 British Airways issued an application to strike out the claim. At the hearing on 15 October 2015, Hausfeld accepted that the claims could not continue for the vast majority of the claimants because only 5,277 could show that they had shipped cargo by air during the relevant period. Hausfeld claimed that 362 clients had returned forms that provided ratification of the claim.

Rose J held that English law applied to the ratification, and that the claimed ratifications were ineffective.[98] The 'only possible course' was to strike the claim out on the basis of lack of authority.

The airlines also submitted that the case should be struck out as an abuse of process, and the judge said that she would 'undoubtedly consider it was appropriate' to do so for several reasons, including that:

— Hausfeld had no grounds for believing at the time they issued proceedings that any particular claimant had shipped air freight over the relevant period.
— The Hausfeld partner's evidence on the basis of the belief that CCOIC was able, as a matter of Chinese law, to authorise them to issue proceedings was 'wholly inadequate'.
— There was 'a complete lack of candour on the part of Hausfeld'.
— Letters sent to the claimants were 'highly misleading in their description of the nature of the claim and of what is required of claimants in proceedings in this court'.
— '… after more than two years' work they have not in fact gathered a litigation group together at all for these proceedings. To allow this claim to proceed would, in my judgment, be manifestly unfair to the airlines and would bring the administration of justice into disrepute among right-thinking people. It is an abuse of process and should be struck out for that reason.'

F. Cases under the 2015 Competition Damages Action

The following cases have been brought under the 2015 follow-on opt-out competition law regime, neither succeeding in the certification stage of a Collective Proceedings Order (CPO).

---

[98] *Bao Xiang International Garment Centre and others v British Airways PLC* [2015] EWHC 3071 (Ch).

Case study: Mobility Scooters

The first application for a CPO in the CAT was for an opt-out action against mobility scooters manufacturer Pride Mobility Products Limited. Pride had been previously found by the Competition and Markets Authority (CMA) in a decision dated 27 March 2014 to have infringed competition law in relation to resale price maintenance. Pride and the eight independent dealers selling its mobility scooters had entered into bilateral agreements or concerted practices covering some or all of the period February 2010 to February 2012, whereby the dealers would not advertise certain models of Pride scooters online at prices below the Recommended Retail Price set by Pride.

The case was brought by the general secretary of the National Pensioners Convention, Dorothy Gibson, as representative claimant. It was estimated that the class included 27,000–32,000 people, and damages between £2.7 and £3.2 million.[99]

The CAT gave an initial judgment in March 2017 in the application for a CPO.[100] The CAT first decided that there was no fundamental obstacle on human rights or EU law grounds to the making of an opt-out CPO in this case. Second, the CAT held that the certification regime was very different from certification of a US class action, and US authorities were irrelevant, whilst some guidance could be drawn from the Canadian regime.[101] Third, the CAT held that only the infringements found by the CMA could be the basis of the follow-on damages proceedings, and other stand-alone allegations could not be included.[102] It followed that the claim would need substantial reformulation to take into account what loss could be claimed by different sub-classes of purchasers who purchased at different periods. Fourth, the CAT granted the applicant an adjournment and the opportunity to amend the Claim Form to propose revised sub-classes and a methodology which focuses on the effects of the agreements that were the subject of the CMA's Decision. The CMA postponed its decision on whether the case would be suitable for a collective proceedings order, noting 'with a potentially more complex economic analysis, the costs of pursuing the proceedings may increase; and in limiting the claim to the losses resulting from the infringements, the aggregate damages estimate may decrease. ... Until a revised approach to assessment is carried out, it is impossible to assess what the total damages might be.'[103]

The case was withdrawn by the representative claimant in May 2017 after deciding 'the case was not worth enough money to proceed given the costs', and she agreed to pay Pride £309,000 in costs.[104]

Case study: MasterCard Class Action

The EU Commission issued a decision on 19 December 2007 that Mastercard had breached Article 101 of the Treaty on the Functioning of the European Union (TFEU) in setting the multilateral interchange fee (MIF) which applied as a fall-back between banks in the UK, without which intercharge fees charged between banks for cross-border transactions and certain domestic transactions would have been lower.

---

[99] *Gibson v Pride Mobility Products Limited* [2017] CAT 9, judgment 31 March 2017, para 93.
[100] ibid.
[101] ibid, para 104.
[102] ibid, para 112.
[103] ibid, para 122.
[104] N Rose, 'First opt-out class action withdrawn after damages found to be insufficient', *LitigationFutures* 5 June 2017.

A claim was issued in the CAT by representative claimant Walter Merricks CBE, former financial services ombudsman, on behalf of 46 million consumers who between 22 May 1992 and 21 June 2008 purchased goods and/or services from businesses selling in the UK that accepted MasterCard cards.[105] He sought an aggregate award of damages for the class, broadly estimated form at around £14 billion, including a substantial element of interest calculated on a compound basis.

The CAT in July 2017 rejected the application for a CPO as an opt-out class action. The tribunal held that the claims were 'not suitable' to be brought in collective proceedings. 'The problem in the present case is that there is no plausible way of reaching even a very rough-and-ready approximation of the loss suffered by each individual claimant from the aggregate loss calculated according to the Applicant's proposed method.'[106] It said:

> 87. This cannot be dismissed as a 'mere' question of distribution, to be addressed only after an aggregate award has been determined. First, it is largely because of the methodology of seeking to calculate the loss on a top-down, aggregate basis, and not on the basis of a common issue concerning loss suffered by each member (or most members) of the class, that the fundamental problem arises. As a result, if, hypothetically, a million people opted out of the proceedings, there would be no proper way of reducing the quantum of damages accordingly (and, conversely, of increasing it if a large number of people now domiciled outside the UK sought to opt in): it would simply lead to everyone in the class getting more (or less) money out of the total pot.

> 88. Secondly, even if it were possible to determine with some broad degree of accuracy the weighted average for pass-through and thus to estimate the aggregate loss for the 35 class each year, it is the significance of the individual issues remaining which mean that it is impossible in this case to see how the payments to individuals could be determined on any reasonable basis.

> … there are three sets of issues which are relevant: individuals' levels of expenditure; the merchants from whom they purchased; and the mix of products which they purchased. There is no attempt to approximate for any of those in the way damages would be paid out. The governing principle of damages for breach of competition law is restoration of the claimants to the position they would have been in but for the breach. The restoration will often be imprecise and may have to be based on broad estimates. But this application for over 46 million claims to be pursued by collective proceedings would not result in damages being paid to those claimants in accordance with that governing principle at all.

The tribunal noted the argument that

> it would be totally impractical for members in the class to bring claims on an individual basis, if the Tribunal declined to grant a CPO a vast number of individuals who suffered loss would get no compensation. However, that is effectively the position in most cases of widespread consumer loss resulting from competition law infringements. It does not mean that an application to bring collective proceedings in such a case must always be granted.

The claimant was refused permission to appeal by the CAT on 28 September 2017,[107] and appealed to the High Court.

---

[105] *Walter Hugh Merricks CBE v Mastercard Incorporated, Mastercard International Incorporated and Mastercard Europe SARL* [2017] CAT 16, judgment of 21 July 2017.

[106] ibid, para 84.

[107] *Walter Hugh Merricks CBE v Mastercard Incorporated, Mastercard International Incorporated and Mastercard Europe SARL* [2017] CAT 21, Ruling (permission to appeal) dated 28 September 2017.

> It was reported that the action[108]
>
> > was initially financed by litigation funder Gerchen Keller Capital, now owned by Burford Capital, which was to provide upfront costs of up to £36m. If successful, the funder stood to make whatever was the greater of £135m or 30% of the proceeds of the case up to £1bn, plus 20% of the proceeds over £1bn. Had the claim had been granted in full, that would have added up to some £3 billion. … Merricks [said]: 'If we do not reverse this decision, I very much doubt if we will see a consumer class claim being brought against companies that have colluded to fix prices. The whole purpose of the new class claim regime, which consumer bodies fought to see introduced, will have been defeated.'

V. Finland[109]

Class actions were introduced in Finland in 2007.[110] Only public actions are allowed, in the sense that only the Consumer Ombudsman, a state authority promoting consumer interests, can bring a class action. Individuals or organisations have no standing. The Act only applies to consumer disputes that fall within the jurisdiction of the Consumer Ombudsman. Disputes concerning the actions of issuers of securities or public purchase offers are excluded from the scope of application. The same is true for environmental damages.

There are three class action prerequisites. The first condition is that several persons must have claims against the same defendant and that these claims have to be based on the same or similar circumstances. The latter do not have to be the same. Also the claims can differ among class members (eg some class members want a price reduction while others want an annulment of the purchase). However, difference between the types of claims can be an impediment when each of the claims types calls for its own detailed investigation.

The second prerequisite is that the hearing of the case as a class action has to be expedient in view of the size of the class, the subject matter of the claims presented in it and the proof offered in it. In other words, that it would be either impractical or costly to hear each of the class members' cases separately. This means that the size of the group should be big enough for the class action to be advantageous. There are no exact limitations on the group size, as long as it is appropriate to hear the case as a class action. Second, substantial differences between the class members can lead to some members being denied membership due to such difference in claims, which could cause unnecessary prolongation and complexity of the hearing. Such prolongation can be caused for example by the individual presentation of evidence when there is little or no collective evidence to be presented. In such cases, the group should be limited only to those persons, claims of whom can be based on collective evidence, which makes the hearing fluent and the class action practical.

The third condition for a matter to be heard as a class action is that the class should be defined with adequate precision.

---

[108]   M Walters, 'Mystery backer funds appeal in £14bn Mastercard claim', *Gazette*, 27 October 2017.

[109]   The author of this section is Johan Pråhl.

[110]   Finnish Act on Class Actions (444/2007). The Act entered into force in October 2007.

The class action is based on an opt-in system. A class member is one who has submitted, within the time limit, a written and signed letter of accession to the class, after which the Consumer Ombudsman shall prepare a supplemented application for a summons, indicating the names and addresses of the class members, the features of their claims and, if necessary, supplemented grounds for the claims.

Ultimately the class action prerequisites are examined by the court. If they are not fulfilled, the court may dismiss the claims. Only the District Courts of Helsinki, Oulu, Ostrobothnia, Northern Savo, Päijänne-Tavastia and Finland Proper have jurisdiction.

The class members are not parties to the litigation and they do not actively take part in the judicial proceedings. Regarding issues such as the disqualification of the judge or rules on testimonies, the members of the group are treated as parties. Therefore, a class member cannot be heard as a witness, but it is still possible to hear a member with an intention to present proof. Although they are not parties, class members have to specify their claims. Consequently, the Consumer Ombudsman cannot claim a lump sum compensation to be divided between the class members.

The Act on Class Actions, as a *lex specialis*, contains a reference to the Finnish Code of Judicial Procedure in relation to the funding of the litigation. The Code contains the general procedural rules in relation to litigation in the general courts of law (District Courts, Courts of Appeal and the Supreme Court). The party who loses the case is liable for all reasonable legal costs incurred by the opposing party, unless otherwise provided.[111] In its final decision, the court has to decide on who will bear the litigation costs. The judgment will include an exact amount, which is based on the parties' claims usually based on the attorneys' bills. Thus, in class action litigations only the parties will have to pay the litigation costs. These are the defendant and the Consumer Ombudsman representing the group of consumers. Because the consumers are not parties to the procedure, they cannot be ordered to pay the litigation costs.

To date, no class action cases have been brought in Finland. This is mostly caused by the fact that the scope of application of the Finnish class action is too limited, and only the Consumer Ombudsman can initiate action.

Case study: Caruna

In the beginning of 2016, the Consumer Ombudsman was flooded with questions by consumers from a specific geographical area claiming that the price increases intended to enter into force on 1 March 2016 by electricity transmission company Caruna had been excessive.

The Consumer Ombudsman monitors the contract terms between electricity transmission companies and consumers in order to guarantee consumer protection. To be considered reasonable, prices can usually be increased by no more than approximately 10–15% at a time. Caruna's announced price increases would have been considerably greater. What made Caruna's price increases especially unreasonable was the fact that electricity is a basic necessity. Switching to another supplier would not have been an option for consumers either, as Caruna has a monopoly on electricity transmission in its area.

---

[111] Ch 21 S 1 of the Finnish Code of Judicial Procedure.

At the end of February 2016, the Consumer Ombudsman and Caruna reached an agreement as a result of their negotiations. Caruna was not going to raise its prices as of 1 March 2016. Instead, Caruna committed itself to reducing its fixed basic prices for electricity transmission by 25% for all customers and both of its network companies for the next 12 months. This compensation was also meant to balance the price increase in 2017. Furthermore, Caruna agreed to not implementing new price increases in 2017. Due to this agreement, the average annual increase in customers' electricity transmission expenses would remain below 15%, calculated based on the total price of electricity transmission including tax.

A class action was one of the options proposed during the negotiations and the Consumer Ombudsman has revealed having seriously considered it in the matter at hand. However, in this case, the option of resorting to filing a class action against Caruna evidently weighed enough in the negotiations, which made it possible for the parties to reach an agreement outside of court litigation.

After the Caruna price increases and negotiations, the Consumer Disputes Board received hundreds of calls where consumers notified that they are not satisfied with the increases or the negotiated solution. The Consumer Disputes Board has outlined the reasonableness of electricity transmission pricing in its plenum. As a result, it came to the conclusion that the average annual increases of less than 15% in consumers' electricity transmission expenses are not to be regarded as unreasonable in general.

VI. France[112]

A. The *Action de Groupe*

In 2014, France adopted a class action mechanism (hereafter, *action de groupe*)[113] after several decades of tense negotiations and controversies.[114] The objective was to facilitate compensation and access to justice.[115] France has followed a sectorial approach. Originally, the mechanism was available in consumer and competition law.

Act no 2014-344 of 17 March 2014 amending the Consumer Law (*Loi Hamon*) introduced a class action mechanism for consumer and competition law matters.[116] Associations are the only entities entitled to claim compensation for individual damage suffered by consumers placed in similar or identical situations. The loss must result from a breach of statutory or contractual obligations by the defendant(s). The class action is limited to material damage affecting consumers' assets. The proceeding cannot be used to compensate losses resulting from physical or psychological harm.

Associations must be representative at national level, have at least one year of existence, show evidence of effective and public activity with a view to the protection of consumer

---

[112] The authors of this section are Alexandre Biard and Rafal Amaro.
[113] We use here the French terminology to describe the functioning of the French class action.
[114] S Amrani-Mekki, 'La rengaine de l'action de groupe', *Gazette du Palais*, 8 September 2012, n°252, 3; A Du Chastel, 'L'action de groupe ou le mythe de Sisyphe', *Petites Affiches*, 23 June 2008, n°125, 6.
[115] Circulaire of 26 September 2014 de présentation des dispositions de la loi n° 2014-344, http://www.textes. justice.gouv.fr/art_pix/JUSC1421594C.pdf.
[116] Arts L.623-1 et seq and R.623-1 et seq of the French Consumer Code (Code de la Consommation).

interests, and have a threshold of individually paid-up members. To date, 15 associations meet these requirements. Lawyers (*avocats*) are not entitled to start class actions of their own motion.[117] However, *ad litem* representation by lawyers remains mandatory in practice. This is because High Courts of First Instance (*Tribunal de Grande Instance*) have exclusive jurisdiction over *actions de groupe*, and representation by lawyers is mandatory before these courts. The competent court is the one where the defendant is established. However, the Paris High Court of First Instance (*Tribunal de Grande Instance de Paris*) has exclusive jurisdiction when the defendant is located outside France.

The proceedings follow a multi-stage process. First, the court decides on liability on the basis of individual model or test cases brought by the association (the liability phase). The court circumscribes the scope of the defendant's liability, the damage to be compensated and the available remedies. The court also determines the criteria that potential claimants must meet to be part of the group, specifies the conditions of its advertisement in the media, and sets cut-off dates to join the group. This period cannot be less than two months or exceed six months after the end of the advertising period. Second, claimants who meet the criteria set down by the court can join the group via an opt-in system (the compensation phase). In other words, the group of class members is constituted only after the decision on liability has been handed down. In theory, judges do not intervene directly during this second phase. Finally, the court terminates the proceeding and addresses any unresolved issues or disagreements linked to the award distribution.

There is also a simplified proceeding (*action de groupe simplifiée*) for situations in which claimants can be identified easily, and the damage is identical for each claimant. The court may order the defendant to compensate claimants individually within a fixed timeframe.

There are no rules on public funding. Nevertheless, the court may order the defendant to provide the association with an advance on payment in respect of the costs and expenses arising out of the compensation phase. The exact amount is left to the court's discretion, but should reflect the nature and the complexity of the work done by the association.

The aforementioned framework also applies to competition law.[118] However, competition class actions can exclusively be 'follow-on' actions, ie they are only permissible when the decision of (national or European) competition authorities or the review court judgment that identified antitrust practices has become final (ie no longer subject to appeal or cassation). Since the infringement of competition law has already been established, the court will only decide on causation, quantum of the loss, criteria for group membership and the way the case will be advertised in the media. Moreover, competition class actions are no longer permissible after a period of five years from the date on which the administrative decision (or the review court judgment) has become final.

In 2016, the *action de groupe* mechanism was expanded to health law.[119] The introduction of class actions in the healthcare sector was part of a broader legislative initiative aimed at reforming the French healthcare system. *Actions de groupe* for health-related cases are

---

[117] As an attempt to circumvent this limitation, several initiatives have been launched by lawyers—included by the Paris *Ordre des Avocats*—to collect claims of individuals potentially involved in mass harm situations via online means (see eg, Ordre des Avocats au Barreau de Paris, 'Actions conjointes des justiciables: les avocats mises sur le numerique', http://www.avocatparis.org/actions-collectives.

[118] Consumer Code (*Code de la consommation*), arts L.623-24 et seq and R.623-1 et seq.

[119] Code of Public Health (Code de la santé publique), art L.1143-1 et seq and R. 1143-1 et seq.

permissible since 28 September 2016. However, they can apply retroactively to damage that took place before that date. The French Constitutional Council has decided that *actions de groupe* must be considered as new procedural tools, which do not create new substantive rights for claimants. Their retroactive application is therefore permissible.[120]

The action is initiated by accredited associations of users of the healthcare system. Associations must be representative at national or local levels (around 500 associations to date). *Actions de groupe* are only permissible for personal injury claims of individuals who are in identical or similar situations. The damage must be the consequence of a breach of statutory or contractual obligations by a producer, supplier or any entity using healthcare products listed under article L. 5311-1 II of the Code of Public Health. In other words, the *action* can be made against pharmaceutical companies, public or private hospitals, healthcare professionals, healthcare organisations producing or using medicinal products, medical devices, biomaterials, cosmetic products, etc. Alternatively, the *action* can also be directed against insurers directly.

The structure of the litigation is similar to that of *actions de groupe* in consumer and competition law. First, the court decides on defendant's liability through the analysis of individual model or test cases. Then, the court determines the scope of the class by defining membership criteria as well as the personal injury covered. The court decides on the way the case will be publicised in the media, and sets cut-off dates to join the group. This period must be between six months and five years. However, it is noteworthy that the court does not determine how individual compensation will be calculated. This is because compensation will be assessed on an individual basis during the second phase, and will generally result from an agreement between the defendant and the claimant. The judge may intervene in case of disagreements or difficulties during the award distribution.

The rules encourage the use of mediation. If parties agree, the court may request the intervention of a mediator for a period of up to three months, renewable once. The composition of the mediation committee is defined by law. The terms of the settlement agreement must specify the type of personal injuries covered, the proposed compensation amounts, cut-off dates to accept the offer and the way the agreement will be advertised in the media to ensure that all potential claimants are adequately informed. The agreement must ultimately be reviewed by the court.

Also in 2016, the class action mechanism was extended to privacy and data protection.[121] Act no 2016-1547 of November 2016 on the Modernisation of Justice created an *action de groupe* for individuals placed in similar situations and suffering from damage that results from a breach of statutory obligations by data controllers or subcontractors. The proceeding can exclusively be initiated to request the court to order the cessation of the unlawful practice. *Actions de groupe* may be filed before civil or administrative courts by (i) associations that have been exercising their statutory activities in the field of privacy and data protection for at least five years; (ii) accredited consumer associations that are representative at national level (if data processing affects consumers' interests); or (iii) trade unions (if data processing affects employees or civil servants' interests). The framework of this *action de groupe* follows the multi-stage process previously described.

---

[120] Constitutional Council, Decision of 21 January 2016, No 2015-727 DC.
[121] French Data Protection Act of 6 January 1978 (Loi n° 78-17 relative à l'informatique, aux fichiers et aux libertés), art 43 ter.

Act no 2016-1547 of November 2016 on the Modernisation of Justice also introduced a class action mechanism for environmental matters for individuals or legal entities placed in similar situations and suffering damage listed under article L. 142-2 of the Environmental Code, which, among other things, covers damage relating to the protection of nature, water, air, soils, sites and landscapes, controls of pollution.[122] The damage must result from a breach of statutory or contractual obligations by the defendant. Environmental class actions are filed before civil or administrative courts by accredited environmental associations, or accredited associations whose statutory activities include the protection of personal injury or the protection of the economic interests of their members. The framework of the *action de groupe* follows the multi-stage process previously described. The action can be used to request the court to order the cessation of the unlawful practice and/or to claim for damages.

Act no 2016-1547 also introduced a class action for individuals suffering from similar direct or indirect discriminatory practices from the same wrongdoer.[123] The framework of the *action de groupe* follows the multi-stage process previously described. *Actions de groupe* are filed before administrative or civil courts by (i) accredited associations that have been exercising their statutory activities in the fields of disability or fight against discriminations for at least five years, or (ii) accredited associations that have been active for at least five years and the purpose of which includes the protection of an interest violated by the discriminatory practice. The action can be used to request the court to order the cessation of the unlawful practice, and, as the case may be, to make a claim for damages.

In addition, the rules allow for an *action de groupe* to deal with discriminatory practices at workplace. It must be noted that, before initiating the procedure, trade union organisations or associations must send an initial notice to the employer requesting the cessation of the alleged unlawful discriminatory practice. Within one month, the employer must inform the work's council (*comité d'entreprise*) and union organisations representing employees of the request. Upon request from the work's council or union organisations, the employer must start discussions to identify the measures that are necessary to stop the discriminatory practices. The *action de groupe* may only be filed six months after the date of the notice that requested the cessation of the practices.

Finally, Act no 2016-1547 also provides for horizontal rules for *actions de groupe* filed before civil[124] and administrative courts.[125] The procedural framework follows the rules and multi-stage process described previously.

B. Case Studies: *Action de Groupe*

Tracking *actions de groupe* in France remains a challenging task, due to the absence of an official registry listing all past and on-going actions. The following table has been put together from the limited information that is available on associations' websites, through press releases and companies' updates, as at November 2017.

---

[122] Environmental Code (Code de l'Environnement), art 142-3-1.
[123] Labour Code (Code du Travail), art 10 of Act no. 2008-496 of 27 May 2008 and Art L.1134-6 et seq.
[124] Act on the modernisation of justice, art 60 et seq.
[125] Administrative Justice Code (Code de justice administrative), art L. 77-10-1 and seq.

Table 3.4: Number of *Actions de Groupe* in France to November 2017

Case	Date	Jurisdiction	Facts	Potential class/ estimated loss	Results
UFC Que Choisir v Foncia	1/10/2014	Nanterre High Court of First Instance	undue fees charged to tenants for sending them monthly rent payment receipts for an amount of €2.30 per month	318,000 individuals estimated total loss: €44 million (individual loss: €27.60. In some cases, hundreds of Euros).	Pending The action followed criminal proceedings in 2013
Confédération Syndicale des Familles (CSF) v Paris Habitat-OPH	13/10/2014	Paris High Court of First Instance	undue charges for the installation of remote monitoring systems	100,000 individuals estimated loss amount: €3 million	Settlement (€2 million for 100,000 individuals)
UFC Que Choisir v Free (telecom company)	2014	Paris High Court of First Instance	Bad quality of 3G mobile services between 2012 and 2015	Around 141,632 individuals	Settlement (approximately €1.7 million) Claimants individually obtained between €1 and €12 (maximum)
Consommation, Logement et Cadre de Vie (CLCV) v Axa and AGIPI (insurance company)	28/10/2014	Nanterre High Court of First Instance	Breach of contractual obligations in connection with a life insurance contract guaranteeing a minimum return-rate	100,000 individuals Estimated total loss: between €300 million and €500 million (individual loss: between €1,500 and €4,000)	Pending NB: in November 2016, the defendants tried to challenge a decision (ordonnance) from the judge in charge of monitoring civil proceedings (*juge de la mise en etat*) before the Court of Appeal of Versailles. The *juge de la mise en etat* had rejected defendants' arguments against the model cases brought by the plaintiff association on the basis that he was not competent to review the admissibility of the action since the definition of group membership is a substantive issue, and not a procedural one. The Court of Appeal of Versailles (CA Versailles, Decision of 3 November 2016, no 16/00463) confirmed the decision

(*continued*)

Table 3.4: (*Continued*)

Case	Date	Jurisdiction	Facts	Potential class/ estimated loss	Results
Confédération Nationale du Logement (CNL) v Immobilière 3F (housing group)	5/01/2015	Paris High Court of First Instance	unfair contractual terms in lease contracts. The contentious provision provides for a financial penalty of 2% in case of delayed payments	480,000 individuals estimated loss: unknown	Judgment delivered on 28 January 2016 and decision no 16/05321 of the Paris Court of Appeal delivered on 9 November 2017 (see case study below)
Familles Rurales v SFR (telecom company)	May 2015	Paris High Court of First Instance	misleading information about the 4G network geographic coverage	1 to 2 million individuals estimated loss: unknown	Pending
Association Familles Rurales v company Manoir de Ker An Poul (camping company)	August 2015	Vannes High Court of First Instance	Abusive practice forcing clients to purchase a new product after 10 years to keep their plot	around 12 families estimated loss: unknown	Pending
Association CLCV v BMW Motorrad France	December 2015	Versailles High Court of First Instance)	problems with defective motorcycles	600 individuals estimated loss: unknown	Pending
UFC Que Choisir v BNP Paribas	September 2016	Paris High Court of First Instance	misleading information concerning the product 'Garantie 3 Jet'	between 2,000 and 5,000 estimated loss: €27.8 million	Pending
CLCV v BNP Paribas Personal Finance (PPF)	November 2016	Paris High Court of First Instance	unfair commercial practices (including misleading information) on mortgages ('Helvet Immo')	around 4,655 individuals	Pending The action followed criminal proceedings in 2015

(*continued*)

Table 3.4: (*Continued*)

Case	Date	Jurisdiction	Facts	Potential class/ estimated loss	Results
Apesac v Sanofi	May 2017	Paris High Court of First Instance	medicine (Depakine) causing malformations in babies and alleged lack of vigilance of the pharmaceutical company	Between 2,000 and 4,000	Pending Preliminary hearings took place in October 2017
Confédération Générale du Travail (CGT) v Safran Aircraft Engines	May 2017	Not applicable yet (still in its pre-mediation phase)	Discrimination at workplace	Around 34	Pending

---

Case study: *CNL v Immobilière 3F* (2014)

In November 2014, *Confédération Nationale du Logement* (CNL), a consumer association, published on its website a press release announcing that it had initiated an *action de groupe* against the housing company Immobilière 3F, which manages more than 190,000 low-income houses in France. The information was extensively relayed in online press and printed newspapers. In December 2014, CNL published on its website a document inviting all potential plaintiffs to contact the association directly. The summons against Immobilière 3F was formally registered on 5 January 2015 before the Paris High Court of First Instance.

CNL argued that Immobilière 3F had inserted unfair contractual terms in its leases. In particular, the association considered that the part imposing a 2% financial penalty in the case of delayed payments was unfair and unlawful. The association took the view that the *action de groupe* potentially involved more than 480,000 tenants.

By contrast, Immobilière 3F argued that the *action de groupe* was inadmissible since the matter was essentially a question of housing law. The claim would therefore fall outside the scope of application as the proceeding is only permissible for consumer law matters. In addition, the defendant took the view that the term in question was not unfair and authoriSed under existing housing rules.

On 27 January 2016, the Paris High Court of First Instance delivered judgment.[126] The Court first declared the action admissible and chose a broad interpretation of consumer law in including housing litigation within the scope of *actions de groupe*. However, the Court dismissed the claim on the ground that the association had failed to produce sufficient evidence to support its allegations. CNL had brought four individual 'model' cases to prove liability. Of the four model cases, the Court dismissed one case because the lease had not been signed with Immobilière 3F. The review of the three remaining cases was ultimately deemed insufficient to hold the company liable.

---

[126] TGI Paris, 27 January 2016, No 15-00835.

> Finally, on 9 November 2017, the Paris Court of Appeal reversed the decision of the Paris High Court of First Instance (decision no 16/05321). It declared the group action inadmissible and retained a narrow interpretation of consumer law that excluded housing litigation.

C. The *Action en Représentation Conjoint*

Act no 92-60 of 18 January 1992 on consumer protection introduced an *action en représentation conjointe* into the French Consumer Code.[127] Its scope was initially limited to consumer law. However, the action was afterwards extended to other sectors, such as environment and securities. Like the *action de groupe*, the *action en représentation conjointe* is initiated by accredited associations and aims to defend the individual interests of several consumers who are in similar situations, and have suffered from the same corporate misconduct. The action follows an opt-in system, and is used to aggregate individual claims into one single process.

If the association prevails, damages are distributed to the individuals who, beforehand, have previously duly authorised the association to act on their behalf. However, if the association fails, represented individuals no longer have the right to file individual lawsuits for the same facts.

Advertising is prohibited and associations cannot approach consumers directly. Therefore, associations may not solicit individuals by means of public announcements on radio or television, tracts or personalised letters. In addition, each consumer must necessarily give his/her consent in writing prior to the beginning of the proceedings. These two obstacles have ultimately impaired the efficiency of the mechanism.

> **Case study: Mobile phone cartel case (2011)**
>
> The mobile phones cartel was a nation-wide price and market sharing conspiracy between the three main French mobile phone operators: Orange, SFR and Bouygues. The cartel extended over a period of three years. The French competition authority issued a €534 million fine against the cartelists.
>
> In 2006, the consumer association UFC-Que Choisir? initiated a lawsuit to obtain compensation for the €1.2 million to €1.6 million of overcharges paid by the 20 million subscribers of Orange, SFR and Bouygues. The association decided to adopt a 'borderline strategy' by launching an *action en défense de l'intérêt collectif*. The objective was to bypass the restrictive rules applying to the *action en représentation conjointe*, and in particular the prohibition on advertising. The association publicly called consumers via a website and invited them to join the action to obtain compensation for their individual loss. As the UFC Director of legal affairs highlighted, 220,000 consumers registered on the website. However only 12,521 of them actually sent the required documents to join the action. Therefore, after costly and time-consuming proceedings, the association only managed to pool 12,521 consumers who represented only 0.06% of the total population of estimated harmed individuals.

[127] Consumer Code, arts L. 622-1 et seq, Environmental Code (*Code de l'environnement*), art L. 142-3 and Monetary and Financial Code (*Code monétaire et financier*), arts L. 452-2 et seq.

In a judgment of 6 December 2007, the Paris Commercial Court decided that the action of the association was inadmissible because it was in reality a disguised *action en representation conjointe*. Yet, rules regulating *actions en representation conjointe* prevent associations from soliciting consumers by public means within the framework of *action en représentation conjointe*. The Court took the view that the association had publicly solicited consumers through its website. The Paris Court of Appeal confirmed this analysis in its decision of 2010,[128] which was also upheld by the Court of cassation in 2011.[129]

VII. Germany[130]

A. Representative Actions for Cease and Desist Orders

Representative entities (eg consumer associations) can sue companies for an injunction (a so-called cease-and-desist order) in the field of unfair standard contract terms,[131] unfair competition or unfair practices violating EU consumer protection rules[132] and copyright law.[133] Judgments, including the name of the defendant, can be made public. Cease and desist court orders have a binding effect on subsequently filed individual claims by consumers against the same defendant with respect to the court's finding of a violation of the law.[134]

Only injunctive relief can be claimed. Court orders can order the removal of impairments. This has to be distinguished from damages awards. Court orders to remove impairments impose on the defendant an obligation to eliminate the source of violation, but not to compensate any damages caused. With respect to unfair standard contract terms courts can also issue an order against associations to withdraw a recommendation of using a particular standard contract term if the term is illegal.

Legal standing is given to all major consumer associations, chambers of commerce, the federal association to combat unfair competition (*Wettbewerbszentrale*) and all representative entities which are on the list of associations that have legal standing under the 2009 Injunctions Directive.[135] Section 4 of the Act on Injunctive Relief lists the criteria for so-called 'qualified representative entities'.

There are no special rules on funding. Representative entities have to pay the costs out of their regular budgets (consumer associations in Germany are mainly funded by tax payers' money). With respect to actions for injunctive relief under the Unfair Competition Act, courts may, upon application, reduce the amount in controversy which is the relevant basis for calculating court fees and lawyers' fees. Applications are often made and granted in order to reduce the procedural risk for plaintiffs.

---

[128] CA Paris 22 January 2010, No 08-09844.
[129] Court of Cassation, Civil Chamber, decision of 26 May 2011, No 10-15676.
[130] The author of this section is Astrid Stadler.
[131] Act on Injunctive Relief, s 1.
[132] ibid, s 2.
[133] ibid, s 2a.
[134] ibid, s 11.
[135] See ch 2.

There are no detailed data about the number of cases. The VZBV (*Verbraucherzentrale Bundesverband*), the umbrella organisation of all German consumer associations, states on its website that they and the regional consumer associations initiate more than 1000 investigations per year.[136] Roughly 50% settled out of court, 20–25% went to court and the VZBV had a success rate in court of more than 80%. Most of the cases relate to the use of unfair and illegal standard contract terms.

B. Actions for Skimming-off Illegally Gained Profits

Representative entities can sue traders or service providers who violated the regulations of the Unfair Competition Act or the Antitrust Act intentionally and gained illegal profits at the expense of a large number of consumers.[137] The action can result in an order to pay the illegally gained profit to the Federal Budget. Legal standing is given to the same entities that can bring representative actions for cease and desist orders. In case of violations of antitrust rules, the national cartel authorities also have legal standing for such an action.[138]

Again, there are no special rules on funding. Representative entities have to pay the costs out of their regular budgets. If the action is successful they can obtain a certain amount from the money paid by the defendant to the Federal budget in order to cover some administrative costs.

C. Case Studies: Actions for Skimming-off Illegally Gained Profits

With respect to section 34a of the Antitrust Act, not a single case has been reported since its coming into force in 2005. One reason could be that the right of representative entities to bring such an action is subsidiary to the cartel authorities' right of skimming-off illegally gained profits from cartelists. Whenever the cartel authorities investigate a case and impose fines on the members of the cartel, they will also consider skimming-off the profits resulting from the cartel (or take these illegally gained profits into account when deciding on the amount of the fines). Because of the selection of cases by the cartel authorities only standalone actions are left to representative entities. Without an official investigation and a binding decision on the existence of the cartel, representative actions for skimming-off illegally gained profits involve an enormous procedural risk and will not be filed.

With respect to section 10 of the Unfair Competition Act, there have been approximately 12 to 15 cases since the coming into force of this provision in 2004. One reason could be the high procedural risk due to the burden of proof with respect to the defendant's intentional violation of competition rules. Another obstacle is the lack of financial incentives for claimants (the amount to be paid by defendants goes to the Federal Budget). The Federal Ministry of Justice now considers to lower the threshold in substantive law (eg to require only gross negligence instead of an intentional violation for example) and to establish a fund into which the money can be paid and from which it would be available for special

---

[136] http://www.vzbv.de/themen/rechtsdurchsetzung/urteile.
[137] Unfair Competition Act, s 10, and Antitrust Act, s 34a.
[138] Antitrust Act, s 33.

consumer protection projects. Details are not yet available and it is very unlikely that a legislative initiative will be started before the federal elections in 2017.

These cases are listed in the Annex at Table B.5.

Unfair Competition Skimming Off Case Studies

No 1: District Court Bonn, 12.5.2005 (12 O 33/05)

The defendant, a retail seller of mattresses, had referred in his advertisements to a 'very good' result of a product test of his mattresses published by *Stiftung Warentest* (a non-profit German consumer organisation conducting independent products' tests). In reality, the test result was only 'satisfactory'. The plaintiff could not prove that the defendant had used the wrong test result intentionally because the defendant was able to explain that it was simply a transcription error by one of its employees. This defence was plausible as the employee had made similar mistakes in the past and had once even used a test result in advertisements that was worse than the one actually awarded by *Stiftung Warentest*. The action was dismissed. There was no appeal.

No 2: District Court Berlin, 25.9. 2007 (16 O115/06)

The plaintiff sued the defendant for the disclosure of information which was necessary to calculate the illegally gained profits for an action under section 10 of the Unfair Competition Act. The defendant had allegedly violated competition rules by using a design of his websites which did not indicate clearly enough for customers that the download of mobile phone ringtones was not free of charge, but led to a subscription for three tones per month for the price of €4.99 per month. The District Court dismissed the action because the plaintiff could not prove that the defendant had violated the law intentionally. The Court held that a previous written warning sent to the defendant could lead to the assumption that the defendant *from then on* was aware of his illegal practice. Such an assumption requires however that the written warning was made with respect to exactly the same (illegal) conduct as the subsequent action under section 10.

No 3: District Court Heilbronn, Settlement 11.12.2008 (23 O 136/05); Court of Appeal Stuttgart, 2.11.2006 (2 U 58/06)

In 2006, the VZBV sued the discounter Lidl because of its misleading advertisement of mattresses. Lidl had used outdated results of product tests by *Stiftung Warentest*. The Court of Appeals in Stuttgart confirmed that Lidl was obliged to disclose information to the plaintiff in order to allow the VZBV to calculate the illegally gained profit. Upon an action for payment filed by the VZBV later on, Lidl settled the case and paid €25,000 to the Federal Budget. The VZBV had estimated that the total amount of the illegal profit was approximately €400,000 but—due to the procedural risk—had sued Lidl only for €25,000.

No 4: District Court Munich I, 22.7.2008 (33 O 17282/07); Court of Appeals Munich, 15.4.2010 (6 U 4400/08)

The regional consumer association in Hamburg (supported by a litigation funder) had sued a telecommunication provider who in 2002 had undisputedly used an illegal method in its invoices in order to convert the former German currency to Euros. There were clear European provisions in this respect and the European Court of Justice (ECJ) had confirmed that the defendant's method was not in line with these rules. The method brought up the price for phone calls to a round figure and thus overcharged customers. The action was dismissed in both instances because the defendant's behaviour was classified as a breach of individual contracts only, but not as competing activity or a violation of competition rules. According to section 10 of the Unfair Competition Act, however, the defendant must have gained the profit by an intentional violation of competition rules.

No 5: Court of Appeals Hamm, 14.2.2008 (4 U 135/07)

The plaintiff filed an action against the defendant for the disclosure of information which was necessary to calculate the illegally gained profits for an action under section 10 of the Unfair Competition Act. The plaintiff alleged that the defendant had violated competition rules by selling a pharmaceutical product 'F' which contained additives that were not allowed in Germany. Again, it turned out to be difficult to prove an intentional violation of the law. The plaintiff argued that the defendant must have been aware of the illegality because of a previous law suit in which the court had ordered the defendant to stop selling a similar product which contained the same additives. The Court of Appeals of Hamm dismissed the action based on the finding that there was only gross negligence on behalf of the defendant. The new product 'F' was imported from the Netherlands where it could legally be put on the market. Therefore—due to EU regulations—the defendant had reason to believe that he was also allowed to sell the same product in Germany.

No 6: District Court Hanau, 17.9.2008 (1 O 569/08)

The VZBV sued an internet service provider who had offered an 'online advent calendar' and had given the impression to users that participation and registration was free of charge. Only from a small footnote it became clear that users had to pay €59. The VZBV had sent a written warning to the service provider and when they did not sign a cease-and-desist undertaking the VZBV obtained a court injunction. The subsequent action based on section 10 of the Unfair Competition Act to disclose all relevant information for the calculation of the illegally gained profit was successful. An action for skimming-off the illegally gained profit, however, was not filed and there is no publicly available information as to the final outcome of the case.

No 7: Court of Appeals Frankfurt, 4.12.2008 (6 U 186/07)

The defendant had offered on his internet website access to art design and poems without clearly indicating that using a confirmation button lead to a subscription of three months and a price of €39 per month. The court held that this was an illegal 'subscription trap' and that the defendant must have been aware of the violation of competition rules. There is no information available on the final outcome of the case.

No 8: District Court Hanau, 1.9.2008 (9 O 551/08)

The VZBV sued 'Online Service Ltd' for the disclosure of information necessary for the plaintiff to calculate the illegally gained profits for an action under section 10 of the Competition Act. The defendant had allegedly violated competition rules by not indicating clearly on his websites that the use of particular services was not free of charge. The action was successful only in part. The District Court held that the defendant had not violated competition rules intentionally before receiving a written warning from the plaintiff. Only once he had received such a warning the defendant must have been aware of the fact that his practice was illegal and must have realised that the previously obtained legal advice from his lawyers was probably not correct.

No 9: Court of Appeals Schleswig Holstein, 26.3.2013 (2 U 7/12)

In this case the plaintiff requested a court injunction against the defendant, a telecommunications service provider, to ban continuing to use several standard contract terms, particularly one which required customers to pay a €10 fee for a return debit note. The action was also for the disclosure of the necessary information required to calculate the profit illegally gained from the use of that practice. As a consequence of a former proceeding the defendant had already reduced the handling fee from almost €30 to €10, but insisted that this practice was lawful. The court of first instance granted the cease-and-desist order, but dismissed the action under section 10 of the Competition Act based on the lack of an intentional violation by the defendant. On appeal, the Court of Appeals confirmed the cease-and-desist order and also granted an order for disclosure. It held that the defendant, a big undertaking with its own legal department, could be expected to know the relevant case law with respect to unfair standard contract terms and therefore had acted at least with *dolus eventualis*. The Court of Appeals did not allow a further appeal on points of law and the respective motion by the defendants to set aside this non-admission was dismissed by the Federal High Court (BGH, 24.7.2014, III ZR 123/13). In a second stage, however, the parties are now litigating the question whether the defendant correctly complied with the order to disclose the relevant information: Federal High Court, 4.5.2016 (I ZR 64/16), Court of Appeals Schleswig Holstein, 25.2.2016 (2 U 7/15), District Court Kiel, 19.6.2015 (17 O48/15). In the enforcement proceedings, the defendants alleged that they had given all information required to an independent certified accountant as ordered by the court. The court thus intended to protect the trade secrets of the defendant with respect to some information (eg the names of customers). However, the Court of Appeals and the Federal High Court held that the information provided to the certified accountant was not detailed enough. Therefore the defendant's motions to stay the execution proceedings and to suspend the enforcement of a penalty payment were dismissed. According to information provided by the VZBV an action for payment is now pending before the District Court Kiel. The defendant has already announced to pay voluntarily an amount of €147,000. The VZBV estimates that the total amount of illegally gained profit is approx. €450,000.

No 10: District Court Munich, 17.9.2014 (37 O 16359/13)

The plaintiff, a professional association of dentists, sued a Munich dentist for the disclosure of information and for the accounting of illegally gained profits. The case was based on the defendant's advertising on his internet website where he offered dental services for prices which were allegedly 'inappropriately low' compared to the official dentists' fee schedule. The action was dismissed because the plaintiff could not prove that the dentist actually gained any relevant profit from this strategy at the expense of his patients. Although the defendant admitted that he had attracted new customers by his advertising this was not sufficient to prove any profit. The defendant may have enticed patients away from other dentists, but the court held that Section 10 Unfair Competition Act required evidence that any profit was made at the expense of consumers. It was not sufficient to simply inflict damage on competitors.

No 11: District Court Hannover, 17.11.2015 (18 O 36/15)

The plaintiff sued a home savings and loan association which administrated approximately 3.5 million buildings savings contracts in 2013. The plaintiff claimed the disclosure of information and accounting of illegally gained profits. The defendant had charged customers with handling fees of at least €10 for each return debit note and thus violated the rules against unfair standard contract terms. The court granted the order and held that there was an intentional violation of the law and that the defendant had acted intentionally—at least since he had received a written warning from the plaintiff in April 2012.

No 12: District Court Darmstadt 13.1.2009 (16 O 366/07), Court of Appeals Frankfurt 4.12.2008 (6 U 186/07)

The defendant was responsible for several websites where consumers could use special search engines. The company canvassed customers with the statement 'today free of charge'. Customers who registered and did not revoke their registration at the same day bought a subscription running 24 months for €7 per month. The VZBV alleged that the advertisement was misleading. The facts were proved by screenshots which depicted the statement 'today free of charge' and showed that customers had to scroll down in order to get the information that by registration they will get a subscription which is not free of charge when the website was used more than 24 hours.

The case started in 2006 when the VZBV sent a written warning to the defendant explaining that its advertisement was illegal and asking for a cease-and-desist undertaking (the normal practice in these cases). The undertaking was signed by the defendant but the practice did not stop. The action filed by the VZBV in 2007 was an 'action by stages' where, in the first stage, the claimant sued for the disclosure of information about the defendant's use of the website, the turnover, costs, taxes and so on, which is information necessary to calculate the illegally gained profit. In the second stage, there is normally an action for the account of profits. In this case there were court proceedings only with respect to the request for disclosure.

The proceedings took from 2007 to 2010 (first instance and appeal). There was an appeal on points of law to the Federal High Court which was not successful, but there is no publicly available information as to the date of the Federal High Court's decision. The court of first instance and the Court of Appeals held that the advertising was misleading and violated the Unfair Competition Act. They also held that the defendant was—at least after receiving the VZBV's written warning— aware of the fact that the practice was illegal. As a number of customers had to pay the monthly fee for the two year period of the subscription there was also profit gained 'at the expense' of a considerable number of consumers. The requirements of section 10 of the Unfair Competition Act were thus fulfilled.

In the first instance, however, the plaintiff's action also covered the use of the allegedly misleading advertising during a period which was before the VZBV had sent a written warning to the defendant. In this respect the action was dismissed (probably because an intentional violation could not be proved for that period).

For the period after the defendant had received the written warning the action for disclosure of the relevant information necessary for the exact calculation of profits was successful. The Court of Appeal did not allow a further appeal on points of law to the Federal High Court. The defendants filed an appeal to the Federal High Court asking to set aside the non-admission, but that appeal was dismissed. In an action for payment (of €400,000) the VZBV was only successful in part. The defendant could prove that from its turnover of €400,000 resulting from the use of the websites, approximately €385,000 had to be deduced because of commissions to be paid to employees and third parties. Defendants were finally ordered to pay only €12,300 and interest.

There was no compensation of the customers (as the action was not for the recovery of damages). According to information provided by the VZBV the defendants finally paid €12,300, but the enforcement was difficult due to the fact that defendant became insolvent.

No 13: District Court Kiel, 14.5.2014 (4 O 95/13), Court of Appeals Schleswig-Holstein, 19.3.2015 (2 U 6/14)

The defendant, a mobile phone service provider, used several standard contract terms which according to the plaintiff were illegal. Particularly two clauses were in dispute. One standard contract term required customers to pay a deposit of €9.97 for securing the return of the SIM card after the termination of the contract. Another contract term required customers to pay a so-called 'no-use-fee' if they did not use (not even partially) a particular service under the contract. With respect to the first contract term (deposit) the plaintiff sued for a cease-and-desist order. With respect to the second contract term ('no-use-fee') the VZBV asked for a disclosure order with respect to the information and figures necessary to calculate the illegally gained profit. The case came to light through several complaints of customers made to consumer associations.

The action was initiated by the VZBV as plaintiff. The defendant was the mobile phone service provider. The action was brought before the District Court in Kiel. The case started in April 2011 when the VZBV sent a first written warning to the defendant, objecting to the use of a standard contract term used by the defendant. With respect to that clause, the VZBV obtained a cease-and-desist order from the District Court Kiel (2 O 136/11, 29.11.2011), which was confirmed on the defendant's appeal by the Court of Appeals Schleswig-Holstein on 3 July 2012 (2 U 12/11).

The defendant then changed the wording of its contract clause with respect to the refund of the deposit. Customers could get the refund although they returned the SIM card only after the period of 14 days, which was the deadline according to the contract. The VZBV, however, still claimed that the contract term was illegal and sent another written warning to the defendant in February 2013. The defendant declined to sign an undertaking not to use the terms in the future on 26 February 2013. As a consequence, on 23 April 2013 the VZBV filed an action for a court order prohibiting the use of the new contract term and for the disclosure of the relevant information necessary to calculate illegally gained profits from the use of the former contract clause regarding the SIM card. The court issued an order for the disclosure of that information and held that the contract terms were unfair. It held that although the defendant remained the owner of the SIM cards he had no legitimate interest to receive them after the termination of the contract. The defendant himself had admitted that the SIM cards were all immediately destroyed and that there was no indication as to any misuse of SIM cards by customers after the termination of the contract.

With respect to the 'no-use-fee' general contract term the VZBV obtained a judgment by default against the defendant in August 2011 according to which the defendant was not allowed to use the contract term any more. Upon the defendant's motion to set aside the judgment by default, the court decision was confirmed and another appeal dismissed by the Court of Appeals in July 2012. Since August 2012 the contract term has not been used any more by the defendant. In December 2012, the VZBV asked the defendant to disclose the amount of the profit illegally gained by the use of the 'no-use-fee' since 1 June 2011, which the defendant declined. With its action filed on 23 April 2013 the plaintiff also sues for the disclosure of the necessary information and for the disgorgement of the profit.

The Court of Appeals rejected the appeal of the defendants and confirmed the illegal use of the standard contract term with respect to the deposit for the SIM card. It also confirmed the decision at first instance with respect to the disclosure of relevant information for the disgorgement of profits. The Court held that the use of unfair general contract terms is relevant for fair competition and confirmed that the defendant acted at least with eventual intent (*dolus eventualis*). In this respect the Court rejected the argument that 'intent' can be assumed only if there was a previous court decision declaring the standard contract term in dispute illegal. In the case at hand, the unfairness of the 'no-use-fee' was obvious. The Court of Appeals did not allow a further appeal on points of law the Federal High Court. The defendants filed an appeal to the Federal High Court asking to set aside the non-admission, but the motion was withdrawn (BGH III ZR 128/15).

There was no compensation of the victims. There was no action filed by the VZBV for the disgorgement of a certain amount of the illegally gained profit. The legal department of the VZBV is still in negotiations with the defendant for a settlement. The amount in dispute is approximately €430,000.

D. Test Case Proceedings by Consumer Associations[139]

Publicly funded consumer associations can enforce consumer claims based on an assignment or power of attorney within their statutory field of responsibility (ie consumer law). If the individual case raises significant legal issues of general relevance, it can be brought up to the Federal High Court (regardless of the amount in controversy) and thus result in an important although not legally binding precedent. The mechanism can be used for a test case proceeding in a single case, but it can also be used for collecting a limited number of consumer claims by pooling them in single action. Due to the high administrative efforts necessary to handle a large number of claims, consumer associations prefer to bring single test cases. The procedure applies to consumer claims only, but is not restricted to consumer contracts. It also applies to consumers' claims arising from, for example, product liability or pharmaceutical cases.

Case study: VZBV Test Case

The VZBV filed an action against one of the big traders of electric appliances. The claim of a single consumer was assigned to the VZBV. The consumer had bought a baking oven from the defendant, but 17 months after the delivery of the oven the enamel coating of the oven started to splinter and a repair was not possible. Due to the defect of the good, the defendant delivered a new one, but asked the consumer to pay a compensation of €70 for the use of the defective oven for 17 months. The consumer paid under reserve. According to the applicable national rules at that time, traders were allowed to claim a compensation for the use of the defective product in cases like this. The VZBV sued the trader for a refund of €70 (an action for declaratory relief would not have been admissible) and took the case up to the Federal High Court. The judges of the Federal High Court referred the question of how to interpret the applicable provisions of the Directive 1999/44 EC on the sale of consumer goods to the European Court of Justice. The ECJ held that according to the Directive traders were not allowed to ask for compensation for the use of defective products (Case C-404/06, *Quelle AG v Bundesverband der Verbraucherzentralen und Verbraucherverbände* [2008] ECR I-02685). Therefore, the German provisions were violating EU law. Accordingly, the Federal High Court ordered the refund of €70 (BGH, 26.11.2008—VIII ZR 200/05). Ultimately, the German legislature changed the national rules in order to comply with the ECJ's interpretation.

E. Capital Market Test Case Proceedings (KapMuG)

The KapMuG was enacted in 2005[140] as a reaction of the German legislature to the Deutsche Telekom case, which involved more than 17,000 claimants and completely clogged the District Court in Frankfurt in 2003–04. In 2012, the KapMuG was amended.[141]

The KapMuG represents a sectoral approach and applies only to claims for damages caused by false, misleading or omitted public capital market information of a company

---

[139] Civil Procedure Code, s 79 para 3 no 3.
[140] Federal Law Gazette 2005 I (no 50), 2437.
[141] For details of the amendments see Federal Law Gazette 2012 I (no 50), 2182.

or for damage caused by false or misleading investment consulting based on such information. The Act also applies to some special claims for performance based on German securities law.

The core of the KapMuG is to establish a model case proceeding with respect to facts or legal issues which are equally relevant to a large number of damages claims filed before courts in Germany. Courts of first instance where damage claims are pending can refer a list of common issues to the Court of Appeals which will decide on these issues in an intermediate stage of the proceedings. The Court of Appeals will appoint a test case plaintiff from the group of investors who have already filed an action for damages. During the test case proceedings before the Court of Appeals, all other individual proceedings are stayed and will be continued only after there is a final decision on the common issues tried in the test case. The final decision of the Court of Appeals or (in case of an appeal) the Federal High Court is binding for all individual proceedings in which the common issues are also relevant.

Investors have to sue the defendant individually in the first place (the KapMuG is not a representative action). If the application for test case proceedings is successful and a minimum of 10 claimants from different proceedings agree to join the test case proceedings, the Court of Appeals will appoint a test case plaintiff. The test case plaintiff is not a representative of the other investors, although the outcome of the test case has a binding effect upon them. Even if an investor who has sued the defendant withdraws his action, he cannot escape the binding effect (for example, if he later files a new action). Plaintiffs whose proceedings have been suspended with respect to the test case are allowed to participate in the test case proceedings as so-called interested parties. They can file motions and submit facts and evidence to the court. Since the 2012 reform, the test case plaintiff has been allowed to negotiate a settlement with the defendant on behalf of all claimants. An opt-out system applies when the test case plaintiff enters into a settlement with the defendant(s). The settlement—once approved by the court—becomes binding for all claimants if they do not opt-out within a certain period after having received a notice of the settlement. Another requirement for the binding effect is that the settlement is accepted by 70% of the investors who have already filed an action against the defendant.

Until the 2012 reform of the KapMuG, the legal representative of the test case plaintiff did not receive any additional remuneration for his engagement in the test case proceedings. Consequently, law firms were not eager for becoming selected for the test case. The 2012 reform changed the rule on costs and allows a (small) additional fee for the legal representative of the test case proceedings. There is no separate accounting of the legal expenses in the test case proceedings, they are part of the individual proceedings for which the test case decision ultimately becomes binding.

F. Case Studies: Capital Market Test Case Proceedings (KapMuG)

The official statistics of the German Federal Office of Statistics identify only those proceedings which are 'real' KapMuG proceedings in the sense of test case proceedings before the Court of Appeals. There is not data available with respect to cases in the first instance where applications for KapMuG proceedings had been filed, but were not successful (either because the District Court dismissed the motion or because the necessary number of 10 applications for test case proceedings was lacking). Therefore, there are only figures available with respect to test case proceedings before the Court of Appeals, as shown in Table 3.5. The latest data is from 2014.[142]

Table 3.5: Number of KapMug Cases

Year	Number of proceedings
2010	56
2011	8
2012	18
2013	89
2014	124

According to the official statistics there were no KapMuG proceedings between 2005 and 2010. This is definitely not correct, because a number of court decisions from KapMuG proceedings have been issued and published since 2006, for example by the Courts of Appeals in Munich, Stuttgart, Cologne and Frankfurt. According to the file numbers used for example by the Court of Appeals in Munich, in 2007 it seems that there were at least 34 KapMuG proceedings pending, two in 2008, and four in 2009. The Court of Appeals in Frankfurt had one in 2006 (Telekom).

The evaluation of the KapMuG (commissioned by the Federal Ministry of Justice) by Halfmeier, Rott and Feess, published in 2010,[143] mentions the following figures: from 2005 (when the KapMuG came into force) to September 2009, 24 cases in which applications for test case proceedings under the KapMuG have been published, in 12 cases test case proceedings actually began before Court of Appeals.

KapMuG Case Studies

No 1: Telekom Case, Court of Appeals Frankfurt

The first case under the KapMuG (enacted in 2005). Approximately 17,000 small investors had sued Deutsche Telekom, the Federal Republic of Germany (as the former main shareholder of Deutsche Telekom AG), KfW (*Kreditanstalt für Wiederaufbau*, a large banking institute), and several banks as members of a consortium for damages. The prospectus used for the third initial public offering in 2000 was allegedly not correct with respect to the accounting profit of €8.2 billion from an intracompany sale of the US subsidiary 'Sprint' and the validation of the value of real estate owned by Deutsche Telekom. The actions were filed in 2003 and 2004 before the District Court in Frankfurt. During the first two years of the proceedings not much happened as the Court was waiting for the German legislature to enact a new law which should help in the handling of such a complex mass litigation.

---

[142] Statistisches Bundesamt, Fachserie 10, Reihe 2.1, Rechtspflege Zivilgerichte 2014, published 16 November 2015.

[143] A Halfmeier, P Rott and E Feess, *Kollektiver Rechtsschutz im Kapitalmarktrecht* (Frankfurt School Verlag, 2010).

After the KapMuG came into force in 2005, the District Court Frankfurt published the decision to refer a list of legal and factual issues to the Court of Appeals Frankfurt for a binding decision in a test case under the new KapMuG (LG Frankfurt 3/7 OH 1/06, 3-7OH 1/06, 3/07 OH 1 06, 3-07 OH 1/06). The Court of Appeals appointed a test case plaintiff, the legal representative was the law firm Tilp & Partners which is specialised in capital market litigation, particularly in KapMuG proceedings. The proceedings in the test case dragged on because the KapMuG allows parties the filing of supplementary motions for new issues at almost any time. Another reason for the lengthy proceedings was that the chairman of the chamber at the Court of Appeals who was in charge of the case retired during the proceedings and—due to a lawsuit among potential successors—it took several months before the chamber could continue with the case. In May 2012, the Court of Appeals Frankfurt finally announced the test case decision. It held that the prospectus used by Deutsche Telekom was correct with respect to all the allegations raised by the claimants (16.5.2012, 23 Kap 1/06). The test case plaintiff appealed and in October 2014 the Federal High Court remanded the case (21.10.2014, XI ZB 12/12). It held that the prospectus was at least partially wrong and misleading. As the Court of Appeals had not yet decided on the requirements of fault and the causal link between the misleading information and the damages caused, the case was given back to the Court of Appeals in Frankfurt. In November 2016, the Court of Appeals handed down a new test case decision (30/11/2016, 23 Kap 1/06) which was completely in favour of the test case plaintiff. The defendants again appealed to the Federal High Court (published in the electronic register 20.6.2017—XI ZB 24/16). Meanwhile the test case plaintiff has passed away, but the proceedings go on. A new test case decision of the Federal High Court can be expected in summer 2018. Once that decision has been made all the proceedings in first instances (which are still suspended as long as the test case proceedings are not finished) will have to be continued in order to decide on the individual damages claims based on the binding test case decision(s). Due to legal interests (which have to be paid from the day proceedings have started) the total sum of compensation claimed by the claimants has doubled by now to an amount of approximately €200 million.

No 2: Conergy AG

In October 2008, the Munich law firm *Rotter* filed actions on behalf of investors against Conergy AG, a company operating in the solar industry, based on alleged violations of accounting rules (the published turnover figures that were too high) and the late public ad hoc announcements with respect to a delay in the delivery of silicium and moduls (both necessary for the production). Ad hoc announcements of October 2007 had caused a breakdown of share prices. Board members had sold their own shares in March 2007 resulting in a profit of a double digit million Euro amount. In June 2010 the District Court of Hamburg decided to refer the case for test case proceedings to the Court of Appeals of Hamburg. The proceedings are still pending. There was also a criminal investigation against board members of Conergy AG resulting in criminal court proceedings based on a possible violation of insider trade rules and manipulation of financial statements.

No 3: Correalcredit Bank AG

From 2006–08 numerous actions for damages based on allegedly omitted ad hoc announcements (in 2004) were filed against Correalcredit Bank AG before the District Court Frankfurt. Upon application of the plaintiffs a model case procedure according to the KapMuG followed. The central issue to be adjudicated upon was whether the defendant had informed the public in due time about their plans to sue former board members who had engaged in derivative activities thus gambling with the existence of the company. On 20 August 2014 the Court of Appeals in Frankfurt confirmed the main issues in favour of the plaintiff's side and dismissed the defendant's applications. An appeal on points of law is pending before the Federal High Court (File no II ZB 24/14).

No 4: Hypo Real Estate

Private and institutional investors sued Hypo Real Estate for a total amount of damages of approximately €1 billion. The actions are based on an alleged failure of Hypo Real Estate to publish ad hoc announcements with respect to insider information. Due to the global financial crisis the Hypo Real Estate Bank almost collapsed in 2008 when it announced considerable write offs for US certificates. The value of its shares dropped by 35%. As a result of the situation of Hypo Real Estate, other banks were also on the brink of insolvency. The Federal Government stepped in and supported Hypo Real Estate by investing more than €100 billion. On 15 December 2014 the Court of Appeals of Munich (Kap 3/10) confirmed that between 8/2007 and 8/2008 HRE had misled investors about the risks of the certificates Hypo Real Estate held with respect to the US subprime market. Hypo Real Estate filed an appeal on points of law to the Federal High Court (BGH XI ZB 13/14, 1.12.2015). Should the Federal High Court confirm the decision of the Court of Appeals of Munich, the law suits against the defendant pending in the first instance and stayed until the model case decision becomes *res judicata* will continue. Plaintiffs still have to prove the causal link between defendant's failure to publish an ad hoc announcement and the damage of investors suffered due to the deterioration of share prices. The model case is still pending before the Federal High Court. In September 2017 (19/9/2017—XI ZB 13/14), the Federal High Court issued a partial judgment on procedural issues and decided that at the level of appeal before the Federal High Court no third-party notice is allowed. A decision on the merits can be expected in 2018.

No 5: VIP 4 GmbH & Co KG Investment fund

VIP 4 is an investment fund for film, media and entertainment. Investors sued the defendant VIP and several others persons responsible for the defendant's prospectus based on allegedly false and misleading information in the defendant's prospectus published in 2004. The District Court of Munich I referred a list of 32 common issues of fact and law to the Court of Appeals in Munich for a binding decision in a model case proceeding (District Ct Munich I, 15.11.2007, 22 OH 2145/07). In its model case decision the Court of Appeals in Munich (30.12.2011, Kap 1/07) confirmed the allegations of the plaintiff only in part. Defendants' filed an appeal on points of law to the Federal High Court. On 27 July 2014, the Federal High Court overturned the decision of the Court of Appeals of Munich with respect to some of its findings (particularly those related to tax law) and referred the case back to the Court of Appeals for a new trial. With respect to other issues the Federal High Court gave a final decision as no further evidence taking was necessary.

No 6: Volkswagen 'Dieselgate'

In September 2015 Volkswagen AG admitted the use of illegal defeat devices installed in numerous VW diesel cars in the USA, in Germany and elsewhere in order to manipulate emission control tests. When this information became public the price of Volkswagen AG's shares dropped by 35%. In October 2015, Tilp law firm, which is specialised in KapMuG proceedings, filed actions for damages on behalf of 278 institutional investors against Volkswagen AG in the District Court of Braunschweig claiming approximately €3.25 billion. Since then several other complaints have been filed. Tilp represents more than 1200 investors who suffered loss with respect to their Volkswagen AG and Porsche shares. The amount of damages claimed in the Braunschweig law suits is thus the highest ever claimed in Germany. On 8 August 2016 the District Court of Braunschweig referred a list of 193 issues of fact and law to the Court of Appeals Braunschweig for a decision in model case proceedings (District Court of Braunschweig 5. 8. 2016 [5 OH 62/16] published on the website: www.bundesanzeiger.de). The KapMuG proceedings started in March 2017 and the Court of Appeals selected Deka Investment GmbH, represented by Tilp, as the test case plaintiff. Nevertheless, the situation of investors is not satisfactory because not all of them wanted to sue Volkswagen AG. As it is, however, possible that for a large part of the investors claims the period of limitation expired on 19 September 2016 (it is a highly controversial issue), claimants needed to stop the limitation period from running. There were only two ways to preserve the claims. Claimants must either have filed an action against Volkswagen AG before 19 September or formally register as a claimant in a KapMuG proceeding. Due to the fact that the model case proceedings could not start officially before 19 September 2016 (and actually started only in March 2017), numerous investors decided to sue Volkswagen AG, whilst others obviously relied on the possibility that a longer period of limitation can apply in this case. The total value of claims filed in Braunschweig is now approximately €8.8 billion. Parallel to the German law suit, damages actions filed by investors are also pending in the USA. In July 2016, one of the plaintiffs in the Braunschweig litigation sued Volkswagen of America (VWoA) in New Jersey and attempted to obtain a discovery order under 28 USC § 1782 against VWoA for the production of approximately 18 million documents which might be useful for the plaintiffs in the Braunschweig proceedings. The motion was granted in early 2017 by the New Jersey courts, and the parties are now in the process of negotiating the extent to which documents must be disclosed and which documents are to be protected as trade secrets by a protective court order.

Case Study: Daimler Aktiengesellschaft

Investors sued Daimler AG for damages based on the failure to publish ad hoc announcements with respect to the fact that the chairman of the supervisory board, Jürgen Schrempp, would resign from his position. Since 17 May 2005 there had been an internal discussion about the resignation of Jürgen Schrempp planned for the end of 2005. In July 2005, the chairman of the workers' council received the information and a formal decision of the supervisory board was scheduled for 27 July 2005. The next day an ad hoc announcement was published resulting in a rise of Daimler's share prices. Plaintiffs argued that an ad hoc announcement should have been made as early as May 2005 and claim recovery of damages which they suffered from selling their shares at a low price.

A group of investors sued Daimler Aktiengesellschaft before the District Court of Stuttgart. In 2006, the District Court referred the case for test case proceedings to the Court of Appeals of Stuttgart (District Ct Stuttgart, 3.7.2006—21 O 408/05). In a first decision published in February 2007 (901 Kap 1/06) the Court declined that Daimler was liable for damages. The test case plaintiff filed an appeal on points of law to the Federal High Court. The Federal High Court overturned the decision of the Court of Appeals in Stuttgart for procedural reasons (particularly a violation of the right to be heard). Therefore, the Court of Appeals in Stuttgart scheduled a new trial and again dismissed the applications of the plaintiffs (Court of Appeals Stuttgart, 22.4.2009, 20 Kap1/08). The main argument was that in case of a step by step development of an event within the company, ad hoc announcement should not be based on intermediate steps. An ad hoc announcement was not necessary before the resignation of Jürgen Schrempp was 'likely to a certain degree'. The judges concluded that this was not the case before the formal decision of the supervisory board on 27 July 2005. Again, plaintiffs filed an appeal on points of law to the Federal High Court. The Federal High Court in November 2010 (II ZB 7/09) stayed proceedings and made a reference to the European Court of Justice for a preliminary ruling on Directive 2003/6/EC on insider trade and market abuse (the Market Abuse Directive).

On 28 June 2012 the European Court of Justice decided (Case C-19/11, *Markus Geltl v Daimler AG* [2012]) that also intermediate steps of an event could raise the obligation of a company to publish an ad hoc announcement. Therefore, the Federal High Court again overturned the (second) decision of the Court of Appeals of Stuttgart and referred the case back

(Federal High Court, 23.4.2013, II ZB 7/09). It emphasised that already a first communication of Jürgen Schrempp to the chairman of the supervisory board in May 2005 could, in principle, require an ad hoc announcement. The Court of Appeals of Stuttgart had to take further evidence with respect to the question of how likely a resignation of Schrempp was in May 2005. The Court of Appeals had to decide whether the conversation between Schrempp and Kopper in May 2005 was only an 'exchange of ideas' or the first clear step to Schrempp's resignation. The Court suggested a settlement and announced a decision for 21 September 2015 if no settlement was concluded. The parties settled the case and all claims have been withdrawn (press release of the Court of Appeals in Stuttgart 16.12.2016). The amount paid according to the settlement was not disclosed.

There were also administrative proceedings initiated by the German Federal Financial Supervisory Agency (BaFin). BaFin had imposed an administrative fine on Daimler AG. The decision was, however, set aside by the Regional Court of Frankfurt. The Court argued that due to the fact that it was not clear whether and when an ad hoc announcement should have been published Daimler AG was mistaken as to the wrongful nature of the act and could not be held liable under criminal and administrative law (15.8.2008, 934 OWi 7411 Js 233764/07). Upon an appeal on points of law, the Court of Appeals in Frankfurt, however, overturned the decision and held that Daimler AG should have published an ad hoc announcement as early as possible. Daimler AG then accepted the administrative fine and there was no new decision by the Regional Court of Frankfurt.

VIII. Italy[144]

A. Class Actions

The Italian class action procedure is laid down in article 140bis of the Consumers' Code.[145] Consumers can bring a class action to protect their homogenous rights, seeking compensation for damages and/or restitution of undue payments. The class action device can be initiated to establish the liability of the defendant and to obtain compensation for damages, but it cannot be used to stop or to prevent a certain conduct by the defendant; such result can anyway be pursued through the different remedy of the Representative Action, as set forth by article 140 of the Consumers' Code (see paragraph (c) below).

Class actions can be brought only to protect:

(a) the contractual rights of multiple consumers and users who find themselves in the same situation in relation to a 'professional' (usually a company), including rights arising out of general terms and conditions;

---

[144] The author of this section is Daniele Vecchi.

[145] The Consumers' Code was introduced by Legislative Decree no 206 of 6 September 2005, which came into force on 23 October 2005. The Consumers' Code is a consolidated act, bringing together and coordinating all existing provisions with regard to consumers' protection. Art 140bis was introduced by Law no 244 of 24 December 2007. The provision was amended by Law no 99 of 23 July 2009 and by Art 6 of Law no 27 of 24 March 2012. Currently, a reform of Art 140bis is under discussion before by the Italian Parliament. A bill for a reformed class action regime has been approved by the Italian Chamber of Deputies (Bill of Law no 1335 of 2015) and is currently pending before the Senate.

(b) the rights that multiple end-users of a product/service have against a manufacturer, even if there is no direct contractual relationship (i.e. product liability) and;

(c) the rights to compensation for the prejudice suffered by consumers and users as a consequence of unfair business practices or unfair competition, including misleading advertising.

Class actions can only be brought before the Tribunals (ie major courts of first instance and not justices of the peace) of the capital of the region where the defendant has its registered office. It has been argued by scholars (no case law presently available) that a class action cannot be brought against a foreign company, since it does not have its registered office in Italy.

Class actions can only be initiated by a consumer or a user who has the same right to claim protection (homogenous rights) as the other members of the class. The consumer or user can bring the class action personally or through a consumer association or a representative body (on purpose *committee*) to which he/she belongs. The law does not specify the legal role of representative bodies and consumer associations within the proceedings, this issue has been dealt with by case law. Although they are not legal entities, representative bodies (*comitati*) may also become the lead plaintiff if they have been set up solely for the purpose of representing class members and if they prove that they have been granted powers by at least one class member, while the role of consumer associations is usually limited to technical support to the lead plaintiff.

The case law is, in any event, not consolidated on the merits. In two cases where claims were filed by some consumers together with a consumer association, the Court ruled that the consumer association could not file the suit because the principals (ie the consumers/plaintiffs) had already filed an action based on the same claim. According to the Tribunal, a principal and its proxy should appear 'alternatively' and not together (*Aduc v and Mr De Francesco vs Banca Popolare di Novara*, case number 5 in Table 3.6, and *Altroconsumo and Mr Gasca vs Intesa S Paolo*, case number 6 in Table 3.6). However, the Court of Appeal, reversing the decision of the Tribunal in case number 6 of Table 3.6, clarified that the proxy granted to the consumer association should be considered as a 'technical proxy' for practical assistance (in addition to the necessary proxy granted to a lawyer) and not as a substantial proxy of rights, thus allowing consumers to appear together with the chosen consumer association.

Each class member may file a claim by initiating a class action and proposing him/herself as lead plaintiff and class representative, or by opting in to a certified class action, or by initiating individual proceedings. In starting a class action, the lead plaintiff is in fact bringing an action also in the interests of other class members. However, the class action is not binding for the other class members until they decide to opt-in. When filing his/her request for opting in, a class member must provide all documents and evidence proving his/her claim and elect a domicile for the proceedings (ie specify the address where he/she wishes to receive all communications).

Having opted in, each class member waives his/her right to file any other action (individual or collective) for restitution/compensation for damages grounded on the same circumstances. Nonetheless, the rights of the consumers or users who have joined the class are not affected if the lead plaintiff withdraws the claim or enters into an out-of-court settlement with the defendant. In such cases, when class members are not willing to waive nor to accept the out-of-court settlement (an express and individual acceptance is required to adhere to the settlement accepted by the class representative), they can file their claim in court again.

The procedure consists of two phases: a certification phase, where the court decides on the admissibility of the class action, and a phase on the merits, which only takes place if the class action is declared admissible, where the opt-in takes place and the case is decided in the merit.

The case starts with the service of a writ of summons on the defendant. 20 days before the hearing (or, in some cases, at the hearing) the defendant is requested to file its defensive brief. At the first hearing the lead plaintiff has to provide evidence that the admissibility conditions have been met and the parties are admitted to discuss admissibility; the Tribunal may allow the parties to file additional briefs and documents. Subsequently, the Tribunal decides whether to certify—and therefore admit—the class action or not. There is no time limit for the conclusion of the first phase of the proceedings; on average this may take from five to seven months. The Tribunal will deny class certification if:

— the rights of class members are not homogeneous, the ie commonality requirement is not met (in the past, before a law reform took place, certification was denied if those rights were not identical);
— the lead plaintiff is unable to adequately take care of the interests of the class;
— there is a conflict of interest between the lead plaintiff and the interests of the class;
— the claim is manifestly ungrounded on the merits.

The order declaring the class action admissible or inadmissible can be challenged before the Court of Appeal. In the event the class action is declared admissible, the appeal does not stay or suspend the proceedings pending before the Tribunal. The Court of Cassation, which is Italy's Supreme Court, has ruled that the decision on appeal on the admissibility/inadmissibility of a class action cannot be further challenged.

After the class action has been declared admissible, the decision is published and advertised pursuant to the admission order and the opt-in period starts running. The Tribunal then has to rule on the merits. The Tribunal may adopt all necessary measures for the collection of evidence/pieces of information, also departing from ordinary procedural rules. The decision on the merits is binding only for the lead plaintiff and the members of the class who opted in. Class members who did not opted in are not affected by the decision.

The decision on the merits can be challenged before the Court of Appeal, in accordance with the general rules on appellate proceedings. The decision of the Court of Appeal on the merits can be challenged before the Court of Cassation, but the Court of Cassation's review is limited to issues regarding the interpretation and correct application of the law and cannot re-examine facts or evidences.

There are no specific rules on funding or financing class actions. The general rules apply. Third-party funding is not frequently used in Italy. This may be due to the absence of punitive damages or specific rewards for the funding person/entity. Lack of an additional award on the lead plaintiff acting as class representatives and on the promoters of the class action could be one of the reasons why the class action mechanism is not very common in Italy. Individual plaintiffs are not motivated to bring a class action because their 'reward' is equal to all other class members, while the lead plaintiff has to cover all legal fees and publication costs and is exposed to the risk of being condemned to refund the other party's legal fees in case of loss (which has been happening more frequently compared to the past. In fact, in the first class actions cases, courts were more inclined to settle fees between the parties when the class members were the losing party rather than condemning them to refund the defendants). A sort of financing mechanism may be found in the support offered to consumers by consumer associations. As already mentioned, one of the conditions for a class action to be declared admissible is that the lead plaintiff is able to adequately take care of the interests of the entire class. Consequently, it may become necessary for a single consumer/user or a small group of consumers/users to have technical or financial support from an association, which may also provide the necessary legal assistance. Even if consumer associations do not receive any additional award, they still have an interest in supporting class actions and in investing human and financial resources in them, because they use class actions as tools not only for protecting consumers' interests and self-advertising, but also for increasing memberships.

B. Case Studies: Class Actions

There are no official statistics related to class action cases brought in Italy. The Ministry of Economic Development dedicates a section of its website to class actions,[146] but this section is not updated regularly and furthermore reports only admitted class actions in order to consent consumers to evaluate opt-in; therefore, because it does not report rejected class action or final outcome, this record is not an adequate tool for a comprehensive analysis.

On the basis of the information collected so far, somewhere between 50 and 100 class actions have been announced. We have been able to track about 50 proceedings, listed in Table 3.6. The following general remarks can be made on these cases. First, data information regarding any proceedings is not publicly available in Italy; as a consequence, the list, as well as some details regarding the above listed class actions, is incomplete. Second, the pieces of information included in this chart have been collected on the basis of direct checks within relevant Clerk Office and whether possible, web pages and national newspapers.

Out of 49 tracked class actions, 19 were not certified and 22 were certified (the other outcomes are not available, or the processing is still pending). In the first years of application of the law, most class actions were not certified, while in the more recent years most of the proposed class actions were certified, probably due to a better understanding and use of the class action tool.

In relation to final outcomes on the merits, six out of seven final decisions (of this cohort of 49) were favourable to the class, and in the seventh case the action was dropped because a settlement was reached. A number of cases in the cohort remain unconcluded.

---

[146] http://www.sviluppoeconomico.gov.it/index.php/it/mercato-e-consumatori/tutela-del-consumatore/class-action/ordinanze-class-action.

Table 3.6: Class Actions in Italy

	Plaintiff/s	Defendant/s	Court	Claim	Decision Date and Outcome	Status of proceedings
1.	Codacons	Intesa San Paolo SpA	Turin	Compensation for damages caused by the introduction of new and more expensive commissions in place of the so called maximum uncovered. The claim relied on a decision of the Italian Antitrust Authority.	Not admitted neither on 1st instance (4 June 2010), on appeal (27 October 2010) and before the Court of Cassation (14 June 2012)	By an order dated 4 June 2010 the Court of Turin declared the action inadmissible. The Court of Turin found that Codacons had no legal capacity to sue as the defendant never applied to the consumer, who was represented in this case, the contractual conditions at issue. Thus, such a consumer had no title to represent the class. The aforesaid order was then challenged before the Court of Appeal of Turin. It was confirmed on 27 October 2010. The order of the Court of Appeal of Turin was then challenged before the Court of Cassation which declared that the order was not challengeable before the Court of Cassation.
2.	Codacons	Voden Medical Istruments SpA	Milan	Compensation for damages caused by the purchase of Ego Flu Test, for self-diagnosis of A and B influenza. The test would in fact not be as reliable as promised.	Admitted (20 December 2010) Adjudicated in the merits (26 August 2013) Appealed before the Court of Cassation	By an order dated 20 December 2010 the Court of Milan declared the action admissible. Voden challenged the order before the Court of Appeal of Milan, which confirmed the first instance decision on 3 May 2011. The action before the Court of Milan continued in the merit. By a decision dated 14 March 2012, the Court of Milan rejected the claim on the merits, founding that the plaintiff failed to provide evidence of her quality of 'consumer' (having her purchased the relevant product for aims related to the proceedings at issue only, and not to actually use it) and the damage claimed due to the allegedly misleading advertising of the same product. The plaintiff was also condemned to refund the defendant with an additional amount as damaged for malicious litigation (art 96 of the Italian Code of Civil Procedure).

(continued)

Table 3.6: (*Continued*)

Plaintiff/s	Defendant/s	Court	Claim	Decision Date and Outcome	Status of proceedings
					The decision of the Court of Milan was challenged before the Court of Appeal of Milan that, by a decision dated 26 August 2013, reverted the decision on the merits, stating the following:
					— the assessment of admissibility of a class action does not rely on the single case filed by the plaintiff, but on the (possible) existence of an homogeneous right of a class; in the case at issue, there was a homogeneous right of all the people who bought Ego Flu Test to ask for the ascertainment of its reliability;
					— on the merits, the discrepancies between what was declared in the leaflet and on Voden's website could mislead the consumers, thus having the right to be refund for damaged (depending on the damages proved)
					— as per the damages suffered by the plaintiff (who was qualified as a 'consumer' and a 'class member', being irrelevant the specific reasons why she bought the Test) she solely proved the purchase of the Test, thus having the right of being refunded of its price (€14.50); as per the sole other consumer who joined in, his claim was rejected for lacking the proof of him purchasing the Test.
					From the information available, the decision on the merits of the Court of Appeals has been challenged before the Court of Cassation.

3.	Codacons	Unicredit SpA	Rome	Compensation for damages caused by the introduction of new and more expensive commissions in place of the so called maximum uncovered. The claim would rely on a decision of the Italian Antitrust Authority.	Not admitted neither on 1st instance (25 March 2011) and on appeal (14 May 2012)	By an order dated 25 March 2011, the action was declared inadmissible, as the facts at issue occurred before the procedural law about class action came into force. That order was challenged by Codacons before the Court of Appeal of Rome which confirmed it on 14 May 2012. Copy of the relevant order is not available. Nonetheless, by the information collected, it results that the Court of Appeal of Rome found the case inadmissible as the relevant contracts, containing the allegedly damaging provisions, were signed before 15 August 2009, when the class action discipline was not into force.
4.	Codacons	BAT Italia SpA	Rome	Compensation for damages caused by consumption of cigarettes under Article 2043 or Article 2050 of the Italian Civil Code.	Not admitted neither on 1st instance (1 April 2011), on appeal (27 January 2012) and before the Court of Cassation	On 1 April 2011 the Court of Rome declared the inadmissibility of the action against British American Tobacco. This order was then challenged before the Court of Appeal of Rome. On 27 January 2012 the challenge was rejected because of lack of identity of rights amongst the consumers (smokers). Codacons challenged it before the Court of Cassation, who declared the decision on admissibility non-challengeable
5.	Mr Marzio de Francesco and Adoc as per mandate ranted to by the former	Banca Popolare di Novara	Turin	Compensation for damages caused by the introduction of new and more expensive commissions in place of the so called maximum uncovered. The claim relied on a decision of the Italian Antitrust Authority.	Not admitted on 1st instance (7 April 2011)	By an order dated 7 April 2011 the action was declared inadmissible by the Court of Turin, that found that: — Adoc had no legal capacity to sue, as it acted on behalf of a consumer who was already party in the proceedings, excluding the existence of an autonomous and several power to act (of consumer as well as the consumer association) under Article 140 *bis*, first and second paragraph of the Italian Consumer Code ('ICC'); and

(continued)

Table 3.6: *(Continued)*

Plaintiff/s	Defendant/s	Court	Claim	Decision Date and Outcome	Status of proceedings
					— Mr de Francesco, a retired person, was not able to guarantee, given his economic status, adequate protection of the interest of the class pursuant to Article 140 *bis*, sixth paragraph, of the ICC. No reference to an appeal of the order was found.
6. Francesco Gasca, Emanuela Lucidi and Filippo Sobrero and Altroconsumo, as per mandate granted by the former	Intesa San Paolo SpA	Turin	Compensation for damages caused by the introduction of new and more expensive commissions in place of the so called maximum uncovered. The claim would rely on a decision of the Italian Antitrust Authority.	Admitted on appeal Adjudicated in the merits (June 2016)	By an order dated 28 April 2011 the Court of Turin declared the action inadmissible. Such order was challenged before the Court of Appeal of Turin, which on 23 September 2011 declared the action admissible finding that: — the consumers, having the support of Altroconsumo, had the economic means to bear the costs of the procedure; — to satisfy the legal requirements a condition of identity/homogeneity is sufficient; a perfect match of all the consumers' claims is not required; — damage to be taken into account are those caused after the entry into force or article 140-bis of the ICC only. No retroactivity is admissible. Intesa San Paolo challenged the admissibility before the Court of Appeal before the Court of Cassation, which rejected the challenge.

					In the merit the Court of Turin on 23 July 2014 has issued its final decision and condemned Intesa San Paolo to refund the consumers, but limiting its decision to three consumers (over 104 opting-in consumers. The exclusion of these latter parties has been due to lack of formal requirements in adhering to the class action. On 30 June 2016 the Court of Appeal of Turin confirmed the first decree merit decision.
7.	Adoc	Gruppo Torinese Trasporti SpA	Turin	Compensation for damages caused by the defendant company, managing bus transportation services, due to continuous and sever delays, and the very low qualities of the vehicles used.	Not admitted neither on 1st instance (31 October 2011) and on appeal (11 January 2012)	The action was declared inadmissible as ungrounded on the merits (lack of *prime facie* groundness) by an order dated 31 October 2011. Albeit the condition of identity was satisfied, the consumers failed to prove the damage claimed. No full text of the relevant order is available. Such order was challenged before the Court of Appeal of Turin. On 11 January 2012 the challenge was rejected because, albeit the condition of identity/homogeneity had been satisfied, the action was declared manifestly ungrounded for failure to prove any damage or loss suffered.
8.	Vincenzo Donvito and Aduc	Microsoft Srl	Milan	Compensation for damages caused by the sale of personal computers with preinstalled-by manufacturer versions of Windows, without granting to the purchaser the possibility to opt for other operating systems.	Not admitted (20 October 2011)	By an order dated 20 October 2011 the action was declared inadmissible for the defendant's lack of capacity to be sued. The claim should have been raised against the seller of the computers where the relevant software was installed and not against the manufacturer of the same software. ADUC was condemned to advertise at its own cost the order on newspapers. No information about challenge is available.

(continued)

Table 3.6: *(Continued)*

Plaintiff/s	Defendant/s	Court	Claim	Decision Date and Outcome	Status of proceedings
9. Altroconsumo	RAI TV	Rome	Compensation for damages caused by the breach of duty to offer an impartial information as provided for by the Agreement for the issue of the relevant Public Service.	Not admitted neither on 1st instance (8 July 2011) and on appeal (8 May 2013)	The action was declared inadmissible at the hearing of 8 July 2011. No copy of the decision is available. Such order was challenged by Altroconsumo before the Court of Appeal of Rome. — It seems on 8 May 2013 the Court of Appeals confirmed the decision of inadmissibility because the class members were not entitled to sue the company.
10. Group of commuters—Comitato Pendolari FR 8 Carrozza di Nettuno	Trenitalia SpA	Rome	Compensation for damages caused by continuous delays of trains along the route between Rome and Cassino.	Not admitted neither on 1st instance (16 September 2011) and on appeal (6 November 2012)	By an order dated 16 September 2011 the action was declared inadmissible because: — lack of identity of rights amongst the consumers (damages should vary in accordance with the price of the ticket; since the consumers paid different prices, they were not considered to be in an identical situation); — the damage claimed did not reach the threshold established by law (the judge qualified the petitioners' condition as a simple discomfort, not amounting to damage). Such order was challenged before the Court of Appeal of Rome, which confirmed the inadmissibility stating that: — Trenitalia's lack of capacity to be sued: the action should have been raised against the Region Lazio; — The case fails to satisfy the condition of identity/ homogeneity; the request for Trenitalia to fulfill the obligation (*i.e.* respect the timetable) is inadmissible, being the class action aimed solely to compensate damages.

11.	Unione Nazionale Consumatori	Wecantour	Naples	Compensation for damages caused by sale of travel packages for a location in Zanzibar.	Admitted (1 October 2011) Adjudicated in the merits (18 February 2013)	On 1 October 2011 the case was certified. On the merits, the Court of Naples admitted the claims raised by the plaintiff and by the consumers belonging to some groups identified in the decision, ordering WT to compensate each member of the class €1,300.00 plus interest and monetary evaluation, corresponding to 80% of the price originally paid.
						In contrast, the Court of Naples rejected the claims raised by other consumers for lack of identity with the class as defined above. The Court of Naples, moreover, noticed that in relation to the claims raised by these consumers no evidence was provided about the actual damage they suffered.
12.	Associazione Utenti Cimiteriali (Naples)	Municipality of Naples	Naples	Compensation for damages for bad management of cemeteries.	No available information	The writ of summons was served in February 2012. No information is available.
13.	Single citizen	Quadrifoglio Servizi Ambientali Area Fiorentina	Florence	Compensation for damages for bad management of the cleaning of the street after snowing (request for refund of the tax paid for the cleaning of the town).	Not admitted neither on 1st instance (30 May 2011) and on appeal (14 December 2011)	By an order dated 30 May 2011 the Court of Florence declared the action inadmissible. No copy of the order is available; nonetheless, for the information at disposal, it seems that the Court of Florence found that the claim at issue was out of the scope of Article 140 *bis* of the Consumers' Code.
						Such order was challenged before the Court of Appeal of Florence, which confirmed the inadmissibility finding that:
						— there was not a contractual relation between the citizens and the Company appointed for the cleaning. The citizens were considered to be 'beneficiaries' and not parties (the sole relation run between the citizens and the Municipality of Florence);

(continued)

Table 3.6: *(Continued)*

Plaintiff/s	Defendant/s	Court	Claim	Decision Date and Outcome	Status of proceedings
					— the payment of the tax the consumer asked to be refund of, was not due because of a contractual relation, but because of the law. The notion of 'product' and, consequently, of 'producer', must not be interpreted in a broad sense (as per Article 3 of the Consumers' code) but in accordance with article 115 of the Consumers' code, which excludes 'public' services (such as the cleaning of the streets) from the definition of products.
14. Assoconsum ONLUS	Banca della Campania spa	Naples	Compensation for damage caused by the unilateral introduction of new clause in the bank account concerning the application of a new commission/fee over the bank account (*commissione per mancanza fondi*).	Admitted (16 November 2011) Adjudicated in the merits (18 February 2013)	By an order dated 16 November 2011, the Court of Naples declared the action admissible assessing: — The identity of rights amongst the consumers (the owners of the bank accounts where said commission /fee was introduced); — the entry of Assoconsumo ONLUS in the list of the Consumers Associations considered as representative of consumers on a national level; — the non-manifest groundlessness of the claims of the Consumers, having the Consumers' association challenged the violation of Law 2/2009 which forbids commissions for maximum uncovered. The order was challenged by Banca della Campania before the Court of Appeal of Naples, which confirmed the admissibility of the action stating that: — the alleged illegitimate behaviour of the bank took place in 2010 and not in May 2009 (ie after the entry into force of the class action);

#	Plaintiff	Defendant	Court	Claim	Status	Notes
						— the requirement of 'identity' of the rights of the consumers can be identified in the fact that they were all owners of the same kind of bank account; — the inclusion the consumers association in the list of Consumers Association representing the consumers at national level entitle Assocunsumo to sue. Apparently in the merit the Court has condemned Banca della Campania to pay compensation of damages to the consumers (October 2012). Such decision is not available.
15.	Altroconsumo	Moby, Snav, Grandi Navi Veloci, Forship	Genova	Compensation for damages for raising of prices of all the ferry boats from/ to Sardinia.	Abandoned	Apparently, with an order dated 4 October 2012 the Court suspended the proceedings because of the pending of a proceedings before the Antitrust Authority on the behaviour of the defendant. From Altroconsumo website it seems the Antitrust Authority has condemned the companies, but the decision was then reformed by the Administrative Court of Lazio Region (as confirmed by the Supreme Administrative Court). Thus, the class action was abandoned for lacking grounds (the violation of competition rules was excluded).
16.	Codacons	Trenitalia	Bologna	Compensation for damages for delays of trains on 1 February 2012.	No available information	No further information is available.
17.	Ferdinando Secchi	Cagliari Calcio (Football Association)	Cagliari	Compensation for damages for the Football Association decision to play football matches in Trieste and not it Cagliari (the supporters could not attend he match).	No available information	Apparently, the case led to a class action, but according to different websites it seems that several hearings were held on 17 October 2012 before the Justice of Peace of Cagliari. Technically, it does not seem to be a proper class action because it seems the Judge is reviewing the situation of each single class member. The pieces of information available are controversial. It seems that there is a conciliation proceeding pending before the 'Associazione Casa dei Diritti'.

(continued)

Table 3.6: *(Continued)*

Plaintiff/s	Defendant/s	Court	Claim	Decision Date and Outcome	Status of proceedings
18. Codici, Unione Nazionale Consumatori, Movimento Difesa del Cittadino, ACU	Autostrade per l'Italia	Rome	Compensation for damages for traffic jam on 17–18 December 2010, due to bad conditions of the weather.	No available information	From the information available on websites, it seems the action has been suspended because of the need to wait for a decision of the Regional Court or Lazio Region. No further information is available.
19. Codacons on behalf of Marta Rossi (also on behalf of her son Filippo De Giuli)	Hospital Policlinico Universitario 'Agostino Gemelli', Rome	Rome	Compensation for damages for tuberculosis of the claimant's child, alleging that the Hospital let a nurse work when probably affected by the disease.	Admitted (20 April 2012)	By an order dated 20 April 2012, the Court of Rome declared the class action admissible. No further information is available.
20. Codacons	Trenord	Milan	Compensation for damages for delays of trains on 10/14 December 2012.	Admitted (April and May 2014) Adjudicated in the on the merits (25 August 2017)	Three proceedings started against Trenitalia by different Consumer associations were consolidated. The Court of Milan has declared the proceedings inadmissible. The Court of Appeal of Milan has admitted the proceedings in April and May 2014. The Court of Milan has rejected the suit in the merit with decision no 426 dated 26 January 2016. All consumers associations appealed, and the appeal proceedings were consolidated.

	Defendant	Court	Subject	Status	Outcome
					With decision no 3756/2017, published on 25 August 2017, RG no 667/2016 the Court of Appeal of Milan admitted the appeal, and condemned Trenord to pay a €100 to a relevant number of consumers (the consumers assisted by Altroconsumo and Codici are about 3,500, while no figures are available with regard to consumers assisted by Codacons), further to pay almost €130,000 for legal fees in favour of the promoting consumers association. Therefore, the class action is worth in aggregate around €500,000.
21. Altroconsumo	Trenord	Milan	Compensation for damages for delays of trains on December 10/14, 2012.	Admitted (April and May 2014) Adjudicated in the on the merits (25 August 2017)	Three proceedings started against Trenitalia by different Consumer associations were consolidated. The Court of Milan has declared the proceedings inadmissible. The Court of Appeal of Milan has admitted the proceedings in April and May 2014. The Court of Milan has rejected the suit in the merit with decision no 426 dated 26 January 2016. All consumers associations appealed, and the appeal proceedings were consolidated. With decision no 3756/2017, published on 25 August 2017, RG no 667/2016 the Court of Appeal of Milan admitted the appeal, and condemned Trenord to pay €100 compensation to a relevant number of consumers (the consumers assisted by Altroconsumo and Codici are about 3,500, while no figures are available with regard to consumers assisted by Codacons), further to pay almost €130,000 for legal fees in favour of the promoting consumers association. Therefore, the class action is worth in aggregate around €500,000.

Table 3.6: (*Continued*)

Plaintiff/s	Defendant/s	Court	Claim	Decision Date and Outcome	Status of proceedings
22. CODICI Onlus	Trenord	Milan	Compensation for damages for delays of trains on 10/14 December 2012.	Admitted (April and May 2014) Adjudicated in the merits on the merits (25 August 2017)	Three proceedings started against Trenitalia by different Consumer associations were consolidated. The Court of Milan has declared the proceedings inadmissible. The Court of Appeal of Milan has admitted the proceedings in April and May 2014. The Court of Milan has rejected the suit in the merit with decision no 426 dated 26 January 2016. All consumers associations appealed, and the appeal proceedings were consolidated. **With decision no 3756/2017, published on 25 August 2017, RG no 667/2016 the Court of Appeal of Milan admitted the appeal, and condemned Trenord to pay €100 compensation to a relevant number of consumers (the consumers assisted by Altroconsumo and Codici are about 3,500, while no figures are available with regard to consumers assisted by Codacons), further to pay almost €130,000 for legal fees in favour of the promoting consumers association.** Therefore, the class action is worth in aggregate around €500,000.

23.	Federconsumatori Campania	INA Assitalia	Rome	Compensation for damage caused by unfair trade practices, notably by the omission of the communication of withdrawal from the insurance contract at least 30 days before the annual expiry of the contract and by the non-delivery of the 'certificate of risk'.	Not admitted (25 June 2012)	By an order dated 25 June 2012, the Court of Rome declared the action inadmissible on the basis of the lack of capacity to sue of the plaintiff, as the relevant Consumers' Association would have not been provided with a proper power of attorney.
24.	Remo Bondioli and other 47 citizens and Codacons	Municipality of Zocca	Pavullo	Compensation for damages caused by the request of payment of Municipality fees that they had already paid but that have been embezzled by an unfaithful employee.	No available information	During the first hearing on 15 December 2011 the Municipality raised a competence issue, namely that jurisdiction does not pertain to the Ordinary Court but to the Administrative Court. Apparently a second hearing has been scheduled for May 2013. No further information is available.
25.	Federconsumatori, CTCU (Centro Tutela Consumatori e Utenti dell'alto Adige)	Apple Italia	Milan	Compensation for damages caused by the inducement to purchase a useless product (namely, the 'AppleCare Protection Plan'), provided that an equal or even stronger guarantee is already due to consumers in accordance with Consumers' Code.	Not admitted (10 December 2013)	The Court declared the proceedings inadmissible with an order dated 10 December 2013.

(continued)

Table 3.6: *(Continued)*

Plaintiff/s	Defendant/s	Court	Claim	Decision Date and Outcome	Status of proceedings
26. Comitato per l'Acqua Bene Comune del Quartiere 4 di Firenze	Publiacqua SpA	Florence	Compensation for damages caused by the charge of a particular fee by Publiacqua SpA provided its supervened unlawfulness by means of a national referendum dated 12/13 June 2012.	Not admitted (31 January 2013)	The Court has declared the proceedings inadmissible because Publiacqua has correctly applied the national and regional rules.
27. Codici	AMA spa	Rome	Refund of the extra fees paid by citizens of Rome for garbage management	Not admitted	Information from the press. No further information available
28. Private citizen+ Federconsumatori	SKY spa	Milan	Compensation for damages for breach of law being the commercials broadcasted on Sky tv (pay per view channels) 'invasive'	Not admitted	Apparently, the class action has been declared inadmissible by the Court of Milan. No further information available
29. 105 citizens	Brugo Spa/ Municipality of Sora, Province of Cassino, Region Lazio	Cassino	Compensation for damages caused by pollution	No available information	The Judge scheduled the first hearing for 12 May 2014. No further information is available.

30.	Altroconsumo	Municipality of Florence	Florence	Refunding of VAT over Waste Tax	Not admitted	The Court has declared the suit inadmissible with order dated 5 March 2014.
31.	Codacons	ATM	Milan	Compensation for damages caused by a strike occurred on 2 October 2012.	Not admitted (19 April 2014)	The proceedings have been declared inadmissible by the Court of Milan with a decision dated 19 April 2014, which has, moreover, condemned Codacons to refund the counterparty (ie the Company in charge charged of public transport) all the costs of proceedings, thus abandoning the common practice of compensating the same costs between the parties when the consumers are the losing party. Such decision has been grounded on the negligence of the Consumers Association in carrying out the proceedings (lack of accuracy and of professionalism in filing the claims), which could also be detrimental to the rights of the consumers represented by the same association.
32.	Comitato tuela Banca Carige	Banca Carige	Genoa	Compensation for damages for unfair commercial conducts	Not admitted (June 2014)	The Court of Genova declared the class action inadmissible for lack of standing of the Comitato Tutela Banca Carige. Said Committee was then condemned to refund Carige legal fees for €11,500. The class members were around 250,000.
33.	CODICI Onlus	Wind	Rome	Compensation for damages—class members: clients of Wind (Telephone, Mobile or internet) 13 June 2014.	Inadmissible (1st instance) Admitted in appeal (February 2016) Abandoned	The Court of Rome had initially declared the class action inadmissible. Said order was challenged before the Court of Appeals of Rome, which declared the action admissible on 8/22 February 2016. The Court of Rome reopened the case, granting terms for advertising the order and for consumer to opt-in. The case was abandoned by all parties for the reaching of an out-of- Court agreement.

(continued)

Table 3.6: *(Continued)*

	Plaintiff/s	Defendant/s	Court	Claim	Decision Date and Outcome	Status of proceedings
34.	Adusbef	MPS	Florence	The class action concerns the assessment and statement of responsibility for incomplete or inaccurate information in the 2010 budget of the bank	Not admitted	The Judge has declared the proceedings not admissible because the investors are not considered consumers but as professionals.
35.	CTCU/CRTCU	Trenta SpA	Venice	The associations ask the Court of Venice to order the company to refund to all consumers or applicants participating in this action, the sums received by way of VAT on the rate of environmental hygiene (Tia) and the Tares.	No available information	No information is available.
36.	Adiconsum and 'Civiltà e Progresso'	Abbanoa	Cagliari	Compensation for damages for Bad management in the provision of water in North Sardinia (water not suitable for drinking)	Admitted (1st instance)	By an order of 12/13 February 2017 the Court of Cagliari declared the proceedings admissible. The class action is open to all consumers who have suffered the consequences of bad management in the provision of water in Porto Torres area between 27 November 2009 and 21 October 2015.

| 37. | Comitato per l'acqua in Sardegna + 6 consumers | Abbanoa | Cagliari | Unfair request of payment, from the regional water company, of compulsory taxes related to the period 2005–2011 (statute of limitation and illegitimate calculation of the amounts, on forfeiture basis) | Not admitted on 1st instance (30 July 2014) Admitted in appeal (30 July 2014) | By an order dated 17 October 2013 the Court of Cagliari declared the action inadmissible. No copy of the order is available. Nonetheless, for the information at disposal, it seems that the Court of Cagliari found that the plaintiffs (a Committee and 6 consumers) didn't prove their capacity to carry out the class action, taking into account the complexity (and the relevant costs) of the phase of evidence-gathering in relation to the claim at issue.

Such order was challenged before the Court of Appeal of Cagliari, which reformed the order of inadmissibility finding that the Committee, expressly created for the class action, could be endowed with enough resources to carry out any necessary activities, also considering that (i) the number of class members—clients of Abbanoa, which operates in the sole Sardinia Region—was limited and (ii) from the allegations of Abbanoa, which recognized troubles in offering its services, technical tests or activities seemed to be unnecessary.

No further information is available |
| 38. | Unidos and Mr Mauro Pili (Member of Parliament) | Abbanoa | Cagliari | Unfair request of payment, from the regional water company, of compulsory taxes related to the period 2005–2011 (statute of limitation and illegitimate calculation of the amounts, on forfeiture basis) | Admitted (December 2018) | After first class action was not admitted, a second class action has been filed against Abbanoa on 28 June 2016, supported by Mr Mauro Pili (a local politician and a Consumers' Committee).

According to the press in December 2017 the Court of Cagliari admitted a class for reimbursement of undue payment. The potential class members are in the order of 750,000. |

(*continued*)

Table 3.6: *(Continued)*

Plaintiff/s	Defendant/s	Court	Claim	Decision Date and Outcome	Status of proceedings
39. Comitato rappresentato da Piero Panu + Mr Giancarlo Rotella	Abbanoa	Cagliari	Bad management in the provision of water in North Sardinia (water not suitable for drinking)	Not admitted (17 December 2016)	By an order of 17 December 2016, the class action was declared inadmissible by the Court of Cagliari for lack of homogeneity and condemned the Plaintiffs to refund Abbanoa with €2,500.
40. 127 citizens of Buggerru Municipality	Abbanoa	Cagliari	Refund of the amount paid by each consumer in the last 5 years for the service of water-cleaning, because not provided by the Company, plus compensation for damages	Admitted on 1st instance (11 October 2016)	By an order of 11 October 2016, the Court of Cagliari declared the class action admissible because the plaintiffs demonstrate the homogeneity of the class. The Court of Cagliari has thus granted new terms for opting it (20 July 2017) and scheduled a new hearing on September 2017.
41. Consumers (citizens of Montenero di Bisaccia, in Molise Region)	Azienda Molise Acque	Rome	Compensation for damages caused by (allegedly) toxic water (presence of trialometani) and for breach of contract, being water not available when the episode took place (December 2010/ January 2011)	Admitted (2 May 2013)	A hearing has been held on 21 September 2015, but no further information is available.

42.	Consumers (citizens of Petacciato, in Molise Region)	Azienda Molise Acque	Rome	Compensation for damages caused by (allegedly) toxic water (presence of trialometani) and for breach of contract, being water not available when the episode took place (December 2010/January 2011)	Admitted (2 May 2013)	A hearing has been held on 21 September 2015, but no further information is available.
43.	Altroconsumo + a single citizen	FCA	Turin	Compensation for unfair commercial practice (selling of cars branded Panda without the features set out in the purchase agreement as per pollution—much higher costs for fuel)	Not admitted on 1st instance Admitted on appeal (17 December 2015)	The Court of Turin declared the class action inadmissible. Said order of inadmissibility was challenged before the Court of Appeal of Turin, which declared the action admissible. Consumers have been granted time up to 15 April 2016 to decide to opt in. According to Altroconsumo, around 21,000 consumers have opted in.
44.	Altroconsumo + 2 single citizens	Volkswagen	Venice	Compensation for unfair commercial practice (selling of some model of cars without the features set out in the purchase agreement—much higher costs for fuel) ('golf-gate')	Not admitted on 1st instance (12 January 2016) Admitted on appeal (19 June 2016)	On 12 January 2016 the first decree Court declared the class action inadmissible for lacking of homogeneity of rights and for lacking of proof on the plaintiffs' side (the report filed to Court with the results of some tests on cars did not involve the defendant, nor it was sufficient to demonstrate some illicit conducts of the defendant). Said order of inadmissibility was challenged before the Court of Appeal of Venice, which declared the action admissible in June 2016.

(continued)

Table 3.6: (*Continued*)

Plaintiff/s	Defendant/s	Court	Claim	Decision Date and Outcome	Status of proceedings
					The Court of Venice will have to re-open the case, defining the 'class', granting a term for advertising and one for opting it. The press reported about 5,000 consumers opted-in. Next hearing scheduled for 6 December 2017.
45. Codacons	Volkswagen	Venice	Compensation for breach of contract (selling of cars without the features set out in the purchase agreement as per pollution—much higher costs for fuel)	Admitted	Information only from the press.
46. CAN	Mercedes Benz Daimler, Volkswagen, Volvo/ Renault;		Compensation for damages claimed by truck owners against truck manufacturers for unfair competition (some truck manufacturers were recently sanctioned by the European Commission for having set the prices and slowed down the implementation of new technologies)	Admitted	Information only from the press.

47.	Altroconsumo	Samsung	Milan	Refund of a percentage of the price of some smartphones/tablets for having their batteries much less endurance than what was declared by Samsung (around 40%). Said claim is grounded on a decision of the Italian Antitrust Agency to sanction Samsung after having ascertained said discrepancy in the endurance of the batteries	Admitted	The Court of Milan has declared the class action admissible on 10 November 2016. Said Order was challenged by Samsung. On 6 June 2017, the Court of Appeal of Milan confirmed said order, rebutting the request of Samsung to reform the admissibility order. It seems the amount claimed is of maximum €304,000 for each consumer (or even less, taking into account that the smartphones/tablets involved are old models). Consumers have time up to 28 November 2017 to opt-in. Next hearing scheduled for 18 January 2018.
48.	Codacons	Municipality of Milan	Milan	Breach of contract for lacking surveillance in the Cemetery of Milan (action filed by the owner of graves).	Admitted	With an Order of 12 April 2017, the Court of Milan has declared the action admissible, granting a term up to 30 October 2017 to consumers to opt-in.
49.	Altroconsumo + 2 single citizens	Volkswagen, Audi, Skoda, Seat	Venice	Compensation for unfair commercial practice (selling of cars without the features set out in the purchase agreement as per pollution—much higher costs for fuel) ('diesel-gate')	Admitted (25 May 2017)	With an order of 25 May 2017, the Court of Venice has declared the action admissible, because there is homogeneity of rights when the 'damaging event' is common to all damaged parties, even if the damages suffered may differ from one another (using the damages suffered as the criterion for deciding on the existence of homogeneity of rights will lead to the impossibility of having a class). According to the press, the number opting-in was over 90,000, with a value over €350 million, it is likely the biggest class action in Europe. Next hearing scheduled for 12 December 2017.

Analysis of Decisions on Inadmissibility

Tribunals and/or Courts of Appeal have declared class actions inadmissible on several grounds:

— the plaintiff, a consumer association, was not able to sue because it had not been provided with a proper power of attorney (*Federconsumatori Campania vs INA Assitalia*, Tribunal of Rome);

— the plaintiff was not a class 'representative' because he had not suffered the same (alleged) damages as the others class members (*Codacons vs Intesa San Paolo*, Court of Appeal of Turin);

— because the situation which the plaintiffs were complaining about did not reach the threshold established by law to be qualified as a 'damage'; rather, the Tribunal concluded that the condition of the class members consisted simply of a discomfort, not amounting to damage (*Group of commuters travelling by train between Rome and Cassino vs Trenitalia SpA*, Tribunal of Rome);

— the plaintiff failed to prove the damage claimed (*Adoc vs Gruppo Torinese Trasporti SpA*, Tribunal of Turin);

— the plaintiff wrongly identified its claim, having asked the Court to order the defendant to fulfil an obligation (in the case at issue, the respect of the timetable in providing railway transport services); pursuant to Article 140bis of the Consumers' Code a class action can be filed solely to obtain a compensation for damages (*Group of commuters travelling by train between Rome and Cassino vs Trenitalia SpA*, Tribunal of Rome);

— the alleged damages took places before the Class Action law was enacted (and the same is not retroactive (*Codacons vs Unicredit*, Tribunal of Rome);

— the defendant was not a 'professional' pursuant to Consumer Law but a public body (*Altroconsumo vs RAI Radiotelevisione*, Tribunal of Rome),

and, mostly because

— there was no identification of rights and/or situation amongst the consumers (*Group of commuters travelling by train between Rome and Cassino vs Trenitalia SpA*, Tribunal of Rome; *Codacons vs British American Tobacco Italia Spa*, Court of Appeal of Rome).[147]

The first class actions cases dealt mostly with breach of contracts. In particular, attention was focused on banks for having applied unlawful contractual conditions to their clients' bank accounts (for instance, *Codacons vs Unicredit*, *Adoc vs Banca Popolare di Novara*, *Codacons vs Intesa San Paolo*). Almost all of these class actions were declared inadmissible due to lack of formal requisites. This could have been due to the fact that the consumer associations which promoted the same actions had no experience with this procedural tool and did not invest sufficient resources to prepare their defences.

Case Study: *Altroconsumo vs Intesa San Paolo*

In 2014, a consumer association, *Altroconsumo*, succeeded in a class action against the biggest Italian bank, *Intesa San Paolo*, obtaining an order of compensation for damages caused by the

---

[147] In 2012, the 'identical rights'-prerequisite was substituted by a 'homogeneous rights'-prerequisite.

introduction of new and more expensive commissions in place of the so-called maximum uncovered. *Altroconsumo* obtained a favourable decision. Nevertheless, the Tribunal ordered to compensate damages in favour of only three out of 104 consumers who had opted in, due to the lack of formal requirement for most of the consumers. Moreover, damages compensated to those three consumers amounted to €200.

Case Study: Volkswagen

Two class actions have been initiated by *Altroconsumo* against Volkswagen because of the 'diesel-gate' affair, the first as a kind of general test involving a model of Golf car, and the second involving numerous models manufactured by Volkswagen, Audi, Skoda and Seat.

Initially, both class actions were declared inadmissible. The relevant orders of inadmissibility, however, were appealed and later reverted. These class actions are still pending in the merit, but the aggregate opt-ins, pursuant to the press, are above 95,000 and the value of the cases is reported as about €400 million.

Case Study: *Codacons vs Policlinico Gemelli di Roma*

Another significant class action case was initiated in 2012. The action was brought by a consumer association, *Codacons*, against a hospital, *Policlinico Gemelli di Roma*. The claim regarded the alleged damage caused by the hospital to some hospitalised children who contracted tuberculosis during their stay in the hospital. Their infection was caused by a nurse, who was affected by the disease and continued working. The Tribunal of Rome certified the class action. The class action was filed by a consumer association in the name and on behalf of a single citizen, Mrs Marta Rossi (as mother of the patient, Filippo De Giuli), but more than 188 families were involved.

From the information available, it seems that the Tribunal of Rome rejected the claim on the merits, but the decision was then appealed. In any event, this class action could be influenced by parallel criminal proceedings filed against the hospital, which has recently led to the ascertainment of a criminal liability for violation of safety rules. On this basis, it could become easier for patients to prove the claimed damages (not only the relevant infection, but also, for those who were not affected by the disease, the exposure to the risk and the psychological impact this could have had on them).

Case Study: Class actions in public services

Some class actions have been filed to obtain compensation for damages caused by delays/inefficiencies in providing a public service. The most significant cases involve the following claims:

— Compensation for damages caused by a company managing bus transportation services, due to continuous and several delays, and the extremely inferior quality of the vehicles used (*Adoc vs Gruppo Torinese Trasporti*—case decided in January 2012). This class action, which was declared admissible by the Court of Appeal of Turin (reforming the inadmissibility order issued by the Tribunal of Turin), was rejected on the merits as it was manifestly ungrounded. The plaintiff failed to prove the damage or losses allegedly suffered.

— Compensation for damages caused by breach of the duty to offer impartial information as provided for by the agreement related to the Broadcast Public Service (*Altroconsumo vs RAI TV*, the national broadcast company—case decided in January 2014). From what the consumer association *Altroconsumo* advertised on its website (no official document is available), almost 55,000 consumers filed their claims, requesting a refund of €500 each. However, both the Tribunal and the Court of Appeal of Rome declared the class action inadmissible as the class members lacked the legal capacity to sue the defendant.

— Compensation for damages caused by continuous delays in train transports services along the route between Rome and Cassino (*Group of Commuters vs Trenitalia*, the national railway company—decided in November 2012). The class action was filed by a 'committee' representing the commuters (their exact number is not available). It was declared inadmissible by both the Tribunal and the Court of Appeal of Rome for several reasons, including (i) lacking the condition of 'identity of rights amongst the consumers', as it was not proved that they all paid the same ticket price (according to Courts, the damage had to be the same; in this case, the class members could not be considered in an 'identical' situation, having paid different prices for their tickets); (ii) the quantification of the damage claimed, which did not reach the threshold established by law (on the contrary, having amounted to a mere discomfort); and (iii) Trenitalia's lack of capacity to be sued, since the action should have been filed against the Region Lazio, which was responsible for the public transport service.

— Compensation for damages caused by inadequate services in train transport services run by the local railways Trenord. Initially all class actions started from three consumers associations were declared inadmissible by the Court of Milan but, contrarily to other cases, the relevant orders of inadmissibility were reverted by the Court of Appeal. The merit proceedings were consolidated and rejected in the merit of lack of commonality. Again the Court of appeal reverted the first decree decision and on August 2017 condemned Trenord to pay €100 compensation to about 3,500 commuters, further to almost €130,000 for legal fees in favour of the promoting consumers association. Therefore as an aggregate figures the class action worth is around 500,000 Euro, by now the most relevant merit decision in Italy.

— Compensation for damages for bad management of streets cleaning after snowing (*a single citizen vs Quadrifoglio Servizi Ambientali Area Fiorentina*, appointed by the Municipality of Florence for the cleaning up of the city—decided in November 2011). This class action was filed by a single consumer, who requested the refund of the tax he paid for his city cleaning. It was declared inadmissible by both the Tribunal and the Court of Appeal of Florence, mainly because, at the time being, article 140bis of the Consumers' Code limited the recourse to class action to cases for damages caused by 'products'. The Courts interpreted said notion strictly, excluding that a 'service', such as the city cleaning up, could be qualified as a 'product'.[148]

— Reimbursement of undue payment for inadequate services. Since 2013 Abbanoa, the Sardinia public water supplier company, was target of several class action proceedings, and was winner of some and loser of others (local class action covering single municipalities) until in December 2017 the Tribunal of Cagliari admitted a major class action covering most of the Sardinia. The potential class members are in the order of 750,000 citizens. The case is still pending in the merit.

---

[148] In 2012, the scope of the class action mechanism was extended to the protection of rights of consumers of services.

Class actions are also suitable for requesting compensation for damages for unfair business practices or unfair competition, especially when said practices have been already ascertained by a decision of the Antitrust Authority. In such cases, the existence of damage has already been assessed by the Antitrust Authority decision. However, not a lot of these class actions have been brought (eg, *Altroconsumo vs Intesa San Paolo* and *Adoc vs Banca Popolare di Novara*). Both cases were based on a decision of the Italian Antitrust Authority, which sanctioned the banks for the application of new and more expensive commissions to their clients' bank accounts.

Another case of this sort was filed by *Altroconsumo vs Moby, Snav, Grandi Navi Veloci, Forship* (all transport companies providing boat trips from/to Sardinia) for compensation for damages due to the increase of ticket prices due to a cartel. When the class action was filed in 2012, a decision from the Antitrust Authority had not yet been issued and the Court decided to suspend the proceedings while waiting for such a decision. Only after the decision of the Antitrust Authority was issued, the Court could have made its decision with regard to the admissibility of the class action. From its website *Altroconsumo* advertised that at conclusion of the relevant procedure the Antitrust Authority condemned the companies. However, the decision of the Antitrust Authority was then reformed by the Administrative Court of Lazio Region. Thus, the class action was abandoned in 2016.

Case Study: *Codacons vs Voden Medical Istruments*

The case was filed before the Tribunal of Milan in 2010 by the consumer association, *Codacons*, in the name and on behalf of a single consumer, Mrs Simona Zacchei, against the company *Voden Medical Instruments SpA* in relation to a device for self-diagnosis of A and B influenza, the so-called 'Ego Flu Test'. According to *Codacons*, all consumers who bought 'Ego Flu Test' were entitled to obtain compensation for damages since the test would not be as reliable as promised (purchase driven by misleading advertising). The amount claimed included both the price for the purchase of the 'Ego Flu Test' (€14.50) and any other damages (personal damages or property loss) suffered by each consumer for the 'psychological impact' a wrong result of the test could have had, included the negative effect to the social and familiar relationships of each consumer wrongly convinced to be affected by A or B influenza.

The Tribunal of Milan declared the class action admissible in December 2010 (it has been the first case to be certified in Italy). The order for the admission of the class action was challenged by the defendant before the Court of Appeal of Milan. The latter confirmed the first decision. The case was then sent back to the Tribunal of Milan, which allowed the plaintiffs to publish the action in national newspapers and granted terms to all class members to opt-in. Only one person, Mr De Francesco (a lawyer) opted in.

In March 2012 the Tribunal of Milan issued its decision on the merits of the case. The Tribunal of Milan rejected the claim on the merits, founding that the plaintiff, Ms Zacchei, failed to provide evidence of her status as 'consumer'. As a matter of fact, Ms Zacchei was a lawyer working for *Codacons* and the defendant was able to show that she purchased the relevant product not to use it, but specifically to start the legal action. The Court upheld the thesis of the defendant which highlighted the peculiar succession of facts: the device was bought on the same day when Ms Zacchei granted to her lawyer the power of attorney for the class action, less than one hour later than the purchase, and this time was not even enough, based on Ms Zacchei's address, for the plaintiff to go home and use the product; on the contrary, Ms Zacchei went directly from the chemist where she purchased the product to the lawyer. Ms Zacchei also failed to provide evidence of the damage claimed due to the allegedly misleading advertising of the same product.

This decision is relevant for several reasons.

First, the Tribunal of Milan carried out an in-depth analysis of the documents/evidence filed by *Voden* to demonstrate that Ms Zacchei was not really a consumer. It took very seriously the scrutiny of this prerequisite, not considering it enough for the plaintiff to 'prove' the purchase of the product at issue, but affirming the necessity to demonstrate that the 'Ego Flu Test' had been purchased for actual use and not as an excuse to initiate a class action.

Second, the Tribunal of Milan not only applied the 'loser pays' principle to the losing plaintiff (until then the trend in Courts was to settle legal fees between parties, when the plaintiffs were the losers), condemning Ms Zacchei to refund *Voden* the amount of €16,180 (plus taxes and Lawyers' Pension Fund contribution) as legal fees and €842 of costs,[149] but also condemned the plaintiff to refund the defendant with an additional and significant amount of €17,022 as damaged for malicious litigation (pursuant to Article 96 of the Italian Code of Civil Procedure).

The decision of the Tribunal of Milan was challenged before the Court of Appeal of Milan. On 26 August 2013, the Court of Appeal reformed the first instance decision on the merits, assessing that the assessment of admissibility of a class action does not rely on the single case filed by the plaintiff, but on the (possible) existence of an homogeneous right of a class. In this case, there was a homogenous right of all the people who bought the 'Ego Flu Test' to ask for the ascertainment of its reliability. On the merits, the discrepancies between what was declared in the leaflet and on *Voden*'s website could really mislead the consumers, thus having the right to be refunded for damages (depending on the damages proved).

As per the damages suffered by the plaintiff (who was qualified as a 'consumer' and a 'class member', being irrelevant the personal reasons why she bought the test) she solely proved the purchase of 'Ego Flu Test', thus having the right of being refunded of its price (€14.50). As per the sole other consumer who joined in, his autonomous appeal against the first instance decision was first declared admissible even if he was not technically a 'party' in the proceeding since the opting in could be qualified as a third-party intervention. On the merits, his claim was rejected for lacking the proof of him having purchased the 'Ego Flu Test'.

The Court of Appeal of Milan, reversing the first decision, condemned *Voden* for having promoted its 'Ego Flu Test' through misleading advertising, hiding the material unreliability of the test. However, as per the quantification of the damages, the Court of Appeal considered the consumers were entitled to have only the purchase price (€14.50) returned, since no other damages have been proved. Because of this upholding of the plaintiff's claims, the Court of Appeal removed the condemnation of the latter to the additional fee due for malicious litigation.

The decision was significant from a procedural point of view: it stated the right of a class member who opted in, although not formally a 'party' in the class action proceeding, to appeal the first instance decision, but solely for the section concerning the condemnation to pay the counterparty's legal fees, since that is the sole section of the decision which affects directly its own rights.

The case did not receive great coverage in the media. This was probably due to fact that (i) it was initially rejected on the merits, thus consumer associations had no interest in advertising it; (ii) on appeal, it simply granted the right to have a very small amount reimbursed; and (iii) it dealt with a very limited number of consumers, the one opted in.

---

[149] The opted-in consumer, Mr De Francesco, was declared as jointly liable with Ms Zacchei for those legal fees and costs, but solely for 50% of the overall amount.

Case Study: *Mr Maggi and Unione Nazionale Consumatori vs Wecan Tour*

The case was initiated in 2010 by Mr Maggi and *Unione Nazionale Consumatori*, a consumer association, against *Wecan Tour di Goa Srl*, a company offering tourist services. Mr Maggi bought from Wecan Tour a so-called 'all-inclusive holiday packet' in Zanzibar (Tanzania) for a week, between 23 December 2009 and 31 December 2009, including a return flight and a stay in a four star lodge, the Uraadi Beach Resort. When he landed in Zanzibar, Mr Maggi was forced to spend the first three days of his stay in a lower class lodge, the Samaki Lodge. After that, he was moved to the Uraadi Beach Resort, he discovered the same was still partly under construction and, in any case, did not meet by far the expected requirements, as previously illustrated by Wecan also by brochures and commercials. Mr Maggi claimed compensation for the pecuniary and not pecuniary damage suffered as a consequence of the conduct assumed by Wecan Tour, which only in part fulfilled its obligation under the relevant agreement, providing a service of a dramatically lower level.

On 7 October 2011 the Tribunal of Naples declared the action admissible and defined the class as all consumers who purchased the all-inclusive holiday packet promoted by Wecan Tour, for a week to be spent in Zanzibar between 23 December 2009 and February 2010 at Uraadi Beach Resort and who were transferred, while in Zanzibar, for some days to the lower class lodge, Samaki Lodge. Almost 40 consumers opted in. Amongst them there were consumers who spent: (i) the entire week of vacation at the Uraadi Beach Resort; (ii) part of that week of vacation, instead at Uraadi Beach Resort, at the Samaki Lodge; and (iii) part of that week of vacation, instead at Uraadi Beach Resort, at a lodge belonging to a lower category.

The Tribunal of Naples issued its final decision in February 2013. The decision was not appealed. The whole proceedings, in first instance, took about three years, which is quite a long time for a sole decree, taking into account that (i) the order of admissibility was not challenged, thus no incidental phase before the Court of Appeal took place, and (ii) no evidentiary phase was carried out. However, the length of a proceedings in Italy may be influenced by the workload of each Court (the Tribunal of Naples, where this class action has been filed, is above the national average as per the length of its proceedings).

The Tribunal of Naples admitted the claims raised by the plaintiffs and by the intervened consumers belonging to groups indicated under point (i) and (ii) above. On the contrary, it rejected the claims raised by the consumers belonging to the group indicated under point (iii) above for lack of identity with the class as defined above and for lacking evidence.

The Tribunal of Naples evaluated the claims raised by the intervened consumers under the criterion of 'identity'. According to the Tribunal of Naples, such a criterion is satisfied whenever the rights claimed are identical from any point of view, in relation to both their ground and their extension, being different only because they belong to a different subject. Significantly the Tribunal of Naples referred to the just approved reform of article 140bis of the Consumers' Code (from 'identical rights' to 'homogeneous' rights) to affirm that: (a) because the reformed text of Article 140bis of the Consumers' Code was applicable only to proceedings initiated since 25 March 2012, in the case at issue the notion of 'identity' still had to be applied; (b) the criterion of 'homogeneity' was no doubt broader than the one of 'identity'; (c) conversely the criterion of 'identity' should be strictly construed and applied (on the idea that the advantage of a sole proceedings lies in the perfect coincidence of the situations and damages suffered by the consumers). Otherwise, said the Court, there would be no reason why the law modification at issue was introduced. In the case at issue, the recent law reform was taken into account by the Tribunal of Naples to ground its interpretation of the criterion of 'identity' and to interpret it 'strictly', thus going in the opposite direction of what the legislator wished to obtain with said law reform.

Nonetheless, from a practical perspective, the Tribunal of Naples seemingly departed from its reasoning. The Tribunal of Naples considered as 'identical' the positions of consumers belonging to groups indicated under points (i) and (ii) above. But those groups were not exactly specular to each other, referring to partly different situations. Some of the consumers fully met the conditions on which basis the Tribunal of Naples defined the class; others only partially did—the former spent the week partly at Samaki Lodge and partly at Uaridi Beach Resort, as the plaintiff did; the latter spent the entire week at Uaridi Beach Resort. These positions appear, in fact, 'homogenous' rather than 'identical'.

This decision is also significant being the first favourable ruling on the merits for consumers in a class action. For this reason, even if did not involve a very high number of consumers, the decision was broadly advertised by the media and by consumer associations. However, the decision had a limited practical effect, as Wecan Tour went bankrupt and its debts remain mainly unpaid.

C. Representative Actions

Consumer associations have the right to bring so-called representative actions: legal actions aimed at obtaining injunctive relief in favour of all consumers (not only their members). These associations are not allowed to claim compensation on behalf of the consumers, but they can ask injunctive relief for the cessation of an unlawful behaviour by the defendant and the removal of the effects of such behaviour. The purpose is to provide consumers or, in general, classes of people with the same rights/interests with an efficient protective tool, especially for cases where the legal costs of the lawsuit exceed the compensation each individual would be entitled to receive.

The representative action is governed by article 140 of the Consumers' Code.[150] The action can be anticipated by an ADR procedure to be initiated before the Chamber of Commerce in the same district of the Court having jurisdiction for the proceedings or before any other ADR agency recognised by the Ministry of Economic Development. In case an agreement is reached, it becomes binding for the defendant.

In accordance with article 140 of the Consumers' Code, a consumer association is entitled to request the court of the place where at least one consumer has its residence to issue an injunction order against the defendant or to impose on the defendant the adoption of measures to avoid/reduce the damages caused or to be caused to the plaintiffs by its behaviour. Only consumer associations are allowed to initiate the action. To identify consumers by name is not required, as the consumer associations act in the name and on behalf of all consumers. As a matter of fact, the injunction order requested will be issued in favour of all consumers affected by the damaging conduct of the defendant.

Only injunctive actions are possible. The consumer association acting in the name and on behalf of the consumers can request both the ceasing of a wrongful conduct for avoiding future damages, or the adoption of measures/conducts to correct, reduce or eliminate any past/present damage. In fact, the issuing of any order of this kind implies the ascertainment of an unfair/illegitimate conduct on the defendant's side.

---

[150] Decree no 206 of 6 September 2005 which came into force on 23 October 2005.

Case Study: Associazione Movimento Consumatori against several banks

A consumer association, Associazione Movimento Consumatori, filed several claims against several banks before several courts seeking the cessation of their alleged unlawful behaviour and the removal of the relevant effects. The Courts of Milan, Roma and Biella ordered the defendant banks to cease the calculation of compounding.

Before the Court of Cuneo the defendant Cassa di Risparmio di Fossano (and others) argued that a request for 'removal of effect' is equal to a request of restitution of interest that was unlawfully cashed and therefore was out of the scope of a representative action as set forth by article 140 of the Consumers' Code and should have been brought in the form of a class action pursuant to article 140 bis of Consumer Code (which requires different formal requirements).

The Court stated preliminarily that the final outcome could be only an injunction order to stop the unlawful calculation of interest and to allow '*restitution only on a going forward basis*' (ie for any further unlawful conduct of compounding interest in violation of the injunction order), but not an order of reimbursement (*Associazione Movimento Consumatori vs Cassa di Risparmio di Fossano and other banks*, decision issued on 11 March 2016).

At the end of most of the proceedings, the Court ordered the banks to restrain calculating compounding interest (*Associazione Movimento Consumatori vs Intesa San Paolom* decision issued on 5 August 2015), but the case law is not consolidated, because other Courts (Cuneo, Bologna, Turin) took a different position.

IX. Lithuania[151]

A. Representative Action Aiming to Protect the Public Interest

These actions can be brought by public authorities and certified organisations (such as associations and other non-profit public entities). The cause of action has to correspond with the statutory aim. These actions can only be used for injunctive or declaratory relief. Compensatory relief as a remedy is not available. The members of the public whose interests are being protected by the action are not parties of the proceedings.

Examples

Article 30 of the Law of Consumer Rights Protection. The State Consumer Rights Protection Authority has the right to protect consumers' public interest. Consumer associations have the same right, but they must satisfy the following criteria:

— being registered in the Register of Legal Entities of Lithuania;
— their statutory aim should be the representation and the protection of consumer rights and legitimate interests;
— they should have not less than 20 members
— they should be independent from business and should have no interests not related with consumer right protection.

---

[151] The author of this section is Renata Juzikienė.

These associations can seek the recognition or the change of a legal relationship, the prohibition (or the termination) of certain actions (or omissions) of a seller or service provider whereby legitimate common interests of consumers are being infringed and which are unfair or are not in compliance with the fair business practice or are in conflict with the provisions of the Lithuanian Civil Code, the Law on Consumer Protection of Lithuania or other legal acts.

Article 7, paragraph 2 of the Law on Environment Protection. This provision stipulates the right to apply to court to protect the public interest by seeking to review the procedural and substantive legality of decisions, acts or failures to act regarding the environment and the protection or exploitation of natural resources. Associations and public legal entities, which are established in accordance with the laws to promote environmental protection, have standing. Standing is also given to natural or legal persons affected, or likely to be affected, by the decision, act or failure to act regarding the environment and the protection or exploitation of natural resources.

Article 18, paragraph 1, subparagraph 6 of the Law on Competition. The Competition Council can bring an action before the court for the protection of the public interest. Organisations representing the interests of traders or consumers are entitled to bring a claim before the court on behalf of traders or consumers, whose legitimate interests are violated by the actions of unfair competition (article 16 of the Law on Competition). Available remedies are: (1) the termination of the illegal actions; (2) making a public statement in which the incorrect information is refuted or providing explanations as to the identity of the trader or its goods; (3) the seizure or the destruction of the goods, their packaging or other means directly related to unfair competition, unless the infringements can be eliminated otherwise.

Article 28, paragraph 2 of the Law on Advertising. Organisations representing the interests of advertising operators or consumers and self-regulatory advertising authorities have the right to bring an action before the court, when rights and interests protected by this law are violated. They can claim the termination of the use of the advertising or can claim the publication of a statements in which the misleading advertising is refuted.

Article 71, paragraph 1, subparagraph 13 of the Law on Markets in Financial Instruments. The Central Bank of Lithuania can bring an action before court for the protection of the public interests and representing investors' interests.

B. Group Actions

The provisions on group actions are laid down in Chapter XXIV[1] of the Civil Procedure Code (CPC).[152] The group action is described as a claim grounded on identical or similar factual circumstances and aimed at protecting identical or similar substantive rights or interests of natural persons or legal entities that form a group.[153] The Law was passed on 13 March 2014 and came into force on 1 January 2015. The group action is of a universal nature and not limited to specific sectors. Injunctive, compensatory and declaratory relief are possible. The group action is an opt-in model. There has to be at least 20 class members. Class members should be represented adequately. The class representative can be a natural person (one of the class members) or a legal person (an association or trade union). In the latter case the class action must relate to the aim and field of activity of the association

---

[152] The provisions on group action were enacted by Law No XII-77-1 Amending Code of Civil Procedure, art 49 and Supplementing the Code with Art 261[1] and Ch XXIV[1]. They entered into force on 1 January 2015.

[153] CPC, art 441[1].

or the trade union. Moreover, at least 10 class members must be members of the association or trade union. The regional courts (as courts of higher instance) have exclusive jurisdiction. The law requires mandatory participation of an attorney-at-law throughout the proceedings.

There are two phases. First, there is a mandatory pre-trial procedure. The class representative must notify the defendant of the intention of bringing a group action. The representative must send a written notice by registered mail to the defendant. The notice must specify the class members and their claims and mention that if these claims are not granted a group action will be initiated. A period of at least 30 days should be given to the defendant. If the defendant does not respond, it shall be deemed that he failed to fulfil the claims of the class members.[154]

Second, there is a certification phase. The following class prerequisites apply:[155]

— numerosity (there should be at least 20 legal or natural persons);
— adequacy of representation; the court will assess honesty, competence, experience, procedural behaviour, conflict of interests and financial capacity of the proposed representative;
— effectiveness of the procedure; the court will assess whether a group action is a more expedient, effective and suitable means for resolving the dispute than an individual action;
— the commonality of the claims (whether the claims are based on identical or similar factual circumstances or identical or similar substantive rights or interest).

If the court certifies the class action, it shall set a term for class members to opt-in. A public notice will be made on a special internet website.

There are no special rules regarding the merits of the case. When there are individual pecuniary claims of each member, there will be a collective phase during which the common issues will be resolved by the preliminary ruling. This preliminary ruling will have a *res judicata* effect for all class members. Next, there will be an individual phase during which the individual issues of the class members will be resolved (eg amount of damages). An 'individual' ruling can be enforced individually by a class member against the defendant. In cases of injunctive or declaratory actions the court shall deliver a 'common' ruling, which is common to all class members.

There are no special provisions regarding the funding of a group action. It is assumed that the procedure will be financed in the same way as an individual procedure. There is no explicit prohibition on third party funding. The general principle of 'loser pays' applies. The class representative can be ordered to pay the litigation costs. Class members are liable for reimbursement of these costs.

The court fee for a group action has to be paid by the class representative. The single court fee of €500 shall be paid for non-pecuniary claim of the group action (equally divided to all class members), the amount of the court fee for each pecuniary claim shall be calculated according to the general rules of CPC. The amount of the stamp duty (court fee) due from each member of the class shall be collected from members of the class according to the

---

[154] CPC, Art 441².
[155] CPC, Art 441⁷.

rules on apportionment of litigation expenses, which shall be approved by the representative. These rules shall comprise a detailed apportionment of litigation expenses among the members of the class action (article 441[16] of CPC). When the court awards fees and costs to the defendant, it shall be deemed that these fees and costs will have to be paid by the class members in equal parts, unless the law states otherwise.

To date, five group actions have been filed. Three of them failed at the certification phase, two others are pending at the certification phase. All judgments dismissing group actions were appealed and the appeals were dismissed. Both of the pending cases are related with claims against insolvent commercial banks.

Case involving shareholders of an insolvent bank

A group of shareholders of an insolvent commercial bank, represented by an investors association, lodged a claim for damages from an auditor for a false and misleading report about the financial status of the bank. The claimants alleged that this report made an essential impact on their decision to make investments and to buy shares of the bank. The shares were bought in 2011 and the bank became insolvent in 2013. The court refused to hear the case as a group action because the prerequisites were not met. The court stated that there was no commonality because the factual circumstances of the class members were not identical or similar. The class members had bought shares at different periods of time, some of them decided to buy shares, and others decided to hold on to already acquired shares. Their investment decisions were made for different reasons, and each investor had different investment experience, education, age. According to the court, it is impossible to make a common decision on the civil liability of the auditor in respect of all class members.

Case involving energy consumers

A group of energy consumers (legal persons and individuals), represented by the district municipality, claimed damages from energy suppliers on the ground of unjust enrichment. The group claimed that part of the payments that the suppliers received was an unjust enrichment because the energy was sold for a higher price than the suppliers were allowed to sell, according to the public tender. The court dismissed the claim at the certification phase on the ground that the prerequisites were not met. The pre-trial procedure was not conducted correctly and the notification sent to the respondent was too abstract and unclear for the respondent to identify the scope of the group and the amount of damages suffered by each claimant. Moreover, the class representative did not have the power to claim compensatory claims on behalf of each class members. Finally, the court stated that there was no commonality because the factual circumstances were not identical or similar as the class members based their claims on different contracts with the defendant.

Case involving investors of an insolvent bank

A group of claimants (more than 1,000 natural persons), represented by an investors association, claimed to declare their contracts on buying bonds of another insolvent commercial bank null and void. They claimed that these contracts were concluded under influence of mistake or misleading, and requested a declaration that money was transferred to the bank as deposits (this legal result has a significant impact on the amount of the associated insurance payment, which differs depending on the status of the underlying money). The court dismissed the action at the certification phase on the ground that the prerequisites were not met. The court stated that there was no commonality because the factual circumstances were not identical or similar. Even though all claimants can be deemed to be non-professional investors, it was impossible to give a common ruling in respect of all class members as each of them bought bonds at different dates, their investment decisions were made for different reasons, each investor had different investment experience, education, age. Since the court would have to evaluate the circumstances in which every contract was concluded, including the preliminary negotiations of each agreements, there was no basis for the group action.

X. The Netherlands

The 2005 Dutch Collective Settlements Act provides for settlement-only class actions.[156] Only when a collective settlement is reached, this procedure can be used. In case no settlement is reached, the procedure does not apply and there is no collective redress. An association or (special purpose) foundation, representing the victims of a mass harm, tries to reach an all-embracing settlement with the wrongdoer. This settlement is then approved by the Amsterdam Court of Appeal, which has exclusive jurisdiction. The court does not approve the settlement *pro forma*. Approval can be denied if the compensation for the class members is not reasonable (in light of the size of the total damages, the simplicity and speed to receive compensation and the possible causes of the damages), if insufficient security has been provided for the payment of the claims of the class members, if the interests of the class members are insufficiently safeguarded, if the association or foundation acting on behalf of the class members is not representative enough, if the size of the class is too small to justify a (collective) homologation etc.

The association and the defendant jointly file a petition with the court to have the settlement approved. Only foundations or associations with full legal competence can conclude a collective settlement. In addition to the existing, and well-established, consumer and shareholder associations, Dutch law also allows for the creation of special purpose foundations. The settlement has to contain some specific provisions (eg a description of the class, the possible identification of the class members, the compensation the class members will receive, the conditions the class members have to meet to receive compensation, how the

---

[156] The procedure is described in Dutch Civil Code, arts 7:900–:910 and Dutch Judicial Code, arts 1013–1018. See WDH Asser, 'New Trends in Standing and Res Iudicata in Collective Suits (the Netherlands)' in AW Jongbloed (ed), *The XIIIth World Congress of Procedural Law: The Belgian and Dutch Reports* (Cambridge, Intersentia, 2008) 17; J Fleming and JJ Kuster, 'The Netherlands' in PG Karlsgodt (ed), *World Class Actions: A Guide to Group and Representative Actions around the Globe* (Oxford, Oxford University Press, 2012), 286; I Tzankova and D Lunsingh Scheurleer, 'The Netherlands' (2009) 622 *Annals of the American Academy of Political and Social Science* 149 and MJ van der Heijden, 'Class Actions' in JHM van Erp and PW Van Vliet (eds), *Netherlands Reports to the Eighteenth International Congress of Comparative Law* (Cambridge, Intersentia, 2010) 197.

compensation will be structured and divided and the name of the person to whom the opt-out notice should be addressed). If the settlement does not meet all of these requirements, the court can give the parties the opportunity to amend or supplement the settlement. All known class members are individually notified of the petition, unless the court orders otherwise. The court can also order notice via other means (eg newspapers and the internet). Other (individual) procedures are suspended during the homologation procedure. The court can appoint independent experts to report on the fairness of the compensation to be awarded. The court organises a hearing where all parties are given the opportunity to make oral submissions.

The court decision approving the collective settlement is (individually) notified to all known class members. Three months after the date of the court decision (when an appeal with the Supreme Court of the Netherlands is not possible anymore), the court decision and the collective settlement are published in one or more national newspapers. Class members who disapprove of the settlement can opt out by sending a written notice to the person mentioned in the collective settlement. If not, they are bound by the court decision approving the settlement.

In 2013, the Dutch Collective Settlements Act was amended.[157] The two most significant revisions are the applicability of the act in bankruptcy cases, and the introduction of a pre-trial hearing. The association or foundation and the alleged wrongdoer(s), can, jointly or at the request of either party, make an appeal to the judge to convene a pre-trial hearing to explore whether a settlement is possible. Parties must appear; if not, they can be ordered to pay the costs of the appearing party. During the hearing, the parties and the judge can discuss a possible settlement track.

The amending act also includes some technical adjustments: instead of ordering the parties to amend the settlement, the judge can do this on his own initiative, with consent of the parties; the rule on the tolling of statutes of limitations for individual class members is revised; the judge can allow the parties to ask class members opting out to provide additional information (the refusal to do so does not affect the validity of the opt-out) and the judge can order the appearance of the parties in any stage of the proceedings to discuss its orderly course and/or to give directions or orders.

In 2012, the Dutch legislator adopted an act amending the Code of Civil Procedure that can facilitate a collective settlement.[158] The Act on Prejudicial Questions to the Supreme Court allows courts[159] to submit a direct request to the Dutch Supreme Court for an interlocutory ('prejudicial') decision on questions of law, if the answer to the question is of central importance to the case. The Act explicitly refers to the situation of a multitude of claims based on the same or similar issues of fact or law. Although the act has a broader application than class settlements, it is expected to enhance the settlement system, as it will enable parties to obtain swift clarification on questions of law.

To date, nine cases have been treated under the Dutch Collective Settlements Act.[160]

---

[157] Collective Settlements Act Amendment of 26 June 2013, *Staatsblad* 2013, 255. The act entered into force on 1 July 2013.

[158] Act on Prejudicial Questions to the Supreme Court of 9 February 2012, *Staatsblad* 2012, 65.

[159] The Amsterdam Court of Appeal ruling on a request to approve a collective settlement, cannot ask a prejudicial question to the Supreme Court.

[160] All decisions are available in Dutch at http://zoeken. rechtspraak.nl/default.aspx.

Table 3.7: Dutch Collective Settlements Act Cases

Case	Year	Type
DES	2006	product liability
Dexia	2007	financial product
Vie d'Or	2009	financial product
Shell	2009	securities
Vedior	2009	securities
Converium	2012	securities
DSB Bank	2014	financial product
DES II	2014	product liability
Ageas (Fortis)	2016 (still pending)	securities

In 2016, Tillema published the following detailed overview of seven collective settlements that were approved by the Amsterdam Court of Appeal.[161]

Table 3.8: Breakdown of Dutch Collective Settlements Act Cases

Case	Year	Nature	Number of class members	Funding	Settlement	Fee for association
DES	2006 2014	Product liability	N/A (17,000 registered)	Subsidies & donations	€38 million	N/A
Dexia	2007	Financial product	300,000 (25,000 opt-outs)	€45 Contribution per class member	€1 billion	N/A paid by Dexia
Vie d'Or	2009	Financial product	11,000	Funding by regulator	€45 million	€8.5 million (maximum) paid by regulator
Shell	2009	Securities	500,000	Funding by Shell	$448 million	$12 million (association) $47 million (US lawyers)
Vedior	2009	Securities	2,000	Contributions	€4 million	€ 212.000 (maximum)
Converium	2012	Securities	12,000	Funding by defendants	$58 million	€ 1.6 million $ 11.6 million (US lawyers)
DSB Bank	2014	Financial product	345,000 (300 opt-outs)	Funding by DSB Bank	€500 million (maximum)	N/A paid by DSB Bank

---

[161] I Tillema, 'Tien jaar WCAM: een overzicht' (2016) 3 & 4 *MvO* 90, at 91–92.

The Dutch Collective Settlements Act was created in order to manage the notorious *DES* case, a pharmaceutical product liability case. At the time of its passage, the Act was envisaged as being used solely for mass exposure and mass disaster personal injury claims. However, from 2009 on, most cases have been security law cases. This is explained by the fact that the Dutch Collective Settlements Act partially became the default international extra-US procedure to settle mass security law cases. After the US Supreme Court's decision in *Morrison v National Australia Bank, Ltd* invalidated class actions brought in the US on behalf of foreign class members,[162] US lawyers had to look for new jurisdictions for their non-US class members. Ultimately, they found and used the Dutch Collective Settlements Act. The Amsterdam court met them with open arms. In its November 2010 decision in the *Converium* case, the court ruled that it had international jurisdiction to approve the settlement for non-US class members, even though the class mainly consisted of non-Dutch class members.[163] In its final decision of January 2012, the court declared the settlement binding on all class members. The court had no problem with the contingency fee arrangement for the American lawyers, which involved up to 20% of the amount of the settlement. Amsterdam clearly has become the settlement hub for claims involving non-US class members in mass securities cases.[164]

XI. Poland[165]

A. Polish Class Actions Act

The Polish Class Actions Act came into force on 19 July 2010.[166] The Act introduced an opt-in procedure that can be brought by a class member or by a regional consumer ombudsman (public body), in the name of at least 10 people with claims of the same kind.[167] The claims must have the same or similar factual basis (such as the presence of the same or similar unfair clauses in consumer contracts, the same tortious conduct, use of a certain product manufactured or imported by the defendant, or the same unfair commercial

---

[162] 130 S Ct 2869 (US 2010) (holding that Securities Exchange Act of 1934, s 10(b) does not provide a private cause of action in cases where foreign plaintiffs sue foreign defendants for misconduct in connection with securities traded on foreign exchanges).

[163] Court of Appeal Amsterdam 12 November 2010, JOR 2011, 46. The Amsterdam Court of Appeals claimed jurisdiction based on arts 2.2, 6.1, and 5.1 of the (old) Brussels I Regulation.

[164] T Arons and WH Van Boom, 'Beyond Tulips and Cheese: Exporting Mass Securities Claim Settlements from the Netherlands' (2010) 21 *European Business Law Review* 857; B Krans, 'The Dutch Class Action (Financial Settlement) Act in an International Context: The *Shell* Case and the *Converium* Case' (2012) 31 *Civil Justice Quarterly* 141–50 and H van Lith, *The Dutch Collective Settlements Act and Private International Law* (Antwerp, Maklu, 2011).

[165] The author of this section is Magdalena Tulibacka.

[166] Dziennik Ustaw (Journal of Laws), Act on Class Actions of 17 December 2009 (*Ustawa o dochodzeniu roszczeń w postępowaniu grupowym*), no 7; item 44, 1, published 2010.

[167] For instance: monetary claims, although there may be two or more types of claims included in the case, for instance a monetary claim and a request to stop certain conduct, as long as these are of the same kind among all class members—this point was confirmed in the certification decision of 26 April 2016 of District Court of Warsaw, XXV C 915/14).

practice by a trader).[168] Unless the representative is a practising lawyer, legal representation is mandatory.[169] The higher judicial tier—district courts—have jurisdiction. A panel of three judges is required.

The class action mechanism has been in operation for over seven years. It introduced into the Polish civil procedure a set of rules, procedures and practices that were unknown or even rejected before: most importantly the very concept of mass litigation, as well as contingency fees for lawyers. It was eagerly awaited, and was also widely expected to facilitate access to justice. The number of cases brought during the seven years of its operation (227) demonstrates how popular the mechanism has become. In fact, several cases were brought within the first few days of its coming into force. The high hopes very soon turned into disappointment with many aspects of the Act: its narrow scope (only consumer protection, product liability and tort claims), the exclusion of claims for the protection of personal interests (for instance personal injury claims), the requirement of standardisation of monetary claims in groups or sub-groups, and lack of precise regulation of requirements for security for costs. Further, some of the greatest sources of disappointment were the opportunities for the parties to delay proceedings, and the resulting length of class action proceedings that is deemed unacceptable by many litigants and by commentators.

The Act was amended on 7 April 2017.[170] The 2017 amendment changes some of the aspects of the class action system that were causing problems and controversies.[171] These reforms are examined throughout this contribution.

B. Scope

Before the 2017 amendment, class actions could only be brought in three areas of law: consumer law, product liability law and tort liability. Further, claims for the protection of personal interests were entirely excluded from the scope of the Act.[172] Thus, class actions could be brought in the following types of cases:

— consumer law cases, including for instance unfair contractual clauses, unfair commercial practices, consumer credit, package holiday, consumer sales. These included contractual liability and unjustified enrichment claims in C2B relations;

— product liability cases based on the implemented Product Liability Directive, as well as on traditional fault-based tort liability provisions of the Civil Code;

— other tort liability cases: including medical negligence, liability of state bodies for actions or omissions while exercising public authority (also for issuing legislative or

---

[168] Class Actions Act, art 1.1 and 4.2.

[169] The Supreme Court judgment of 13 July 2011 held that mandatory legal representation also applies to consumer ombudsmen (uchwała SN z dnia 13 lipca 2011 r., sygn. akt III CZP 28/11). Interestingly, the Court went against the express statement in the official justification for the Act, mentioned above (published in the Parliamentary Note No 1829 of 26 March 2009), that no legal representation is required when the consumer ombudsmen represent classes.

[170] Dziennik Ustaw, 'The 2017 amendment', item 933, published 12 May 2017. The amendment came into force on 1 June 2017.

[171] The Explanatory Note to the 2017 Amendment, available on the website of the Polish Parliament: http://sejm.gov.pl/Sejm8.nsf/druk.xsp?nr=1185.

[172] Class Actions Act, art 1.2. See below for explanation of the notion 'personal interests'.

administrative decisions), liability for actions or omissions of another person, or for damage caused by an animal, and, as far as they concern tortious acts: liability within the areas of environmental protection law, competition law, intellectual property (IP) law, labour law.

They could not be brought in the following types of cases:

— contractual B2B claims.
— unjustified enrichment B2B claims. The result of this limitation was that a class bringing a contractual liability or an unjustified enrichment claim could only consist of consumers. This was difficult because it is not always possible to determine at the start of the action whether all those involved are consumers.
— claims in the areas of environmental protection, competition, IP and labour law that did not involve tort liability.
— claims concerning protection of personal interests, whether in consumer cases, product liability or tort liability cases. These include personal injury claims.
— Personal interests are listed in the Civil Code: they include health, freedom, dignity and good name, conscience, name, image, correspondence, home and creative output.[173] The list is non-exhaustive. Claims for the protection of personal interests can have a pecuniary nature (such as costs of treatment or lost earnings in cases of personal injury) or a non-pecuniary nature (such as pain and suffering). The exclusion of claims for the protection of personal interests from the scope of the Class Actions Act meant in practice that no personal injury claims could be brought using the procedure.

Case study: Katowice International Trade Hall

In April 2011, the Warsaw District Court refused to certify a class action of victims of the collapse of the Katowice International Trade Hall.[174] In September 2011 the Warsaw Court of Appeal rejected the complaint against this decision, making it final. The District Court interpreted Article 1.2 of the Act as meaning that a class action was admissible only if class members had non-personal claims (in this context: claims not related to personal injury or death). The Court held that, as only five out of 16 class members had such claims, it was not possible for the class to be certified. The decision confirmed the fears of some academic writers who argued that the exclusion of protection of personal interests unduly limited the use of class actions in the very cases that the legislator intended to cover—relatively small value personal injury cases. On the other hand, the Court seems to have been open to the possibility of certifying the class by limiting it to those with non-personal claims instead of rejecting the entire suit. In 2012 the claimants in this case brought cassation proceedings before the Supreme Court. The Court refused to consider the cassation.[175]

---

[173] Civil Code, art 23. E Baginska and M Tulibacka, 'Poland' in I Boone and A aan den Rijn (eds), *International Encyclopaedia of Laws: Tort Law* (Alphen aan den Rijn, Kluwer Law International, 2014) 194–98.

[174] Decision of 8 April 2011, II C 121/11. Not published. The collapse caused deaths and injuries. 16 victims and their families brought the class action in 2010. The judge made it clear that his decision by no means reflects the value of individual claims of each victim/family. His decision only concerned suitability of the class actions procedure for these claims.

[175] The Supreme Court considers cassations from final decisions of ordinary courts. They are brought by parties to litigation or by certain public bodies (for instance the Public Prosecutor), where the allegation is a breach

The 2017 amendment broadened the scope of the Act. The procedure still covers consumer protection claims, product liability claims and tort claims. Contract law B2B claims and unjustified enrichment B2B claims have now also been added.[176] Further, the exclusion of 'personal interests' no longer includes personal injury claims.[177] Thus, personal injury claims (the literal translation from Polish is 'damage to body or injury to health'), as well as claims by family members of persons who died as a result of personal injury, are admissible under the Act. The extension of the scope of the class action procedure was somewhat moderated by the requirement that monetary claims concerning personal injury, including those of family members, must be brought as 'liability-only suits' (declaratory relief suits).[178] The amended Class Actions Act requires that, in declaratory relief cases, these monetary claims should be listed in the claim form, albeit there is no obligation to provide precise amounts.[179]

C. Standardisation Requirement for Monetary Claims

The Class Actions Act includes a very interesting commonality requirement, which appears to be unique among class action models. If monetary claims are sought, a class action is possible only if the amount claimed by each class member is made equal with the others (this may be done in sub-classes of at least two people).[180] Before the 2017 amendment, the Act required that the standardisation be done taking into account all the circumstances of the case. Courts requested that class members justify the standardisation by specifying the exact factual and legal similarities between members of standardised groups or sub-groups.[181] Not many succeeded. In practice, if a case involved class members with different levels of damages caused by the same or similar event, lawyers representing class members advised them to circumvent the requirement by limiting the claim to declaratory relief only. This option is expressly allowed by the Act: in cases involving monetary claims the suit may be limited to a mere declaratory relief, and then followed by individual lawsuits.[182] This can be illustrated with four cases.

---

of substantive law (its interpretation or application) or procedural law (if it had a material impact on the impact of the case) by the court making the decision. The fact that the Supreme Court did not get involved in this issue means that, for the time being at least, the status quo remains as understood by the courts in this case.

[176] The Act, new art 1.2.

[177] The new arts 1.2a and 1.2b.

[178] Art 2b.

[179] The new art 6.1a.

[180] Art 2.1 and 2.2.

[181] Decision of the Court of Appeal of Krakow of 7 December 2011, I ACz 1235/11, unpublished, quoted in the Explanatory Note to the 2017 Amendment, available at http://sejm.gov.pl/Sejm8.nsf/druk.xsp?nr=1185, at 65 and 66.

[182] The Act, art 2.3 and the new art 2.4. The judgement concluding a declaratory relief class action may be used in further individual litigation or ADR proceedings seeking individual redress. After the 2017 amendment, the judgement will need to contain a list of issues that are common to the class and that are the basis for subsequent individual monetary claims by class members.

Case study: Flood defences in Sandomierz

The first case concerns flood victims and was brought against the public authorities whose duty it was to maintain flood defences in the Sandomierz area.[183] Initially the 17 class members' claims amounted to the sum of exceeding nine million PLN. The class was divided into sub-classes: one claiming 100,000 PLN, another 400,000 PLN, another 600,000 PLN, and yet another: one million PLN. However, the issue of certification of the class ended up in the Court of Appeal which demanded that the quantification of damages and specification of sub-classes be more precise. Following this direction from the Court of Appeal (2011) the lawyers and the class representative decided to change the claim to a mere declaratory relief. The barrister leading the case (Mec Agnieszka Trzaska) reported that it was very difficult to quantify the claims as per the Court of Appeal's request. There is no doubt that each victim's losses were different, and grouping them in some larger sub-classes would be extremely challenging. The class was certified in September 2012, and the court set the time limit for opting in to be 6 March 2013. There were around 300 victims (physical and legal persons), and yet not all of them joined the class. In September 2013 the district court of Krakow finalized the class, which consisted of 27 members: physical and legal persons, with claims valued at 17.3 million PLN. Ultimately 26 class members continued with the proceedings. One person died. The class won the case. On 19 October 2017 the District Court of Krakow decided for the claimants, thus confirming liability of the State for their losses.

Case study: ZUS mis-information to small businesses

In the two other cases the law firm representing the class representative decided to limit the claims to declaratory relief straight away. The second case concerned 19 small business owners who claim they suffered losses by being misinformed by ZUS (the Office for Social Insurance). They had been initially informed that when they officially suspended business their obligation to pay social insurance contributions with respect to the business would be suspended too. ZUS changed its interpretation of law after some time and demanded back payments with interest. This class action was not certified, as the court held that class members did not meet the criteria of the same or similar factual basis for their claims.[184] The third case involved victims of flood, this time in another region of Poland (Płock), suing public authorities for neglect in management and supervision of flood defences.

Case study: Consumer Ombudsman and BRE-Bank

In a decision of the district court of Lodz a class action was brought by the Regional Consumer Ombudsman for Warsaw against BRE-Bank (now MBank). The court decided for the class (3 July 2013). It confirmed that the Bank used an unfair clause in mortgage contracts that resulted in the class members overpaying the interest on their mortgages. The justification of the decision

---

[183] Case brought against the State Treasury (and precisely: against the Wojewoda of the Świętokrzyski district, as well as the Regional Director of Water Management in Kraków) and against the local authorities of the Świętokrzyski district responsible for management and maintenance of water infrastructure in the district.

[184] http://www.lex.pl/czytaj/-/artykul/pozew-zbiorowy-przeciw-zus-nie-zostal-rozpatrzony.

provided by the court contains a statement that one of its aims should be facilitating individual actions of class members against the Bank to recover the amounts overpaid, as well as possibly enticing the parties to settle with no need for further litigation.

However, there were still cases where class members do standardise their claims. Usually, these were cases straightforward enough for such standardisation.

Case study: Amber Gold

An example is an illustrious case against an investment company. Amber Gold invested in gold and some other commodities and, promising returns exceeding 10%, had thousands of investors including politicians, celebrities, and many ordinary people. It operated since 2009, and it seems that since mid-2010 the financial supervision authorities had some knowledge of dubious practices taking place within the company. In August 2012 the company announced its liquidation and offered no money back to investors. The decision followed press and television coverage of the suspected failure of the business and financial crimes of its owner. The owner and his wife were arrested and face many years in jail. Prosecutors received over 4000 complaints, and the law firm dealing with the class action was contacted by over 3000 investors within two weeks. By the end of August 2012, the class action (containing 700 people collectively claiming 41 million PLN) was lodged in the Gdańsk District Court. It is estimated that the total loss to all investors exceeds 200 million PLN. The class was divided into more than 100 sub-classes, claiming between a few thousand and a few hundred thousand PLN. It was clear how much people invested and thus their losses were easy to quantify and probably relatively straightforward to standardise with others. The future of this litigation was uncertain for some time because the company has since been declared insolvent. A new suit was brought against the state, alleging that public prosecutors failed to act in a timely manner in reaction to a public enquiry into the company's finances. In March 2016 the Court of Appeal certified this class action. It involves over 170 people with losses exceeding 21 million PLN. Again, their claims were standardised. More class members could still join until 14 December 2016. At the same time, a criminal suit against the couple has also finally commenced, and criminal courts in Poland have the power to order perpetrators of crimes to compensate their victims. Commentators are speculating that the civil suit will be concluded faster, as the prosecutors are planning to examine testimony of 430 witnesses.

The 2017 amendment eliminated the requirement to consider all the circumstances of the case when justifying standardisation of claims, which should make bringing compensation claims under the Act easier.[185]

D. Contingency Fees

The Act allows lawyers representing the class to agree to a success fee, with the upper limit of 20% of the amount recovered for the class.[186] There is not much evidence of such

---

[185] The Act, the new art 2.1 and 6.1.2.
[186] Art 5.

arrangements actually being concluded in practice. There is anecdotal evidence of several agreements having been concluded in class actions led by sole practitioners. Lawyers acting in class actions, however, prefer to use traditional cash remuneration. Many see class actions as too risky to invest in. The procedure has not yet been tested fully and the cost exposure for lawyers, especially in complex cases, is unknown. Further, the possibility of agreeing to a success fee virtually disappears in cases where declaratory relief is sought. There is no 'amount obtained for the class' to set as the basis of the fee. Even in cases where claims have been standardised and it would be possible to conclude a contingency fee agreement, lawyers demand money up-front. In the case against the investment company Amber Gold (analysed above), the law firm demanded an up-front fee the amount of which depends upon the amount claimed by each class member. The law firm demanded between 3.3% and 9.8% of the value of each person's claim as remuneration payable up-front, in addition to collecting 2% of the value of each claim to cover court fees. To summarise, it is extremely rare for class members to be able to join a class action without paying quite a considerable fee to their lawyers. Other potential costs of class litigation, and the 'loser pays' principle, further increase the cost exposure for class members.

E. Other Costs and Funding Issues

The Act does not allow class representatives to obtain legal aid (in Poland legal aid consists of legal assistance nominated by court and a waiver of court fees). It sets the court fee for lodging the case at 2% of the value of the claim, which is lower than in most other types of litigation and yet may be a high amount considering the potentially high numbers of people involved. In cases where a regional consumer ombudsman is a class representative, the court fee is waived.

F. Security for Costs

The Act provides the possibility for defendants to request that the class provide security for costs. Article 8 allows for such requests to be made at the latest during the first procedural step. The decision on whether security ought to be provided is within the court's discretion, and can be appealed. The court also sets the deadline for payment (up to one month). The maximum amount of security is 20% of the value of the case. Article 8 became the focus of criticism by scholars and legal practitioners. Its main weakness was that it did not provide the criteria to be used by courts when deciding whether requiring the class members to pay security for costs was indeed appropriate. Further, if the security was not paid on time, the court was to reject the claim. This was seen as a disproportionately severe penalty. The 2017 amendment addressed these criticisms. First of all, in line with the original rationale behind the provision,[187] Article 8 now requires the defendant to demonstrate that the case

---

[187] The Explanatory Note to the Class Actions Act, Parliamentary Note no 1829, quoted by the Explanatory Note to the 2017 Amendment, at 83.

against him is weak, and that recovering the costs from the class will be very difficult or impossible if the security for costs is not provided. These issues are to be examined by the court when considering the defendant's request. The court is also not to decide on security for costs before the certification decision becomes final (before the amendment there was no clear indication when the decision was to be made). Further, after the amendment, the court cannot reject the suit immediately after the deadline for paying the security for costs expires. The provision now requires that the proceedings be initially suspended for three months, thus giving the class members more time to consider their options and possibly still pay the required amount.

G. Proceedings

The class action procedure starts with a lawsuit brought by a class representative with the assistance of a lawyer. The court notifies the defendant of the lawsuit, waits for the defendant's response, and considers whether all the requirements have been met and thus whether the class action can be certified. It is also during this stage, and more precisely at the time of the first procedural activity (which in most cases would be the response to the suit), that the defendant can ask for security for costs. The case will not progress further before the final decision on the issue of security for costs has been finalised (here either party can appeal the decision to the court of appeal). The decision to certify the class action, which can be appealed, concludes the first stage. The decision contains information about the action, the class representative, arrangements concerning remuneration of lawyers, and the names of class members who joined so far.

After the certification decision becomes final (either because it has not been appealed or the appeal did not succeed), the court coordinates activities aimed at notifying all potential class members of the class action. It can also decide that no further notification is required if all potential claimants joined the class already. The 2017 amendment made the requirements concerning publicity more flexible, allowing the judge to select the means of publication that are best suited to the circumstances of the specific case. The new article 11.3 allows the court to select the means of publication: including the official bulletin of the court, websites of the parties, or the national or local press. Further, the new article 11a requires that the Minister of Justice should publish information about all class actions in which the statement on the commencement has been issued (as well as all completed procedures) in the official information bulletin of the Ministry. Courts are required to send information on proceedings where the statement was issued to the Ministry, and the latter should immediately update the bulletin. No such information has been published yet by the Ministry.

The second stage focuses on these activities within the time period set out by the court for joining the class. After the time limit passes, the court decides on who the class consists of. The defendant can question class membership of specific persons as well as appeal the final decision on the members of the class.

The first two stages are considered to be non-flexible, formalistic and long.

Case study: BRE-Bank

The issues of formality and duration can be illustrated by the timeline in this case:

20 December 2010	Class action lawsuit brought before district court
6 May 2011	District court certifies class
28 September 2011	Appeal court denies the defendant's appeal against certification—certification final
28 December 2011	The district court issues a decision on the text of the public announcement and its placement in *Gazeta Wyborcza* (a daily newspaper)
31 January 2012	Publication of the announcement in *Gazeta Wyborcza*
6 September 2012	Decision of the district court confirming the final membership of the class
29 November 2012	The Court of Appeal denies the defendant's request for security for costs
16 June 2013	The first substantive hearing
3 July 2013	First instance decision in favour of claimants
30 April 2014	The Court of Appeal confirms the first instance decision

Thus, it took 30 months from bringing the case for the first hearing on the substance to take place. The whole procedure from bringing the case to the Court of Appeal decision took 40 months. When compared with the average district court case length of 7.8 months this is striking, even considering that class actions are normally more complex than litigation in individual cases. Another problem with this particular case, similar to many other class actions brought in Poland, is that this was a liability-only claim. Each individual claimant had to subsequently approach the Bank and individually request payment of compensation. In some cases further litigation (this time in individual cases) took place, or is still taking place.

Before the amendment, the court's decision finalising the second stage of the proceedings (the decision finalising the class) could be appealed, and the third, substantive stage could not start before the appeal proceedings were completed with a final decision. The 2017 amendment makes it clear that the appeal on this issue does not suspend the proceedings. The new article 17.2a provides that immediately after issuing the decision the court must set the time for the hearing on the substance of the case or continue with the proceedings in some other appropriate manner.

The 2017 amendment also introduced a number of other reforms aimed at making the first two stages run more efficiently. First of all, the court no longer will need to hold a separate hearing devoted to a certification decision. This decision will now be taken at a non-public session, at which the court will either decide to certify, or refuse to certify and thus reject the class action (article 10.1 and 10.1a). Before this session is held, the court will request that the defendant submit an official response to the claim. Further, once the certification decision is final, the certification issue can no longer be considered again during the proceedings (this is unclear under the current Act) (the new article 10a). The certification decision as well as the decision to refuse certification can be appealed, and subsequently the cassation proceedings can be brought before the Supreme Court. In the amendment, the Supreme Court has been given the power to cancel the decision refusing to certify the class action, and by doing so also to certify the class (the new article 10b).

After the decision is final, the third stage: the proceedings concerning the substance of the case, begins. The proceedings are concluded by a judgment on substance as well as a decision on costs.

The fourth and final stage, after the judgment becomes final, is enforcement. The court judgment, naming all class members and specifying their claims and the amount of damages attributed to them (if any), is the execution title.

H. Statistical Information

The Ministry of Justice provided the statistical information in Table 3.9 concerning numbers of class actions brought before district courts (first instance) in civil cases between 2010 and end of June 2017.[188]

Table 3.9: Number of class actions in Poland before district courts in civil cases between 2010 and end of June 2017

Year	Brought	Processed				Remaining
		Altogether	Including			
			Rejected[189]	Denied[190]	Returned[191]	
2010	21	.	.	.	.	.
2011	37	21	4	–	11	20
2012	35	20	6	1	10	33
2013	22	26	5	6	5	29
2014	41	19	9	2	7	51
2015	32	31	9	2	7	52
2016	30	23	5	2	10	59
2017 (January–30 June)	9	13	2	1	3	55

Further, in the same time period a small number of commercial cases were also brought before district courts (first instance), noted in Table 3.10.

---

[188] https://isws.ms.gov.pl/pl/baza-statystyczna/opracowania-wieloletnie/.

[189] Rejected suits are those that do not meet formal requirements for group claims, and thus they were denied certification.

[190] Denied claims are those where the claimants lost the case.

[191] Suits returned to the claimant because of some formal deficiency.

Table 3.10: Number of class actions in Poland before district courts in commercial cases between 2010 and end of June 2017

Year	Brought	Processed					Remaining
		Altogether	Including				
			rejected	denied	returned		
2010	–	.	.	.	.		.
2011	1	.	.	.	.		.
2012	4	1	1	–	–		4
2013	–	2	1	–	–		2
2014	1	2	2	–	–		1
2015	1	–	–	–	–		1
2016	–	–	–	–	–		2
2017 (January–30 June)	–	–	–	–	–		2

Since 19 July 2010 227 class actions were brought (amounting to the average of around 32 cases per year) in civil cases, and seven in commercial cases. While this may seem like a significant number, one needs to put it in perspective: in 2015 the number of claims brought before civil courts in Poland was around 6.5 million. The most common defendants in class actions are banks, other financial and insurance institutions, the state (specifically, local authorities), some internet-based service providers and residential builders.

Of the 227 civil and seven commercial claims, around 153 and five respectively were completed. 40 civil claims and all five commercial suits were rejected (refused certification because they did not meet the conditions set out by the Act), and 53 civil suits were returned because of various formal inadequacies. Only 38% of the civil claims actually went through the phase of substantive adjudication. A large number of those claims are still in the system. Only around 11 were concluded with final judicial decisions.

XII. Sweden[192]

A. Group Actions

The Swedish legal system has a collective redress mechanism in the form of an opt-in group action.[193] Its scope of application is universal and includes all civil claims that can be dealt

---

[192] The authors of this section are Peder Hammarskiöld and Sigrid Törnsten.
[193] The legal basis for the Swedish group action is the Group Proceedings Act (2002:599) (Sw. *lagen (2002:599) om grupprättegång*), which was enacted on 30 May 2002 and came into on 1 January 2003. The Act can be found in English at http://www.government.se/government-policy/judicial-system/group-proceedings-act/.

with by a general court in accordance with the rules as laid down in the Swedish Code of Judicial Procedure (*Rättegångsbalken*). The following class action prerequisites apply:

— the action is based on circumstances that are common or similar to all class members;
— the group action does not seem inappropriate in light of the differences between the claims of the class members;
— the majority of the claims cannot be equally well pursued in individual proceedings by the class members;
— the class is well defined in terms of size and delimitation and;
— taking into account the plaintiff's interest in the substantive matter, the plaintiff's financial capacity to bring a group action and the circumstances generally, are appropriate to represent the class members.

The group action can be of an injunctive, declaratory or compensatory nature. In environmental disputes, the available remedies are injunction and damages.

A group action can be initiated by any natural or legal person having a civil claim. It can also be initiated by non-profit associations protecting the interests of either consumers or wage-earners in disputes between consumers and traders. In some instances, eg when the public interest is at stake, public authorities, such as the Swedish Consumer Ombudsman, may initiate group actions. Non-profit associations safeguarding nature conservation or environmental protection or associations of professionals in the fishing, agricultural, reindeer or forestry industries have standing to bring an injunctive or compensatory group action under the Swedish Environmental Code. The plaintiff is the class representative and will act on behalf of the class. It is only the plaintiff who is a party to the proceedings.

Once the group action is approved by the court, any class member can opt in by giving personal notice to the court stating that he/she shall be bound by the final ruling. The class members who have opted in do not become parties. However, they may intervene and appeal the judgment, in which case they are considered as parties. The judgment is binding both for and against all class members who have opted in. Those who have not can pursue their claim individually in separate proceedings.

The Group Proceedings Act contains some specific case management rules. For example, the claim form addressed to the court must contain information relevant for the court's consideration of whether a group action is appropriate for the dispute. Another example is that group members can opt-in during the proceedings at a later stage. However, this can only be done without causing any significant delay to the case and without any other substantial inconvenience for the defendant.

The general rules on litigation costs in the Swedish Code of Judicial Procedure apply. However there are some specific rules on the funding and financing of group actions. The general rules provide that the losing party has to pay the costs of the proceedings. In a group action, this means that the class representative, as plaintiff, will have to pay these costs if the group action fails. Class members can only be held liable for litigation costs corresponding to the benefits they obtain from the proceedings, or if they have incurred additional litigation costs. There is also a specific rule making it possible for the plaintiff to enter into a contingent fee agreement with a lawyer if the court considers this to be reasonable with regard to the nature of the claim. In such a contingent fee agreement, the parties agree that the size of the lawyer's remuneration will be reduced if the case is lost or will be increased if the case is won. However, the contingent fee agreement cannot be approved if the size of the fee is solely based on the value of the claim.

B. Case Studies: Group Actions

In October 2008, the Swedish government issued a complete review of the functioning of the Group Proceedings Act. At that time, 12 group actions had been initiated. There are no official statistics on how many cases have been brought to date (probably between 30 and 50). Below are a number of examples.

District Court of Stockholm, T 3515-03, moved to District Court of Nacka, T 1281-07, January 2003, Bo Åberg ./. Elefterios Kefalas

The case involved claims for damages due to crime (fraud). The defendant was the owner of an airline company that later went bankrupt. Several hundred passengers had been left stranded at different airports due to the bankruptcy. 500 of 700 affected passengers opted in. The total claim for compensation was approximately SEK 3 million. The dispute was settled with a payment of SEK 810,000 by the defendant.

District Court of Stockholm, T 6341-03, April 2003, Mattias Larsson et al ./. Falck Security AB

The plaintiff sued a security company and sought compensation for damages because the company was accused of having set up an illegal database covering 658 suspected graffiti vandals. The claim was for SEK 25,000 per person. The intention was to convert the proceedings to a group action but since the defendant refused to disclose the names in the database, this was not possible due to insufficient Swedish rules of discovery. Ultimately, the dispute was litigated as an ordinary individual civil dispute.

District Court of Stockholm, January 2004, T 97-04, Grupptalan mot Skandia ./. Skandia AB

The dispute concerned a claim for compensation to policyholders of a life insurance company due to suffered injury when proceeds of the sale of the subsidiary's assets management business were transferred to the parent company. The plaintiff was an association with approximately 15,000 class members. However, the total claim for the 1.2 million affected policyholders was estimated to be several billion SEK. The group action was withdrawn and the dispute was ultimately settled in an arbitration procedure.

District Court of Stockholm, January 2005, T 17333-04 (and T 10992-04), Linus Broberg and Henrik Skeppland ./. Aftonbladet Nya Medier AB

The dispute concerned compensatory damages for eight participants who could not take part in an online game, because of data transmission problems. The application for group action was dismissed by the Court because the case did not fulfil the requirements to be litigated as a group action. The Court stated that the majority of the claims in the group action could be equally well be pursued in individual proceedings by the group members and also concluded that the plaintiff's financial capacity to bring a group action was not appropriate to represent the group members in the case.

District Court of Gothenburg, July 2005, T 7247-05, Lars and Vuokko Elner ./. Göteborgs Egnahems AB

The dispute concerned the ownership of an electric heating facility located on the plaintiffs' property. The group consisted of 30 property owners. The dispute was settled out of Court and the group action was withdrawn.

District Court of Stockholm, March 2006, T 5254-06, Devitor AB ./. TeliaSonera AB

The dispute concerned claims for a refund from a phone operator. The District Court dismissed the case because the plaintiff failed to define the members of the group action. The plaintiff appealed to the Svea Court of Appeal but the plaintiff did not pursue its appeal since the defendant took corrective action in accordance with the plaintiff's claim.

District Court of Stockholm, June 2006, T 9593-06, Peter Lindberg ./. Municipalities of Storstockholm

The dispute concerned compensatory damages due to poor care in municipal orphanages. The municipalities of Storstockholm had removed 41 children from their homes and placed them into foster care, which, according to the claim, had caused them damages. The Court dismissed the application for group action because the case did not fulfil the requirements to be litigated as a group action since it was needed that all individual claims had to be investigated separately.

Environmental Court of Nacka, August 2006, M 1931-07, Carl de Geer et al ./. Air Navigation Services of Sweden

The dispute concerned a claim for damages due to aviation noise. The group action was initiated by seven group members and consisted of approximately 20,000 persons. The Court confirmed an out of court settlement in which the Air Navigation Services of Sweden was obliged to allocate funds for research to reduce aviation noise.

Svea Court of Appeal, December 2009, T 3552-09, Olivia Rozum ./. Sweden

The dispute concerned damages due to gender discrimination by the university in the admissions process. The plaintiff claimed SEK 100,000 in compensation due to the discrimination. The Court ordered the defendant to pay SEK 35,000 per person in damages to the plaintiff and the other 43 group members due to the gender discrimination. The case was appealed by the defendant and the judgment was affirmed by the Svea Court of Appeal.

District Court of Malmö, March 2010, T 9330-09, Elin Sahlin ./. Sweden

This dispute also concerned damages due to gender discrimination by a university in the admissions process. The dispute was settled out of court and the Court confirmed the settlement in which the plaintiff and 23 group members received SEK 35,000 per person.

District Court of Nacka, June 2011, T 3385-09, Tobias Karlsson ./. Svenska Handelsbanken AB

The dispute concerned damages due to negligence by the defendant, a bank, when a person, who did not have the right to do so, was allowed to withdraw money from a bank account. The dispute was settled out of court and the settlement was confirmed by the Court. The bank was obliged to pay a total amount of SEK 200,000 to the plaintiff and 10 group members.

District Court of Gothenburg, February 2012, T 7211-03, Guy Falk & Lisbeth Frost ./. NCC AB

The dispute concerned a demand for performance of a contractual obligation by the defendant to build a marina. Due to the fact that the defendant had not built the agreed marina, the market value of 33 affected real estate properties in the area had decreased by approximately SEK 500,000 each. The District Court permitted the application for a group action. The defendant appealed the decision to the Court of Appeal for Western Sweden which affirmed it. The dispute was withdrawn from the District Court due to an out of court settlement. The settlement was not confirmed by the Court since the plaintiff and the other group members were settled individually and not as a group. Therefore, no information is available.

District Court of Stockholm, November 2010, T 17420-10 et al, John Helms Gandrup et al ./. Acta Kapitalförvaltning filial till Acta Kapitalforvaltning AS Norge

The dispute concerned the right for compensation to 194 plaintiffs due to the purchase of bonds which lost their value in the financial crisis. The average claim was for SEK 140,000. The plaintiff wanted to apply for a group action but instead the group members applied for an action against the defendant separately which resulted in a large number of individual cases. The dispute was settled out of court and the claims were withdrawn.

The Gota Court of Appeal, June 2013, Ö 3152-12, Intresseföreningen för Spararna i Habo Finans ./. Ola Claesson

The applying association's members had lost money in the bankruptcy of a finance company and claimed compensation from the auditor of the finance company due to the auditor's negligent audit. The total claim for compensation was SEK 63 million with an average claim of SEK 140,000. The application was dismissed since the majority of the claims in the group action could be pursued in individual proceedings.

District Court of Nacka, April 2014, T 1982-14, Reclaimjustice vs Sweden ./. Sweden

The dispute concerned the right for compensation due to a claimed violation of the European Convention on Human Rights by the State. The plaintiff claimed that there was no legal protection against slander and defamation because a webpage, Lexbase.se, had published the identities of convicted criminals who were members of the plaintiff's association. The plaintiff claimed SEK 20,000 in compensation for each member of the association. The Court dismissed the application because a non-profit association is not allowed to have standing in a group action against the State.

Announced group action, Sveriges Aktiesparares Riksförbund ./. Swedbank Robur Fonder AB

The dispute concerns the overcharge of management fees by an asset management company. According to the website of the association that has announced a group action, there are over one million potential group members with a total claim of SEK 7 billion. In September 2016, no group action had been filed.

District Court of Umeå, November 2011, T 5416-04, The Consumer Ombudsman ./. Stävrullen Finance AB

The dispute concerned damages due to the defendants' failure to supply electricity at the agreed price. The Consumer Ombudsman applied for a group action on behalf of nearly 7,000 affected consumers in the District Court of Umeå on 15 December 2004. The case was brought against Stävrullen Finance AB. The contractual breach had caused the consumers additional costs when they had to enter a less favourably agreement with a different company. The alleged damage was between SEK 1,000 to SEK 10,000 per consumer.

The District Court of Umeå permitted the application for a group action. According to the Court a group action was the most suitable option due to the fact that a large number of consumers was affected and that most of them would not be able to pursue their claim individually. The Court further stated that the fact that the damages had to be calculated on an individual basis, and did not rule out the possibility of a group action. The decision was appealed and later affirmed by the Court of Appeal for Northern Norrland.

In an intermediate judgment regarding the liability of the defendant, the District Court of Umeå found that the company was obliged to compensate the consumers for damages due to the company's failure to supply electric power. The intermediate judgment was appealed and it was affirmed by the Court of Appeal for Northern Norrland. The Supreme Court affirmed the latter decision.

The parties settled the case out of court before a final judgment regarding the amount and the calculation of the damages for each consumer. On 13 November 2014, almost 10 years after the case was initiated, the District Court of Umeå confirmed the settlement in which the company was obliged to pay SEK 3,342,542 to the Consumer Ombudsman. The Consumer Ombudsman distributed the amount to the affected consumers. 1,881 of the 7,000 consumers were entitled to compensation in the end.

This is the only case where a public body has initiated a group action.

Before the judicial proceedings, there was an ADR group action between the parties at the National Board for Consumer Disputes regarding the same dispute. The ADR group action resulted in a recommendation which the company did not follow, hence the Consumer Ombudsman's group action.

District Court of Nacka, November 2005, T 1286-07, Torkel Jörgensen ./. Sweden

The dispute concerned the liability for damages. The plaintiff (a natural person) claimed compensation for damages from the State on behalf of a group of people who had privately purchased alcoholic beverages online to be delivered to Sweden from abroad. The alcoholic beverages were confiscated by the Swedish Customs. The plaintiff claimed that the Swedish prohibition against such imports violates EU law.

The group members had created an association to finance the group action. Each group member had paid a member fee to the association in order to pay for the litigation costs. The case was brought on 30 November 2005 before the District Court of Nacka. The Court divided the class into three subgroups: (i) members who had recovered their goods by paying customs but claimed that the goods were deteriorated; (ii) members who refused to recover the goods due to the fact that the consumption date of the goods had expired; and (iii) members who could not recover their goods as they had been destroyed by the customs authorities.

Initially the group consisted of approximately 400 members. A number of group members opted out during the proceedings. In the end, there were 97 class members. The plaintiff claimed that the State should compensate the group members with a total amount of almost SEK 500,000 (each claim was between SEK 800 and SEK 10,000 per person).

The District Court permitted the group action and concluded that the Swedish import prohibition for alcoholic beverages did violate EU law. However, the State was not held liable for damages since its misinterpretation of EU law was not made intentionally and the State had not manifestly and gravely misjudged its margin of discretion. The District Court concluded that it was not possible to grant compensation for damages since the infringement was not sufficiently clear. The plaintiff appealed the District Court's judgment which was affirmed by the Svea Court of Appeal on 30 March 2012. As the losing party, the plaintiff was ordered to pay the defendant's litigation costs which were SEK 150,000 in the District court of Nacka and SEK 30,000 in the Svea Court of Appeal.

4

Criminal Compensation: Stand-alone and Consecutive Piggy-back

I. Belgium

A. *Partie Civile* Technique

In Belgium, victims can formulate their civil claim either before[1] or during[2] criminal proceedings via the so-called '*partie civile*' technique.[3] As a result, they become formal parties to the criminal proceedings.[4] Besides the general conditions to commence an action,[5] the admissibility of the civil claim of the *partie civile* depends on the admissibility of the criminal proceedings and whether or not the civil party alleges to have been prejudiced.[6] One should note that assessing the condition of alleging to have been prejudiced includes the prerequisite of a personal harm. Consequently, the *partie civile* technique cannot be applied to claim redress for a third party's harm, although there are statutory exceptions.[7] For instance, Unia (the former Interfederal Centre for Equal Opportunities)[8] can initiate legal proceedings for the benefit of an affected person within the framework of the Act of 30 July 1981.[9] Almost all statutory exceptions allow associations to promote a collective interest which transcends the individual (level). The correlate, however, is that mainly prohibitory injunctions are possible, instead if compensation on behalf and to the benefit of the actual victims. On some occasions, associations are allowed to claim compensation, albeit not on behalf and to the benefit of the actual victims.

---

[1] Code of Criminal Procedure, art 63.

[2] Code of Criminal Procedure, art 67.

[3] S Voet, 'Public Enforcement and A(O)DR as Mechanisms for Resolving Mass Problems: a Belgian Perspective' in C Hodges and A Stadler (eds), *Resolving Mass Disputes: ADR and Settlement of Mass Claims* (Cheltenham, Edward Elgar, 2013) 280–81.

[4] S Voet, 'Cultural Dimensions of Group Litigation: The Belgian Case' (2012–2013) 41 *Georgia Journal of International and Comparative Law* 446.

[5] Judicial Code, arts 17–18 contain the legal requirements of legal capacity and interest. The legal capacity is '*the authority (the power), the basis of which allows an action to be initiated.*' The interest must be existing, immediate (or preventing the infringement of a right seriously threatened), personal and direct.

[6] M Franchimont, A Jacobs and A Masset, *Manuel de procédure pénale* (Brussels, Larcier, 2012) 174 et seq.

[7] ibid, 184 et seq.

[8] See its website: http://unia.be/en/about-unia.

[9] Act of 30 July 1981 for the punishment of certain actions motivated by racism of xenophobia, art 14, §2.

The major advantage for the civil party is the possibility to 'piggyback' the evidence provided by the Public Prosecutor who has to demonstrate a violation of the law, so that the civil party only needs to prove damages and causation.[10] If all three conditions for civil liability[11] (damages, causation and a fault, ie violation of the law) are met—the victim only has to prove that the first two are met—the criminal judge will grant damages to the civil claimants.

The technique can be used to obtain compensation for harm suffered, regardless of the nature of the criminal case. The aim of a civil party using the *partie civile* technique is obtaining compensation for the harm suffered as a result of the criminal offence. As a result, the criminal court will grant compensation (if the conditions are fulfilled). Yet, even in case of rejecting the civil claim, the finding of law violation provides a certain declaratory effect for cases pending before civil courts. In that regard, civil judges have to suspend civil cases against the same defendant as the concurrent criminal case, until the criminal judge has ruled on the criminal case,[12] which is expressed as follows: '*le criminel tient le civil en état*'.[13] Given the aim of preventing conflicting decisions by the civil judge and the criminal judge and given the principle of *res iudicata* from the criminal judge to the civil judge, the decision by the criminal judge takes priority, which thus leads to the suspension of the civil case when confronted with a concurrent criminal case.

Although, in general, everyone harmed by a criminal offence can make use of the *partie civile* technique, the legislator has prevented a civil party from initiating legal proceedings against certain categories of persons by formulating its civil claim before a criminal judge prior to any criminal proceeding. For instance, a civil party cannot initiate criminal proceedings against minors, ministers or members of parliament.

During the criminal proceedings, no court costs or fees are required for the *partie civile* technique. As a result, the procedure is very accessible. Given the far-reaching possibility for the victim to initiate the criminal proceedings, a counterweight exists precisely when the victim initiates the criminal proceedings before the examining judge (*juge d'instruction*) or by means of a direct summons before the criminal judge. In those two particular cases, consignation is generally due by the victim to ensure (partial) cover of the legal costs if the defendant were not to be sentenced. Whether the civil party initiated the criminal proceedings or merely took part in already ongoing criminal proceedings also plays a role with regard to the 'procedural cost indemnity' (*rechtsplegingsvergoeding*). This is the fixed compensation of the costs and fees of the lawyer of the party in whose favour the case was decided.[14] A civil party who loses the case, will only have to pay the procedural cost indemnity when the civil party herself initiated the criminal proceedings.

Two additional mechanisms can be mentioned briefly: the amicable settlement with the Public Prosecutor and mediation in criminal cases. A defendant has no right to an amicable

---

[10] S Voet, 'Consumer Collective Redress in Belgium: Class Actions to the Rescue?' (2015) 1 *European Business Organization Law Review* 121, 122; Voet (n 4) 433, 447.

[11] Civil Code, art 1382.

[12] Preliminary Title Code of Criminal Procedure, art 4, first para.

[13] Voet (n 3) 270, 281.

[14] Judicial Code, art 1022, first para.

settlement with the Public Prosecutor. Only if certain conditions are met—mainly relating to the nature of the criminal offence—the Public Prosecutor can decide that the defendant will not be (further) prosecuted in exchange for a lump sum.[15] What's most interesting in the context of this report, is the prerequisite of an agreement between the defendant and the victim on both the scope of the loss and the redress settlement.[16] Furthermore, redress must have been offered for the loss suffered (or at the least the non-disputed part) and the defendant must have recognised (in writing) his civil liability.[17] This might prove a useful tool in dealing with mass disputes, since it shifts the redress settlement to out-of-court negotiations while at the same time ensuring redress. A final mechanism is mediation in criminal cases[18] in order to prevent criminal proceedings. The Public Prosecutor can request the defendant to receive a particular training or to follow a treatment, but the Public Prosecutor must always also request redress.

B. Special Masters

Gellingen Case

The case of Gellingen (in French: Ghislenghien) concerned a gas explosion on 30 July 2004.[19] The setting concerned a building site for a new construction factory on behalf of the public limited company Husqvarna Belgium (formerly Diamant Boart), master builder, in the economic activity zone of Ath (Ghislenghien). The building site was crossed by two underground gas pipes containing natural gas under high pressure, which ran next to each other over a distance of approximately 460 metres. The gas pipes were exploited by the public limited company Fluxys (formerly Distrigaz), transporting the gas. The building had to be constructed at a distance from the gas pipes, but the surroundings—particularly the roads and parking places—had to be installed above the pipe lines or close to them. During ground stabilisation works involving the use of a Bomag engine, the rotor of the engine violently hit an obstacle, ie one of the gas pipes. The result of the damaged gas pipe was a gas leak, which in turn led to an explosion. On the day of the explosion, in the early morning, the workers on site noticed a suspicious smell. The fire brigade arrived about an hour and a half later. Eventually, the ground started to tremble. A gas cloud emerged and caught fire. 24 people were killed, many more were injured and harmed.

Criminal proceedings were initiated. No less than 23 (physical and legal) persons appeared as defendant before the chambers (Raadkamer/Chambre du Conseil) of Tournai. Afterwards,

---

[15] Code of Criminal Procedure, art 216*bis*.
[16] Code of Criminal Procedure, art 216*bis*, §2, para 6.
[17] Code of Criminal Procedure, art 216*bis*, §4.
[18] Code of Criminal Procedure, art 216*ter*.
[19] See for a statement of the facts: F Lagasse and M Palumbo, '*Ghislenghien*: catastrophe technologique au carrefour du droit pénal et du droit civil' (2013) 4 *Droit pénal de l'entreprise* 37–40; P Moreau, 'Extraits du jugements du 22 février 2010 du Tribunal correctionnel de Tournai dans l'affaire de la catastrophe de Ghislenghien—note introductive' (2010) 1 *Revue pratique de l'immobilier* 215; D Philippe, 'La responsabilité civile en matière d'énergie—Volume 2: L'affaire de Ghislenghien, l'indemnisation du client final envers le gestionnaire de réseau et la responsabilité civile nucléaire' in X, *Responsabilités. Traité théorique et pratique*, Titre III, Livre 32*bi* (Alphen aan den Rijn, Kluwer, 2015) (1) 8, no 107; J-P Renard, 'Observations. Arrêt Ghislenghien' (2012) 1 *T.Aann* 35.

14 defendants were referred to the magistrates' court (Correctionele Rechtbank/Tribunal correctionnel), including Husqvarna Belgium, Fluxys, the legal person responsible for elaborating the project and supervising the execution, the architect, the security and health coordinators as well as the company contractually responsible for the security and health coordination. The principal charges were unintentional homicide and unintentional assault and battery. By means of the *partie civile* technique about 600 persons became a civil party.

In the first instance, most defendants were acquitted (including Husqvarna Belgium and Fluxys) and a few others got a suspension of the sentence. The Public Prosecutor (as well as some defendants and civil parties) appealed to the Court of Appeal of Mons so that 14 defendants appeared before the Court of Appeal.

On appeal, Husqvarna Belgium and Fluxys were fined, while other defendants were either acquitted or got a suspension of the sentence.[20] When dealing with the civil claims, criminal judges generally appoint doctors as expert witnesses to give an estimate of the injuries. The Court of Appeal of Mons noted the large number of civil parties and the need for medical expert reports. It adopted a liberal interpretation of the rules on court-appointed expert witnesses and established an expert committee.[21] Furthermore, the court appointed two '*experts coordinateurs et conciliateurs*' (coordinating and reconciling experts, so-called special masters[22]) who (a) had to coordinate the expert operations, (b) operated as intermediaries between the court and the experts and (c) had to work towards global settlements.[23] The coordinating experts succeeded in their intentions.[24] The lawyers of Fluxys (the deep-pocket defendant)[25] and those of the victims ultimately reached an agreement. The amounts were kept secret, although Fluxys had set aside 10 million euros to compensate the victims.[26]

The Gellingen case led to a legislative initiative. In the summer of 2017, the Act of 8 June 2017 Regarding the Coordination of Court Appointed Experts was published.[27] The new Article 964 of the Judicial Code stipulates that if the court appoints more than one expert, he can appoint a coordinating expert. His mission is to coordinate the activities of the other experts and to try and reconcile the parties.

---

[20] Mons (15th ch) 28 June 2011, No 2010/H/130, *Ius & actors* (2012) issue 1, 113 et seq and *T.Aann* (2012) issue 1, 12 et seq, also available online: http://corporate.skynet.be/rt002598/Arret28062011.pdf.

[21] D Mougenot, 'Une expertise sur mesure pour Ghislenghien' (noot onder Mons (15th ch) 28 June 2011) (2012) 1 *Ius & Actores* 121–22, nos 2–3; X 'Fluxys condamné et 'préoccupé' (29 June 2011), http://deredactie.be/cm/vrtnieuws.francais/infos/1.1054844.

[22] See: D Rosenberg, 'Of End Games and Openings in Mass Tort Cases: Lessons from a Special Master' (1989) 69 *Boston University Law Review* 695 and WD Brazil, 'Special Masters in Complex Cases: Extending the Judiciary or Reshaping Adjudication?' (1986) 53 *University of Chicago Law Review* 394. Compare in the US: Rule 53 Fed.R.Civ.P.

[23] Mougenot (n 21) 121, 122, no 5.

[24] S Voet, 'Mechanisms for resolving mass problems: a Belgian perspective' at the Rüschlikon (Zürich, Switzerland) Conference 'Building effective markets—the role of an integrated legal system' of 29 and 30 January 2013, slide 10, available at https://www.law.ox.ac.uk/sites/files/oxlaw/voet.pdf. Also see the conference summary at p 15: https://www.law.ox.ac.uk/sites/files/oxlaw/executive_summary.pdf.

[25] Voet (n 3) 270, 283.

[26] Rédaction en ligne, 'Catastrophe de Ghislenghien: les victimes enfin indemnisées' (3 February 2012), http://www.nordeclair.be/292403/article/regions/tournai/actualite/2012-02-03/catastrophe-de-ghislenghien-les-victimes-enfin-indemnisees.

[27] *Moniteur Belge* 21 juni 2017.

II. United Kingdom

A. Compensation Orders in Criminal Proceedings

There has been a general trend towards resolving breaches of criminal (and hence regulatory) law by agreement. Deferred Prosecution Agreements (DPAs), used extensively in the USA,[28] were given a statutory basis in 2013,[29] supported by a Code of Practice[30] and general principles in the Code for Crown Prosecutors.[31] A DPA must be approved by the Crown Court in a declaration that the DPA is in the interests of justice, and the terms of the DPA are fair, reasonable and proportionate.[32] The DPA approach to settlement has commended itself to UK Government as a means of securing guilty pleas earlier in the prosecution process, improving efficiency, reducing paperwork and process times, and alleviating the burden on witnesses and victims of crime, resulting in increased use of deferred prosecution agreements.[33]

B. Disgorgement of Profits

We should note a somewhat different approach that might not per se result in payment of redress, but should achieve one part of the similar outcome that the defendant does not retain the illicit gains that have resulted from an infringement. This occurs under a power to 'skim off' such illicit profits.

Leading examples exist in German competition law,[34] although it has apparently never been invoked there,[35] in the UK under criminal enforcement provisions discussed above,[36]

---

[28] See S Oded, *Corporate Compliance: New Approaches to Regulatory Enforcement* (Cheltenham, Edward Elgar, 2013).

[29] Crime and Courts Act 2013, s 45 and Sch 17. See *Deferred Prosecution Agreements Government response to the consultation on a new enforcement tool to deal with economic crime committed by commercial organisations* (Ministry of Justice, 2012), Cm 8463.

[30] Issued under Crime and Courts Act 2013, Sch 17, para 6. See *Crime and Courts Act 2013: Deferred Prosecution Agreement Code of Practice. Consultation on draft Code* (Serious Fraud Office, 2013).

[31] *The Code for Crown Prosecutors*, available at http://www.cps.gov.uk/publications/code_for_crown_prosecutors.

[32] Crime and Courts Act 2013, Sch 17 para 8. A major example was the DPA agreed between the Serious Fraud Office and Rolls-Royce plc in relation to extensive practice of bribery of foreign officials, and a fine of £239,082,645.00 (including a discount of 50% for exceptional collaboration) and costs of £13 million approved by the court: *Serious Fraud Office v Rolls-Royce PLC and Rolls-Royce Energy Systems Inc.* Judgment of Sir Brian Leveson P, 17 January 2017, at https://www.judiciary.gov.uk/wp-content/uploads/2017/01/sfo-v-rolls-royce.pdf.

[33] *Deferred Prosecution Agreements Government response to the consultation on a new enforcement tool to deal with economic crime committed by commercial organisations* (Ministry of Justice, 2012), Cm 8463.

[34] German Act Against Restraints on Competition (GWB), art 34. See W Wurmnest, 'A New Area for Private Antitrust Litigation in Germany? A Critical Appraisal of the Modernized Law Against Restraints of Competition' (2005) 6 *German Law Journal* 1173; T Lübbig and M Le Bell, 'Die Reform des Zivilprozesses in Kartellsachen' (2006) *Wettbewerb in Recht und Praxis* 1209. See also S Peyer, 'Myths and Untold Stories—Private Antitrust Enforcement in Germany', University of East Anglia, Centre for Public Policy, Working Paper 10-12, July 2010, at http://ssrn.com/abstract=1672695.

[35] Information kindly supplied by S Peyer after discussions with the Bundeskartelamt.

[36] Various general powers are available to UK criminal prosecutors, notably a Confiscation Order or Recovery Order under the Proceeds of Crime Act 2002, ss 6–13 and 240–43.

and specific financial services powers,[37] and in the United States of America, such as in antitrust enforcement.[38] The disadvantage of this approach is that it only deals with one outcome: removing the profits does not by itself rectify victims' losses. There needs to be a further ability to achieve the redress outcome. Under the German law, the illicit profits are paid to public funds, so although the power is exercisable by the consumer associations, they have no incentive to use it, and have not done so.

In 2016/17, the Financial Conduct Authority (FCA)'s Accredited Financial Investigators worked on confiscation investigations concerning 99 individuals under the Proceeds of Crime Act 2002. As at 31 March 2017, restraint orders were in place against 30 suspects or defendants. In 2016/17, the FCA obtained eight confiscation orders totalling £2,440,413, of which £2,127,675 was used to compensate the victims of the defendants' crimes.[39]

Disgorgement from a Company

In 2014, the Financial Conduct Authority fined Barclays £52.3 million, as disgorgement of the amount that Barclays generated from the illegal transaction, and a further penalty of £19,769,400.[40]

Confiscation Order and Restitution relating to an Individual

Shay Reches controlled professional indemnity insurance schemes that were carried out without approval, leading to three insurance companies going into administration and 1,300 law firms being at risk of operating without indemnity cover. Reches was banned from any FCA-regulated activity in future, fined £1.05 million and agreed to pay £13.13 million to the three insurers that went into administration.[41]

---

[37] Skimming off can be achieved through a compensation order, for such sum as appears just, where profits have accrued to a person as part of a contravention of the requirements and a person has suffered loss as a result, and seize infringers' assets: FSMA 2000, ss 382, 383.

[38] The SEC ordered recoveries of $2.8 billion per year in 2010 and 2011: See *SEC's Financial Statements for Fiscal Years 2011 and 2010* (Government Accountability Office, 2011) GAO-12-219, at 57.

[39] *Enforcement annual performance account. Annual report 2016/17* (Financial Conduct Authority, 2017).

[40] Press release, *FCA fines Barclays £72 million for poor handling of financial crime risks.* FCA, 26.11.2014, https://www.fca.org.uk/news/press-releases/fca-fines-barclays-%C2%A372-million-poor-handling-financial-crime-risks<u>. The failings related to a £1.88 billion pound transaction (Transaction) that Barclays arranged and executed in 2011 and 2012 for a number of ultra-high net worth clients. The clients involved were politically exposed persons (PEPs) and should therefore have been subject to enhanced levels of due diligence and monitoring by Barclays, which the bank failed to apply. The FCA calculated the fine in this way:

Step 1: disgorgement:	£52,300,000
Step 2: the seriousness of the breach	level 4, £52,300,000
Step 3: mitigating and aggravating factors	increase Step 2 figure by 20%
Step 4: adjustment for deterrence	£28,242,000
Step 5: Settlement discount	30% to the Step 4 figure
Hence financial penalty:	£72,069,400.

[41] J Hyde, '£15.5m penalties for PII that put 1,300 law firms at risk' *Gazette* 1 February 2016.

Action taken by the FCA against individuals responsible for a fraudulent collective investment scheme was expected to lead to investors receiving in excess of £2.9 million, which equated to approximately 55% of the capital sums that were owed to them.[42] The owner of the scheme, Alex Hope, was sentenced to seven years' imprisonment in January 2015, was subject to a confiscation order of £166,696 under the Proceeds of Crime Act 2002. In 2016 he was also ordered to return to investors within three months almost £2.65 million, representing his benefit from his involvement in the fraudulent scheme, failing which he would serve a further 20 months' imprisonment.

---

[42] Press release, '£2.9 million to be returned to investors following FCA prosecution' Financial Conduct Authority, 12/02/2016.

5

Regulatory Redress

I. Concept

Regulatory redress is a generic term that describes the outcome of redress being paid, or made, as a result of the intervention of a public authority. We consciously choose to refer to the wide concept of 'intervention' by a public authority, since experience has shown that redress may in practice be achieved by less formal means than being 'ordered' by an authority or court.

In England and Wales, the power for public authorities that enforce market regulatory law or consumer protection law to make orders that traders should make redress to consumers, individually and collectively, has developed strongly since around 2012 and has now become the primary mechanism for delivering collective redress to consumers, clearly eclipsing private enforcement by or on behalf of consumers.[1] It has become typical practice in some sectors for traders and enforcers to agree redress arrangements as one element of a package of measures that settle infringement, behavioural actions and redress elements. It is now rare for such settlements to be fought in court: many are agreed between trader and regulator, even if the arrangement then has to be approved by the court in order to trigger its binding effect and enable independent oversight.

In this chapter, we will analyse the range of mechanisms that can be used to deliver regulatory redress, and then look in detail at some of the leading States where the technique has been used.

II. The Range of Mechanisms of Regulatory Redress

Hodges noted in 2015 that the redress power may take a number of forms, and he identified a typology of them,[2] which shows that the activities of public authorities range from 'soft'

---

[1] See R Money-Kyrle, 'Collective Enforcement of Consumer Rights in the United Kingdom' in M Schmidt-Kessel, C Strünck and M Kramme (eds), *Im Namen der Verbraucher? Kollektive Rechtsdurchsetzung in Europa* (Jena, Schriften zu Verbraucherrecht und Verbraucherwissenschaften, Band 5 Jenaer Wissenschaftliche Verlagsgesellschaft, 2015); C Hodges, 'Mass Collective Redress: Consumer ADR and Regulatory Techniques' (2015) 2 *European Review of Private Law* 829; C Hodges, *Law and Corporate Behaviour: Integrating Theories of Regulation, Enforcement, Culture and Ethics* (Oxford, Hart Publishing, 2015) ch 10; C Hodges and N Creutzfeldt, 'Transformations in Public and Private Enforcement' in H-W Micklitz and A Wechsler (eds), *The Transformation of Enforcement* (Oxford, Hart Publishing, 2016).

[2] Hodges, 'Mass Collective Redress' (n 1) 841.

influence (akin to resolution 'in the shadow of the law') to 'hard' enforcement (through the formal exercise of enforcement powers). The individual mechanisms might be grouped under the following functional headings, where the public authority acts on the parties, especially the defendant, through influence, approval or coercion. We will now examine these techniques in greater detail, noting first three broad categorisations in the way that powers may be used: influence, approval and coercion.

A. Influence

The most obvious situation would be where the behaviour of a payer is influenced by the persuasive intervention of a public authority, perhaps backed by a coercive power. The authority might simply have influence by intervening as a neutral third party, akin to a conciliator or mediator, and persuade the payer to offer or make a payment.

The influence of the authority would, clearly, be increased where it has a number of powers that it could choose to use against the payer, such as to start an investigation or an enforcement action, culminating in imposing a fine or commencing a prosecution. The existence of such power or powers—including powers to coerce making redress—should clearly be influential, and form the background to a less formal or swifter resolution. Some enforcement authorities refer to having a 'toolbox' of enforcement powers that contains multiple weapons. Not only might it be advantageous to have the ability to select individual effective tools, but the combined effect of a range of effective tools should also be helpful.

In addition to the ability to rely on coercive powers, authorities may deploy effective 'nudge' or encouragement techniques. For example, they might be able to take into account, in deciding on imposing or asking a court for a sanction, the mitigating circumstances relating to the defendant's conduct, such as whether he had taken swift and effective action to make voluntary redress. Criminal courts typically take into account defendants' behaviour in mitigation or aggravation of offences in deciding on the size of sanctions.[3] This technique offers a clear financial incentive for infringers to implement redress speedily.

A similar technique might be the ability to interrupt an enforcement process after the investigation stage and interpose a 'time out' period before taking a decision on imposition of sanctions. This would incentivise defendants to agree (perhaps through alternative dispute resolution (ADR)) voluntary redress payments, especially so as to seek a reduction in the level of a public penalty. This 'nudge' was suggested by Andreas Schwab MEP in 2013 as Rapporteur of the European Parliament Report in relation to enforcement of competition law.[4] He suggested that after the statement of objections (and thus before a decision

---

[3] In competition enforcement, the European Commission and some national authorities have either reduced or even waived fines after firms have paid compensation, see A Ezrachi and M Ioannidou, 'Public Compensation as a Complementary Mechanism to Damages Actions: from Policy Justifications to Formal Implementation' (2012) *Journal of European Competition Law Practice* 1.

[4] Draft Report of the Committee on Economic and monetary Affairs on the proposal for a directive of the European parliament and of the Council on certain rules governing actions for damages under national law for infringements of the competition law provisions of the member States and of the European Union, COM(2013)0404-C7-0170/2013—2013/0185(COD), 3.10.2013; Rapporteur, Andreas Schwab MEP.

regarding the fine for infringement), an authority could define a time frame in which the infringers could voluntarily seek a settlement with their victims. If the authority considered that the compensation paid were accurate and lawful, it should subsequently take it into account when setting its fine. The Rapporteur noted that this solution 'seems to provide the fastest and most cost-efficient way' to compensate victims.

A further technique applies where the authority has power to accept an undertaking by a prospective defendant that it will make redress. Such undertakings have been used in connection with resolution of enforcement actions by agreement rather than full—and hence lengthy—formal enforcement proceedings. Examples are Deferred Prosecution Agreements (DPAs), introduced in the UK in 2013,[5] supported by a Code of Practice.[6] This technique incentivises speedy and comprehensive resolution of behavioural and redress aspects of the enforcement activity.[7] It might be used where the principle of redress is agreed by a defendant, but the detailed distribution of redress to all individual recipients might take time, and can be agreed to occur under an approved mechanism or scheme.

The European Commission adopted the approach in enforcement of competition law in 2013 by proposing to accept commitments from a trader that include introduction of a new pricing system and paying some customers compensation.[8,9]

B. Approval

There can be situations in which a public authority might itself approve redress arrangements, or might agree to place or recommend a redress arrangement before a court for its approval. The power to approve a compensation scheme has been used by the UK Financial Conduct Authority, as illustrated below.[10] This mechanism may incentivise one or more of the parties to propose a redress arrangement.[11]

---

[5] Crime and Courts Act 2013, s 45 and Sch 17. See *Deferred Prosecution Agreements Government response to the consultation on a new enforcement tool to deal with economic crime committed by commercial organisations* (Cm 8463: Ministry of Justice, October 2012), available at https://consult.justice.gov.uk/digital-communications/deferred-prosecution-agreements/results/deferred-prosecution-agreements-response.pdf.

[6] Issued under Crime and Courts Act 2013, Sch 17, para 6. See *Crime and Courts Act 2013: Deferred Prosecution Agreement Code of Practice. Consultation on draft Code* (SFO, 27 June 2013), http://www.sfo.gov.uk/press-room/latest-press-releases/press-releases-2013/deferred-prosecution-agreements-consultation-on-draft-code-of-practice.aspx.

[7] DPAs have increased been used in USA since 2004. See JM Anderson and I Waggoner, *The Changing Role of Criminal Law in Controlling Corporate Behaviour* (Santa Monica, RAND Corporation, 2014); J Arlen and M Kahan, 'Corporate Governance Regulation through Non-Prosecution' (2016) *New York University Public Law and Legal Theory Working Papers* 551.

[8] Press release: *Antitrust: Commission market tests commitments proposed by Deutsche Bahn concerning pricing system for traction current in Germany* (European Commission, 15 August 2013), IP/13/780. The company proposed to pay railway companies that it does not own a one-time retroactive refund of 4% of their latest annual traction current invoice, and to provide the Commission with the necessary data to assess if the price levels charged under the new pricing system would lead to a margin squeeze.

[9] Such a separate oversight mechanism was implemented in 2017 for UK competition damages, see below.

[10] See s III.D.iii.a below.

[11] In UK consultation discussions, The Office of Fair Trading favoured this option, as it operates on a 'high level basis' and avoided involvement in any aspect of quantifying individual loss, and in overseeing the satisfactory implementation of any payment scheme, and that the authority should only approve proposals put forward voluntarily by firms in general terms: *Response by the OFT to Consultation on Private Actions in Competition Law* (Office of Fair Trading, 2012) para 4.4.

It may be thought that this mechanism would be little used unless it occurs against the backdrop of a power to compel a defendant to create or propose a redress arrangement. However, there may be a national culture of settlement, as has been identified in the Netherlands, or there may be several reasons why it would be advantageous for a defendant to propose a settlement—such as speed, closure, mitigation of damage to reputation of the risk of sanctions, or just to do the right thing. The cases under the Dutch Mass Claims Settlement Act show that the technique can be useful and effective in some situations. Some of those Dutch cases approved settlement agreements reached spontaneously by the parties, and some cases related to the need to resolve all cases that occurred outside the USA, after the intra-USA cases had been settled there.[12]

There are indications that the mere existence of the power can act as an incentive for parties to short-circuit litigation and move straight to settlement discussions. This power can obviously be used together with other coercive powers. The advantage of official approval is to afford independent scrutiny that the terms are fair, especially if the agreement thereby becomes binding on all class members.

C. Coercion

A power that orders redress might take one of a number of forms.

One power might be for an authority to propose a redress scheme. Such a scheme might subsequently be approved by the authority and/or by the court, or by some independent (eg ADR) body.

There may be a power to order a defendant to negotiate, or some other regulatory pressure that incentivises a business to propose to make redress.[13] An example of this arises under the 2017 revision of the Consumer Protection Cooperation Regulation, discussed in chapter 2 above, is where competent authorities are to have power to seek or obtain remedial commitments from the trader for the benefit of affected consumers.[14]

There may be a power for an authority to bring court proceedings for an order that redress be paid to those harmed. One example of this is the ability of the Consumer Ombudsman

---

[12] F Weber and WH. van Boom, 'Dutch Treat: The Dutch Collective Settlement of Mass Damage Act (WCAM 2005)' (2011) 1 *Contratto e Impresa/Europa* 69; B Krans, 'The Dutch Class Action (Financial Settlement) Act in an international context: The *Shell* case and the *Converium* case' (2012) 31(2) *CJQ* 141; XE Kramer, 'Enforcing Mass Settlements in the European Judicial Area: EU Policy and the Strange Case of Dutch Collective Settlements (WCAM)' in C Hodges and A Stadler (eds), *Resolving Mass Disputes. ADR and Settlement of Mass Claims* (Cheltenham, Edward Elgar, 2013).

[13] In Italy Decision no 173/07/CONS of the Public Authority for Telecommunication required that there must be a mandatory attempt at settlement before local administrative bodies, or before the Chambers of Commerce, or through a conciliation body on which representatives of telecommunication companies and the consumers associations sit. If a settlement is not reached, any party could refer the case to be decided by the Public Authority for Telecommunication, which operates on an arbitration basis. Separate procedures for settlement of telecom disputes exist for mobile phones, which can be activated also through the internet, and for normal phones. See http://www2.agcom.it/operatori/operatori_utenti.htm. The decision was overturned by the Constitutional Court but reinstated in 2013.

[14] Regulation (EU) 2017/2394 of the European Parliament and of the Council of 12 December 2017 on cooperation between national authorities responsible for the enforcement of consumer protection laws and repealing Regulation (EC) No 2006/2004, art 9.4(c).

of Denmark to bring a class action in the Market Court on behalf of affected consumers, on an 'opt-out' basis.[15]

The most obvious powers are where the authority may order a person to pay redress, or order a redress scheme to apply. The former power is similar to where a criminal court has power to order a defendant who is convicted to pay redress, such as under a compensation order. A public regulatory authority might have a similar power. However, the simple redress order is more likely to be applicable in circumstances where there is certainty over the identity of the recipient of the redress, the number of recipients is small, and the amount payable to each recipient is known or easily ascertainable. In more complex circumstances, involving a large number of potential recipients and/or uncertainty over who is entitled to what amount of money, an order to create a redress scheme offers a solution. The parameters of the redress scheme might be fixed in advance (by agreement or order) or certain details might be left for later resolution (for example by the administrator of the scheme).

As discussed below, many UK regulatory authorities have revised enforcement policies to require them to achieve redress.[16] The UK financial services regulator has power to order a consumer redress scheme or its equivalent on several or an individual provider.[17] An example of this power was where the Office of Fair Trading agreed that the 50 infringing independent schools that had colluded on prices should not pay a fine (since that would close them all down, and be funded by future innocent parents) but instead make *ex gratia* payments totalling £3 million to create an educational trust for the pupils whose fees had been fixed.[18] This approach has the obvious limitation that all the details need to be known, so does not on its own have the flexibility to cope with situations where the exact quantification of loss due to each identifiable recipient is unknown. However, where it applies, it should be highly efficient and speedy.

It will be seen that there are various options as to how a redress power and an approach towards redress might be designed and used. None of these options need stand alone. Indeed, the effectiveness of the technique is enhanced where several of the powers listed above are combined—whether with each other, or with other powers in the enforcement toolbox, or other options such as ADR techniques, as discussed below. As Hodges has said:

> Functionally, there are three main elements. First, a power to order redress, or to seek a court order for redress. Second, a power to approve the fairness of a proposal to make redress. Third, a power to reduce a penalty where redress is paid. Individually and together these elements incentivize but also facilitate the outcome of redress.[19]

---

[15] See P Kiurunen, N Lindström and M Bylov Rath, 'Denmark' in PG Karlsgodt (ed), *World Class Actions. A Guide to Group and Representative Actions around the Globe* (Oxford. Oxford University Press, 2012) 194.

[16] Regulatory Enforcement and Sanctions Act 2007, Part 3.

[17] Financial Services and Markets Act 2000, s 404 and 404 F(7).

[18] *Exchange of Information on Future Fees by Certain Independent, Fee-Paying Schools* (OFT, 2006). See *Evaluation of an OFT intervention. Independent fee-paying schools* (Office of Fair Trading, May 2012), OFT1416; and A Ezrachi and M Ioannidou, 'Public Compensation as a Complementary Mechanism to Damages Actions: from Policy Justifications to Formal Implementation' (2012) *Journal of European Competition Law and Practice* 1. See case study at p 62 above.

[19] Hodges, 'Mass Collective Redress' (n 1) 829.

III. Examples of the Powers

This section illustrates examples of the principal types of powers that have been identified in the previous section.

A. Belgium

There are multiple public enforcers or regulators in Belgium, but generally their powers regarding restitution or civil sanctions are limited.[20] The focus is on deterrence rather than restitution.[21] Nevertheless, victims can claim compensation following a public enforcement decision (*follow-up*), arguing that the tort (or at least the fault element) has been proven by the findings of a violation.[22]

However, some remarks have to be made regarding two important regulators and their link with redress, namely the Financial Services and Markets Authority (FSMA)[23] and the Commission for the Regulation of Electricity and Gas (CREG).[24] A first remark relates to the general finding that restitution and civil sanctions are not the main focus of public regulators or enforcers.[25] One could take the example of the FSMA. When a supervised trader does not comply with the regulations in place, the FSMA has a wide array of instruments to deal with this non-compliance and to sanction the trader.[26] The (administrative) sanctioning has to be situated in the relationship between the FSMA and the supervised trader, not vis-à-vis the financial consumer.[27] Although a consumer's complaint might trigger an investigation and administrative action, a harmed financial consumer will need to have recourse to other instruments outside the regulatory framework.[28]

---

[20] S Voet, 'Public Enforcement and A(O)DR as Mechanisms for Resolving Mass Problems: a Belgian Perspective' in Hodges and Stadler (n 12) 270 at 274 and 279.

[21] S Voet, 'Collectieve afwikkeling van consumenten-massaschade. Pleidooi voor een geïntegreerde aanpak' (2013) 3 *DCCR* 201, 210.

[22] See, for competition law: T Schoors, T Baeyens and W Devroe, 'Schadevergoedingsacties na kartelinbreuken' (2011) 239 *NjW* 198, 199, no 4.

[23] See: http://www.fsma.be/. The FSMA is an autonomous supervising entity responsible (together with the National Bank of Belgium) for the regulatory supervision of multiple players in the field of Belgian financial business.

[24] See: http://www.creg.be/nl/index.html. The CREG is one of the four regulators in the Belgian energy sector. It is the federal regulator which (among other tasks) looks after the essential consumer interests, although consumers are referred to the Energy Ombudsman for complaints.

[25] Voet (n 20) 270, 279.

[26] For instance, require the publishing of a correction, inspections, publishing warnings, suspend trading, striking an intermediary from the register, revoking authorisation, imposing fines or penalties.

[27] This also seems true for the Directorate-General Enforcement and Mediation (part of the Federal Public Service Economy, SMEs, Self-Employed and Energy) which can arrange the transactional settlement of violations for some legislations and in the framework of some legislations has the power to offer the offender the opportunity to pay an amount of money to halt further prosecution, but this doesn't directly concern the relationship with the harmed consumer. See for a list of the regulator's powers: Annual Report 2011, http://economie.fgov.be/en/binaries/Annual_report_E7_2011_tcm327-200828.pdf, 31.

[28] R Houben and D Vanderstraeten, 'De bescherming van de financiële consument door de FSMA' (2016) 111(21) *DCCR* 60, no 49.

One should nevertheless pay attention to the possibility of including the consumer indirectly in a settlement between the FSMA and the non-complying trader. The fact that the consumer is not a party to that settlement, does not imply that the consumer cannot be kept in mind when drafting the terms of the settlement. A settlement concerning interest rate derivatives to cover variable rate loans to SMEs between the FSMA and a number of financial institutions provides an excellent example.[29] After inspection, the FSMA concluded that not all rules regarding the duty of care and the supply of information were observed by the financial institutions concerned so the FSMA pressed for several interventions. Some only regarded the institutions, such as their duty to make sure that their employees are qualified to assume the responsibility imposed onto them. Yet, the consumer was not forgotten. The financial institutions concerned agreed to pay each client a certain amount of money by way of commercial compensation. That way, compensation is provided to the consumers although the settlement was only reached between the FSMA and a number of financial institutions.

In addition to including consumers' redress in settlements, the statutory framework can also provide some assistance to financial consumers. In that regard, Article 30*ter* of the Act of 2 August 2002[30] comes to mind. It contains a rebuttable presumption that in case a financial consumer is harmed by a transaction and a trader listed in the next paragraph of the provision has committed a certain breach as a result of that transaction, the transaction at hand is presumed to be the result of the breach. This means that the presumption entails that the investor would not have made the same decision without the breach.[31]

A second remark concerns the CREG. The statutory framework provides for the creation of a Dispute Resolution Chamber which would resolve disputes between the network administrator and the network users regarding the duties of the network administrator, the distribution network administrators and the administrators of closed industrial networks within the context of the Law on the organization of the electricity market (and its implementing orders), except for disputes regarding contractual rights and obligations.[32] The (administrative) decision of the Dispute Resolution Chamber is binding.[33] The *law in the books* certainly leaves room for offering redress to consumers, but the *law in practice* has not yet developed since the Dispute Resolution Chamber is currently unable to operate due to a lack of appointment of its members.[34]

---

[29] See: http://www.fsma.be/en/in-the-picture.aspx, 19-05-2015, 'Interest rate derivatives to cover variable rate loans to SMEs' (only available in Dutch and French).

[30] Law of 2 August 2002 on the supervision of the financial sector and on financial services, *Official Gazette* 4 September 2002.

[31] T Van Dyck and L Denturck, 'De burgerlijke sanctie van artikel 30*ter* van Twin Peaks II/ De tanden van een papieren tijger?' (2013) 6 *Bank Fin R* 274, 275.

[32] Art 29 Law of 29 April 1999 on the organization of the electricity market, *OG BS* 11 May 1999.

[33] Art 29, §3 *in fine* Law of 29 April 1999 on the organization of the electricity market, *Official Gazette* 11 May 1999.

[34] See: http://www.creg-ar.be/2015/report-en.html#principales (p 82 of the report).

B. Denmark

i. The 'Opt-out' Class Action[35]

The four Nordic states—Denmark, Finland, Norway and Sweden[36]—each have a public official responsible for enforcement of consumer law called a Consumer Ombudsman. It is important to realise that this use of the term 'Ombudsman' differs from its use in non-Nordic states, since the functions of Ombudsmen differ, as appears below. In the Nordic model, the Consumer Ombudsman is the principal national enforcement officer of consumer law, with power to initiate prosecutions for breaches of the national Marketing Practices Act, and usually brings cases in the Market Court.[37] Each of these states has introduced a class action mechanism, as noted in chapter 3 above, but the Danish Law differs from that of the other states. In Denmark, Norway and Sweden, a member of the class may commence an application to the court for a class to be ordered, but in Denmark such a class can only be constituted on an opt-in basis. Unlike the other Nordic states, Denmark permits an application to be made for an opt-out class action, but restricts the power to make such an application solely to the Consumer Ombudsman.

In Finland, the application may only be made by the Consumer Ombudsman, and not by a class member or anyone else.[38] The reason for this restriction was 'to diminish suspicions concerning the possible misuse of the new act' and 'to ensure the actions could not be taken for the purpose of blackmail or damage'.[39] The fundamental point is that the intermediary—here, the Consumer Ombudsman—has to be trusted to exercise the redress power independently in the public interest. The Nordic Consumer Ombudsmen do not have a conflict of interest by the potential to benefit from the action.

The Consumer Ombudsman of Denmark is constantly active in taking preventative or enforcement action, such as issuing opinions, negotiating with traders and trade associations, or instituting prosecutions. The Consumer Ombudsman has strong powers, but is subject to a 'principle of negotiation', which is a typically Nordic approach: he or she must 'seek by negotiation to influence traders to act in accordance with good market practices'.[40] The class action power may only be used by the Consumer Ombudsman where two conditions apply, both of which were included in the legislation to emphasise the exceptional nature of this mechanism. First, the case must concern claims that are individually so small that it is evident that they cannot generally be expected to be brought through individual actions. Such claims are stated normally to involve under DKK 2,000. Second, an opt-in class action must be deemed to be an inappropriate method of examining the claims. This will be the case if the class includes a very large number of persons so that the practical administration of opt-in notices will require a disproportionate amount of resource. The normal rules on 'loser pays costs' apply to a class action.

---

[35] This section draws on C Hodges, *The Reform of Class and Representative Actions in European Legal Systems. A New Framework for Collective Redress* (Oxford, Hart Publishing, 2008).

[36] A fifth Nordic state is Iceland, which does not have a Consumer Ombudsman.

[37] eg Danish Class Actions Act 2007, Act No 181 of 28 February 2007; Finnish Consumer Protection Act 34/1978.

[38] Act of Class Actions 444/2007.

[39] HE 154/2006, p 16. Information kindly supplied by K Viitanen.

[40] Marketing Practices Act, s 23.

However, since the Consumer Ombudsman was awarded the power to initiate a class action on 1 January 2008, no such applications have been brought, although this has been threatened regularly. The redress power is regarded as just one tool in the enforcement armoury of the Consumer Ombudsman, to be deployed alongside other tools on cessation of infringements, undertakings as to future conduct and so on. The Consumer Ombudsman has resolved a series of cases, of which leading examples are given below. Most of these are summaries, but in one case we quote the text of the Settlement Agreement by way of illustration.

ii. Case Studies

Cases

Translations kindly made available by the Consumer Ombudsman[41]

Investment Bonds

DiBa Bank sold portfolio management agreements concerning investments in ScandiNotes and Kalvebod bonds to customers. Nine holders of the bonds made claims against the bank through the ADR body, the Danish Complaint Board of Banking Services (Pengeinstitutankenævnet), eight of which were upheld. However, unusually, the bank refused to accept the decisions of the Complaint Board. The Financial Services Authority criticised the bank's hedge fund for its written marketing material and the bank itself for the financial advice it had given, stating that both were against the requirements of good financial practices. The Consumer Ombudsman then instituted proceedings at Næstved District Court, based on his power to take action, including a class action, against breaches of honest principles and good practice, under the Financial Business Act section 348(1). Following grant of free legal aid, the unit trust decided to bring a class action against the bank and the hedge fund.

In June 2013 the Consumer Ombudsman concluded a Settlement Agreement with DiBa Bank A/S that included the following terms:

1. The bank would pay compensation to all present and former customers who had a low-risk profile according to the relevant portfolio management agreements (low-risk and/or risk score 1 to 4 referred to as either 'low risk' or 'moderately low risk' in the portfolio management agreements).

2. Customers classified as medium-risk customers who can be reclassified into low-risk customers according to the current practice of the Danish Complaint Board of Banking Services or, subject to agreement by the Parties, who are in an equal position. The Agreement did not include any other medium-risk, moderately high-risk or high-risk customers or customers with risk scores between 5 and 10.

3. The compensation would be 80% of the customers' losses on ScandiNotes and Kalvebod notes. The loss was computed as a whole for all ScandiNotes and Kalvebod notes as the difference between the purchase price, exclusive of transaction costs, and the market value on 21 June 2013, exclusive of transaction costs. Any notes sold, redeemed or written down were included in the computation as the difference between the purchase price and the value on sale, redemption or write-down. To perform the Settlement Agreement, DiBa Bank bought the notes from those

---

[41] Henrik Øe, and colleagues Benedikte Havskov Hansen and Diane Svanholm Kvist.

existing customers who accept the settlement, and paid the market value at 21 June 2013 with the addition of the above amount of compensation. No deduction will be made for interest paid, and the amount of compensation will not accrue interest from the date of the purchase of the notes.

4. For customers who had switched to another bank and therefore no longer held the notes in a custody account with DiBa Bank or had any portfolio management agreement with the Bank, the loss on all ScandiNotes and Kalvebod notes as a whole was computed as the difference between the purchase price, exclusive of costs, and the market value on the date of cessation of the customer relationship with DiBa Bank.

5. Schedule 1 of the Agreement provided four computation examples for existing customers who held notes, existing customers who had sold their notes, former customers who had sold their notes and former customers who still held notes.

6. The offer of compensation was in full and final settlement of any claim by the customer against DiBa Bank concerning investments in ScandiNotes and Kalvebod notes made under the portfolio management agreement.

7. Individual customers, including customers who have authorised others to conduct their legal action, were free to decide whether to accept the offer of compensation made by DiBa Bank.

8. DiBa Bank made the offer of compensation by means of a letter to the customers appended as Schedule 2. The offer was binding on DiBa Bank for three months from the date and publication of the Settlement Agreement. DiBa Bank could withdraw the offer during the three months if the offer was not accepted by a substantial number of the customers to whom it is made.

9. The legal actions before Næstved District Court were withdrawn.

Agreement concluded by Sampension KP Livsforsikring a/s ('Sampension'), the Danish Consumer Ombudsman and Ydelsesgarantiforeningen ('the Association')

1. Preamble

In 2011, the Danish Consumer Ombudsman commenced an investigation of the revocation by Sampension of average interest rate guarantees (*ydelsesgarantier*) based on the agreements made by Sampension and the parties to relevant collective agreements. Based on this investigation, the Consumer Ombudsman is of the opinion that Sampension was not entitled to revoke the average interest rate guarantees with retroactive effect without the consent of the individual customer.

Sampension and the relevant collective agreement parties have maintained against the Consumer Ombudsman that Sampension was entitled to revoke the average interest rate guarantees in the manner done.

Together with the Association [an association representing the class action plaintiffs against Sampension], the Consumer Ombudsman and Sampension have examined the possibilities of reaching a forward-looking settlement that will take into consideration the policyholders of Sampension, whether individually or collectively, as an alternative to a lengthy legal action.

On that basis, the Parties have agreed on the terms and conditions described in this document.

2. Transfer of own funds to individual special provisions

Sampension and the Consumer Ombudsman have considered how to ensure that the financial reserves on which the average interest rate guarantees were based before the revocation will also in future benefit the policyholders.

The Parties have jointly reached a solution according to which Sampension shall transfer part of its own funds to individual special bonus provisions allocated to the policyholders.

The following has been agreed for the policyholders of those pension plans with Sampension for which a revocation of the guarantees and a transfer of the pension plans to a declaration-of-intention scheme have been agreed with the relevant collective agreement parties or effected on 1 January 2011 or a subsequent date. Also comprised are the customers who have switched from the average interest rate product to the 3-in-1 Life-long Pension product (*3 i 1 Livspension*) before or after the revocation of the average interest rate guarantee.

As at 1 January 2014, Sampension will transfer an amount equal to 5% of each policyholder's account balance on 1 May 2013 from Sampension's own funds to individual special bonus provisions as detailed in the Addendum to the Agreement. This amount corresponds to the typical solvency margin applicable to the average interest rate guarantees under the current Solvency I regime.

The Consumer Ombudsman, the Association and Sampension all find that the transfer of an amount equal to 5% of each policyholder's account balance to individual special bonus provisions is an attractive offer to such policyholder as an alternative to a lengthy legal action. The policyholders can choose whether or not to accept the offer, see clause 3, and the offer is thus without prejudice to those who may want to pursue any individual potential claims contesting Sampension's revocation of the average interest rate guarantees. If an individual pursues such potential claim, his or her entitlement to individual special bonus provisions will cease, see clause 3 below.

The policyholders who will receive part of Sampension's own funds as individual special bonus provisions will be informed thereof in a way to be agreed between the Parties.

3. Renunciation

Individual policyholders with pension plans pursuant to a declaration-of-intention scheme who cannot accept this Agreement can renounce the transfer to individual special bonus provisions by notifying Sampension of their renunciation within four weeks of the date of the notice informing the policyholder of the transfer. Upon renunciation, the policyholder will be in a position as if the average interest rate guarantee had not been revoked on 1 January 2011 as regards contributions made prior to that date.

In case of renunciation of this Agreement, the relevant policyholder forfeits the entitlement to individual special bonus provisions under clause 2.

Any policyholders who individually give notice of renunciation of this Agreement after expiry of the said time limit of four weeks will not recover their rights under the average interest rate guarantee.

Any policyholder who takes legal steps by complaining to the Danish Insurance Complaints Board (*Ankenævnet for Forsikring*), issuing a writ, joining a class action or taking similar steps with the aim of contesting the revocation of the average interest rate guarantees without having first renounced this Agreement is deemed to have renounced this Agreement. Under such circumstances, the relevant policyholder will forfeit the entitlement to individual special bonus provisions under clause 2, and individual special bonus provisions already transferred will be charged back as regards such policyholder.

4. Renunciation by the Consumer Ombudsman and the Association of the right to take legal action concerning the revocation of average interest rate guarantees

The Consumer Ombudsman and the Association renounce the right to take, join or intervene in any legal action against Sampension under the rules of the Danish Financial Business Act (*lov om finansiel virksomhed*), the Danish Marketing Practices Act (*markedsføringsloven*) or on any other basis, whether in their own names, as class action representatives, as third parties or advocates to the court or as authorised agents, relative to any claim concerning the revocation of average interest rate guarantees other than issues concerning the performance of this Agreement.

5. Sampension's right of withdrawal

Sampension may withdraw from this Agreement in full or in part.

If Sampension withdraws from this Agreement in full, the Agreement will cease to exist in its entirety.

If Sampension only withdraws from this Agreement in part, the Agreement will cease to exist only for the policyholders comprised by the withdrawal.

If Sampension withdraws from the Agreement, whether in full or in part, the renunciation by the Consumer Ombudsman and the Association of their right to take legal action, see clause 4, ceases to exist in its entirety, and this settlement is without prejudice to any such legal actions in all respects.

Within three months of the signing of this Agreement, a written notice of withdrawal must be given to the Consumer Ombudsman and to each policyholder affected by the withdrawal.

6. Suspension of limitation, etc

Sampension declares that all time limits for limitation and inactivity, also relative to any failure to complain, will be suspended on the part of the Consumer Ombudsman and customers of Sampension for three months as from the signing of this Agreement.

If Sampension withdraws from this Agreement, whether in full or in part, no claim will be statute-barred due to limitation or inactivity for the first three months after Sampension's written notice of its withdrawal from this Agreement.

As regards legal steps commenced only after expiry of the said time limits, Sampension may rely on limitation and inactivity under the general rules, always provided that the period of suspension commencing on 13 March 2013 is included in a determination of whether a claim is statute-barred due to limitation/inactivity.

7. Performance of the Agreement

The Parties undertake to use their best endeavours to implement a settlement out of court in accordance with this Agreement.

If a dispute arises on the interpretation of this Agreement or other issues after the conclusion of this Agreement and a Party wishes that the Parties to this Agreement should reach a common position, such Party may request the Consumer Ombudsman to arrange a meeting, whereupon the Consumer Ombudsman shall arrange such meeting. The Parties shall seek in good faith to come to an agreement on the relevant issue.

8. Press release

The Parties agree to issue a joint press release on conclusion of the Agreement.

9. Condition

The Association will be bound by this Agreement only if it is approved by an extraordinary general meeting of the Association.

2 May 2013

[Signed by the CEO of *Sampension KP Livsforsikring A/S, the Consumer Ombudsman, and others*]

Share sales in Roskilde Bank A/S

Roskilde Bank A/S engaged in aggressive sales campaigns to sell its own shares between January 2006 and August 2008. It was warned repeatedly by the Danish Financial Supervisory Authority (*Finanstilsynet*) that its business conduct was more risky than that of comparable banks in a number of central areas, but this was not made public.

A number of customers complained to the Consumer Ombudsman, who launched an investigation in August 2010. He was afforded access to all relevant documents on request. He found that two share campaigns, in August–September 2006 and March–April 2007, had involved letters sent to a very large number of customers that did not comply with the rules on good practice in section 43 of the Financial Business Act, by emphasising the advantages but not providing a balanced description of the advantages and disadvantages. It was agreed in December 2013 between the Consumer Ombudsman and Finansiel Stabilitet A/S, the publicly-owned banking compensation scheme, that the latter would offer private customers who had bought shares on the basis of the invitation in the campaign letters compensation of 60% of their net loss. It was taken into account that capital losses were suffered on bank shares generally during the relevant period. The settlement agreement set out various criteria under which particular classes of purchasers would qualify. They were given 12 weeks to accept the offer from the date of the offer letter, after which they would be deemed to have refused the offer.

Jyske Bank

Investors started individual actions and an opt-in class action over the purchase of and investment in a product marketed by Jyske Bank called the Jyske Invest Hedge Markedsneutral-Obligationer ('JIHMO'). The Consumer Ombudsman also started enforcement proceedings in the Western High Court. Meetings were held in May–August 2012 between the Consumer Ombudsman, the Investor Association and Jyske Bank that resulted in agreement on three Conditional Offers, each involving different classes of investors.

The Consumer Ombudsman and an attorney acting for investors undertook to send out the Conditional Offers 2 and 1, to collect acceptances, and send them to Jyske Bank before or immediately following the expiry of the time limits for acceptance of the two conditional offers.

The Investor Association undertook to suspend the enrolment of new members as from the date of publication, and to send out the Conditional Offer 1 and convene a general meeting for the purpose of achieving a final and irrevocable dissolution of the Investor Association, which would result in the abatement of the class action (B-284-11) at the Western High Court (*Vestre Landsret*). The parties to the class action agreed that an attempt to reschedule the appeal proceedings (H-65/12) at the Supreme Court (*Højesteret*) must be made immediately following the conclusion of the Agreement, but that the appeal would not be withdrawn until the abatement of the class action at the High Court (B-284-11) was final and any time limit for appeal had expired without the initiation of any appeal proceedings. Additionally, the Association undertook, either prior to or simultaneously with the dissolution of the Investor Association, to authorise the attorney to be in charge of all kinds of practical and administrative initiatives related to the implementation of the Conditional Offer 1 and the abatement of the class action.

The Consumer Ombudsman undertook to withdraw legal actions B-1083-11 and B-1082-11 from the Western High Court on the condition that each party would bear its own costs when and if the eight plaintiffs in action B-1083-11 accepted Conditional Offer 2 and Jyske Bank declared that all the conditions of Conditional Offer 2 had been fulfilled.

Distribution of telephone directories

Many customers were unlawfully charged for so-called 'extra entries' in a telephone directory. When challenged by the Consumer Ombudsman, the company was not able to substantiate that a contractual relationship did in fact exist in all the cases brought forward. The settlement, made in 2009, eventually comprised all consumers who had been unlawfully charged for the extra entries. As part of the settlement the company committed itself to send out an individual letter to the customers affected, thereby also enabling customers who had not lodged a complaint to come forward and claim the money.

C. Finland[42]

The Consumer Ombudsman can initiate a group action for injunction in consumer matters before the Finnish Market Court, which was established to handle issues regarding competition, public procurement and consumer disputes related to general terms and conditions as well as disputes regarding marketing between companies and between authorities and companies. If the Consumer Ombudsman refuses to take action, a registered association representing either of the parties can also file a petition. In addition, foreign authorities and organisations also have the right to initiate such proceedings.

An injunction order is imposed by the Market Court if the trader's marketing practice is considered unfair. Usually, a conditional fine is imposed and has to be paid if the trader does not comply with the Court order. The Court may also order the trader to take corrective measures. The Market Court cannot impose criminal sanctions or award damages in individual cases.

Both parties, the Consumer Ombudsman and the trader, bear their own costs. There is no requirement to define the group represented by the Consumer Ombudsman, since the litigation is related to injunction and no individual damages are awarded.

The Market Court keeps an accurate database of all the cases solved. While the majority of cases handled are related to public procurement and intellectual property disputes, a fair amount of cases related to unfair business practices and consumer protection are brought annually. During the last four years, the Market Court has annually decided on issuing an injunction in approximately 20 cases related to unfair business practices and approximately two cases related to consumer protection. The processing times have decreased under the last few years, from an approximate eight to nine months in 2010 to approximately five to six months in 2015.

The most recent and most notable cases are related to marketing contrary to the Finnish Consumer Protection Act, unfair business practices, misleadingness and acceptability of marketing and fairness of contractual terms.

Cases

Decision no MAO:185/13 relates to marketing contrary to the Consumer Protection Act. In this case, the Consumer Ombudsman had demanded that the Market Court should prohibit Nokian Tyres plc from using a mark specifying the parameters of the tyres in the marketing of the tyres,

---

[42] The author of this section is Johan Pråhl.

if such mark is not clearly differentiated from a similar mark in accordance with the EU regulation no 1222/2009. The Consumer Ombudsman also demanded the injunction to be enforced by a conditional fine of €100,000. In the Market Court's decision an injunction was issued, since the mark used by Nokian Tyres plc was similar to the official EU mark and that a consumer might mistake the mark used by the company for an official mark in accordance with the EU regulation, even though there were slight differences in the styles of the marks. Such misleading nature of marketing is prohibited in the Consumer Protection Act, especially when it has the ability to affect the consumer's purchase decision. The Consumer Ombudsman's demand for a conditional fine was dismissed since Nokian Tyres plc had announced that it had already stopped using the mark in the tyre marketing, and thus there was no need for the fine.

Decision no MAO:372/13. In this case the Market Court addressed the fairness of a consumer contract term used by Oy Parknet Ab, according to which the company has the right to increase the amount of a parking supervisory fee of €40 by 50% after it has fallen due. The Consumer Ombudsman demanded that Oy Parknet Ab should be prohibited from using this term or any similar terms, which entitle the company to charge more for a fee that has fallen due than what they are entitled to according to the Finnish Act on Collecting of Receivables. The Market Court decided to issue an injunction based on the fact that the term used by the company was against the mandatory provisions of the Finnish Interest Act, not the Act on Collecting of Receivables, as claimed by the Consumer Ombudsman. According to the Court, if a term in a consumer contract is unlawful, it is to be deemed unfair from the point of view of consumers, and thus the use of such term is to be prohibited. Since Oy Parknet Ab had already stopped using the unfair contract terms, the demand for a conditional fine was dismissed.

In a more recent decision given in November 2015 (no MAO:829/15) the Market Court addressed the misleadingness of price comparisons and special offer prices used by the sport and recreation equipment retailer XXL Sports & Outdoor Oy. The Consumer Ombudsman demanded that XXL should be prohibited from, inter alia, promising the customers price difference refunds should they find a certain product for sale for a cheaper price somewhere else and thus creating an image that XXL is the most affordable option on the market, and from making groundless statements about certain products being sold for a special offer price, even though the same product is normally sold at the same price. One of the demands was also that XXL should be prohibited from comparing the prices of the products to the recommended retail prices of suppliers and distributors. The Consumer Ombudsman's demands were accepted partially, since the price difference refund promises were not deemed unlawful. Comparing the prices to the recommended retail prices misled the consumers into thinking that the actual price level of the products was higher than it really was, as did the false statements about certain products being for sale for a special price for a limited time. The amount of the conditional fine was halved from the €200,000 demanded by the Consumer Ombudsman, taking into account the solvency and the effectiveness of the fine.

Decision no MAO:18/03 dealt with identification of advertising. A Finnish vehicle inspection company Etelä-Suomen Autokatsastus Oy marketed its services by sending letters to consumers, reminding them about the mandatory inspection and containing an invitation. The letters also included pre-filled bank transfer forms, which the consumers were advised to use to pay for the inspection. The Consumer Ombudsman claimed that such marketing is contrary to the Finnish Consumer Protection Act, since it is not clearly identifiable as an offer made to the consumer, and thus demanded that the company should be prohibited from using such unidentifiable marketing and from including the bank transfer forms, through which the consumer can accept the company's offer, in the marketing letters. The Market Court accepted the Consumer Ombudsman's demands since from the point of view of a consumer the nature of the letters was indeed unclear. The Market Court issued an injunction in accordance with the Consumer Ombudsman's demands and enforced them with a conditional fine of €50,000.

The Market Court has addressed the issues of unfair practice and marketing targeted at children already in the 1980s—in December 1987 the court gave its decision no MT:1987:13, in which the Consumer Ombudsman demanded that McDonald's Oy should be prohibited from using the form of the packaging as a primary message of the advertisement instead of the product itself and from using children in essential roles in the advertisements. The company used a toy boat as a packaging and a tray for a hamburger meal, and the advertisements were focused on the boat, thus bringing the consumers' attention away from the meal itself. In addition to that, children in advertisements were directly asking their parents to buy them the meal, thus urging the children targeted by and affected by the advertisement to act in a similar manner. The Market Court issued an injunction prohibiting the company from using the packaging as the main point in the advertisements and from using the children in advertisements in such central roles, where the children express a direct invitation to purchase the product or otherwise suggests purchasing the product. Use of children as such in the advertisements was not prohibited. This decision was the first case concerning cross-border marketing solved by the Market Court. The television advertisements in the case were broadcast from outside of Finland on behalf of McDonald's System of Europe Inc based in Frankfurt. Since the target of the television advertisements was to facilitate sales of products of McDonald's Oy, and the advertisements were similar to and in a temporal connection with the advertisements on the radio and the on the posters, both ordered by the Finnish McDonald's Oy, the Market Court concluded that the television advertisements were also broadcast on behalf McDonald's Oy.

D. Italy

The decisions of regulatory authorities may affect or involve the rights of a high number of people, who may have been damaged by another entity's unlawful conduct. Some of these are noted below, particularly those acting in sectors where mass protection may be an issue. In general terms, the decision of these authorities may consist of a relevant basis, in terms of evidence, for the affected consumers to bring an action in Court and obtain compensation of the damages suffered.

i. *The Italian Competition Authority*

The *Autorità Garante della Concorrenza e del mercato* (AGCM) is an independent body established by Law no 287 of 1990. The Authority enforces rules against anticompetitive agreements among undertakings, abuses of dominant position, concentrations (eg mergers and acquisitions, joint ventures) as well as misleading advertising, which may create or strengthen dominant positions detrimental to competition. Its decisions are directed only towards the 'damaging' party, and they do not give rise to an automatic 'right' to compensation for damages to all citizens having been affected by the unlawful conducts ascertained by the Authority. However, any citizen (or group of citizens) who considers himself affected by an unlawful conduct, ascertained by a decision of the Authority, may claim compensation for damage before a civil court (but he/she will need to prove both the damages suffered and the causal link between said damages and conduct).

AGCM is granted quite a number of enforcement powers in the interest of consumers. The AGCM can protect consumers against unfair commercial practices used by traders, as well as against unfair contract terms; it has also enforcement powers aimed at shielding micro-enterprises from unfair commercial practices used by traders in case of misleading and illegal comparative business-to-business advertising by competitors. The powers of enforcement granted to AGCM as regards consumer protection have been extended by a statutory instrument (no 21 of 2014) issued as implementation of Directive 2011/83/EU on consumer contract and consumer rights.

The Authority carries out its enquiries against companies on the basis of (i) its own research, (ii) complaints received by private citizens/companies or (iii) self-denunciation by companies.

The AGCM can begin an investigation, acting *ex officio* or pursuant to a complaint lodged by an interested subject or entity (individual consumers or consumer associations, but also public entities). The investigation follows the procedure laid down by specific regulations adopted by the AGCM itself, a procedure aimed at safeguarding the right to be heard and a full scrutiny of the evidence produced. During the investigation, interim measures can be issued with a view to halting temporarily unfair commercial practices, insofar as reasons of urgency make that advisable. If the outcome of the investigation is against the trader, the AGCM shall issue a decision by which the trader is ordered to refrain from the unfair commercial practices, and to pay a fine whose amount may range from €5,000 to €5,000,000, depending on the seriousness and the duration of the infringement. Furthermore, the trader can be ordered to give public notice of the decision, for instance having it published in the most appropriate media. Additional penalties can be imposed in case of non-compliance with the decision (or interim measures) issued by AGCM. It is worth mentioning that the investigation conducted by AGCM can be stopped if the trader commits himself to putting an end to his illicit practices, provided that this commitment is deemed to be serious enough and is made known to the public.

Every year this Authority issues several decisions against companies for unfair competition, however without directly granting the consumers any right to compensation.

In 2015 the Authority conducted 123 investigations, of which 104 led to decisions finding infringements of the rules of the Consumer Code and related legislation (73 unfair commercial practices; six misleading and illegal comparative business-to-business advertising; 18 failures to comply with previous decisions issued by the Authority; seven violations of consumer rights pursuant to statutory instrument 21 of 2014). Investigations were begun upon complaints brought by individual consumers in 89 cases and consumer associations in 11 cases; in six cases AGCM acted *ex officio*. The total amount of fines imposed was €32,692,000.

The economic sectors in which infringements were found were: energy and industry, 36%; communications, 29%; financial and insurance sector, 16%; services, 12%; food, pharmaceutical and transportation sectors, 7%.

A recent and significant case regards 'dieselgate'. On 4 August 2016 the Authority issued a decision against Volkswagen for unfair competition. Said decision was grounded on the ascertainment (also due to a self-denunciation of Volkswagen) that around 11 million vehicles sold worldwide were equipped with software, the 'defeat device' in relation to the production of pollution of the same vehicles. Because of this, the Authority condemned the company to a sanction of €5 million. However, said decision has not a direct impact on consumers: each owner of the vehicles equipped with the software could claim compensation for damages within a civil court, supporting his/her claim with what has already been ascertained by the Authority.

As anticipated, a class action is already pending before the Court of Venice and said Authority sanction could have an impact on its final decision on the merits.

ii. The Italian Regulatory Authority for Electricity Gas and Water

The Italian Regulatory Authority for Electricity Gas and Water (AEEGSI) is the independent regulatory body of the energy markets and the integrated water services. It was established by Law no 481 of 14 November 1995, with the purpose of protecting the interests of users and consumers, promoting competition and ensuring efficient, cost-effective and profitable nationwide services with satisfactory quality levels in the electricity and gas sectors.

Amongst its services, it monitors the conditions under which the services are provided, with powers to demand documentation and data, carry out inspections, obtain access to plants and apply sanctions, and to determine those cases in which operators should be required to provide refunds to users and consumers.

Upon its activities, it may sanction companies, but also condemn them to refund their clients amounts they have unlawfully charged. In these latter cases, the clients should receive automatically said refund by those companies (which are obliged to present proof of the refunds to the authority, under penalty of other sanctions).

In such cases, all clients falling within the field of application of the decision of the Authority will benefit from a refund, without the need to file a judicial claim.

Those decisions of the Authority may be encouraged by a single consumer, groups of consumers, or through consumers' associations, who may file a complaint to the Authority (such a complaint must identify an irregular conduct or a violation of the law or any other unclear behaviour; the Authority carries out enquiries, requests clarifications etc and, should it not be satisfied or should it assess a violation, it may sanction the company or order it to refund amounts).

The AEEGSI uses two instruments of collective redresses in the electricity and gas services that it regulates. In addition, AEEGSI operates an effective ADR system for electricity and gas customers (and TLC as well) targeted at individual dispute resolution.

First, both suppliers and DSOs are required to pay automatic compensation to customers when quality standards set by the regulator are broken. In Italy, 155,769 such compensation payments were made in 2016 for breach of the rules on continuity of electricity supply (ie for long interruptions of supply), plus 54,238 for violation of commercial quality standards. When customers are not satisfied by this compensation, they can apply to ADR bodies (such as that of AEEGSI) or courts to ask for additional damage reimbursement.

Table 5.1: Automatic reimbursements to final customers for violation of continuity of supply and commercial quality standards as set by the Energy Regulator AEEGSI[43] (2016)

2016–ELECTRICITY		
	Number	**(M€)**
Long interruptions—low voltage customers	155,769	10.1
Long interruptions medium voltage customers	2,542	2.2

Source: Annual AEEGSI report.   (*continued*)

---

[43] Annual Report (AEEGSI, 2016).

Table 5.1: (*Continued*)

	Number of people repaid	Amount repaid (€ million)
Commercial quality standards violations and economic reimbursements to final customers	18,986	1.7
Low voltage customers		
— Budgeting for execution of works on the BT network in relation to ordinary connections	2,586	
— execution of simple works for ordinary connections	1,965	
— Execution of complex works	391	
— Supply activation	2,424	
— Supply disactivation 5 working days	1,348	
— Reactivation due to default 1 working day	3,888	
— Area of timeliness relating to postponed customer appointments	103	
— Reactivation of supply following fault of the measurement unit	818	
— Communication of the outcome of the verification of the measurement unit 15 working days	702	
— Replacement of the faulty measurement unit 15 working days	79	
— Communication of the outcome of the verification of the supply voltage 20 working days	74	
— Reinstatement of the correct supply voltage 50 working days	134	
— Budgeting for execution of works on the BT network in relation to new permanent ordinary connections	1,418	
— execution of simple works on the BT network in relation to new permanent ordinary connections	1,144	
— execution of complex works on the BT network in relation to new permanent ordinary connections	315	
— Budgeting for execution of works on the BT network in relation to temporary connections	254	
— execution of simple works in relation to temporary connections with maximum power before and after activation within 40kW and maximum distance of 20m from the existing permanent network installation	122	
— execution of simple works in relation to temporary connections with maximum power before and after activation in excess of 40kW and/or distance in excess of 20m from the existing permanent network installatio	7	

(*continued*)

Table 5.1: (*Continued*)

	Number of people repaid	Amount repaid (€ million)
Medium voltage customers		
— Budgeting for execution of work on MT network	199	
— Execution of simple works	6	
— Execution of complex works	3	
— Activation of supply	35	
— Deactivation of supply	58	
— Reactivation of supply consequent to overdue payments 1 working day	63	
— Timeliness range in relation to postponed customer appointments	2	
— Communication of the outcome of the verication of the measurement unit 15 days	27	
— Replacement of the faulty measurement unit 15 working days	3	
— Communication of the outcome of the verification of supply voltage 20 working days	6	
— Reinstatement of correct range of supply voltage 50 working days	0	

Source: Annual AEEGSI Report.

2016–GAS		
	Number of people repaid	Amount repaid (€ million)
Commercial quality standards violations and economic reimbursements to final customers	35,252	1.8
— Budgeting for simple works	5,579	
— Budgeting for complex works	86	
— Execution of simple works	5,131	
— Activation of supply	1,921	
— Deactivation of supply	3,616	
— Reactivation following discontinuation of supply due to overdue payments	3,171	
— Verifications of measurement unit	251	
— Verification of pressure of supply	1	

(*continued*)

Table 5.1: (*Continued*)

2016–GAS	Number of people repaid	Amount repaid (€ million)
— Timeliness range in relation to postponed customer appointments	12,977	
— Reinstantement of the supply due to potential threat to public safety	774	
— Replacement of measurement unit	1	
— Postponed appointments	1,744	
— Reinstatement of compliance pressure value	0	

Second, where AEEGSI has opened regulatory proceedings aimed at the imposition of sanctions against a supplier or DSO, the company may, within 30 days, propose 'commitments' (economic compensation or other) in favour of those customers who were affected by regulation violation, so as to avoid or reduce sanctions from the AEEGSI for violation of the rules.[44] The approval of commitments by the Authority ends the sanctions procedure without proof of the infringement and without the imposition of the sanction. In order for commitments submitted to be eligible, the company has to provide evidence of the end of the misconduct, and must also demonstrate the suitability of the proposed commitments to restore the interest prior to the infringement or to eliminate, at least partially, any direct and immediate consequences of the violation. These features, therefore, ensure that the commitments both protect the public interest in compliance with the regulation and provide for the compensation of private interests affected by the misbehaviour. The fact that the commitments should be able to remove the injurious effects of the offence, namely to restore the interests before the violation, makes this institution a tool capable of satisfying compensatory damages suffered by third parties, in most cases consumers, because of the violation.

Two Examples of Redress Commitments Accepted by AEEGSI

By deliberation 92/2014/S/gas AEEGSI approved the commitments offered by ENI SpA (ENI) in proceedings initiated for delay billing against about 86,000 customers, both the gas and the electricity sector. The measures contained in the commitments provided:

1. compensation of €25 to all customers involved in disruptions for whom, on 31 December 2013, there was a delay billing; another compensation of €10 to customers for whom, on 31 December 2014, there was a further delay billing;

---

[44] The commitments procedure arises under art 45, para 3, of Legislative Decree 93/2011. The proceedings for evaluation of commitments was defined by AEEGSI in decision 14 June 2012, 243/2012/E/com (arts 16 and subsequent of Allegato A to that decision).

2. for all cases of delay billing, automatic extension and interest free instalments (in a number of monthly payments equal to the not issued invoices) on the owed sum, in order to reduce the inconvenience caused to customers;
3. ENI's various initiatives aimed to stimulating the customers self-reading of consumptions;
4. ENI's adherence to the 'Energy Customers Conciliation Service' instituted by the Authority with deliberation 260/2012/E/com.

By deliberation 529/2016/S/eel AEEGSI approved the commitments offered by Acea Energia SpA (Acea Energia) in proceedings initiated for no or late provision of automatic compensation for failure to comply with specific commercial quality standards against about 8,700 customers. The measures contained in the commitments provide:

1. compensation of €15 to customers that in second semester 2012 and year 2013, were compensated over a period of eight months expected by Testo Integrato della Qualità dei servizi di Vendita (TIQV);
2. compensation of €15 to customers that starting from year 2014 had gained the right to compensation provided by article 18 of TIQV until the date of presentation of the commitments and have not received it within eight months expected by article 20 of TIQV.

iii. Institution for the Supervision of Insurance

As of 1 January 2013 the new Insurance Supervisory Authority (IVASS) assumed all the powers, functions and competencies of the former authority ISVAP. Established under Law no 135 of 2012 ratifying, with amendments, Law Decree no 95 of 2012, IVASS is charged with ensuring the stability of the Italian insurance market and the protection of consumers who have suffered damages from the unlawful conduct of insurance companies, agents or brokers.

Complaints can be filed by the policyholder, the insured party, the beneficiary of an insurance contract or the injured party and by consumer organisations with a legitimate interest in protecting consumers.

If IVASS finds out that there has been a breach of the rules in force by the supervised entities, it starts a sanctioning procedure. However, if a violation is identified, the Authority decision does not give all individuals who deem to have suffered damages by said unlawful conduct the right to be compensated: a judicial claim must be filed in order to have that right to compensation recognised.

iv. The Italian Data Protection Authority

This is an independent authority set up to protect fundamental rights and freedoms in connection with the processing of personal data, and to ensure respect for individuals' dignity. It was set up in 1997, when the former Data Protection Act came into force.

Amongst its several functions, it supervises compliance with the provisions protecting privacy and private life; handling claims, reports and complaints lodged by citizens; it may also ban or block processing operations that are liable to cause serious harm to individuals, check, also on citizens' behalf, into the processing operations performed by police and intelligence services and carry out on-the-spot inspections to also access databases directly.

Once a complaint is received, the Authority carries out its enquiries. A mechanism of opting-in/opting-out is not set out, but it may happen that the Authority receives more complaints for the same unlawful behaviour or that a complaint is filed by a group of people allegedly damaged by an unlawful conduct or by a consumers' association. Should the violation be ascertained, the Authority may prevent unlawful data processing and impose sanctions to the damaging party, but it is not endowed with the powers to condemn the same party to refund amounts/to compensate for damages those citizens having been affected by said illicit conduct.

There are no specific rules on 'funding' or 'financing' these procedures, since the damaged party is 'involved' solely at the first stage, when the complaint is filed (this filing does not involve any costs). The damaged party has no more access to the files of the sanctioning procedure, which is confidential (only the person/company under investigation may have access to them). However, all final decisions are made public on the Authority's website.

v. The Italian Central Bank

According to the Italian Consolidated Banking Law, the Bank of Italy (*Banca d'Italia*) oversees the disclosure and the fairness in the relations among banks/other financial intermediaries and their respective customers. Article 128-ter of the Italian Consolidated Banking Law, which entered into force in 2010, provides that the Bank of Italy:

a.   can hinder banks and other financial intermediaries from keeping going with the violations noticed in its control activity related to disclosure and fairness in the relationship among regulated entities and their respective customers;
b.   can order regulated entities to redress customers for sums unduly paid; and
c.   can intimate any further measures required.[45]

An order to redress (under b) above) is issued when, following the controls performed by the Bank of Italy as the Italian Authority responsible for the disclosure and the fairness in the relations among banks/other financial intermediaries and their respective customers, violations emerge that impinge on the customer protection legal framework.

The Bank of Italy can publish on its website any orders issued under article 128-ter of the Italian Consolidated Banking Law—including the order to redress—and may mandate any further publicity needed (eg on newspapers).

Pursuant the law the Bank of Italy is not mandated to define in detail neither the customers to be redressed, nor the amounts to be precisely disgorged to each of them. However, the orders issued so far by the Bank of Italy include a duty for the regulated entity involved to identify in detail the customers to be redressed and the sums to be refunded, and to provide the Bank of Italy with updates on the execution of the order.

Should the regulated entity fail to comply with the order, the Bank of Italy may impose a fine. It is worth noting that the law does not specify whether the customers may sue the regulated entity for being restored solely on the basis of the 'order to redress'.

---

[45] Authors' translation.

Banca d'Italia redress cases

Since 2012, the Bank of Italy has initiated seven proceedings pursuant to article 128-ter of the Italian Consolidated Banking Law, addressed to seven different regulated entities. In four cases, the proceedings had been filed before the issuance of an order to redress because the regulated entity involved promptly refunded their customers, or consented to provide the Bank of Italy with detailed information about their initiatives. It is worth noting that in those cases customers have been granted refunds for a total amount of €692,345.67.

In 2014, the Bank of Italy has issued two redress orders concerning mistakes in the calculation of interest, for a total amount of €118,506,000.

The Bank of Italy, when discharging its supervisory duties under the Italian Consolidated Banking Law, usually asks regulated entities to adopt initiatives in order to refund customers for sums unduly paid, even without initiating a proceeding pursuant to article 128-ter of our Consolidated Banking Law. In 2015, refunds stemming from informal requests by the Bank of Italy totalled around €65,000,000.

---

vi. Evaluation

All these Authorities issue several decisions per year, all published on their respective websites. As noted, the procedure of enquiries which may lead to a condemnation/sanctioning decision is not made public. Moreover, even where Decisions of an Authority found that there was unlawful conduct that may have an impact on a high number of individuals in terms of loss, no information is available about cases where this has led groups of consumers to judicial remedies, apart from those already mentioned above (and the Antitrust Authority decisions).

However, with reference to the Italian Regulatory Authority for Electricity Gas and Water, as noted above, some decisions may have that 'direct impact' on consumers. We mention only two of them as examples. In 2011 the AEEG Authority carried out enquiries against ENI on the basis of a high number of complaints (the number is not available in the final decision) for continuous delays in the recognition and application of tariffs adjustments to its clients. Having ascertained the violation, the Authority condemned ENI to pay a sanction of almost €700,000 and to update and complete all the tariffs adjustments, giving then proof of the fulfilment of both those obligations to the same Authority.

Similarly, in 2011 the AEEG Authority issued a decision condemning 71 water providers to return €55 million to around 11 million consumers, because of the unlawful cashing of amounts as return on capital (*remunerazione del capitale*), for five months, even if those amounts had been abolished by a national referendum. Those companies where thus obliged to refund their respective clients in the bill following the issuance of that decision.

IVASS issues a very high number of sanctioning decisions every year (around 50 advisors are sanctioned, and around 300 sanctions are issued each month). It is thus very difficult to map how many decisions, amongst them all, may directly affect consumers (for example, some sanctions are dealing with irregular data management, some with unfair conduct, some with lack of transparency towards their clients). However, these sanctions, even if adopted after an enquiry conducted upon a consumer's complaint, do not lead to a condemnation of the advisor to refund the damaged party, who must sue the advisor judicially. Up to now, we have not detected any decision of the Authority which has led to a mass litigation phenomenon, where a high number of individuals were involved and decided to file mass claims to Court.

E. United Kingdom

i. Development of Regulatory Redress

The 'regulatory redress' technique is used to a great extent in the UK. It is now a mainstream consideration of many regulatory authorities, as an integral part of their oversight of markets and of the behaviour of traders towards consumers and others. The technique has spread quickly, starting from use by regulatory authorities in particular sectors (financial services, then energy, water, environment and others) and then mandated on a generic basis for consumer trading under the Consumer Rights Act 2015. A redress power was first introduced as part of the major reform of the regulation of financial services in 2000, alongside the creation of a powerful Financial Services Ombudsman (discussed later in this book). The power was significantly upgraded in 2010 as a response to the financial crisis, and was copied into the legislation governing the regulatory system for energy in 2013. In parallel, a movement occurred towards including redress in the functions and hence powers of enforcers responsible for consumer protection generally, and this led to the codification and extension of powers in the Consumer Rights Act 2015, which firmly included redress as one of the 'enhanced consumer rights' powers.

The general development of regulatory policy beyond just 'enforcing' the law and towards ensuring that markets are returned to fair balance after breaches, are continuously monitored, and that consumer confidence in markets is maintained—hence that redress is made where it is due—can be seen to have had a broad development from the 1960s and especially from 2000.[46] A sequence of official Reports gradually shifted the enforcement approaches, policies and duties on almost all of the public regulatory authorities, which has included delivering 'restorative justice' as one of their formal objectives. As a result, most authorities are now delivering mass compensation as standard practice in an increasing number of situations, and are able to do so remarkably quickly, cheaply and effectively.

An important milestone was the 2006 Review by Professor Richard Macrory of regulatory enforcement penalties,[47] which included in its six objectives the aims of eliminating any financial gain or benefit from non-compliance and restoring the harm caused by regulatory non-compliance. Duties on regulators to consider such wide outcomes were

---

[46] For a broad review, see C Hodges, *Law and Corporate Behaviour: Integrating Theories* (n 1).

[47] R Macrory, *Regulatory Justice: making sanctions effective* (HM Treasury, 2006); reprinted in R Macrory, *Regulation, Enforcement and Governance in Environmental Law* (Oxford, Hart Publishing, 2010). Underlying this approach are 'restorative justice' and 'responsive regulation' policies: see I Ayres and J Braithwaite, *Responsive Regulation: Transcending the Deregulation Debate* (Oxford, Oxford University Press, 1992). J Braithwaite, *Restorative Justice and Responsive Regulation* (Oxford, Oxford University Press, 2002). C Hodges, 'Encouraging Enterprise and Rebalancing Risk: Implications of Economic Policy for Regulation, Enforcement and Compensation' [2007] *EBLR* 1231.

included in the Regulatory Enforcement and Sanctions Act 2008 (RESA),[48] together with the ability for individual authorities to be awarded restorative powers as civil sanctions. In the event, that awarding regime was overtaken by later developments that widened the same general approach. Regulators were made subject under RESA to a Regulators' Compliance Code,[49] which included an express aim of eliminating any financial gain or benefit from non-compliance. Although this aim disappeared when the Code was revised and shortened in 2013,[50] there was no change in policy. Indeed, the Enforcement Policies subsequently published by many regulatory and enforcement authorities, as required by the Code,[51] expressly include statements of intention to focus on delivering outcomes and redress.[52]

Under RESA, certain regulators may apply to their minister to be granted general civil sanctions in addition to existing criminal sanctions.[53] The civil sanctions include accepting undertakings to restore the position to what it would have been or to pay money to benefit a person harmed by the offence.[54] Approved regulators may make a 'discretionary requirement', which can include a 'compliance requirement',[55] designed to secure that the offence does not continue or recur,[56] and a 'restoration requirement',[57] to take steps specified by the regulator, within a stated period, designed to secure that the position is restored, so far as possible, to what it would have been if no offence had been committed.[58] The process for issuing discretionary requirements specifies that the regulator should serve a proposed notice, and give an opportunity for the business to make representations, before exercising discretion by issuing a final notice, after which the business may appeal to a tribunal.

---

[48] See J Norris and J Philips, *The Law of Regulatory Enforcement and Sanctions: A Practical Guide* (Oxford, Oxford University Press, 2011). On further implementation see P Rogers, *National enforcement priorities for local authority regulatory services* (Cabinet Office, 2007).

[49] *Regulators' Compliance Code: Statutory Code of Practice for Regulators*, (Department for Business Enterprise and Regulatory Reform, 2007), para 8.3. The Code is made under s 22 of the Legislative and Regulatory Reform Act 2007. As mentioned above, the same approach was previously mandated under 'Purpose (e)' of the purposes of sentencing set out in s 142 of the Criminal Justice Act 2003: 'Any court dealing with an offender in respect of an offence must have regard to the following purposes of sentencing … (e) the making of reparation by offenders to persons affected by their offences.'

[50] *Regulators' Code* (Department for Business Innovation & Skills, 2013).

[51] 2013 Code, para 6.2(d).

[52] For an analysis of various Enforcement Policies see C Hodges, *Law and Corporate Behaviour: Integrating Theories* (n 1).

[53] Empowering Orders may be made by ministerial order under Part 3 of RESA to 118 regulatory bodies and 400 local authorities. The principles that the Government would, in general, observe when considering whether to make Orders under the RESA to provide a regulator with powers to impose certain civil sanctions as an alternative to prosecution were published in: *Written Ministerial Statement—Department for Business, Innovation and Skills: Use of civil sanctions powers contained in the Regulatory Enforcement and Sanctions Act 2008* (Department for Business, Innovation and Skills, November 2012), available at http://www.parliament.uk/documents/commons-vote-office/November_2012/08-11-12/1.BIS-Use-of-Civil-Sanctions-Powers.pdf.

[54] RESA, s 50.

[55] RESA, s 42(3)(b).

[56] *Regulatory Enforcement and Sanctions Act 2008: Guidance to the Act* (BERR, 2008) para 44.

[57] RESA, s 42(2)(c).

[58] *Regulatory Enforcement and Sanctions Act 2008: Guidance to the Act* (BERR, 2008) para 44.

Under an 'enforcement undertaking'[59] a regulator who reasonably suspects that a person has committed an offence may accept an undertaking from that person 'to take such action as may be specified in the undertaking within such period as may be so specified'.[60] The action that a firm can offer to undertake must be:[61]

i.   action to secure that the offence does not continue or recur;
ii. action to secure that the position is, so far as possible, restored to what it would have been if the offence had not been committed;
iii. action (including the payment of a sum of money) to benefit any person affected by the offence; or
iv. action of a prescribed description.

Thus, an enforcement undertaking could provide for reimbursement, compensation to be paid, or other redress be made. The undertaking mechanism is technically voluntary but can in practice be reached by negotiated agreement, in substitution for the institution of a prosecution, which would trigger the mandatory compensation order mechanism.

In relation to mass or collective redress, the Coalition Government in 2012 *rejected* a litigation approach to consumer redress (and a collective action procedure) and favoured voluntary redress schemes, ADR, encouraging and backed by new powers for regulators.[62] Although collective litigation was a theoretical option, the government was 'concerned about the scope for such mechanisms to create incentives for intermediaries, the economic cost of such intermediation and the very heavy burden which a proliferation of such cases may impose on businesses.'[63]

In the event, few regulators were granted RESA powers, as the civil sanctions regime was overtaken by a wider regime under the Consumer Rights Act 2015, which we now describe.

ii. The 2015 Consumer Redress Powers

Enforcement powers in relation to consumer protection were codified and updated in the Consumer Rights Act 2015. The basic enforcement powers available to domestic enforcers[64] are as follows. First, there is power to require *the production of information* specified in a notice,[65] for the purpose of ascertaining whether there has been a breach of the enforcer's legislation,[66] either where the enforcer is a market surveillance authority, or where an officer reasonably suspects a breach.[67]

---

[59] RESA, s 50.
[60] ibid, s 50(2).
[61] ibid, s 50(3).
[62] *Civil enforcement remedies: consultation on extending the range of remedies available to public enforcers of consumer law* (Department for Business Innovation and Skills, 2012).
[63] ibid, para 3.10. The exception it made related to competition law, see below.
[64] Domestic enforcers are contrasted with EU enforcers, as defined in Sch 5 arts 3 and 4 respectively.
[65] Consumer Rights Act 2015, Sch 5, art 14.
[66] ibid, Sch 5, art 13(4).
[67] ibid, Sch 5, art 13(5) and (6).

Second, there is a *toolbox of general powers*, which may be exercised subject to specific purposes and in specified circumstances. The toolbox comprises powers to purchase products, to observe carrying on of business, to enter premises without a warrant, to inspect products and take copies of records or evidence, to test equipment, to require the production of documents, to seize and detain goods, to decommission or switch off fixed installations, to break open containers or access electronic devices, to enter premises with warrants, and to require assistance from persons on premises.[68]

Supplementary provisions include an offence of obstruction or of purporting to act as an officer, a right of persons to access seized goods and documents, a requirement for notice to be given of the testing of goods, a right to appeal against detention of goods and documents, and a requirement on officers to pay compensation to any person with an interest in goods seized for loss or damage caused by the seizure or detention if the goods have not disclosed breach and the power was not exercised as a result of any neglect or default of the person seeking compensation.[69]

The Consumer Rights Act 2015 amended Part 8 of the Enterprise Act 2002[70] to allow specified enforcers (and many authorities were designated)[71] to attach remedies focused on behavioural undertakings ('enhanced consumer measures') to Enforcement Orders and undertakings.[72] Where an enforcer accepts an undertaking from a business, the remedies to be attached to the undertaking are to be agreed between the parties. *Enhanced consumer measures* can fall within three categories: the redress category, the compliance category and the choice category.[73]

— *redress*: including (a) measures offering compensation or other redress to consumers who have suffered loss as a result of the conduct which has given rise to the enforcement order or undertaking, (b) offering consumers the option to terminate (but not vary) a contract, and (c) where such consumers cannot be identified, or cannot be identified without disproportionate cost to the subject of the enforcement order or undertaking, measures intended to be in the collective interests of

---

[68]   ibid, Sch 5, arts 19–35.

[69]   ibid, Sch 5, arts 36–42.

[70]   Consumer Rights Act 2015, s 79 and Sch 7.

[71]   The Enterprise Act 2002, s 213 provides for four categories of enforcer: *general* (the Competition and Markets Authority, Trading Standards Services in Great Britain; Department of Enterprise, Trade and Investment in Northern Ireland); *designated* (see SI 2003/1399 as amended SI 2005/917 and SI 2013/478: the Civil Aviation Authority, Director General of Electricity Supply for Northern Ireland, Director General of Gas for Northern Ireland, Ofcom, The Water Services Regulation Authority, The Gas and Electricity Markets Authority, the Information Commissioner, ORR, the Consumers' Association and the Financial Conduct Authority); *community* (a qualified entity for the purposes of the Injunctions Directive EC 98/27); and *CPC* (various bodies designated as national contract points under Regulation (EC) No 2006/2004 on Consumer Protection Cooperation).

[72]   Available under Part 8 of the Enterprise Act 2002, ss 215, 217 and 219. An enforcement order that the infringer stops engaging in the conduct in question is issued by a court, and either a court or an enforcer may accept an undertaking from the business that it will not engage in conduct that involves an infringement. For a useful explanation of the three objectives of redress, compliance and choice, and illustrative caser studies, see *Enhanced Consumer Measures: Guidance for enforcers of consumer law* (Department for Business Innovation & Skills, May 2015).

[73]   Enterprise Act 2008, s 219A, inserted by the Consumer Rights Act 2015, Sch 7, art 8.

consumers. Such measures are subject to a cost proportionality requirement[74] and certain safeguards.[75]

— *compliance*: measures intended to prevent or reduce the risk of the occurrence or repetition of the conduct to which the enforcement order or undertaking relates (including measures with that purpose which may have the effect of improving compliance with consumer law more generally).

— *choice*: measures intended to enable consumers to choose more effectively between persons supplying or seeking to supply goods or services.

It will be noted that these definitions of enhanced consumer measures are deliberately wide and purposive, and allow flexibility for businesses and enforcers in deciding, and negotiating, what actions and undertakings are appropriate in the circumstances in responding to the underlying and future behaviour and in providing redress. However, any enforcement order or undertaking may include only enhanced consumer measures as the court or enforcer considers to be just and reasonable.[76]

In introducing these enhanced consumer remedies, the government sought to encourage businesses to put in place *schemes* aimed at providing redress to consumers collectively when a breach of consumer law arises and causes consumers significant losses.[77] The government cited three examples:

— *Where a trader has access to a list of all customers*, the trader could write to all customers informing them of their right to a sum of money if they send back tear-off slip within a set time period. Terms and conditions should not be complex. The trader would reimburse every consumer who responds within 30 days. *Enforcers would check that letters had been sent out and all claims answered within 30 days.*

— *Where a trader has no list of customers but there is likely to be take-up if advertised*, the trader could take out adverts in national, regional or specialist press. Advertising would be proportionate, targeted and effective. The advert would operate in a similar way as product recall where if people showed they were affected by the issue they would receive a sum of money. Additionally, the availability of redress could be flagged to consumers complaining to the Citizens Advice consumer helpline. *Enforcers would monitor that adverts had been placed and compensation paid to claimants.*

— *Where individual consumers cannot be identified*, however, alternative measures may be effective, such as advertising that consumers (who can prove they were affected by the issue) can claim an agreed sum of money from the company or from an appointed ADR provider or offering discounts to all future consumers for a fixed period of time to mitigate against any financial gain arising from the breach.

---

[74] An enforcement order or undertaking in the redress category may only include redress measures in a loss case and if the court or enforcer is satisfied that the cost of such measures to the subject (excluding administrative costs) is unlikely to be more than the sum of the losses suffered by consumers as a result of the underlying conduct: Enterprise Act 2008, s 219B (2), (4) and (5).

[75] Enterprise Act 2008, s 219C.

[76] Enterprise Act 2008, s 219B(1).

[77] *Civil enforcement remedies: consultation on extending the range of remedies available to public enforcers of consumer law* (Department for Business Innovation & Skills, 5 November 2012).

iii. Redress Powers in Selected Sectors

a. Financial Services[78]

A major reform of financial services regulation was undertaken in 2000 (the 'big bang'). The legislation created the Financial Standards Authority (FSA) as regulator, and included a provision for the Treasury to order the regulator to establish and operate a multi-firm scheme for reviewing past business.[79] That mechanism was cumbersome,[80] and not formally used in the subsequent decade, although a significant number of cases where it might have been used were resolved through settlements that resulted in agreed payment of redress. The authority was reluctant to get involved in mass redress issues[81] and the Labour government did not wish it to get involved. However, pressure to resolve mass cases mounted as the number of complaints to the Financial Ombudsman Service rose in relation to payment protection insurance (PPI) products. In September 2009, the authority set out a proposal for Guidance on the fair assessment and redress of complaints related to sales of PPI, and *rules requiring firms to re-assess*, against the proposed new guidance, complaints about PPI sales.[82] The banks then challenged the Guidance through judicial review, but lost.[83]

The Labour government proposed to introduce a representative claim in the courts in 2009, to be a mechanism of last resort,[84] but it was unacceptable to the Conservative opposition[85] and was dropped in the swift 'wash up' of Parliamentary business when the general election was called in early 2010. However, a proposal to expand the regulator's power to impose a redress solution survived.

---

[78] This summary is from C Hodges, 'Mass Collective Redress: Consumer ADR and Regulatory Techniques' (2015) 23 *European Review of Private Law* 829, which itself draws on Hodges (n 35) and C Hodges, *Law and Corporate Behaviour: Integrating Theories* (n 1), especially 274–301. See earlier C Hodges, 'Developments in Collective Redress in the European Union and United Kingdom 2010' at http://globalclassactions.stanford.edu/sites/default/files/documents/1010%20Class%20Actions%20UK%202010%20Report.pdf.

[79] Financial Services and Markets Act 2000, s 404.

[80] For example, s 404(1)(b) required consumers to have a private law remedy, and the FSA was required to implement detailed rules. The restitutionary powers under ss 382–84 are less unwieldy and were invoked on occasion by the FSA. However, voluntary arrangements were not impeded by such barriers.

[81] The effort involved was minimal compared with that required for private litigation: The Financial Services Authority estimated in 2012 that a typical section 404 case required 0.4FTE of legal work and 0.1 FTE of policy work for a period of around three months. *Impact Assessment. Private Actions in Competition Law: A Consultation on Options for Reform* (Department for Business Innovation & Skills, 2012).

[82] http://www.fsa.gov.uk/pages/Library/Corporate/Annual/ar09_10.shtml. See *Reforming Financial Markets* (HM Treasury, 2009).

[83] *R (on the application of the British Bankers' Association) v Financial Services Authority* [2011] EWHC 999 (Admin).

[84] Financial Services Bill, cl 18–25, which proposed that an individual may bring representative proceedings on behalf of others who are entitled to bring proceedings of the same, similar or related issues of fact or law, subject to the court approval of a collective proceedings order. The court would decide on whether an opt-in or opt-out model would apply. Extensive subsidiary regulations and rules are envisaged: see Draft court rules for collective proceedings by the Civil Justice Council at http://www.civiljusticecouncil.gov.uk/files/CJC_Draft_Rules_for_Collective_Actions_Feb_2010.pdf.

[85] The Labour government was also greatly concerned about introducing a collective action procedure, since it would at that stage have exposed every local government authority to equal pay collective actions. In the subsequent Equality Act, a proposed collective action procedure was dropped, and instead the mechanism that was passed imposed a duty on local authorities to have a stated policy on equal pay, which would equalise pay over time and could be policed through judicial review.

The FCA currently has a sequence of redress powers that support the imperatives for firms to take voluntary actions. First, by 2011 the Authority was empowered with four linked measures to require firms to take pro-active steps to deliver collective redress:[86]

1. an obligation on firms to carry out proactive reviews of their complaints and sales in the complaints handling rules;[87]
2. a requirement that when assessing complaints they take account of decisions of the FOS.[88]
3. requiring firms to provide the FCA with complaints handling data;[89]
4. a requirement for a firm to appoint an 'approved person' with official responsibility for oversight of the firm's compliance with complaints handling rules.[90]

Second, the FCA may apply to the court for a Restitution Order,[91] or use its powers to require restitution itself where it is satisfied that an authorised person has contravened a relevant requirement, or been knowingly concerned in the contravention of such a requirement, and either that profits have accrued to him as a result of the contravention, or that one or more persons have suffered loss or been otherwise adversely affected as a result of the contravention.[92]

Third, the FCA has two procedures for putting in place procedures for handling mass claims, where the regulator considers a widespread problem exists and a court would award redress to consumers.[93] The first of these is under a '*consumer redress scheme*' (section 404) that can apply to multiple firms,[94] and the second is a *single firm scheme* (section 404F(7)).[95]

---

[86] DISP 1.4.2G and DISP 1.10.1R were first introduced in 2007. Then see Consultation Paper CP11/10. By November 2010, published contents covered more than 90% of FOS' caseload, so firms should be able to judge what complaints FOS is likely to uphold.

[87] DISP 1.3.6G. This was first introduced as DISP 1.3.5G in guidance in November 2007, but left it to firms to decide when proactive redress would be appropriate; the September 2011 guidance provided further details of when proactive reviews are required.

[88] Under the guidance in DISP 1.4.2 G 'factors that may be relevant in the assessment of a complaint … include … appropriate analysis of decisions by [FOS] concerning similar complaints received by the respondent …' This refers back to the more general guidance in DISP 1.3.2A G.

[89] The complaints data return form was updated as of 30 June 2016, as part of the changes implemented by PS15/19. The revised form was intended to provide greater transparency for consumers and higher quality of data for FCA supervisory purposes. The FSA had in 2010 identified concerns around firms' quality of complaints handling, and all firms needed to ensure that they focus on improving standards in this area: *Financial Risk Outlook 2010*, FSA, March 2010, 69.

[90] DISP 1.3.7R.

[91] FSMA, ss 382–83. Amounts received by the FCA under restitution orders must be paid or distributed as ordered by the court to multiple 'qualified persons' to whom the profits are rightly attributable, or who have suffered loss. An example is *Financial Services Authority v Anderson* [2010] EWHC 1547 (Civ), in which £115 million was recovered. See Money-Kyrle (n 1).

[92] FSMA, s 384.

[93] FSMA, s 404, The FSA decided not to apply for civil sanction powers under RESA since it concluded that having them would not make a material difference to the effectiveness of its enforcement action.

[94] FSMA, s 404(1) as amended by Financial Services Act 2010, ss 14 and 26(3). The new rules were brought into force from 12 October 2010 by The Financial Services Act 2010 (Commencement No 1 and Transitional Provision) Order 2010/2480. The FSA decided not to apply for civil sanction powers under RESA since it concluded that having them would not make a material difference to the effectiveness of its enforcement action.

[95] FSAM, s 404F(7).

Under either approach, the initial complaint handling and spontaneous repayment is to be undertaken by the relevant firm(s), and dissatisfied consumers may then apply to the Financial Ombudsman Service (FOS). In either case, the FOS's basis of decision is effectively amended by the regulator to that of applying the terms of the scheme.[96] A single firm scheme under section 404F(7) is effected by the FCA altering a firm's permissions or authorisation to operate,[97] and can be done either *at the request of the firm* or on the FCA's initiative. The FCA may include the same requirements on the individual firm as under a section 404 scheme, and apply the Ombudsman's jurisdiction as under section 404B. Public accountability for a redress scheme exists through the regulator, who has to consult on rules before imposing the scheme, and through firms' right of appeal to the Tribunal.

A consumer redress scheme may be ordered where it appears to the FCA that there has been a widespread failure to comply with applicable requirements and as a result, consumers have suffered loss or damage in respect of which, if they brought legal proceedings, a remedy or relief would be available.[98] The regulator can make rules which may include requirements for the firm to:

— investigate whether, on or after a specific date, it has failed to comply with particular requirements that are applicable to an activity it has been carrying on;
— determine whether the failure has caused (or may cause) loss or damage to consumers;
— determine what the redress should be in respect of the failure; and make the redress to the consumers.[99]

The result is that, both under a 'consumer redress scheme' under section 404(1) or a single firm scheme under section 404F(7), a procedure for handling mass claims is put in place. Under this procedure, the initial complaint handling and spontaneous repayment is to be undertaken by the relevant firm(s), and consumers may then apply to the Ombudsman. In either case, the Ombudsman's basis of decision has been effectively amended by the regulator to that of applying the terms of the scheme. The Ombudsman may, of course, consider cases which fall outside the scope of the scheme or variation of permission, on the normal basis (applying the criterion of fairness).

Public accountability for a redress scheme exists through the regulator, who has to consult before imposing the scheme, and through firms' right of appeal to the Tribunal.

---

[96] FSMA, s 404B. The award is subject to the Ombudsman's upper limit, but he may recommend that the firm pay a larger amount: s 404B(5) and (6). The Ombudsman may, of course, consider cases which fall outside the scope of the scheme or variation of permission, on the normal basis (applying the criterion of fairness).

[97] The FCA Register states firm's permissions.

[98] FSMA s 404, as amended by Financial Services Act 2010, s 14: the power for the Authority to make rules requiring each relevant firm (or each relevant firm of a specified description) to establish and operate a consumer redress scheme arises where it appears to the Authority that there has been a widespread failure to comply with applicable requirements and as a result, consumers have suffered loss or damage in respect of which, if they brought legal proceedings, a remedy or relief would be available.

[99] FSMA, s 404 (4)–(7). A firm may apply to the Tribunal for a review of any rules made by the Authority: s 404D. See also *Guidance note No 10* (2010) (The FCA has now issued guidance, the Consumer Redress Schemes Sourcebook (CONRED), that supersedes the Guidance Note), at http://www.fsa.gov.uk/Pages/Library/Policy/Guidance/index.shtml.

Guidance[100] expands on the statute, and states that a consumer redress scheme is a set of rules under which a firm is required to take one or more of the following steps:

— investigate whether, on or after a specific date, it has failed to comply with particular requirements that are applicable to an activity it has been carrying on;
— determine whether the failure has caused (or may cause) loss or damage to consumers;
— determine what the redress should be in respect of the failure; and make the redress to the consumers.

Fourth, it can also be noted that under the FCA's enforcement action leading to a penalty or public censure, the decision-making process for considering the full circumstances of each case when determining whether or not to take action for a financial penalty or public censure lists, among the factors that will be taken into account are any remedial steps that the person has taken in relation to the breach.[101]

In this context, the FCA may be involved in discussions on the appropriateness of voluntary redress schemes created by a regulated firm in relation to one of its activities inside or outside the regulatory perimeter. One example of a voluntary redress scheme covered Interest Rate Hedging Products, and another was the 2016 scheme for small business customers of RBS's Global Restructuring Group.

In a 2016 consultation on its future mission, the FCA confirmed that it sees its role as 'to bring firms which have breached regulatory requirements to account and to ensure that redress follows, so consumers who have suffered because of this breach are compensated.'[102] It summarised its approach thus:

> We believe the financial conduct regulator, alongside the Financial Ombudsman Service and the Financial Services Compensation Scheme, has a role in ensuring consumers can receive redress through cheaper and quicker routes than the courts. We also believe these routes are important for market confidence.
>
> We will use the following criteria to help inform our decisions about whether or not to effect redress:
>
> — how quickly and urgently the redress is needed
> — the number of consumers affected
> — if the activity that led to the harm occurs inside or outside our regulatory perimeter.[103]

Noting that the courts deliver redress too slowly, and that cost issues can deter those harmed from claiming, the FCA said:

> Consumers, firms and regulators judge how successful these alternative routes are based on their ability to deliver fair outcomes more quickly and cheaply than through the courts. We commonly seek injunctions, prosecute and obtain redress for victims of unregulated businesses through the courts. This has been a major part of our work for many years.[104]

---

[100] Guidance note No 10 (2010), available at http://www.fsa.gov.uk/Pages/Library/Policy/Guidance/index.shtml.
[101] *Decision Procedure and Penalties (DEPP) Manual* (Financial Conduct Authority), DEPP 6.2.1G(2)(d).
[102] *Our future Mission* (Financial Conduct Authority, 2016), 27.
[103] ibid, 5.
[104] ibid, 27.

In 2016, the newly created Payment Systems Regulator announced that it would adopt the approach of approving voluntary redress schemes as applied under the Competition Act 1998 (see below), although applying its own enforcement policy.[105]

The 2011 enforcement policy of the Financial Conduct Authority (FCA) included 'in the area of consumer protection, holding firms to account for misconduct and requiring them to make good on the losses they cause consumers.'[106] The FCA said that it would 'require firms to provide prompt and effective redress' and 'ensure that firms are not benefiting from exploitation of market failures'.[107] The authority may place requirements on a firm's permission, and this may affect behaviour and redress. In 2011–12 a total in excess of £150 million was secured by the FSA in redress for consumers, excluding compensation for payment protection insurance.[108]

Redress was again afforded a central place in the FCA's 2016 Consultation on its role.[109] This is worth quoting at length.

Consumer redress

As we know from experience, there are times when the harm caused to consumers through inappropriate provision of financial services should be compensated through the provision of financial redress. This redress can take a number of forms, depending on the facts of the case.

We believe the financial conduct regulator, alongside the Financial Ombudsman Service and the Financial Services Compensation Scheme, has a role in ensuring consumers can receive redress through cheaper and quicker routes than the courts. We also believe these routes are important for market confidence.

We will use the following criteria to help inform our decisions about whether or not to effect redress:

— how quickly and urgently the redress is needed
— the number of consumers affected
— if the activity that led to the harm occurs inside or outside our regulatory perimeter.

…

---

[105] *Approval of voluntary redress schemes under Competition Act 1998* (Payment Systems Regulator, 2016). The Payment Systems Regulator said that it would adopt the *Guidance on the approval of voluntary redress schemes for infringements of competition law* (Competition and Markets Authority, 2015), https://www.gov.uk/government/publications/approval-of-redress-schemes-for-competition-law-infringements, but would apply its own *Administrative Priority Framework*, https://www.psr.org.uk/administrative-priority-framework instead of the Competition and Markets Authority's *Prioritisation Principles*.

[106] *The Financial Conduct Authority: Approach to Regulation* (Financial Services Authority, 2011) para 1.1. The instances cited included personal pensions, mortgage endowment policies, split capital investment trusts and payment protection insurance (PPI). 'Millions of consumers have suffered detriment on a large-scale and, together, the industry has had to make compensation payments of approximately £15 billion, with most PPI redress still to come. Such outcomes would be regarded as unacceptable in other sectors of the economy.'

[107] *The Financial Conduct Authority: Approach to Regulation* (Financial Services Authority, 2011) Ch 1, para 5.40.

[108] *Enforcement Annual Performance Account 2011/12* (FSA, 2012), para 19, at http://www.fsa.gov.uk/static/pubs/annual/ar11-12/enforcement-report.pdf.

[109] *Our future Mission* (FCA, October 2016), https://www.fca.org.uk/news/press-releases/fca-mission-consultation. The subsequent policy, which was more general, was *Our Mission 2017. How we regulate financial services* (FCA, 2017), https://www.fca.org.uk/publication/corporate/our-mission-2017.pdf.

7. Protecting consumers ….

Our role in delivering consumer redress

In financial markets, as with any other market, sometimes things go wrong and a consumer feels that a promise has not been kept or they have been unfairly treated. When this happens consumers can claim redress through the courts if the law has been broken or they have suffered a breach of contract. But such claims can take time, be expensive to pursue and involve complex issues of law and fact.[110] Some consumers, particularly the most vulnerable, will not seek redress through the courts as lack of time, money and understanding of the process create large obstacles.

FSMA enables consumers to be given additional protection through simpler and cheaper routes to redress. These alternative routes are also an important source of market confidence and integrity. Consumers are likely to be more willing to engage with financial services if they are confident that they can effectively and quickly challenge unfair treatment and get a remedy. And other firms are likely to have greater confidence that competitors' wrongdoing will be exposed through easy-to-access systems for redress. Consumers, firms and regulators judge how successful these alternative routes are based on their ability to deliver fair outcomes more quickly and cheaply than through the courts. We commonly seek injunctions, prosecute and obtain redress for victims of unregulated businesses through the courts. This has been a major part of our work for many years.

In our view, the financial conduct regulator has a role in ensuring that consumers receive redress, although the nature and extent of the role varies depending on the particular type of redress. The way redress can be provided is varied:

— complaints led, such as PPI and the Financial Ombudsman Service
— specific statutory powers, such as consumer redress schemes under FSMA, for example the Arch cru scheme which related to unsuitable advice given to investors in Arch cru funds
— voluntary schemes which can occur when the actual harm comes from a regulated firm undertaking an activity either inside or outside the regulatory perimeter. Examples of a voluntary redress scheme include Interest Rate Hedging Products and when firms agree to pay redress as part of an enforcement settlement, and
— schemes of arrangement under the Companies Act 2006, where we may also use our statutory powers for arrangements made between a company and its creditors to pay redress, such as the scheme set up to deal with mis-selling of card/identity protection by Card Protection Plan

Our role is to bring firms which have breached regulatory requirements to account and to ensure that redress follows, so consumers who have suffered because of this breach are compensated.

Most FCA redress programmes are likely to involve the following key stages:

1. a past business review (PBR), either by the firm or an independent third party, to identify the consumers who might have suffered from the firm's non-compliant conduct and so could be eligible for redress
2. assessing whether redress is required
3. calculating and paying redress

---

[110] Although the small claims court process which deals with cases whose value is £10,000 or less mitigates some of these difficulties.

An FCA redress scheme will typically involve us both setting out the test for whether redress should be paid and the relevant arrangements for calculating and paying it. This may include requiring firms to appoint skilled persons to supervise the scheme. However, individuals can still go to the Financial Ombudsman Service if there is an industry-wide scheme. The Financial Ombudsman Service will decide the complaint based on the scheme's provisions.

Financial Ombudsman Service

In financial services, individual consumers, micro-enterprises, small charities and trusts have the right to complain to the Financial Ombudsman Service if they are unhappy with the way a firm has handled their complaint. Generally, the vast majority of complaints to the Financial Ombudsman Service involve issues that are specific to the individual complainant and do not indicate a wider, systemic problem. There are, however, clear exceptions, such as PPI complaints. Our role is to set the rules that govern how complaints are referred to the Financial Ombudsman Service and what kinds of complaint can be referred to it. We do not get involved in substantively deciding the claims because this is an independent and impartial judgement made by the Financial Ombudsman Service.[111]

FCA and redress schemes

We set the rules for how firms must handle complaints. Effective, accessible and trusted internal complaints systems operated by firms themselves are of fundamental importance to treating consumers fairly. These systems, if set up and run efficiently, remove the need for consumers, firms and regulators to use great resources on more formal and binding redress mechanisms. Firms have a responsibility to take complaints seriously and provide appropriate redress when necessary. Our involvement in these schemes can, however, be more direct, such as using our power to approve voluntary schemes of arrangement set up by firms which have demonstrated anti-competitive behaviour.

We can also require firms to identify customers who have suffered detriment and provide compensation when there has been a widespread or regular failure by firms to comply with their regulatory requirements. We have a statutory duty to supervise the firms we authorise and the power to discipline those which do not comply with their regulatory requirements. An appropriate outcome of this kind of supervision, either through a formal enforcement process or as part of more general supervisory duties, may be a requirement for the firm to offer redress.

We are also involved in voluntary redress schemes which do not involve a direct use of our powers to compel firms to provide redress. These schemes come under our Competition Act powers and allow us to seek agreement from firms to pay redress for breaches of competition law that fall outside our regulatory perimeter. We discuss our approach to such perimeter issues in the next section.

We need to be clear about the scope of the redress exercise and our role in the exercise, both with firms and the wider public. We must also ensure our decisions and requirements are consistent and communicated clearly, and that the affected consumers and firms feel that they have been treated fairly throughout.

---

[111] Although there is some nuance on this point. For example, we have rules on how firms should consider PPI complaints and what redress they should pay and the Financial Ombudsman Service is required to take our rules and guidance into account.

Challenges and issues relating to redress

There are a number of challenges and issues for redress schemes on which we would like views:

How quickly redress is needed – We are more likely to undertake a redress exercise if factors such as the vulnerability of consumers make it more important that they can get redress quickly. Just as our work on the vulnerability of some consumers[112] highlighted the importance of supporting access to financial services, it is equally important to ensure they can get a speedy remedy. It is precisely these consumers that are most likely to have suffered both financially and emotionally from the wrongdoing and who will have greatest need for redress that is both simple to access and quick to provide a remedy. We must seek to ensure our redress schemes are set up where possible to deliver redress faster than available through the courts, given the number of consumers involved.

Number of affected consumers – We will be more likely to make arrangements for providing redress if large numbers of consumers have been affected. An example of this is PPI. Prioritising such large arrangements creates challenges in ensuring valid claims are met, communicating the arrangements to all eligible claimants and ensuring appropriate finality and certainty for firms and claimants on when the scheme will end.

Activity outside our regulatory remit – In the past we have sometimes taken enforcement action where harm has come from regulated firms undertaking unregulated activities, given our remit covers firms' behaviour more generally. However, unless a firm agrees, we are unlikely to be able to deliver a redress scheme if the wrong-doing involves activity outside our regulatory perimeter. Instead, our approach has been to seek to ensure that the firm puts an acceptable voluntary scheme of redress in place.

Communication – In past schemes we have had complaints that we have not been clear at the start about how long the redress exercise will take, who it will cover and its basis within our powers. In future we will communicate this information clearly at the outset. Because many financial products are long-term there are challenges in informing as many potential complainants as possible about the scheme. If, for example, a particular product was mis-sold many years ago, a consumer may no longer have the evidence. Ensuring comprehensive, accurate and widespread communication is a role for firms and us, but other organisations, such as consumer organisations, also have an influential role to play.

Treatment of individual complainants

Despite the FCA or firms employing independent reviewers, some complainants still feel that the redress procedure is not transparent enough and does not give them the same level of personal attention they would get from the individual complaint procedure through the Financial Ombudsman Service or courts. We welcome feedback on how we could improve how consumers feel about the redress process without reducing its relative speed and low cost.

13. Our approach to enforcement

Our public sanctions must also encourage or require full remedy of both the causes and the consequences of misconduct, including for customers or other affected victims. When we assess sanctions and penalties we take into account how much someone has cooperated with us, is prepared to acknowledge what has gone wrong and to remediate the causes and address all the consequences, including through paying redress.

---

[112] FCA Occasional Paper 8 (2015).

In the decade in which the original powers under FSMA 2000 applied, redress was paid in a number of significant cases that resulted from enforcement action by the FSA,[113] usually as a result of agreed settlements and any redress element was given little publicity, so little information is identifiable.[114] Cases often involved a voluntary agreement to pay redress rather than being agreed as part of the settlement of official action (such as in the Abbey case). Over time, the FSA became keener to publicise the redress element of a settlement.[115]

Major cases are listed in the Annex to this book. Cases listed there in 2016 and 2017 involve £1.3 billion in redress.

As noted above, a new regulatory regime was adopted from 2010, after which a number of cases were resolved through the intervention of the regulator with firms, in different ways. The amount of redress the firm has to pay can be well in excess of the fine.[116] First, a series of cases was dealt with under the *single firm scheme* of section 404F(7).

Financial services single firm schemes: section 404F(7)

The interest rate applied to Halifax tracker mortgages was Bank of England base rate plus a percentage, which varied. The regulator considered that the variations were applied in a questionable way. The regulator reached agreement with the Bank of Scotland, the owner of the firm involved, that letters were to be sent to all customers and that it would automatically compensate some borrowers.[117] Possibly £20 million was paid in compensation fairly quickly and without any consumers having to complain.[118] Significantly, the FSA agreed the scope of the compensation programme with the bank. That formal agreement therefore pre-empted other litigation.

Welcome Financial Services Ltd got into severe financial difficulties after mis-selling PPI. It reached an agreement with the Financial Services Compensation Scheme and the FSA.

---

[113] See Egg Banking (PPI misselling, Dec 08), see para 2.6(5), at http://www.fsa.gov.uk/pubs/final/egg.pdf; AWD Chase de Vere (unsuitable advice regarding its pension transfer, pension annuity and income withdrawal business, Nov 08), see para 2.5(4), at http://www.fsa.gov.uk/pubs/final/awd.pdf; Alliance and Leicester (PPI misspelling, Oct 08), see para 2.7(5), at http://www.fsa.gov.uk/pubs/final/alliance_leicester.pdf; GE Capital Bank (PPI misspelling, Jan 07), see paras 2.4 and 2.6, at http://www.fsa.gov.uk/pubs/final/gecb.pdf;

Abbey National (complaints mishandling, May 05), see para 2.9(1), at http://www.fsa.gov.uk/pubs/final/abbey_25may05.pdf; Capita Trust Company (precipice bonds misspelling, October 04), see para 2.9(3), at http://www.fsa.gov.uk/pubs/final/capita_20oct04.pdf.

[114] Note that redress can also be agreed with a firm without preceding enforcement action.

[115] See recently *Enforcement Annual Performance Account 2010/11* (FSA, 2011) para 21, at http://www.fsa.gov.uk/pubs/annual/ar10_11/enforcement_report.pdf.

[116] See eg the CPP press release: http://www.fsa.gov.uk/library/communication/pr/2012/102.shtml. In 2012 the FCA secured over £150 million in redress for consumers.

[117] See paras 10–18 of the October 2012 BoS Final Notice for details re the SVR and cap issue. The firm was fined for its failure to keep accurate records which had affected the compensation programme: https://www.fca.org.uk/publication/final-notices/bank-of-scotland.pdf. Details of the compensation programme can also be found in this document, which describes the requirements included in the firm's permission ie the variation of permission: http://www.fsa.gov.uk/pubs/other/vvop.pdf.

[118] The Notice mentions that £20 million was erroneously paid out to customers and the firm reportedly stated that it would set aside £500 million for compensation: https://www.lovemoney.com/news/11197/halifax-to-pay-500m-to-overcharged-customers-.

Three arrangements related to the manager and two depositaries involved in Arch Cru funds, which promised high returns and were in fact speculative investments made through Guernsey. The facts were complicated and there was no proof that the managers, Capita, had done anything wrong. However, the following variations in permissions providing compensation arrangements were agreed: Capita Financial Managers Ltd agreed voluntarily to contribute (ie £32 million towards £54 million payment) to compensation without admission of liability,[119] together with HSBC, depositary of one of the funds; and BNY Mellon, depositary of another of the funds.

Second, a *consumer redress scheme* was made under section 404 in relation to intermediaries involved in Arch Cru funds.[120] Third, various *other arrangements* were agreed 'in the shadow' of the rules, without formal powers being invoked. The National Audit Office commented with approval in 2016 on the extent to which the FCA had encouraged firms to enter voluntary redress arrangements, whereby firms accept terms of redress agreed with the FCA.[121] It gave the example of redress in relation to interest rate hedging products for businesses. Between April 2014 and November 2015, the FCA established 21 informal redress schemes, which it estimates provided £131 million in compensation to consumers.[122]

Financial services voluntary redress arrangements

IRHPs

Interest rate hedging products (IRHPs) were sold to small and medium sized firms. An FSA review in 2012 found serious failings in the sale of IRHPs by four banks. After discussions, those four banks, followed by nine others, had agreed to review their sales. A pilot review of sales to 'non-sophisticated' customers from the first four banks found that over 90% did not comply with one or more regulatory requirements, and that the involvement of independent reviewers plays a vital role in ensuring that outcomes for customers are fair and reasonable. The banks undertook to continue their internal reviews and to achieve fair and reasonable redress in each non-compliant case, according to a set of principles about outcomes, depending on whether the customer would have purchased the same product in any event, or would not have done so, or would have purchased a different product.[123]

ATMs

Customers withdrawing cash from automatic telling machines (ATMs) might walk away from the ATM leaving the money behind, after which the machine swallowed it and the customer's

---

[119] See Capita FML Final Notice dated Nov 2012: https://www.fca.org.uk/publication/final-notices/capita-financial-managers.pdf.

[120] *Consumer redress scheme in respect of unsuitable advice to invest in Arch cru funds: Consultation Paper* (FSA, CP12/9, April 2012), available at http://www.fsa.gov.uk/static/pubs/cp/cp12-09.pdf.

[121] *Financial services mis-selling: regulation and redress* (National Audit Office, 2016) HC Paper No 851, para 4.5.

[122] This excludes the interest rate hedging products scheme and other schemes which were established in 2013.

[123] *Interest Rate Hedging Products. Pilot Findings* (FSA, 31 January 2013), http://www.fsa.gov.uk/static/pubs/other/interest-rate-swaps-2013.pdf.

account remained debited. A voluntary arrangement was applied by retail banks to credit relevant customers in relation to ATM withdrawals covering a certain period from 2009 and the date of new rules. It appears that the banks' voluntary action occurred after regulators approached the banks against the background of the regulator's powers to go further.

Payday Loans

CFO Lending Limited (CFO) launched a platform in 2009 for High Cost Short Terms Credit ('payday loans'). It traded as Payday First, Flexible First, Money resolve, Paycfo, Payday Advance and Payday Credit. After widespread concern about firms in this market, and an investigation by the FCA, in 2014 HCSTC providers Wonga Group Limited, Ariste Holding Limited and CFO voluntarily agreed to stop seeking to collect outstanding debts. CFO was required to carry out an independent review to investigate whether its debt collection practices and automatic customer balance calculations had caused loss to its customers.

The investigations determined that CFO had engaged in a series of unfair practices, dating back to 2009. Failings included:

— The firm's systems not showing the correct loan balances for customers, so that some customers ended up repaying more money than they owed
— Misusing customers' banking information to take payments without permission
— Making excessive use of continuous payment authorities (CPAs) to collect outstanding balances from customers. In many cases, the firm did so where it had reason to believe or suspect that the customer was in financial difficulty
— Failing to treat customers in financial difficulties with due forbearance, including refusing reasonable repayment plans suggested by customers and their advisers
— Sending threatening and misleading letters, texts and emails to customers
— Routinely reporting inaccurate information about customers to credit reference agencies
— Failing to assess the affordability of guarantor loans for customer.

CFO entered a redress scheme agreement with the FCA in September 2016 to provide over £34 million in redress to nearly 100,000 customers, comprising writing off £31.9 million in outstanding balances and making £2.9 million in cash payments to customers.[124]

Further Cases

1. In 2014, the FCA fined Credit Suisse International £2,398,100 and Yorkshire Building Society £1,429,000 for failing to ensure that promotions of a structured product were clear, fair and not misleading, since the financial promotions highlighted the maximum return whilst the chances of investors receiving it were 'close to zero'.[125] Both companies agreed to contact customers who bought the product between 1 November 2009 and 17 June 2012 to offer them the chance to exit the product without penalty and with interest paid up to the date of exit.[126]

---

[124] Press release, 'Payday firm CFO Lending to pay £34 million redress' (FCA, 2016), https://www.fca.org.uk/news/press-releases/payday-firm-cfo-lending-pay-34-million-redress.

[125] The Cliquet product, which was designed to provide capital protection and a guaranteed minimum return with potential for significantly greater return if the FTSE 100 performed consistently well. The fines were set to reflect settlement by the banks at an early stage (Stage 1 of the prescribed procedure), therefore qualifying for a 30% discount.

[126] FCA Press release at http://www.fca.org.uk/news/fca-fines-credit-suisse-and-yorkshire-building-society-for-financial-promotions-failures.

2. In 2015, customers of Affinion International Limited approved a compensation scheme agreed voluntarily by the company and the FCA in relation to various card security products sold from 2005 at an average cost of £25 each.[127] The High Court approved the scheme, and it was closed in March 2016, after £108.2 million of compensation had been to 533,000 claimants, an average of £203 per claim.[128]

3. In November 2016, Motormile Finance UK Ltd, a debt purchase and collections firm, entered into an agreement with the FCA to provide redress to more than 500,000 customers for historic failures in its due diligence and collections process.[129] Its inadequate systems and controls produced failure to conduct sufficient due diligence upon the purchase of a debt portfolio to be satisfied that the sums due under customer loan agreements were correct. This in turn led to unfair and unsuitable customer contact for recovery of those sums. The redress was £154,000 in cash payments to customers and the writing-off of £414 million of debt where the firm was unable to evidence the outstanding debt balance is correct and properly due. Additionally, in February 2015, the FCA appointed a skilled person to conduct a review of Motormile's (which also trades as MMF, MMF Debt Purchase and MMF UK) existing loan portfolios and collections processes, including its due diligence. Motormile had since amended its processes, systems and controls to mitigate the risks identified. It had also implemented major changes including a bespoke new IT system and the appointment of a new Chief Executive Officer, which the FCA considered should be sufficient to ensure compliant standards are maintained. Customers did not need to take any action, as MMF would contact affected customers by February 2017, and set up a dedicated page on their website to provide further information to customers.[130]

4. RBS established to a voluntary redress scheme for small businesses (SMEs, as opposed to consumers), following its treatment of SMEs in financial difficulty, leading to allegations of excessive and aggressive charging that forced some businesses unnecessarily into insolvency.[131] In January 2014, the FCA appointed Promontory as a skilled person under section 166 of the Financial Services and Markets Act 2000 to review RBS's treatment of SME customers transferred to its Global Restructuring Group (GRG) between 2008 and 2013. Promontory, with the assistance of its sub-contractor Mazars, provided its final report to the FCA in September 2016, and identified a number of areas of inappropriate treatment of customers, some of which were systematic. After discussions with the FCA (the key aspects of the activity were not directly subject to FCA regulation),[132] the bank issued a public apology in November 2016 and created an independent complaints process overseen by a retired High Court judge and instigated an automatic refund for complex fees charged to SME customers in GRG, estimated to amount to approximately £400 million to be paid in Q4 2016.[133]

---

[127] See *Compensation—card security product holders invited to vote on scheme* (FCA, 2015), at https://www.fca.org.uk/news/affinion-scheme-for-card-security-product-holders.

[128] Compensation Scheme results - https://www.fca.org.uk/news/news-stories/card-security-product-holders-compensation-scheme-now-closed.

[129] Press release, 2 November 2016, https://www.fca.org.uk/news/press-releases/debt-purchaser-motormile-finance-agrees-redress-package.

[130] http://www.mmile.com/RedressProgramme.aspx.

[131] Press release, 8 November 2016, https://www.fca.org.uk/news/press-releases/review-royal-bank-scotland-treatment-customers-referred-global-restructuring-group.

[132] House of Commons Treasury Committee, oral evidence of Financial Conduct Authority, 8 November 2016, HC 812.

[133] Press release, 8 November 2016, http://www.rbs.com/news/2016/november/GRG.html.

Regulatory Guidance and Redress

The Financial Conduct Authority issued a guidance consultation (GC16/6) in late 2016 on the fair treatment of mortgage customers in 'payment shortfall', or arrears.[134]

In June 2010, the Financial Services Authority introduced a rule that firms must not automatically capitalise a payment shortfall where the impact on the customer would be material.[135] The FCA subsequently identified that some lenders automatically included customer arrears balances within their monthly mortgage payments.

It published a case study drawing attention to the practice, which it estimated potentially affected 750,000 customers. It consulted on rule changes, but also issued a remedial framework that firms could apply voluntarily, against the stated expectation that firms should start identifying affected customers and then contact them, in advance of the final guidance.

Voluntary Redress

1. HSBC voluntarily agreed in January 2017 to set up a redress scheme for customers who may have suffered detriment by paying an unreasonable debt collection charge imposed by HFC Bank Ltd (HFC) and John Lewis Financial Services Limited (JLFS), the Financial Conduct Authority (FCA) has announced today. Both HFC and JLFS are now part of HSBC Bank Plc.[136]

2. In the first use of powers under FSMA section 384 to require a listed company to pay compensation, Tesco plc and Tesco Stores Limited (Tesco) agreed in July 2016 that they committed market abuse in relation to a trading update published on 29 August 2014, which gave a false or misleading impression about the value of publicly traded Tesco shares and bonds. Tesco agreed to pay compensation to investors who purchased Tesco shares and bonds on or after 29 August 2014 and who still held those securities when the statement was corrected on 22 September 2014.[137] The scheme would to be launched by 31 August 2017, administered by KPMG,[138] and accepted claims until 22 February 2018. About 10,000 retail and institutional eligible investors would be eligible for compensation, who between them purchased approximately 320 million shares during the period. Each net purchaser was entitled to compensation of 24.5 pence per share purchased. The FCA estimated that the amount of compensation would be £85 million, plus interest.

3. As part of the FCA's 'High Cost Credit Review',[139] and after working with the FCA since 2014, BrightHouse undertook in October 2017 to pay over £14.8 million (in the form

---

[134] *FCA to consult on mortgage payment shortfall remediation guidance*, Rosling King LLP, 17 November 2016.

[135] Mortgages and Home Finance: Conduct of Business Sourcebook (MCOB), ch 13.

[136] Press release, 'HSBC voluntarily agrees to provide approximately £4m redress for historical debt collection practices' FCA, 20 January 2017, https://www.fca.org.uk/news/press-releases/hsbc-voluntarily-agrees-provide-approximately-4m-redress-historical-debt.

[137] Final Notice, Financial Conduct Authority, 28 March 2017, which set out agreed details of the infringement and the scheme. See also press release, 'Tesco to pay redress for market abuse' FCA, 28 March 2017, https://www.fca.org.uk/news/press-releases/tesco-pay-redress-market-abuse.

[138] An online claims portal was established for claimants, who were required to provide identification documents, a bank account statement for the account to which payment was requested, and evidence of the transactions, eg broker statements and contract notes.

[139] See https://www.fca.org.uk/publications/feedback-statements/fs17-2-high-cost-credit.

of cash payments and balance adjustments) to 249,000 customers in respect of 384,000 agreements for lending which may not have been affordable and payments which should have been refunded.[140] The rent-to-own firm provided household goods to customers on hire purchase agreements.

In response to these concerns that the firm's lending application affordability assessment processes and collections processes did not always deliver good outcomes for customers particularly those who were at a higher risk of falling into financial difficulty, BrightHouse undertook an extensive programme of work to improve its lending application assessment to ensure that loans are affordable and customers are treated fairly throughout the collections process, including revising its late payment fee structure.

   In addition, BrightHouse has identified customers that may have been treated unfairly where its processes fell short of FCA expectations and has committed to putting things right for these customers.

   The firm proposed redress for customers in two sets of circumstances:

— customers whose circumstances had not been assessed properly at the outset of the loan to determine whether they could afford it and may have had difficulty making payments. Customers who handed back the goods will be paid back the interest and fees charged under the agreement, plus compensatory interest of 8%. Customers who retained the goods would have their balances written off. This redress totals around £10.1 million for 114,000 agreements entered into between 1 April 2014 and 30 September 2016, covering 81,000 customers.

— customers who made the first payment due under an agreement with the firm which was cancelled prior to the delivery of the goods. This first payment was not returned to all customers. BrightHouse agreed to refund this first payment plus pay compensatory interest of 8%. This redress totals around £4.7 million for 270,000 agreements entered into after 1 April 2010 covering 181,000 customers.

BrightHouse agreed to write to all affected customers, some of whom are affected by both sets of circumstances, to explain the refund or balance adjustment that they will receive. Customers were advised by the FCA that they did not need to take any action until they were contacted by BrightHouse.

b. Communications

The Office of Communications (Ofcom) has a number of means that clearly incentivise the making of redress by suppliers.[141] Consumer complaints are referred to an approved ADR body. A notification of contravention of conditions by a provider of electronic communications networks or services is to include not just the condition contravened but must also specify a period within which the provider may address the contravention and

---

[140] Press release, 'Rent-to-own provider BrightHouse to provide over £14.8 million in redress to around 249,000 customers' Financial Conduct Authority, 24 October 2017.

[141] See *Speech by Ed Richards*, Chief Executive of Ofcom, 16 September 2013, specifically highlighting redress and ADR for consumers.

remedy its consequences.[142] The 2011 Penalty Guidelines include 'any steps taken for reme-
dying the consequences of the contravention' as one of the matters to be taken into account
in establishing a penalty.[143]

The approach of combining enforcement and restitutionary compensation was adopted,
even if unintentionally, by the UK's Ofcom in its response to a GMTV consumer overcharge
'skimming off'.[144]

Case study: GMTV competitions

The television channel GMTV Ltd included viewer competitions in its programmes between
August 2003 and February 2007. The communications regulator, Ofcom, found GMTV to be in
breach of various provisions of the Broadcasting Code (not conducting competitions fairly, prizes
should be described accurately, and making rules clear and appropriately made known) and the
ITC Programme Code (not retaining control of and responsibility for the service arrangements,
including all matters relating to their content). Ofcom imposed a fine of £2,000,000 and required
GMTV to broadcast a statement of Ofcom's findings on three occasions.

In its decision,[145] Ofcom stated that the financial penalty would have been higher had
GMTV not put in place such an extensive programme of reparations and remedies. These
included that GMTV did not intend its competitions to be conducted in a way that was not
compliant with the relevant Codes. GMTV co-operated willingly and fully with Ofcom's investigation and had taken extensive steps to remedy the consequences of the breaches. These
included:

— the decision by its Managing Director to take full responsibility for GMTV's failures and
  therefore to resign from his post, along with the Head of Competitions;
— offering refunds on a potential 25 million entries, a number which it believed was 'certainly
  far higher than the number of people who would have actually been disenfranchised';
— setting up a Freephone number for viewers to request a claim form, which could also be
  downloaded from its website;
— promoting the refunds every day on GMTV for a five-week period and taking out advertising
  for the refunds in national and regional newspapers;
— holding 250 new free prize draws, each with a £10,000 prize, for all entrants on the refund
  database, at a total cost of £2.5 million; and
— making a £250,000 donation to the children's charity ChildLine, to take account of the data
  it had not been able to retrieve.

In addition to the reparations and remedies, GMTV had introduced improved internal codes of
conduct and compliance for any future premium rate activities.

---

[142] Communications Act 2003, s94.
[143] *Penalty Guidelines* (Ofcom, 2011), para 4 (iv).
[144] A similar approach was adopted in a number of subsequent similar cases against other companies, see
Sanctions Committee Adjudications dated 8 May 2008 at http://www.ofcom.org.uk/tv/obb/ocsc_adjud visited
26 May 2008.
[145] Decision of Ofcom Content Sanctions Committee, 26 September 2007 at www.ofcom.org.uk.

The result in this case should have produced,[146] as a result of voluntary action by the company, restitution of loss to consumers, an improved system to guard against future non-compliance, retribution for those held responsible, and imposition of a public penalty. The public penalty was based on both responsive and restorative approaches: if the risk of future infringement was low, there was a low need for individual deterrence. General deterrence was provided by swift publication of these actions. But this approach would not be possible under an approach in which general deterrence is deemed to be the paramount enforcement goal, as it is in competition policy. This begs the question of which approach is more just and more effective in controlling behaviour. The individual approach is clearly more just. The behavioural outcome could only be answered by lengthy empirical observation, not by assertion.

> Ofcom required a telephone company that had been billing customers for services that had been cancelled to repay the customers and to pay compensation where it was appropriate. As a result, some 62,000 customers received a total of around £2.5 million in refunds and goodwill payments. Ofcom also imposed a fine of over £3 million.[147]

c. Gas and Electricity

The Gas and Electricity Markets Authority, acting through the Office of Gas and Electricity Markets (Ofgem),[148] operates a licensing regime for suppliers. Ofgem's priority is always putting things right for those consumers directly harmed, including doing this quickly (including without taking formal enforcement action).[149] Redress may arguably

---

[146] As at 2008, it appeared that GMTV may not have repaid consumers in full: see R Taylor at www.ofcomwatch.co.uk, visited 11 May 2008. The lesson to be drawn would be that the regulator should have the power to accept enforceable undertakings or some other power so as to oversee the repayment.

[147] *Consultation on a proposed new power for Ofgem to compel regulated energy businesses to provide redress to consumers* (Department of Energy and Climate Change, 2012) para 13.

[148] See http://www.ofgem.gov.uk.

[149] The Consultation *Allocation of voluntary redress payments in the context of enforcement cases* (Ofgem, June 2016) said: '1.6. The last few years have seen Ofgem conduct more investigations, and there has been a corresponding increase in the number and value of both direct compensation to affected consumers and voluntary redress payments to charities, trusts and organisations. For example, during the four financial years from 2010–11 to 2013–14, compensation paid directly to affected consumers and voluntary redress payments to third sector organisations was on average 43.7% of the total penalty value. This figure rose to 93.2% in 2014–15 and effectively 100% in 2015–16.

1.7. The importance of the payments to charities, trusts and organisations can be seen from the numbers of consumers who benefitted. Taking just the financial year 2014-15, our analysis shows that over 218,000 consumers and nearly 600 small and medium enterprises benefitted through support funded by this money. ...

1.13 Over the last two years, we have received a growing amount of feedback on the process of allocation of voluntary redress payments. Feedback has come from several sources, including from attendees at our Enforcement Conference in June 2015, recipients of voluntary redress payments (including through monitoring reports sent to us on the use of the money), potential funding recipients and other third sector stakeholders, and from our regular stakeholder engagement with licensees.

1.14 This feedback has generally been positive, and has been supportive of the extra efforts that Ofgem has made to ensure energy consumers are supported through our approach to voluntary redress payments

be taken into account under the requirement on Ofgem to issue a final compliance order where it is satisfied that a licence holder is, or is likely to be, in contravention of a condition or requirement so as to secure compliance.[150] Ofgem's 2014 Enforcement Guidelines on complaints and investigations cover sanctioning for breaches of licences or licence conditions.[151] Customer complaints are required to be handled by companies under strict complaints handling standards[152] within eight weeks and may then be referred to the Energy Ombudsman.[153]

In order to improve both payment of redress to consumers, and the regulator's leverage in bringing about redress, the Energy Act 2013 copied the regime used in the communications sector and included powers to secure direct redress for customers, whether domestic or businesses, pursuant to breaches of regulatory requirements, through a consumer redress order.[154] Under these provisions, Ofgem is required to give notice to the company and any other affected party at least 21 days before making the order for redress. When giving notice, Ofgem is required to set out which condition has been breached, how in its view the licensee has breached it, and the remedy it deems appropriate. The licence holder has a minimum of 21 days to make representations to Ofgem regarding the proposed order for redress. Enforcement Guidelines set out more details.[155]

In the financial year 2015–16, nearly £43 million was secured as a result of Ofgem enforcement investigations. Almost all that money was paid either as compensation to affected consumers, or through voluntary redress payments where companies allocate redress to charities, trusts or organisations in lieu of paying a financial penalty to HM Treasury.[156] During this period Ofgem completed 13 investigations with an average case length of less than one year.

Ofgem's voluntary redress policy is unique amongst comparable UK economic regulators and has seen over 218,000 domestic consumers and nearly 600 small and medium enterprises benefit through schemes funded by voluntary redress payments in 2014 and 2015 alone.[157]

(i.e. by providing voluntary redress as an option, instead of having all penalties go to Treasury). There have also been suggestions for what we could do to further maximise consumer benefits, which we have taken on board and are now considering.'

[150]   Gas Act 1986, s28 and Electricity Act 1989, s 25.

[151]   *Enforcement Guidelines* (Ofgem, 2014). See also M Forbes, *Review of Ofgem's enforcement activities— consultation on strategic vision, objectives and decision makers* (Ofgem, 2013). See previously *Enforcement Guidelines on Complaints and Investigations* (Ofgem, June 2012).

[152]   The Gas and Electricity (Consumer Complaints Handling Standards) Regulations 2008 (SI 2008/1898).

[153]   See C Hodges, I Benöhr and N Creutzfeldt-Banda (eds), *Consumer ADR in Europe* (Oxford, Hart Publishing, 2012) 307–11.

[154]   As principally set out in the Electricity Act 1989, s 27G, and the Gas Act 1986, s 30G, inserted by the Energy Act 2013, s 144 and Sch 14. See *Consultation on a proposed new power for Ofgem to compel regulated energy businesses to provide redress to consumers* (Department of Energy and Climate Change, 2012), 2D/060.

[155]   *Enforcement Guidelines* (Ofgem, 2014); *The Gas and Electricity Markets Authority's 'Statement of Policy with respect to Financial penalties and Consumer Redress under the Gas Act 1986 and the Electricity Act 1989'* (2014).

[156]   *Ofgem: Enforcement Overview 2015/16* (Ofgem, June 2016), 2.

[157]   *Allocation of voluntary redress payments in the context of enforcement cases* (Ofgem, June 2016) 6.

The 2014 Enforcement Guidelines provide for resolving cases, either before they are open or during an investigation, through 'Alternative Action'.[158] Direct redress and voluntary redress may be applicable to an 'Alternative Action', although Ofgem has no formal powers to impose redress in this instance. This mechanism would result in cessation of a formal investigation without a finding of breach of the regulations.

Ofgem uses similar powers in relation to wholesale transactions. It included a clear incentive for companies to agree restitution in implementation of the EU 'REMIT' Regulation,[159] which includes requirements on market participants to notify the national authority without delay if they reasonably suspect that a wholesale energy market transaction might breach the prohibitions on insider trading or market manipulation, and to publicly disclose inside information in an effective and timely manner.[160] Ofgem's 2013 Statement of Policy included the objectives of ensuring that no profits can be drawn from market abuse, and protecting the interests of consumers in wholesale energy markets and of final consumers of energy, including vulnerable consumers.[161] Ofgem proposed to 'take full account of the particular facts and circumstances of each case when determining whether to impose a financial penalty and/or issue a statement of noncompliance.'[162] Included in the factors relevant to determining the level of penalty were 'the amount of any benefit gained or loss avoided as a result of the breach (financial or otherwise, potential or actual)' and 'the degree of harm or increased cost incurred or potentially incurred by consumers or other market participants *after taking account of any restitution paid to those affected*'.[163] One of the resolution options open to the Authority would be its early resolution Settlement Procedure:

> The aim of settlement is to reach agreement on the nature and extent of breaches, an appropriate level of penalty and, where appropriate, proposals for restitution. Ofgem may agree other terms with the person as part of settlement. Where agreement is reached on the breaches, Ofgem will seek to agree the amount of the financial penalty and/or restitution to those adversely affected.[164]

Private sector bodies can raise or investigate complaints from consumers if they are of wider public interest. Citizens Advice or the Energy Ombudsman are relevant here, and have a Tripartite Agreement with Ofgem to improve coordination and ensure consumers are receiving timely and appropriate redress via our coordinated efforts. Until it ceased in 2014, Consumer Futures successfully negotiated with energy companies to secure redress for consumers, for example, securing payments of £70 million for Npower customers in 2010 when the company made changes to its tariff structure without giving adequate notification to its customers.[165]

---

[158] Enforcement Guidelines (2014), paras 2.9 and 3.26.

[159] Regulation (EU) No 1227/2011 of 25 October 2011 on wholesale energy market integrity and transparency.

[160] ibid, arts 15 and 4.

[161] *Consultation decision—REMIT penalties statement and procedural guidelines* (Ofgem, 2013).

[162] *The Authority's Statement of Policy with respect to financial penalties under REMIT* (Ofgem, 2013) para 3.2.

[163] ibid, para 4.2, emphasis added.

[164] *Proposed Procedural Guidelines on the Authority's use of its Investigatory and Enforcement Powers under REMIT* (Ofgem, 2013) para 8.6.

[165] *Consultation on a proposed new power for Ofgem to compel regulated energy businesses to provide redress to consumers* (Department of Energy and Climate Change, 2012) para 11.

The influence that Ofgem is able to wield, given its ability to amend or remove licences and to attract publicity to energy issues, means that redress can often be achieved through settlement or an informal agreement. A series of cases has been swiftly and effectively resolved by this route in the past four years. The figures for enforcement action alone, apart from a range of other compliance work to put things right for consumers, were recently summarised as follows:

3.6. To give an idea of the numbers of consumers who benefitted from the above voluntary redress payments, our analysis, based on post-allocation monitoring and projections just for cases in 2014 and 2015 that resulted in settlement (excluding alternative action cases), estimates that approximately 522,000 consumers received direct compensation worth a total of £20.1 million and a further £73.5 million was given to charitable organisations.[166] Those charitable recipients used the money to provide support, including providing energy advice services such as advice on energy efficiency, switching and prepayment meters, and the provision of good and services such as home safety checks, emergency heating, methods of alerting consumers when the temperature in their home drops and the installation of insulation and new boilers.11 The work undertaken by charitable organisations as a result of voluntary redress funding ultimately benefited a further 223,000 consumers.[167]

It can be seen from Table 5.2 that whilst there has been a strong shift to achieving redress for consumers, this has been accompanied by a reduction in fines.[168]

Table 5.2: Shifts in fines and voluntary redress involving Ofgem 2010–15

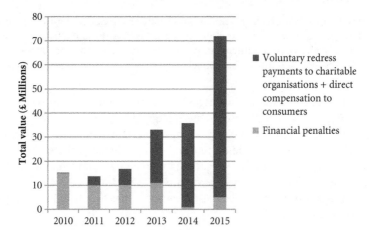

Ofgem started to produce redress outcomes before it was given formal redress power, as a result of its influence, given its ability to amend or remove licences and to attract publicity to energy issues.

---

[166] These figures do not include the £26 million that npower agreed to pay as compensation to customers and to charitable organisations which was announced in December 2015, as that case was not officially closed until January 2016.

[167] *Allocation of voluntary redress payments in the context of enforcement cases* (Ofgem, June 2016).

[168] *Allocation of voluntary redress payments in the context of enforcement cases* (Ofgem, June 2016) fig p 12.

Ofgem issued its first Enforcement Overview in 2015, which identified that redress was used as an enforcement tool, and that redress represented 92.5% of the volume of penalties imposed in 2014/15.[169] In the 13 cases concluded in 2015/16,[170] £43 million was or would be paid out by licensees. Almost all of that money was paid either as compensation to affected consumers, or voluntary redress payments to charitable organisations (along with nominal penalties totalling £15). An additional amount of £3 million was secured through alternative action.[171] Of this £46 million, £26.4 million was or will be made available to compensate directly affected customers (and former customers). Any unclaimed consumer compensation was or will be paid to charitable organisations. The remaining £19.3 million took the form of payments to charities or other third sector organisations in lieu of financial penalties.[172]

More than 630,000 consumers benefitted from remediation schemes set up with money following seven investigations completed in 2015–16 and 12 investigations completed in 2014–15. Of those customers, around two thirds received a direct compensation payment while the remaining third benefitted from projects set up by charities and other third sector organisations who received voluntary redress payments.

Case durations are shown in Table 5.3.

Table 5.3: Duration of Ofgem enforcement cases 2010–15 in months

Financial year	No of cases completed	Shortest	Longest	Average
2010	2	17	61	39
2011	14	4	30	16
2012	4	17	41	25
2013	7	23	55	34
2014	13	3	51	24
2015	13	3	22	11

---

[169] *Enforcement Overview 2014/15* (Ofgem, 2015).

[170] *Enforcement Overview 2015/16* (Ofgem, 2016). See M Canto-Lopez, 'Ofgem's Recent Trends in Enforcement: Settlements, Redress and the Consumer's Interest' (2016) 21(2) *Utilities Law Review* 66.

[171] Where appropriate, voluntary payments to charitable organisations have also formed a part of alternative action work. Perhaps most notably, Ofgem used alternative action to secure a payment of £3 million from National Grid to the fuel poverty charity National Energy Action, because National Grid had failed to meet its target for repairing non-urgent gas escapes on its gas distribution networks. In July 2015, another piece of alternative action work resulted in securing free energy for over 1,000 directly affected customers. The customers received free energy until the supplier involved had fully implemented Energy Ombudsman remedies that had previously been agreed for those customers.

[172] These were paid to entities such as Citizens Advice Scotland, Citizens Advice England and Wales (includes funding for Citizens Advice Bureau programmes such as Energy Best Deal Extra and Energy Best Deal Extra Prepayment meter project), the Carbon Trust, StepChange and Business Debtline.

An example of a CERT Investigation case

In March 2015 Ofgem found Drax and InterGen to have breached the Electricity and Gas (Community Energy Saving Programme) Order. The companies were fined £25 million[173] and £11 million[174] respectively. From these penalties, £26.2 million was allocated to National Energy Action (NEA) in the form of voluntary redress.[175] NEA used these funds to launch the Health and Innovation Programme (HIP) with the aim of bringing affordable warmth to over 6,500 fuel poor and vulnerable households in England, Wales and Scotland.[176]

An example of how Alternative Action is used

In October 2016, Ofgem announced that Co-Operative Energy had agreed to pay £1.8 million to customers affected by issues relating to Co-Operative Energy's implementation of a new IT system.[177] In this instance Ofgem chose not to open a formal investigation into Co-Operative Energy, but did engage with the company to oversee the steps taken to restore customer service levels. Ofgem agreed the compensation package of £1.8 million with Co-Operative Energy. Any compensation that could not be distributed to Co-Operative Energy customers would be allocated to the charity StepChange, to help energy consumers who are in financial difficulties.

Some Ofgem Cases

On 9 March 2012 Ofgem accepted an offer from EDF Energy to invest £4.5 million to help vulnerable customers and consequently reduced a penalty for breach of marketing rules to £1.[178]

In November 2012, Ofgem secured a commitment from E.ON to pay back around £1.4 million (an average rebate of £14.83, including 8% interest) to approximately 94,000 consumers who were incorrectly charged exit fees or overcharged following price rises that were incorrectly implemented too early.[179] In addition, E.ON agreed to make an additional payment of around £300,000 as a goodwill gesture to a consumer fund which they run in partnership with Age UK.[180]

In August 2013 E.ON paid a £500,000 penalty and £2.5 million to benefit customers in fuel poverty after incorrect claims under the Carbon Emissions Reduction Target.[181]

---

[173] https://www.ofgem.gov.uk/publications-and-updates/notice-decision-impose-financial-penalty-following-investigation-compliance-drax-article-141-electricity-and-gas-community-energy-saving-programme-order-2009.

[174] https://www.ofgem.gov.uk/publications-and-updates/notice-decision-impose-financial-penalty-following-investigation-compliance-intergen-article-141-electricity-and-gas-community-energy-saving-programme-order-2009.

[175] Ofgem's first priority in allocating redress is to compensate customers directly affected by the breach identified. In these cases however no customers were directly affected by the breach identified, therefore redress was allocated to charities.

[176] https://www.ofgem.gov.uk/system/files/docs/2016/11/voluntary_redress_consultation_response_-_nea_aug_2016.pdf, 9. More information about the HIP can be found at http://www.nea.org.uk/hip/.

[177] https://www.ofgem.gov.uk/publications-and-updates/co-operative-energy-pay-1-8-million-customer-service-failings.

[178] Details of Ofgem's decision are available at: http://www.ofgem.gov.uk/Media/PressRel/Documents1/EDF%20press%20notice%20March%209%202012.pdf.

[179] Press release, 'Ofgem secures £1.7 million for consumers following E.ON error' (Ofgem, 27 November 2012) http://www.ofgem.gov.uk/Media/PressRel/Documents1/20121127_EON_Press_Release.pdf.

[180] The Engage Fund run in partnership with Age UK Group helps fund services to maximise incomes of older people by providing benefits advice and financial help through benefits health checks carried out either face to face or by telephone in local Age UK offices enabling some to be lifted out of fuel poverty.

[181] *Annual Report and Accounts 2013-14* (Office of Gas and Electricity Markets, 2014) 11.

In October 2013, ScottishPower agreed with Ofgem that it had misled customers in sales approaches, and agreed to pay £7.5 million to around 140,000 vulnerable consumers (identified under the Warm Home Discount Scheme) estimated to be £50 each and establish a £1 million compensation fund for customers to access.[182]

In December 2013, Npower agreed to pay £3.5 million under a similar arrangement after breaches on telesales and face-to-face marketing,[183] and separately apologised to customers and agreed a £1 million payment.[184]

In February 2013, Ofgem called on the energy companies to return credit balances retained after customers had switched suppliers.[185] It estimated 3.5 million domestic and 300,000 business accounts were affected, involving £202 million and £204 million respectively. It issued advice to customers to contact their suppliers, which was given wide publicity.[186]

In July 2014 British Gas repaid £130 to around 4,300 customers (totaling £566,000) and paid £434,000 to the British Gas Energy Trust in relation to a further 1,300 customers it had been unable to trace, following misleading statements that customers would save money by switching.[187]

The Npower group upgraded its computerised billing system, which was used by seven companies in the group, following which major problems occurred, including sending incorrect and late bills. Many customers complained but the companies' complaint handling system was poor.[188] The group acknowledged that its practices fell far short of requirements in relation to its billing and complaints handling, and that it had breached various Standards of Conduct (SLC 25C.5 on treating customers fairly, and SLC 27.17 on provision of final bills) and regulations (3(2), 4(6), 6(1), 7(1)(a)–(b) and 10(2) on complaints handling). Ofgem accepted that Npower had made significant improvements in these areas during the investigation and improved its performance. Ofgem acknowledged that Npower's senior management took action to remedy the contraventions, particularly on the billing issues, and did not consider that Npower's senior management had intentionally contravened the requirements. However, the actions taken were not enough to stop the contraventions from happening, nor did the actions stop them quickly enough to minimise the consumer impact. In late 2015 Npower undertook to take a series of improvement actions, to comply with a series of specific targets, and to make consumer redress payments totalling £26 million. Penalties of £1 each were imposed on seven companies in the group.

[182] Press release, 'ScottishPower agrees to pay customers £8.5 million following Ofgem sales investigation' (Ofgem, 22 October 2013).

[183] Press release, 'Npower agrees to pay customers £3.5 million to help vulnerable customers following Ofgem energy sales investigation' (Ofgem, 20 December 2013).

[184] Press release, 'Npower publishes apology and promises to pay £1m to vulnerable consumers after Ofgem intervened on poor service' (Ofgem, 3 December 2013).

[185] Press release, 'Ofgem calls on suppliers to take action on over £400 million they hold from customers' closed accounts' (Ofgem, 28 February 2014), at https://www.ofgem.gov.uk/press-releases/ofgem-calls-suppliers-take-action-over-%C2%A3400-million-they-hold-customers-closed-accounts.

[186] Press release, 'Closed account balances—advice for consumers' (Ofgem, 28 February 2014), at https://www.ofgem.gov.uk/news/closed-account-balances-%E2%80%93-advice-consumers; 'Energy firms told to return £400m from closed accounts', *BBC News*, 28 February 2014.

[187] Press release, 'British Gas to compensate customers over mis-selling' (Ofgem, 4 July 2014), at https://www.ofgem.gov.uk/news/british-gas-compensate-customers-over-mis-selling.

[188] *Notice of intention to impose a financial penalty pursuant to section 30A(3) of the Gas Act and 27A(3) of the Electricity Act 1989* (Gas and Electricity Markets Authority, 18 December 2015).

Ofgem sets Guaranteed Standards for suppliers, which include customer service standards where suppliers need to visit a customer's premises. Where a supplier fails to meet a performance standard, they must pay compensation to the affected customer. The supplier Guaranteed Standards in force at the time of the failures in question were set under the Gas (Standards of Performance) Regulations 2005 and the Electricity (Standards of Performance) Regulations 2010. Those Regulations were later superceded by the Electricity and Gas (Standards of Performance) (Suppliers) Regulations 2015.

In 2014 E.ON voluntarily informed Ofgem that its agents had missed some appointments with customers, and hadn't then paid compensation to affected customers as required by the Guaranteed Standards. The company and Ofgem worked together to ensure, first, that the supplier improved its customer services processes and would make sure that, when things go wrong, customers receive the compensation they are entitled to; second, that E.ON would pay £1.2 million to affected customers and will pay £1.9 million to energy charities; and third, that the company would also pay £1.9 million to charity to help consumers in need. This includes helping service personnel through National Energy Action's 'Help for Heroes' scheme. The arrangements were announced after the first two actions had been implemented.[189]

The watchdog Consumer Futures can investigate complaints from consumers if they are of wider public interest. It has no legal powers to secure redress on their behalf,[190] but it has successfully negotiated with energy companies to secure redress for consumers, for example, securing payments of £70 million for Npower customers in 2010 when the company made changes to its tariff structure without giving adequate notification to its customers.[191] An example of a case by a predecessor body, Consumer Focus, is given below.

Consumer Focus and Npower

Consumer Focus published this case study in 2012.[192] It argued that all early settlements should be judicially approved by the court, but it can also be argued that various other forms of oversight and approval also exist.

In 2007 the energy group, npower changed the way it applied charges for the first block of higher priced gas units that households paid. These changes were not properly communicated to customers and some 1.8 million customers ended up paying for more of these high priced units than they had expected. Some customers complained to Ofgem, which launched an investigation, and in February 2009 npower was made to repay an average of £6 each to 200,000 customers.

---

[189] Press release, *E.ON pays £3.1m after its agents missed appointments* (Ofgem, 22nd September 2016), https://www.ofgem.gov.uk/publications-and-updates/e-pays-3-1m-after-its-agents-missed-appointments.

[190] See http://www.consumerfutures.org.uk.

[191] *Consultation on a proposed new power for Ofgem to compel regulated energy businesses to provide redress to consumers* (Department of Energy and Climate Change, April 2012) para 11.

[192] *Response to Consultation on Private Actions in Competition law* (Consumer Focus, July 2012).

… Without-prejudice talks with npower were being held concurrently and in February 2010, a Sunday Times article came out which implied that litigation could be on the cards if an agreement was not reached between Consumer Focus and npower. After about four months, npower agreed to calculate each overpayment made by the affected customers. The individual payments ranged from £1– £100 and the total figure to be repaid was £63 million plus VAT.

d. Water

Some regulatory mechanisms do not require any specific power in relation to consumer redress, but have grown out of a general policy of delivering fair services and outcomes to consumers, supported by power to impose penalties under a supervisory licensing regime. Any financial penalties go to HM Treasury rather than being retained by the regulatory authority, whereas various regulators have instead delivered money back to customers.

Ofwat has power under section 22A(1) of the Water Industry Act 1991 (as amended), subject to certain conditions being met, to impose a penalty on a water and sewerage undertaker which Ofwat is satisfied has contravened or is contravening any Condition of its Appointment. Ofwat has used this power in a case in 2014 to impose a nominal fine on the basis of an undertaking by a water company to reduce prices to consumers and make additional payments for the benefit of consumers (see case study).

Ofwat Cases

On 9 June 2011 Ofwat served a Notice on Thames Water Utilities Limited (Thames Water)[193] stating that it appeared to Ofwat that, when it submitted information on 11 June 2010, Thames Water may have contravened Conditions of its Appointment (namely Condition J and/or M in respect of regulatory reporting), and requiring Thames Water to produce certain documents and to furnish certain information specified and described in the Section 203 Notice. After considering the position, including representations by Thames Water, Ofwat issued a Notice stating that it was satisfied that Thames Water had submitted unreliable and inaccurate information on 11 June 2010 in its June return and thereby contravened Condition J of its Conditions of Appointment. In subsequent discussions, Thames Water committed to a package of measures for its customers. Ofwat gave notice of its intended actions,[194] and received representations from two stakeholders (the Consumer Council for Water and an individual consultant), both supportive of the proposed action.

On 22 July 2014, Ofwat issued a Notice[195] stating that it was satisfied that the measures pledged by Thames Water (together with a nominal penalty of £1) would be of greater benefit to customers

---

[193] Under the Water Industry Act 1991, s 203(2).

[194] Notice in writing dated 5 June 2014, under and in accordance with s 22A(4) WIA91, of its proposal to impose a nominal penalty of £1 on Thames Water.

[195] Available at http://www.ofwat.gov.uk/wp-content/uploads/2016/02/not_fne20140722tmssewerflood.pdf.

than the penalty Ofwat had been minded to impose absent these measures. Thames Water had committed to:

— accept a £79 million (2012–13 prices) reduction by Ofwat to its regulated capital value (RCV)1, plus a financial adjustment to remove any benefit Thames Water received from this expenditure being included in its RCV during 2010 to 2015. This resulted in lower bills for Thames Water's 14 million sewerage customers for years to come; and
— spend £7 million on customers, over and above what it would otherwise have spent, over the next five years through:
    — increasing the amount of money available to the Trustees of the Thames Water Trust Fund (£2 million) to assist customers who are having difficulty paying their bills; and
    — investing £5 million to support additional community projects such as local programmes to better protect rivers and improve the natural environment.

e. Railways

Railway operators are regulated by the Office of Rail Regulation (ORR) and subject to licences and conditions. A new enforcement policy issued in 2012 allowed ORR to take account of reparations made when setting a penalty but only if the reparations are made unconditionally (so, for example, without knowing how they will be treated).[196] The prior consultation proposed a policy of accepting 'reparations' where there had been a breach, to encourage rail operators to spend money within the industry to 'make good' the harm brought about by a breach of licence instead of paying a financial penalty.[197] This approach received widespread industry support, and would 'incentivise compliance and change future behaviour no less than a penalty without reparations would, but with the added advantage that operators will be actively encouraged to think directly about the impact the have had on their customers and their customers' needs.[198] Two main changes were proposed to the policy statement. First, the requirement that reparations must be offered unconditionally was removed. Second, ORR would be prepared in principle to reduce a penalty '£ for £' to reflect reparations offered where appropriate. These changes were also to bring ORR more into line with the approach adopted by other regulators, such as Ofgem's acceptance of 'alternative reparation'.[199] ORR expected that these changes would give it more flexibility to accept reparations in lieu of a financial penalty than it had previously, and that it would be more likely an operator would offer to make good the harm brought about by a breach of its licence obligations as an alternative to paying a financial penalty.

> The reform should incentivise compliance and change future behaviour no less than a penalty without reparations would, but with the added advantage that operators will be actively encouraged to think directly about the impact they have had on their customers and their customers' needs.[200]

---

[196] *Economic enforcement policy and penalties statement* (Office of Rail Regulation, 2012) paras 1.9 and 4.6.
[197] *Rail operator penalties to benefit customers, proposes regulator* (ORR, 14 May 2012), available at http://www.rail-reg.gov.uk/server/show/ConWebDoc.10919.
[198] ibid, 2.
[199] ORR had previously said that it was not minded to reduce a penalty '£ for £'.
[200] ORR letter, 14 May 2012, above.

ORR cited that the change would be compliant with the Macrory principle that penalties should aim to restore the harm done by non-compliance.

From 1 October 2016, rail customers were given the right to claim redress under the Consumer Rights Act 2015 legislation if train operators:

— fail to provide a passenger service reasonable care and skill;
— breach other consumer rights provided under the CRA.

A number of pre-existing rail industry compensation schemes continued to be available after 1 October 2016, and remained the main means of redress for customers. The government is expected to enhance passengers' negotiating power by introducing a single railways ombudsman. The ORR enforcement policy was updated in 2017, and repeated the policy of encouraging licence holders and operators to make reparations to those harmed as early as possible.[201]

f. Environmental Protection

The Environment Agency and English Nature were the first (and one of the few) authorities to be awarded the RESA Part 3 power to impose civil sanctions, as of 6 April 2010.[202] The two authorities were granted the full range of powers, including not only the ability to impose financial penalties,[203] but also the ability to issue a Compliance Notice, requiring specified steps within a stated period to secure that an offence does not continue or happen again;[204] issue a Restoration Notice requiring specified steps within a stated period to secure that the position is restored, so far as possible, to what it would have been if no offence had been committed;[205] issue a Stop Notice, which will prevent a person from carrying on an activity described in the notice until it has taken steps to come back into compliance;[206] accept Enforcement Undertakings, which will enable a person, who a regulator reasonably suspects of having committed an offence, to give an undertaking to a regulator to take one or more corrective actions set out in the undertaking;[207] a person may give a Third Party Undertaking to compensate persons affected by an offence, and the regulator if it accepts the undertaking must take it into account in determining the variable monetary penalty.

The Environment Agency makes regular use of its powers to impose civil sanctions (including redress) or agree enforcement undertakings under which firms make voluntary restoration.[208] The majority of civil sanctions applied so far are enforcement undertakings

---

[201] *ORR's economic enforcement policy and penalties statement—Great Britain* (Office of Rail and Road, 2017) paras 97–104.

[202] The Environmental Civil Sanctions (England) Order 2010/1157 and The Environmental Civil Sanctions (Miscellaneous Amendments) (England) Order 2010/1159.

[203] An upper limit of £250,000 has been imposed on variable monetary penalties for 'either way' offences.

[204] The Order, Sch 2.

[205] ibid.

[206] The Order, Sch 3.

[207] The Order, Sch 4.

[208] Under the Environmental Civil Sanctions (England) Order 2010/1157. See *Environment Agency enforcement, sanctions and offences* (Environment Agency, 2017).

volunteered under the producer responsibility legislation. The primary purpose of the enforcement undertaking is to allow the offender to restore and remediate any environmental damage they have caused.

From 28 January 2017 to 31 August 2017 civil sanctions totalling around £60 million were paid by 44 companies, of which 21 were reactive cases where the company contacted the agency.[209] The money was paid predominantly to local charities that had objectives to protect the local environment that had been harmed by the infringing emissions. In the previous period from 1 August 2016–27 January 2017, total financial contribution to charities was £1,564,761 by 26 companies or individuals.[210]

g. Gambling

In the 10 months to June 2016, the Gambling Commission concluded a wide range of cases leading to over £3.74 million in penalty packages.[211]

Gambling Commission and Betfred

On 14 June 2016 the Gambling Commission agreed a regulatory settlement with Betfred in relation to failures by the company's anti-money laundering and social responsibility policies. A Betfred customer had previously been jailed for three years and four months after admitting stealing from his employer. A significant proportion of the stolen money was spent with Betfred. Under the settlement, £443,000 was paid to the victims of the criminal activities, £344,500 was paid to socially responsible causes in lieu of a financial penalty, and the company agreed to reimburse the Gambling Commission's investigation costs. The company also agreed to conduct an independent third party review and audit of its anti-money laundering and social responsibility policies.

---

h. Competition

The Consumer Rights Act 2015 gave the CMA power to approve voluntary redress schemes in cases where competition law has been infringed.[212] The regime for approval of redress schemes involves the infringer making a proposal to appoint an independent board that will oversee the detailed assessment and delivery of damages to those harmed.[213]

Compared with the far more flexible powers available to other enforcers of consumer law, the competition redress power is surprisingly cumbersome and unattractive. It has

---

[209] *Enforcement Undertakings accepted by the Environment Agency* (Environment Agency, 2017), https://www.gov.uk/government/uploads/system/uploads/attachment_data/file/647669/LIT_5789.pdf.
[210] *Enforcement Undertakings accepted by the Environment Agency* (Environment Agency, 2016), https://www.gov.uk/government/uploads/system/uploads/attachment_data/file/546750/LIT_5789.pdf.
[211] Press release 'Betfred to pay over £800,000 following licence review' Gambling Commission, 14.6.2016.
[212] Competition Act 1998, s 49C, as amended by the Consumer Rights Act 2015.
[213] Competition Act 1998 (Redress Scheme) Regulations 2015/1587. See *Guidance on the CMA's approval of voluntary redress schemes* (Competition and Markets Authority, 2015).

apparently not been used, in contrast to the CMA's fining and other 'hard' enforcement powers.[214] Its introduction was part of a package that introduced individual and collective actions for damages.[215] The government's 2012 consultation on introduction of the regulatory power anticipated that the majority of cases in which a regulatory power for competition damages could be used would in fact primarily benefit consumers,[216] noting that:

> Some cases would be much more appropriate for the use of such a power than others: in particular, this procedure would likely be most appropriate for cartel cases involving large numbers of undifferentiated products bought by many consumers, such as milk or football shirts. As it happens, these are cases where there is often most consumer detriment in aggregate, and where bringing cases before the UK courts can be most difficult.[217]

In response, both Citizens Advice and Which? called for the authorities to have the power to require businesses to compensate affected consumers as part of the standard enforcement process.[218] Neither the government nor the Office of Fair Trading (as it then was) was particularly keen on a redress power, but the Government had recognised that:[219]

> there are some situations where it may be appropriate for the public enforcement body to consider mechanisms for redress, as part of its administrative settlement of cases. For example, in its case against certain independent schools, the OFT decided to impose a fine on the schools found to be price-fixing but also agreed that they would establish a series of trust funds to benefit the pupils who attended the schools during the academic years in which the infringement took place.[220]

The focus in relation to enforcement of competition law through promoting damages claims mirrors the general approach to enforcement of competition law, whether by public or private enforcement, of clinging to an enforcement policy based solely on strong ex post deterrence,[221] despite mounting evidence that such a policy is ineffective.[222]

---

[214] See *CA98 register of directions and commitments currently in force*; and *Consumer outcomes secured by the CMA since April 2014*, and *Consumer outcomes secured by the OFT from January 2008 to March 2014*, at https://www.gov.uk/government/news/cma-publishes-details-of-enforcement-and-advocacy-outcomes.

[215] Consumer Rights Act 2015, s 8 and Sch 8.

[216] *Private Actions in Competition Law: a Consultation on Options for Reform—Government Response* (Department for Business, Innovation and Skills, 2013) para 6.34.

[217] Response to Consultation, para 6.36. The Response to the Consultation by R Mulheron and V Smith agreed that power 5 would apply 'typically in those cases where a cartel has substantially affected individual end-consumers' and that an opt-out class action would not work in such a situation.

[218] Responses to Consultation, available at https://www.gov.uk/government/consultations/private-actions-in-competition-law-a-consultation-on-options-for-reform.

[219] *Private Actions in Competition Law: A Consultation on Options for Reform* (Department for Business, Innovation and Skills, 2012) para 6.27.

[220] See OFT press release 166/06, 23 November 2006. It should be noted that this was a settlement in lieu of a higher fine being imposed; it was not a settlement that would have protected the school against subsequent private actions.

[221] G Becker, 'Crime and Punishment: An Economic Approach' (1968) 76 *Journal of Political Economy* 169–217; GJ Stigler, 'The Theory of Economic Regulation' (1971) 2 *Bell Journal of Economics and Management Science* 3–21; WM Landes, 'Optimal Sanctions for Antitrust Violations' (1983) 50 *The University of Chicago Law Review* 652; RA Posner, *Antitrust Law* 2nd edn (Chicago, University of Chicago Press, 2001) vii–ix; M Faure, A Ogus and N Philipsen, 'Curbing Consumer Financial Losses: the Economics of Regulatory Enforcement' (2009) 31 *Law & Policy* 161–91.

[222] See CJS Hodges, *Law and Corporate Behaviour: Integrating Theories* (n 1). For data on levels of cartels and recidivism at http://ec.europa.eu/comm/competition/ecn/statistics.html. See also E Combe, C Monnier and

It is noticeable that enforcement of competition law has not adopted the modernised 'responsive regulation' approach and, as a result, is one of the few areas that is out of step with the approach in many other sectors. The CMA's 2014 enforcement policy made no mention of Macrory, or a regulatory objective of ensuring that victims were paid back.[223]

An improvement to the mechanism was announced in August 2017, when the CMA consulted on various changes to its *Penalties Guidance*, which included introduction of a possible discount when setting a fine for breach of competition law where the CMA considers approving a voluntary redress scheme.[224] This change was made under the power to approve voluntary redress schemes and grant a penalty reduction where such a scheme is approved contained in the Consumer Rights Act 2015, section 49C.

R Legal, 'Cartels: The Probability of Getting Caught in the European Union', BEER paper no 12, available at http://www.concurrences.com/article.php3?id_article=13955; ME Stucke, 'Am I a Price-Fixer? A Behavioral Economic Analysis of Cartels' in C Beaton-Wells and A Ezrachi (eds), *Criminalising Cartels: A Critical Interdisciplinary Study of an International Regulatory Movement* (Oxford, Hart Publishing, 2010).

[223] *Vision, values and strategy for the CMA* (Competition & Markets Authority, 2014).
[224] *Draft revised CMA guidance on the appropriate amount of a penalty. Consultation document* (Competition and Markets Authority, 2017) paras 5.2 and 5.28–5.32.

6

Ombudsmen

I. Typology

A great deal of attention has been focused in recent years on the benefits of alternative dispute resolution (ADR) bodies for resolving consumer–trader disputes, based on evidence that consumer ADR schemes can typically be far more swift, efficient and effective than court procedures in resolving individual claims. In relation to *collective* consumer redress, however, the critical design insight is that general ADR entities are unable to deliver mass redress since they are not designed to aggregate individual cases. Consumer ombudsmen schemes, in contrast, are typically able to deliver collective redress. This is a simple issue of system design. Schemes and procedures that are designed to deliver binding individual outcomes—such as court proceedings or arbitration—have difficulty when faced with multiple similar cases. But consumer ombudsman schemes have various ways in which they can resolve mass cases.

The following typology can be discerned:

1. *A procedure for processing multiple claims*. This can often be remarkably similar to a court-based collective action procedure, in which individual claims are stayed whilst preliminary issues, common issues or test cases are decided, after which the court applies its decisions to the individual cases.
2. *Feeding back information* to traders, sectors, regulators, consumers and others that directly affects the behaviour of an individual trader or a group of traders. An example might be where a trade practice is held by the decision to be in breach of the law or a code or practice. This technique goes beyond the situation where a court makes a decision. First, the ombudsman's decision may be about law or may be about *fairness or practice* (individual schemes differ in their constitutional provisions). Second, there is typically a permanent, continuing and strong channel of communication between an ombudsman and a sectoral regulatory authority, which identifies an issue quickly and triggers action to change behavioural practice. Such change can occur far more quickly than can occur after a court decision on a point of law, and on a scale that can affect the practice of many traders. Third, there is typically an equally strong arm's length channel of communication between the ombudsman and individual companies, which highlights the volume and nature of complaints or consumer requests for advice received by the ombudsman, and how the trader might take action to change its behaviour and reduce the incidence of problems.

3. *Legislation and rule changes.* Providing information that triggers a change in the law or rules. Examples are noted below from Belgium and the UK.

II. National Ombudsmen Schemes

A. Belgium

i. Consumer Mediation Service

Belgium's residual ADR entity is the Consumer Mediation Service.[1] It is an autonomous public body with legal personality, which is composed of a front office and a service for the out-of-court resolution of consumer disputes.[2] The Consumer Mediation Service has a particular structure, in the sense that it is composed of the existing federal economic ombudsman services and two private ombudsman services.[3] The latter two were chosen not only because they administer a large number of complaints, but also because their services are similar to the public ombudsman services.

Every year, the Consumer Mediation Service publishes an activity report,[4] which it makes available on its website.[5] Besides statistical information about the number of complaints, this report can contain recommendations about systematic or significant problems that occur frequently and lead to consumer disputes. These structural recommendations can indicate how such problems can be avoided or resolved in the future. The goal is to enhance traders' performance and to facilitate the exchange of information and best practices.

This statistical information can play a key role in detecting mass cases and in exposing rogue traders. They can give rise to regulatory interventions (ie investigations, the imposition of (administrative) sanctions or criminal prosecution). It is vital that these entities and regulators have access to the collected data. The Consumer ADR Directive pays attention to the cooperation between ADR entities and national consumer regulators. Article 17 states that this cooperation includes mutual exchange of information on practices in specific business sectors about which consumers have repeatedly lodged complaints. It also includes the provision of technical assessment and information by such national authorities to ADR entities where such assessment or information is necessary for the handling of individual disputes and is already available.

---

[1] http://www.consumerombudsman.be//en. The Service is operational since 1 June 2015.
[2] CEL, art XVI.5.
[3] Two members of the Telecom Mediation Service, two members of the Ombudsman Service for the Postal Sector, two members of the Ombudsman Service for Energy, two members of the Mediator for Rail Passengers, the Ombudsman in Financial Matters and the Insurance Ombudsman.
[4] CEL, art XVI.7.
[5] CEL, art XVI.14.

The data from the 2016 report are shown in Table 6.1.[6]

Table 6.1:

total number of treated cases	7105
total number of cases for which the Consumer Mediation Service was competent	4342
total number of cases for which the Consumer Mediation Service was not competent	2763
total number of cases that were referred to another competent entity	2374
total number of cases that could not be transferred to another competent entity (eg, for non C2C cases)	389

How complaints are filed is shown in Table 6.2.

Table 6.2:

the FPS (Federal Public Service) Economy (ie, the regulator)	45%
the online form on the website of the Consumer Mediation Service	30%
Email	22%
Other means (letter, fax, visit)	3%

Classification per category is shown in Table 6.3.

Table 6.3:

guarantee	839
undelivered product	511
defective product	327
product does not correspond to order	325
unjustified billing	194
breaking the contract	181
partial delivery	142
wrong billing	1036
consumer service	96
other problems	67

---

[6] http://www.consumentenombudsdienst.be/sites/default/files/content/download/files/cod-jaarverslag_2016-nl-def-hr.pdf.

Referred complaints are displayed in Table 6.4.

Table 6.4:

ECC	1316
Ombudsfin	91
Ombudsman for Insurances	36
Telecommunications	241
Energy	115
Postal sector	34
Notary	4
Construction Sector	244
Travel Sector	141
Federal Ombudsman	5
Flemish Ombudsman	19
Walloon Ombudsman	9
Automoto	109
Lawyers	8

Top 10 Sectors are shown in table 6.5.

Table 6.5:

electronics (ICT)	390 (15.7%)
maintenance and repair of the house (goods)	390 (15.7%)
furniture	384 (15.4%)
maintenance and repair of the house (services)	305 (11.8%)
electronics (no ICT)	264 (10.6%)
appliances	260 (10.5%)
clothes and shoes	162 (6.2%)
second hand vehicles	157 (6.1%)
airlines	149 (6%)
sports	126 (5%)

Reasons for inadmissibility are shown in Table 6.6.

Table 6.6:

bankruptcy	64
other entity dealt with case	19
legal proceedings	51

(*continued*)

Table 6.6: (*Continued*)

no residual consumer dispute	70
facts are over a year old	8
unidentifiable complaint	61
incomplete complaint	1231
total	1504

Results mediation files are shown in Table 6.7.

Table 6.7:

settlement	1307 (50%)
complaint stopped	342 (13%)
recommendation	956 (37%)

Recommendation follow-up figures are shown in Table 6.8.

Table 6.8: Recommendation follow-up figures

Recommendation followed	Recommendation partially followed	Recommendation not followed	No answer
14,4%	3,6%	20,2%	61,8%
138	34	193	591

The Consumer Mediation Service has three main functions:[7]

— informing consumers and traders about their rights and obligations, particularly about the options available for the out-of-court resolution of consumer disputes;
— receiving all requests for the out-of-court resolution of consumer disputes and, if applicable, transferring them to an existing ADR entity;
— handling all requests for the out-of-court resolution of disputes when no ADR entity is competent.

Regarding the first function, the Service establishes a front office.[8] The six ombudsman services that form the Consumer Mediation Service physically sit in the same office and share the same front office. For the consumer, the referral to one address, one office and one phone number is easier. Moreover, it is also cost efficient in the sense that one single front office means that the six existing ombudsman services can save on logistics.

The other mission of the Consumer Mediation Service is receiving, referring and, if necessary, handling requests for the out-of-court resolution of consumer disputes. A request can be made offline (via paper, fax or phone), online or in person.[9] Referral will only take place if these entities are competent to deal with the dispute. The applicant is informed

---

[7] CEL, art XVI.6.
[8] CEL, art XVI.13.
[9] CEL, art XVI.15, §1, at 16.

and the contact details of the ombudsman service or ADR entity in question are notified. Referring a dispute does not imply a decision by the Consumer Mediation Service about the admissibility of the request.[10]

When a request concerns a dispute for which no ADR entity is competent, the Consumer Mediation Service will deal with the request itself.[11] These are the residual consumer disputes. The Consumer Mediation Service can only mediate between a consumer and a trader. When the Consumer Mediation Service has reached a settlement, it will close the case. The same applies when no settlement is reached. In this case, the Consumer Mediation Service can issue a recommendation for the trader. When the trader does not follow this recommendation, he can formulate a reply or answer.[12]

When the Consumer Mediation Service examines the case, it can visit the offices of the trader, it can order access to all documents relating to the dispute (for example letters, reports, etc), it can claim information from staff members and it can appoint an (objective) expert to conduct technical or other investigations.[13] All information is treated confidentially and can only be used for the out-of-court resolution of a specific dispute or for (anonymously) processing in the annual activity report.[14]

Finally, it should be mentioned that the Consumer Mediation Service also has standing to bring a consumer class action.[15] The Consumer Mediation Service only has standing to initiate a class action and to negotiate a collective settlement.[16] If a settlement cannot be reached, and the court has to decide the merits of the case, a consumer association has to step in to continue the procedure.[17]

ii. Ombudsmen

Table 6.9 shows the statistics for the most important and well-known ADR entities in Belgium.

Table 6.9: Leading Market Ombudsmen in Belgium

2013	Total number of complaints (including complaints transferred from past year)	Files closed in 2013	Percentage of (founded) complaints ending in positive result for complainer	Company/ Product most complained about	Principal subject of the complaints	Average processing time (in working days)
The Office of the Ombudsman for the Postal Sector	14,405 (834 transferred)	13,333	69.2%	BPOST	Treatment of dispatches	38 days

(continued)

[10] CEL, art XVI.15, §2.
[11] CEL, art XVI.15, §3.
[12] CEL, art XVI.17, §2.
[13] CEL, art XVI.19.
[14] CEL, art XVI.20.
[15] Ch 3, s II.A and CEL, art XVII.40.
[16] CEL, art XVII.39, 3°.
[17] CEL, art XVII.40.

Table 6.9: (*Continued*)

The Office of the Ombudsman for insurances	4,817	4,177	50%	Insurance companies: car insurances (civil liability insurance)	Contract management (termination)	/
The Office of the Ombudsman for insurances	2,523	684	88.01% (private persons) 61% (traders)	Payments and checking accounts (private persons) Funding loss (traders)	Disputed transactions after loss/ theft of card (private persons) Funding loss (traders)	/
The Office of the Ombudsman for Energy	6,657 (1,705 transferred)	2,659	89.5%	Electrabel, Luminus and Eandis Electricity	Meter problems	/
The Office of the Ombudsman for Telecommunication	21,519 (complaints in writing)	29,450	95.65%	Belgacom/ Proximus	Billing	/
The Ombudsman for train travelers (Ombudsrail)	5,504	2,629	54%	NMBS	Delays	/

2014	Total number of complaints (including complaints transferred from past year)	Files closed in 2014	Percentage of (founded) complaints ending in positive result for complainer	Company/ Product most complained about	Principal subject of the complaints	Average processing time (in working days)
The Office of the Ombudsman for the Postal Sector	16,421 (1,072 transferred)	15,551	68%	BPOST	Treatment of dispatches	32 days
The Office of the Ombudsman for insurances	5,003	4,022 (by end of January 2015)	52%	Insurance companies: car insurances (civil liability insurance)	Contract management (termination)	/

(*continued*)

Table 6.9: (*Continued*)

The Ombudsman in financial conflicts (Ombudsfin)	2,633	702	91.2% (private persons) 68% (traders)	Payments, checking accounts and credits (private persons) Funding loss (traders)	Cards and non-mortgage credits (private persons) Funding loss (traders)	/
The Office of the Ombudsman for Energy	4,819 (1,491 transferred)	2,046	90.9%	Electrabel and Eandis Electricity and natural gas	Meter problems	/
The Office of the Ombudsman for Telecommunication	19,383 (complaints in writing)	20,450	93.43%	Proximus/ Belgacom	Billing	/
The Ombudsman for train travelers (Ombudsrail)	4,610	1,565	57.3%	NMBS	Delays and railway passes	/

2015	Total number of complaints (including complaints transferred from past year)	Files closed in 2015	Percentage of (founded) complaints ending in positive result for complainer	Company/ Product most complained about	Principal subject of the complaints	Average processing time (in working days)
The Office of the Ombudsman for the Postal Sector	16,787 (870 transferred)	15,447	72%	BPOST	Treatment of dispatches	32 days
The Office of the Ombudsman for insurances	5,171	4,886 (by end of January 2016)	52%	Insurance companies: car insurances (civil liability insurance)	Contract management (termination)	81 days
The Ombudsman in financial conflicts (Ombudsfin)	3,375	925	96.40% (private persons) 32.6% (traders)	Payments and checking accounts (private persons) Funding loss (traders)	Disputed transactions after loss/ theft of card (private persons) Funding loss (traders)	52 days

(*continued*)

Table 6.9: (*Continued*)

The Office of the Ombudsman for Energy	4,211 (1,152 transferred)	1,702	81.9%	Luminus & Eandis Electricity and natural gas	Meter problems	/
The Office of the Ombudsman for Telecommunication	17,741 (complaints in writing)	18,932	94.21%	Proximus	Billing	52 days (mediation) or 19 days (telephonic stalking)
The Ombudsman for train travelers (Ombudsrail)	6,260	2,129	53.3%	NMBS	Delays	/

Sometimes, collective ADR procedures can be provided. The Office of the Ombudsman for the Postal Sector (OMPS), for instance, allows a representative collective ADR procedure. Private persons as well as companies, administrations, associations or organisations can file a complaint whilst having themselves represented, on the condition that representative has a mandate and that the identity of both the client(s) and the representative can be established.[18] Also other ombudsmen accept complaints filed by means of representation, such as Ombudsrail (the Office of the Ombudsman for Train Travelers),[19] the Office of the Ombudsman for Telecommunications,[20] the Office of the Ombudsman for Energy,[21] the Office of the Ombudsman for Insurances,[22] Ombudsfin (the Ombudsman in Financial Conflicts)[23] and the Consumer Mediation Service.[24]

The Office of the Ombudsman for Energy

In March 2014, a residential consumer living in Brussels, Mr M, received a €5,200 bill from his supplier, covering the period from 5 December 2009 to 27 October 2013. This late invoicing caused great harm to Mr M, and is not justified by the supplier. The consumer tried to find an arrangement with the supplier but did not succeed. Mr M formulated a complaint towards the Energy Ombudsman Service.

The supplier acknowledged a non-compliance with its general terms but offered only a payment plan in 48 months (covering the period without invoicing), as well as a €520 credit note as a gesture of goodwill (ie 10% of the disputed bill). The supplier said Mr M never explicitly claimed his annual bills and therefore is also responsible for such a situation. The complainant refuted this statement and refused the supplier's proposal.

---

[18] See: http://www.omps.be/en/679/FAQ/Frequently_asked_questions/Frequently_asked_questions.aspx.
[19] See: http://www.ombudsmanrail.be/nl/faq.html?IDC=73.
[20] See art 21 of the Rules of Procedure of the Telecommunications Ombudsman's Service (09/20/2015), available at: http://www.ombudsmantelecom.be/en/how-to-submit-a-complaint.html?IDC=106.
[21] See: http://www.mediateurenergie.be/fr/faq (2nd question).
[22] See: http://www.ombudsman.as/nl/complaint/form.asp.
[23] See art 10 of the Rules of Procedure, available (in French) at http://www.ombudsfin.be/sites/default/files/Nouveau%20r%C3%A8glement%20de%20proc%C3%A9dure%20Ombudsfin.pdf.
[24] See art 21 of the Rules of Procedure of the Consumer Ombudsman's Office, available at http://www.consumerombudsman.be/sites/default/files/content/SMCDocuments/anglais_-_smc_-_reglement_de_procedure.pdf.

The Ombudsman consulted with the DSO and they analysed that the invoicing should only take into account the period from 2012 to 2013, as the last meter reading dated back to 7 September 2013 and the previous was up to 8 August 2012. The Ombudsman issued a recommendation arguing that the Technical Regulation in Brussels was not correctly applied by the supplier. The Technical Regulation provided that the consumer has two years to challenge the meter reading indexes. Therefore, the supplier should not charge the consumer for the years 2009, 2010 and 2011.

The supplier proposed to grant a 30% discount on the consumption from December 2009 to August 2010; a 20% reduction on the consumption from August 2010 to September 2011 and a 10% reduction on the consumption from September 2011 to September 2013. This leads to a commercial gesture of €1,695. The supplier also offered a payment plan in maximum 48 instalments to clear the remaining open balance. The complainant accepted this proposal.

Impact on policy

The Belgian ombudsman suggested adapting the consumer agreement. Consequently, it become impossible to have a period of more than 12 months from the reception of meter data by the distribution system operator in which the provider would still be able to charge a consumer. The same principle applied in France. In Act No 2015-992 of 17 August on the energy transition as part of a renewable growth (Official Journal RF No 0189 of 18 August 2015), the same principle was laid down in Article 202 of the law: except exceptional cases, no electricity or gas consumption older than 14 months before the latest meter reading can be charged to the consumer.

The Office for the Ombudsman for Telecommunication

1. Introduction

The Office of the Telecommunications Ombudsman has the competence to mediate in complaints against telecom operators. The Office of the Ombudsman receives among other things complaints against mobile phone operators about the billing of premium SMS and M-commerce services. These are services that are not organised by telecom operators, but which use the operator's network, whereby the operator acts as the collector of the amounts due. The providers of those services, which are offered worldwide to telecom users, are often foreign companies, which are difficult to reach for Belgian consumers, also due to a possible language barrier. The content of these 'third-party services' is very diverse: ringtones, quizzes and contests, astrology, information messages, televoting, eroticism, dating, chatting, etc. Since 2002, the issue of the complaints about the billing of premium SMS services and (since 2013) of M-commerce services has many times been raised by the Office of the Ombudsman in its annual reports. Each time recommendations were formulated (and repeated) based on findings during the treatment of several thousands of appeals. Those complaints (and recommendations) have induced the sector to take self-regulating initiatives. In general, this has entailed structural improvements, which we discuss in more detail in this note. Nevertheless, there are still a number of challenges to be faced by the sector. Indeed, after years of declining numbers of complaints the Office of the Ombudsman again has been noticing a certain rise of disputes since 2015. As a matter of fact, it turns out that certain service providers do not entirely observe the existing directives and therefore violate consumer rights. As a result, the Office of the Telecommunications Ombudsman continues to closely follow this issue based on new complaints and will not fail to share its experiences and to make suggestions to the sector and policymakers.

The Office of the Telecommunications Ombudsman mainly uses its annual reports to make public structural problems that surface while treating appeals. This instrument is regularly consulted by all stakeholders and policymakers with a view to establishing provisions of a legal and/or self-regulating nature, as will be shown in this note. This also applies to the issue of premium SMS and M-commerce complaints. In addition, since the phenomenon started in 2002, the Office of the Ombudsman has continuously had contacts with the Government, the regulator, the FPS Economy and evidently also the operators and even service providers, regarding this important issue.

2. *Examples of complaints*

Example 1 (premium SMS complaint from 2009)

> I reacted to a contact advertisement by way of an SMS at number 7404. The advertisement said that each text would cost me € 1.50, without any further explanation. My bill of 16 April 2009 amounted to € 1,273.50. Apparently I also pay for messages received …

Example 2 (premium SMS complaint from 2009)

> On 30/12/2008 I received from Proximus a bill on which was mentioned '30 received from 9989 Ring Logo Euro 49.5870'. I immediately called the Proximus customer service. They assured me that this service would be closed down. They also informed me that the company involved in this fraud was Eldorado. Through the Internet I managed to get hold of a telephone number of that company. The latter assured me that my cell phone number would be deleted from its lists. However, a month later, the same amount was billed again … Surely this must be pure fraud and therefore I want to submit a complaint. I will also go to the police.

Example 3 (M-commerce complaint from 2013)

> My 13 year old son has had a mobile phone since over a year and had acquired during the first months (by way of Internet access) a so-called free game. His mobile phone charges are indicated on a joint bill to my name. After the first bill from Proximus, on which we discovered that this game actually cost a lot of money nonetheless, we pointed out the costs to him and he had promised not to buy anything anymore. The deal was that he would have to pay the charges himself. After that month we blocked his Internet access. At first the indications on the bill were not clear to me: 'BOKU 282080471 (Game) 4400 P4F Funds'. No idea what this means (game, updates …?). BOKU would be a payment service operating as an intermediary between the user and the provider. Yet, we kept on being charged regularly for this game on our next Proximus bills. We thought our son had continued to make purchases through that service. I called Proximus several times in order to stop that payment service. Each time I was promised that it had been stopped. For a month things were OK, until the amounts started to appear on our bills again. … But, is it normal for such a service to be offered to minors? I have not had to give my consent in any way to activate that service, but I have had to make every effort to block it.

3. *Discussion*

In 2002, the Office of the Telecommunications Ombudsman was faced for the first time with complaints about the charging of premium SMS services. In the following years thousands of times an appeal was to be made to the Office of the Ombudsman by users claiming not to have requested those services, yet to be charged for them by their operators.

The first time the Office of the Ombudsman drew attention to this issue was in its 2002 annual report and again in its 2003 annual report. In 2004, the sector took the initiative to draw up a code of conduct (the GOF Guidelines for SMS/MMS/LBS services) for the providers of premium SMS services.

This first version of the GOF Guidelines provided in many aspects an answer to the complaints. It was pointed out to providers that activation of premium SMS services was only allowed following an express request from users. Providers were also obligated to inform users by means of a standardised formulation by SMS about the tariffs for sending and receiving SMS messages. Moreover, the tariff indications in advertisements were regulated ('Graphic Charter'). Finally, the third important measure was that premium SMS services had to be stopped upon simple request from the user. In that context a universal opt-out method was created, ie sending a stop code. However, this first version of the GOF Guidelines did not give solace for the numerous complaints about extremely high costs sometimes resulting from participation in chat sessions through premium text messages. Indeed, that type of services was not or insufficiently regulated.

Although the first version of the GOF Guidelines was a fair initiative to avoid the activation of unsolicited services on the one hand and to better inform users on the other, the number of complaints submitted to the Ombudsman continued to rise unabated from 100 in 2003, 467 in 2004, 720 in 2005 up to 1,412 in 2007 and 1,586 in 2008.

In the 2005, 2007 and 2008 annual reports the Office of the Telecommunications Ombudsman again and again formulated and repeated recommendations based on what were observed to be structural problems during the treatment of complaints. The sector reacted, specifically by adapting the GOF Guidelines.

In the course of 2008 new codes of conduct (an update of the existing GOF Guidelines) became valid. The adaptations undeniably aimed at informing consumers in the best possible way, not in the least because providers of subscription services were from then on forced to use the so-called 'double opt-in'. In theory the principle is that from that moment on each user had to reconfirm his subscription to a premium SMS service and was at the same time informed by the provider in a transparent manner using a standard message about all terms, including the tariffs.

Despite the amendment to the GOF Guidelines a record amount of 1,931 complaints about premium SMS services was submitted the following year (2009) to the Office of the Ombudsman. As from 2010 however, there was a turning point, so that in general there was a sharp fall in the number of complaints to 400 in 2014.

This positive tendency can partly be explained by a late implementation of the renewed GOF Guidelines (which were slightly adapted in 2011), but just as well by the Royal Decree laying down the Ethics Code for telecommunications taking effect on 9 February 2011.

The most important new provision benefiting users included in the Ethics Code was that from then on, service providers were under the obligation to warn the customer by means of a free SMS message about every expenditure of €10. In case of a subscription service this SMS notification also had to mention the terms to opt-out. This measure offered a solution for the many complaints mentioned by the Office of the Ombudsman in its previous annual reports, when users were not aware of the high consumption charges when knowingly participating in premium SMS services. This was specifically the case for chat services, which could sometimes result in telecom bills of hundreds, even thousands of Euro. Such dramatic bill shocks as the subject of a complaint submitted to the Office of the Ombudsman had not or had hardly existed since the Ethics Code had come into force.

Compared to 2014 (400 complaints) the Office of the Ombudsman again registered an increase up to 518 complaints in 2015. In 2016 there were 1034 complaints. This still means a sharp fall compared to the record year of 2009 (1,931 complaints), though. Treatment of recent complaints shows that certain service providers violate the GOF Guidelines and the Ethics Code. Mediation in these cases almost invariably leads to crediting the disputed charges, precisely because it can be proven that the service provider has not followed the guidelines.

From mid-2013 onwards, the Office of the Ombudsman received complaints about 'third-party services' being charged denominated as 'M-commerce' or 'MPay'. The issue was almost identical to that of the premium SMS complaints: hundreds of users reported not to have any clue what-soever about what the contested charges related to, to be kept guessing about the possibility to stop those unsolicited services and not to get any cooperation from their telecom operators. In its 2013 annual report the Office of the Ombudsman raised this new issue and formulated recommendations to the sector. It is very probable that these recommendations have led to the drafting of a code of conduct specifically aimed at M-commerce services (the GOF Guidelines for 'Direct Operator Billing'). By analogy with the guidelines applicable to premium SMS services, this code of conduct mainly focused on the major difficulties, ie the activation of a service with the client's express consent, correct and transparent information about the tariffs and simple terms for opting out, among other things.

Provided that the sector observes the codes of conduct mentioned above, it can be said that they have entailed a structural improvement based on recommendations and policy suggestions from the Office of the Telecommunications Ombudsman. Especially for M-commerce a sharp fall of the number of complaints was noted a few months after the introduction of the first version of the GOF Guidelines. In the case of premium SMS messages, the positive effect (a decrease of the number of complaints) of establishing a code of conduct was not noticeable until various adaptations of the terms over a six-year period. In that case the coming into effect of the Ethics Code played a decisive role in the decrease of the number of complaints. In addition, thanks to the mediation by the Office of the Ombudsman a solution can often be reached in disputes about premium SMS charges, precisely because violations of the Guidelines are very frequently found.

The recent rise in the number of complaints refocuses our attention back on the issue of premium SMS complaints specifically. Based on the current and future complaints the Office of the Telecommunications Ombudsman will continue to detect structural difficulties and inform and advise both the sector and policymakers.

Structural improvement following recommendation and policy suggestions by the Office for the Ombudsman for Telecommunication regarding customer support services by telecom operators

1. Introduction

The Office of the Telecommunications Ombudsman acts as an appeal body. That means that this office can only intervene after the user has tried to reach an agreement with the telecom operator involved as regards the dispute. In principle a user can contact his operator through different channels: by calling the customer support service; by writing a letter, fax or e-mail or by means of the website and in some cases personally by visiting the offices or points of sale.

In this context it is crucial to know whether the customer has indeed been successful in contacting the telecom operator within a reasonable period of time and in an easily accessible fashion. If the user is indeed able to communicate with the operator, he will rely on an efficient and customer-friendly attitude from the company involved with a view to an actual solution of the dispute. The user also expects that contacting his operator will not entail expenses.

A person contacting the Office of the Ombudsman is asked to share his experience with his operator's customer support service. These testimonies revealed diverse structural problems the users are faced with during (attempts to make) primary contacts with telecom operators. These structural issues constituted the subject of various articles in the Ombudsman's annual reports, repeating recommendations for the sector several times. In addition, the Ombudsman repeatedly dealt with recurring problems regarding customer support services in contacts with the government, the regulator, the FPS Economy and of course the operators. We suspect that this repeated input of information regarding the difficulties the users are facing to contact their telecom operator is one of the reasons for the various initiatives that have finally resulted in a more optimal customer support service. One thing and another does not mean that the Ombudsman no longer receives complaints revealing that operators are hard to reach and/or do not treat primary complaints in a correct manner.

This article briefly describes the findings and recommendations of the Ombudsman on complaints about the telecom operators' customer support services since 2002 as well as the initiatives that have been taken by the sector and the government to curtail the problem.

2. Examples of complaints

Example 1 (complaint from 2002)

Mr D, a customer of NetNet's, filed a complaint in December 2002 contesting certain calls made. During the ensuing paper war NetNet states: 'This customer's comments are a waste of time to us. Or [the complainant] pays or we'll send his file to a collection agency. Within 8 days his telephone line will be disconnected.'

Example 2 (complaint from 2004)

Ms M complains about the attitude of one of the Belgacom customer support service's employees. He had hung up after having reacted aggressively when she asked for more information about calls invoiced.

Example 3 (complaint from 2008)

Mr T complains that he was not able to reach the free number of Voo all day. He had been trying to call this number between 8.30 am and 20.45 pm.

Example 4 (complaint from 2009)

Following some uncertainty regarding a recent invoice Ms D called Telenet for more details. She tried to reach the customer service repeatedly but always got the same message 'all our lines are exceptionally busy, waiting times can reach up to …'. In practice it was well nigh impossible to contact Telenet's customer support service. Because Ms D did not pay her invoice in time, she was given a € 7 fine.

Example 5 (complaint from 2016)

In November 2015 Mr. T. received a message from the number 9599. On his following Proximus invoice he saw that the receipt of this uncalled message had been charged. Mr. T. took the invoice contested to a Proximus store at K. The clerk looked at the invoice and said 'everything looks normal'. Mr. T. asked to block the 9599 no. because he continued to receive these premium rate messages but the Proximus clerk sent him off empty-handed. As a result the problem continued and additional costs were charged on Mr. T's invoice every time.

3. Discussion

The Office of the Ombudsman already mentioned the recurring problem of unanswered primary complaints by different operators in its 2002 annual report. In this context the Office of the Ombudsman insisted that each telecom operator makes available a well-functioning, customer-friendly customer support service that users can reach by telephone in an optimal fashion.

In the 2004 annual report attention was paid to the complaints evolution at the alternative operators (Scarlet, Tele2, Euphony and Versatel), who at that time were going through major changes regarding their offer and customer base. The numerous complaints showed that the service provided by these companies to existing customers was still considered to be the Achilles tendon par excellence. These operators' after sales services seemed to be incapable of coping with the developments. There was an ever-increasing demand for a better accessibility by telephone and curtailment of the waiting times. The fact that some of these operators could only be contacted by means of very expensive numbers created ill-feeling among many users as well. The Ombudsman therefore suggested to implement a system in which the waiting times would be free of charge.

During the following year, 2005, a legal provision came into effect regarding the operators' customer support services for the first time. Since the implementation of the Act of 13 June 2005 on electronic communications each operator has been obliged to provide the end-users with a 'service for support by telephone'. Apart from a good accessibility this Act did not lay down specific goals regarding the functioning of a support service. In addition, the Act stipulated that the operators were no longer allowed to impose expensive numbers such as 070 and 090X numbers to contact their support services. To this effect the legislator clearly took into account the Office of the Ombudsman's recommendation in the 2004 annual report.

In the 2007 annual report the Office of the Ombudsman evaluated the implementation of the Act of 13 June 2005 on electronic communications by the operators. The aspect of customer support services was also dealt with therein. The Ombudsman concluded that this specific legal provision was largely productive, especially after Tele2 changed the expensive 070 number for its customer support service to a 02 number (zonal tariff) in 2006.

In spite of this globally positive development it appeared that customer support services provided by telecom operators ranked in the top five of the major complaint themes at the Office of the Ombudsman both in 2008 and in 2009. The complaints indeed showed that there was a tendency for both the accessibility and the quality of primary support by the operators to decrease. Apart from the inaccessibility by telephone the fact that many operators apparently did not respond to written complaints or even complaints sent by registered letter was also cause for a lot of ill-feeling among the consumers. The consequences of a customer service that could not be reached were detrimental to the user as he was no longer able de facto to contest his invoices to the primary support service or report a malfunction. It is no coincidence that this negligence by the operators translated to a record number of appeals filed with the Office of the Ombudsman for Telecommunications. The problem however did not only lay in the difficulty to reach the operators. The quality of the primary complaints handling was below par as well. A great number of complaints filed with the Ombudsman showed that a lot of primary support services contradicted the customer's complaints without any justification and in case of contact by telephone, interrupted the call. In the 2009 and 2011 annual reports the Office of the Ombudsman consequently felt compelled to conclude that the operator's support services were in urgent need of a reassessment because of their non-negligible value. Their reputation could only be improved if an optimal accessibility and a more qualitative primary treatment of disputes were strived after. In order to avoid the communication channels available to the customers to become scarcer the Office of the Ombudsman advised all operators to always provide the users with the possibility to transmit questions and complaints in a written form. On the bright side, the Office of the Ombudsman noted in its 2011 annual report that the complaints showed that the customer support service employees had increasingly less the urge to sell additional products to the customer when the latter contacted them.

Moreover, in 2011 multiple initiatives were taken with a view to a structural improvement of the customer support service of telecom operators. First, an Act came into effect (the Act of 31 May 2011 pertaining to various provisions regarding telecommunications) obliging operators to run a customer support service that was from then on subject to a number of qualitative criteria with a view to an optimal guarantee of the consumer's interests. In June 2011 more than 21 companies, including the major telecom companies, furthermore signed the thus entitled 'Charter for customer-friendliness'. The Charter provided, among other things, for a maximum waiting time of 2.5 minutes for telephone calls by consumers to the customer support service. The text also provided for the possibility of a free call back in case this waiting time was exceeded. Operators also committed themselves to answer letters and e-mails within five days and to suspend the collection of the part of the invoice that had been contested. The call centre's menu had to be simpler and certain oral agreements had to be confirmed in writing at the customer's request.

These particular commitments by the major operators to a large extent met the laments the users had been uttering for a decennium following their appeal filed with the Office of the Ombudsman.

One thing and another did not keep the Office of the Ombudsman from having to reiterate the attention to structural problems with the primary customer support services in its 2012 annual report. The recommendations issued to the telecom operators in this context were repeated time and time again and boiled down to these companies being invited to correctly implement the Charter for customer-friendliness.

In the following years the Office of the Ombudsman noticed that the operators had begun to pay increasingly more attention to a solid customer support service. This in turn translated into positive statistics. The Office of the Ombudsman still registered 1,565 complaints regarding customer support services in 2012, while this decreased to 834 and 710 cases respectively in 2013 and 2014. In 2015 this positive trend continued and the Office of the Ombudsman only noted 372 complaints regarding customer support services. For 2016 there were 340 complaints. It should come as no surprise that these numbers also reflect the influx of appeals with the Office of the Ombudsman: a person who receives primary help by his operator in an efficient manner, will not file a complaint with the Office of the Ombudsman.

The time when the Office of the Ombudsman was flooded by complaints from users who were not able to contact their operator seems to belong to the past. The Office of the Ombudsman can thus concentrate on complaints regarding actual disputes and fully play its role as an appeals body.

The above does not mean there is no more room for improvement. It still occurs that certain users address the Office of the Ombudsman because the waiting times at the operators' customer support services upon contact by telephone are too long or because primary complaints are not being followed up in a serious manner. Especially regarding the primary complaints on the invoicing of services by third parties (such as premium rate text messages) there is room for improvement because the operators—who are the invoicing party—all too often refer their customers empty-handed to the service providers, who themselves are very hard to contact.

Structural improvement following recommendations and policy suggestions by the Office of the Telecommunications Ombudsman regarding TV games/forbidden games of chance

Introduction

In the spring of 2004 the Office of the Telecommunications Ombudsman recorded a new category of complaints. Viewers who participated in a number of new programmes such as 'Puzzeltijd' on VTM, 'Play today/Play tonight' on Kanaal 2, 'Toeters en bellen' on VT4 and 'Allo Cadeaux' and 'Le Mot Gagnant' on RTL-TVI, were faced with high bills. Those were TV games where viewers were invited to send the solution to the question by texting to an SMS short number or by calling to an 0905 number. However, giving the right answer was not enough to win a prize. In some cases the participant had to be the 'tenth person sending an SMS' or the 'tenth caller' for instance.

Only then was one invited to give the answer and state his or her phone number. Those data were collected and at the end of the game someone was called back at random. That person was then given the opportunity to win a large sum of money in the course of the programme itself. If the participant was not the tenth person, he was encouraged to have another try. As part of another game it was possible to have one's data registered for each call, thus enhancing the chance of being selected at random as the 'lucky one', and of (possibly) winning a gift or a sum of money. In any case the common factor in these games was the instigation to make several calls. It was also striking that these games mainly focused on a very vulnerable public such as young, unemployed or elderly people, ie people who were often short of money and at times when they were at home when the programmes were on television (in the afternoon and at night). The questions were so easy that anyone could find the solution. Therefore the impression was given that the sum of money or the gift was easy to win. Each call usually cost €1, regardless of the duration of the call; for calls from a mobile phone the mobile operator charged an extra set-up cost. Text messages also cost €1.

Many people submitted a complaint to the Office of the Ombudsman against their high bills, after having contacted their operators and being informed that the bill was correct and had to be paid. All persons who submitted such a complaint thought they had not made the large number of calls mentioned on the bill. They mostly claimed they had heard a busy tone or a fast busy tone, which in their opinion was billed unjustly. However, all operators who billed 0905 connections denied that busy or fast busy tones were billed and thought the billing was done correctly and that the invoices had to be paid.

The Office of the Ombudsman started to receive these complaints from March 2004, shortly after the new programmes were televised. The number of complaints peaked between April 2004 and July 2004. Each time, recommendations were formulated (and repeated) based on findings during the treatment of several hundreds of appeals.

The Office of the Ombudsman also raised this issue of complaints on billing text messages to a short number/ the billing of calls to an 0905 number in its annual report.

Discussion

In 2004, the Office of the Telecommunications Ombudsman was faced for the first time with complaints about the charging of costs for TV games. Considering the large number of complaints submitted to both the Office of the Ombudsman and the Gaming Commission the latter started an investigation. This Commission forwarded some 50 complaints to the Brussels public prosecutor's office. The fact is, the Office of the Ombudsman was convinced that the case involved a game of chance for which the television channels had no licence.

For the following reason the Office of the Ombudsman thought a game of chance was involved:

Under Article 2 of the Act of 7 May 1999 on games of chance the following elements are required to define a game of chance:

— there has to be a game or a bet
— there has to be a stake of any kind
— there has to be a loss or a gain for one or more players, betters or organisers
— the element of chance, no matter how secondary, has to be present.

All of these elements were clearly present in the games concerned.

Under Article 4 of the same Act games of chance must not be operated without a licence.

Regardless of the question whether a game of chance was involved, also the billing and registration of the calls were questionable. A few complainants witnessed in their case before the Office of the Ombudsman that they had learned over the telephone from both Belgacom and Telenet employees that busy tones were also charged. Not a single operator has confirmed this in writing though. The telecom operators insisted that busy and fast busy tones are not charged.

However, because so many viewers turned to the Office of the Ombudsman for that reason, the cause could also lie elsewhere. If it was indeed true that busy and fast busy tones were not charged, it was possible that the dial-up system of the television channels concerned functioned in another way than could be expected. The TV game participants may have been listening to a tape with a busy tone, which could explain the billing of busy tones. Another possibility was the fact that after making the connection nothing could immediately be heard, so that the participant could have suspected that he did not have a connection, put the receiver down and tried again. However, those possibilities have never been confirmed or observed.

The Office of the Ombudsman looked for a solution for the victims and had to make a distinction between Belgacom (now Proximus) and the other operators. Indeed, the 0905-8 … lines were lines belonging to Belgacom. Belgacom makes its lines available so that participation in these games was possible. The other operators only charged the registered 0905 calls.

The Office of the Ombudsman recommended all operators to credit the calls to 0905 numbers, since the games were forbidden games of chance.

Belgacom was also given the recommendation to start an investigation into the dial-up system of the television channels concerned. It was the opinion of the Office of the Ombudsman that callers should at all times be able to determine whether or not they have established a connection. It was Belgacom's task, as the owner of the line, to see to that. If this was not done, Belgacom had to take the necessary measures and stop making those lines available for those types of games.

Moreover, the Office of the Ombudsman was of the opinion that the operators had the task of better informing their customers about the price and the prohibition for minors to participate in games through a spoken message, in accordance with the provisions of the then valid Act of 14 June 1991 on commercial practices and the information and protection of consumers. Following this message, the caller had to be given another opportunity to break the connection free of charge.

In 2004, the sector took the initiative to draw up a code of conduct. In the 'Code of conduct regarding the offer of certain services through telecommunications for the protection of consumers' the platform members (telecom operators and service providers) stipulated that this message was only required with 0908 and 0909 numbers, because in this case, the price per minute exceeded €1.12.

The Office of the Ombudsman considered this code restricted the information obligation too much.

Belgacom preferred to wait for the results of the meetings with the Gaming Commission before starting to credit. Until then those who had submitted a complaint did not have to pay the disputed amounts.

In October 2004, Telenet decided to credit just for once the disputed 0905 calls to the account of all customers who had submitted a complaint to the Office of the Ombudsman, based on commercial considerations and also awaiting a final decision by the prosecutor's office and/or the Gaming Commission. At the same time, Telenet set an 090X restriction on the line, so that high bills resulting from participating in such games would no longer be possible in the future. If the customer had this restriction removed again, he was responsible for the consequences of further calls to those numbers.

All other operators (eg Proximus, Tele2, Euphony, Scarlet) said they were not prepared to credit the 0905 calls.

In the meantime, the Minister of Justice had the amendment to Article 3 of the Act of 7 May 1999 on the games of chance, installations of games of chance and the protection of the players included in the Programme Act of 27 December 2004 (Belgian Official Gazette of 31 December 2004).

The Royal Decree of 21/06/2011 (Belgian Official Gazette 807/2011) organises the implementation of this provision and regulates the TV games as to provision of information, protection of minors, measures against excessive calling and proper treatment of complaints.

Structural improvement following recommendations and policy suggestions by the Office of the Telecommunications Ombudsman regarding the charging of cancellation fees

Introduction

Since 2002 termination of mobile or fixed telephony contracts has been an almost inexhaustible source of disputes. The number of complaints relating to the cancellation of contracts for which the Office of the Telecommunications Ombudsman was regularly called in was proof of the acute nature of the problem. In 2002, the Office registered about 1,000 appeals. This number continued to rise over the years. In 2011, over 5,000 complainants submitted an appeal of this type to the Office. The peak was reached in 2012 with 5,500 complaints relating to this issue.

The disputes mostly resulted from a lack of information. Analysis of the complaints showed that the operators were giving unclear information about certain terms of the contract, mainly about the duration of the contract. The failure to provide clear information was also observed regarding the amount of the cancellation fees. Yet, informing the end-user about the cancellation fees is a very important matter. It is important for end-users to proceed with caution before they cancel their contract. That is only possible if they have transparent, comparable, correct and up-to-date information about the charges due at the moment of cancelling the contract.

Because of the level of the cancellation fees they could on the one hand constitute a real obstacle and an important and discouraging element to some end-users to fully use the chances offered by the liberalisation of the telecommunications market, specifically to subscribe to the most advantageous offer on the market. On the other hand, the financial burden represented by those fees did sometimes have consequences for the budgetary balance, possibly causing trouble for end-users having a low or moderate income.

The Office of the Ombudsman has continuously pointed out the issue of the complaints about the charging of cancellation fees in its annual reports. In addition, since the phenomenon had started, the Office of the Ombudsman has continuously had contacts with the Government, the regulator, the FPS Economy and evidently also the operators. Each time recommendations were formulated (and repeated) based on the findings during the treatment of the several thousands of appeals. In general, this has entailed structural improvements, which we discuss in more detail in this note.

Nevertheless, there are still a number of challenges to be faced by the sector. In 2015, the Office of the Telecommunications Ombudsman received about 1,200 complaints regarding this problem. The Office of the Telecommunications Ombudsman continues to receive complaints from companies that contest the cancellation fees charged, as well as from consumers who challenge the residual value of their devices taken into account (in case of a conditional sale), even though they were entitled to cancel their contract without any cancellation fees charged, for instance because of network problems. Still today it is difficult to switch to another operator with a total telecom package. Therefore, the Office of the Telecommunications Ombudsman continues to closely follow this issue based on the new complaints and will not fail to share its experiences and to make suggestions to the sector and policymakers.

Examples of complaints

Example 1 (from 2005)

> Mr and Mrs V have transferred their respective cell phone numbers to another mobile telephony operator. The previous mobile telephony operator charged €203.81 of cancellation fees to Mrs V. As a compensation an amount of €244.52 was charged to Mr V. Mr and Mrs V do not remember having signed a fixed-term contract with Proximus. They do admit they have received bills on which 'promotion' was mentioned, but claim not to know what this indication related to exactly.

Example 2 (from 2011)

Mr D switched his call number to BASE because of problems with his subscription. Mr D was convinced he had no more contractual obligations vis-à-vis de Proximus. Imagine his surprise when he received a bill on which the cancellation fee charged was stated. The complainant contested the fact that a contract renewal existed and challenged the high cancellation fee charged by Proximus for early termination of the contract.

Discussion

In 2002, the Office of the Telecommunications Ombudsman was faced for the first time with appeals about the charging of cancellation fees. In the following years, thousands of times users were to call in the Office of the Telecommunications Ombudsman despite the criticism from this Office in its annual reports (2002–11) and the negative opinion from the Consultative Committee for telecommunications (September 2003).

The cancellation fees represent the compensation an end-user has to pay in case of early termination of the contract. The amount of those charges mainly depended on the duration of the contract. The longer the duration, the higher the charges could therefore be in case of early termination.

Also the moment when the termination took place was decisive. The earlier the termination compared with the expiry date of the contract, the higher the amount claimed because of the termination of the contract could be.

It was therefore of great importance for end-users to be clearly informed about the duration of their contract, so that they would have an idea of the charges that could be claimed from them in case of early termination.

In this context in the issue of 23 November 2009 of the Belgian Official Gazette, a Ministerial Order of 12 November 2009 fixing the level of detail of the detailed basic invoice for electronic communications was published, which abolished the Ministerial Order of 27 April 2007.

In Article 4 this Ministerial Order stipulates that for every fixed-term contract the basic invoice has to indicate the expiry date of the contract in a clearly legible manner. This provision came into effect on 1 August 2010, the day when the Ministerial Order of 12 November 2009 abolishing the Ministerial Order of 27 April 2007 and fixing the level of detail of the detailed basic invoice for electronic communications entered into force.

This provision undeniably meant a step forward in better informing consumers and should therefore definitely be highlighted.

The issue of the cancellation fees had not escaped the notice of the European legislator either. Indeed it was the subject of one of the 12 measures in the new regulatory package regarding networks and telecommunications services (Directive 2009/136/EC of the European Parliament and of the Council of 25 November 2009) which had to be transposed into national law by May 2011.

The third telecom package was finally transposed into Belgian law in the Act of 10 July 2012 pertaining to various provisions on electronic communications (Telecom Act, Belgian Official Gazette, 25 July 2012, page 40969). The new provisions regarding charges inherent to early termination of contracts for electronic communications services were effective from 1 October 2012.

Those new provisions meant in many aspects an improvement compared to the situation that existed before.

The Office of the Ombudsman has pleaded several times for closing the gap between the situation of consumers on the one hand and that of certain categories of end-users, such as self-employed people, the liberal professions, non-profit organisations, SMEs and micro-companies on the other hand.

Before that, the cap on cancellation fees only applied to consumers. In most cases that cap was €150. Following new provisions in the Act of 13 June 2005 on electronic communications there is also a cap on the cancellation fees for subscribers who do not have more than five call numbers.

Under Article 111/3, § 3, paragraph 1 of the Act of 13 June 2005 on electronic communications the operator is no longer allowed to claim from a consumer or from a subscriber who does not have more than 5 call numbers a compensation for terminating a permanent contract or for early termination of a fixed-term contract upon expiry of the sixth month following the start of the contract.

The extension of the cap on cancellation fees to subscribers having no more than five call numbers meant a great step forward and is therefore worth mentioning. By contrast, the situation remains the same for end-users having more than five call numbers.

Before, the contract duration was also a factor in the charges for early termination. The longer the contract duration, the more the cancellation fees could run up.

Article 111/3, § 3 of the Act of 13 June 2005 on electronic communications lays down that the contract duration has less impact from now on.

The operator is allowed to claim compensation when the early termination takes place during the first six months (Article 111/3, § 3, second paragraph of the Act of 13 June 2005 on electronic communications). Yet, the compensation an operator is allowed to claim in this case mustn't exceed the subscription fee that would still be due until the expiry of the sixth month following the entry into force of the contract if that contract were not terminated early.

The determining element is now the moment when the termination takes place. The important factor is whether the early termination takes place during or after the first six months of the contract. In the latter case no cancellation fees are claimed in principle. If on the contrary the contract is terminated early in the first six months, cancellation fees can be charged.

The new provisions of the Act of 13 June 2005 on electronic communications have led to a structural improvement of the sector, also based on recommendations and policy suggestions from the Office of the Telecommunications Ombudsman. The operators started to launch formulas without any loyalty period.

Only a few months after the introduction of the new Telecom Act a sharp drop in the number of complaints before the Office of the Ombudsman was already noted. From 5,500 complaints in 2012 the number of complaints about charging cancellation fees dropped to a little more than 2,000 in 2013, 1,500 complaints in 2014 and 1,200 complaints in 2015. In addition, thanks to the mediation by the Office of the Ombudsman a solution can often be reached in disputes about cancellation fees.

Based on the current and future complaints the Office of the Telecommunications Ombudsman will continue to detect structural difficulties and inform and advise both the sector and policymakers.

iii. Belmed

In 2011, the FPS Economy launched Belmed, which is an abbreviation for *Bel*gian *Mediation*.[25] It is a digital portal (platform) on ADR and online dispute resolution (ODR) which wants to promote and make more accessible the use of out-of-court options (including, but not limited to, mediation services). Belmed consists of two pillars: offering

---

[25] http://economie.fgov.be/belmed.jsp. For an analysis see S Voet, 'Belgium' in C Hodges, I Benöhr and N Creutzfeldt-Banda, *Consumer ADR in Europe* (Oxford, Hart Publishing, 2012).

information on ADR and providing ODR for consumers and traders. Belmed is available in Dutch, French, German and English.

The information part contains a guide on how to settle a dispute in an amicable way. It not only explains what a formal notice, a consumer dispute,[26] a third party, and ADR are, but also offers concrete examples of a formal notice, a general purpose registered letter, a registered letter dealing with a product breaking down and a registered letter to terminate a contract.

The information part also offers a convenient outline of all existing ADR entities in Belgium.[27] It gives an overview of all Belgian arbitration, conciliation, mediation and ombudsmen agencies.[28] All this information is offered per sector (consumer goods, general consumer services, financial services, postal services and electronic communications, transport services, leisure services, energy and water, health and education). The information outline of each entity is similar. At a single glance, all relevant information can be consulted: the address, the website, for which problems the entity is competent, the admissibility criteria, how the process works, a complaint form, the rules, and the costs.

Second, and this is the second pillar, Belmed offers the possibility of making an online application for arbitration, conciliation or mediation.[29] Its objective is to operate as a single digital portal, or access point, for the consumer and trader. After an application is made, the Belmed system automatically sends it to the competent ADR entity. So, the consumer or trader do not have to find out, in advance, which entity is competent for their dispute.

The consumer or trader who visits the Belmed platform for the first time is faced with two 'accessibility criteria'. On the one hand, an application can only be made when one has already contacted the other party to report the problem and has tried to solve it amicably. If not, the applicant is referred to the aforementioned guide in the information part, which contains an example of a formal notice. On the other hand, an application can only be made if there is no court proceeding pending. If so, the applicant receives (very limited) information about court-connected mediation.

If the applicant has contacted the other party (without result), and there is no court proceeding pending, he can log in and register. There are two ways to register. First of all, every Belgian resident can use his or her electronic ID card or can use his or her token with the federal authentication portal to register. Second, every Belgian resident and every European consumer/trader can create a personal Belmed account. All European consumers can use the system, but for the moment only when they have a dispute with a trader that is registered in the Belgian Register for Companies.

---

[26] 'With 'consumer disputes' we mean a problem that appears during a business transaction between a consumer and a merchant. Belmed can handle such disputes, but does not deal with disputes between private individuals. Belmed cannot be used either for: cases of fraud, cases of swindle, disputes in the context of tax or social law. Belmed does cover disputes between businesses.' (http://economie.fgov.be/en/disputes/consumer_disputes/Belmed/what_is_it/guide/commercial_dispute/Consumer_dispute/#.VwQQA3lf2po).

[27] http://economie.fgov.be/en/disputes/consumer_disputes/Belmed/what_is_it/help/search_sector/#.VvBgb7v5OM8.

[28] See above s II.A.ii.

[29] http://economie.fgov.be/en/disputes/consumer_disputes/Belmed/mediation_request/#.VvBhabv5OM8.

Every private individual, or trader, can create a personal Belmed account. The applicant has to fill out the following information: email, password, name, first name, street, house number, zip code, city, country, phone, language (Dutch, French, German or English), and gender.

A new request can be made in three capacities: as a private individual consumer, as an intermediary for a private individual consumer and as an intermediary for a company (for example a lawyer or accountant). The two aforementioned questions are asked once again: 'have you contacted the trader/consumer concerned to report your problem?' and 'did you take the matter to court?'. The applicant has to provide information about the trader (there is a tool to search for the traders' business number), or, if the application is done by a trader, information about the consumer (who for example did not pay an invoice). The request information itself is vital, because based on this, the system sends the application to the competent ADR entity. The applicant has to fill out:

— the sector (and subsector) where the problem has occurred: consumer goods, education, energy and water, financial services, general consumer services, health, leisure services, postal services and electronic communications, or other;
— zip code of the location of the dispute;
— the sales method: distance, face to face, online, outside business premises;
— the type of problem: contracts and sales, delivery of goods/provision of services, invoicing/billing and debt collection, price/tariff, privacy and data protection, provider change/switching, quality of goods and services, redress, safety (covers both goods (including food) and services), unfair commercial practices, warranty/statutory guarantee and commercial guarantees, or other issues;
— financial loss estimation.

Finally, there is an unlimited empty field ('description') where the applicant can provide additional information. It is also possible to add scanned documents (for example an invoice, pictures, a letter etc), which can also be sent by regular mail.

When the applicant clicks on 'send', the application is sent, via the Belmed system, to the competent ADR entity. From that moment on, this entity will deal with the case: they will contact the applicant, examine the admissibility of the application, contact the other party, explain the ADR process, etc. Belmed only serves as an administrator, a 'serving-hatch'. It does not see the identity of the applicant, nor does it read the application, nor does it interferes in the ADR process.

B. France[30]

ADR mechanisms have progressively pervaded the French legal system,[31] and ADR mechanisms as tools to resolve mass claims have gained in popularity. In particular, rules on

---

[30] The authors of this section are Alexandre Biard and Rafael Amaro.
[31] Act no 2016-1547 of November 2016 on the modernisation of Justice has recently significantly contributed to the development of ADR.

collective settlements have progressively emerged from practice. In 2009, CMAP (The Paris Mediation and Arbitration Center) participated in a mediation process to resolve a dispute arising between the bank Crédit Foncier and several associations representing consumers. The dispute dealt with erroneous and misleading information on variable rate housing loans.[32] Parties managed to reach an agreement in only six months, which was perceived as a success.[33] Based on this first experience, CMAP developed a set of rules aimed at facilitating the collective settlement of mass claims.[34]

Rules regulating collective settlements have formally been enshrined into French law in 2014, together with the creation of *actions de groupe* in consumer and competition law.[35] In October 2016, the Act on the modernisation of Justice introduced a general framework for settlement of mass claims. Association(s) and defendant(s) can agree to settle their case. The settlement is then submitted to the court for review. Worth noting is the fact that the court must conduct an in-depth evaluation of the terms of the proposed settlement agreement. In particular, judges must make sure that the interests of all potential class members are adequately protected. In other words, judges are required to endorse '*fiduciaries duties*' vis-à-vis absentees.[36] The settlement agreement must then be advertised in the media to allow individuals to opt in.

A report of the French Market Authority dated January 2011 for instance highlighted the relevance of ADR for the treatment of mass securities litigation.[37] The Financial Markets Ombudsman (Autorité des Marchés Financiers, here AMF) has resolved mass cases in 2012 and 2016 as detailed below.[38] It is striking how the AMF Ombudsman acted proactively in managing the process of resolution, contacting relevant lawyers and institutions. The Ombudsman's actions also led to a change in the information provided by various companies in subsequent practice. The two case studies also contrast in the outcomes of the disputes: the Ombudsman basically upheld the claimants in the first case and not in the second.

---

[32] A Outin-Adam, 'La médiation collective pour résoudre les litiges liés à la consommation?', *Les Echos*, 10 November 2001, http://archives.lesechos.fr/archives/cercle/2010/11/10/cercle_31799.htm#P2zUWcRAJG1kThv6.99.

[33] 'Mediation du Credit Foncier: un accord exemplaire selon l'AFUB', http://www.cbanque.com/actu/13284/mediation-du-credit-foncier-un-accord-exemplaire-selon-afub; 'Le credit foncier trouve un compromise pour ses taux variables', http://tempsreel.nouvelobs.com/immobilier/marche-immobilier/20091117.OBS2845/le-credit-foncier-trouve-un-compromis-pour-ses-taux-variables.html.

[34] CMAP, Règlement de médiation collective en matière de consommation, http://www.cmap.fr/le-cmap/reglement-de-mediation-collective-en-matiere-de-consommation/?lang=en; L Ascensi and S Bernheim-Desvaux, 'La médiation collective, solution amiable pour résoudre les litiges de masse' (2012) No 8–9 *Contrats Concurrences et Consommation* étude 9.

[35] Art L623-22 and L623-23 Consumer Code; M Brochier, 'La transaction de groupe—Les particularités de la transaction dans l'action de groupe', *La semaine juridique entreprise et affaire*, 4 December 2014, No 49; L Visscher and A Biard, 'Dutch mass litigation from a legal and economic perspective and its relevance for France', Rotterdam Institute of Law & Economics, 2014/02, available at https://papers.ssrn.com/sol3/papers.cfm?abstract_id=2418974.

[36] The judges' fiduciaries duties with regard to class action settlements have been discussed in the context of US class actions, see: *Reynolds v Beneficial National Bank*, 288 F.3d 277, 279–80—7th Cir 2002 (Judge Posner stating 'we and other courts have gone so far as to term the district judge in the settlement phase of a class action suit a fiduciary of the class, who is subject therefore to the high duty of care that the law requires of fiduciaries').

[37] *Rapport relatif à l'indemnisation des préjudices subis par les épargnants et les investisseurs* (Autorité des Marchés Financiers, 2011).

[38] Information kindly contributed by Marielle Cohen-Branche, Le Médiateur, Autorité des Marchés Financiers.

Failure to give Warnings to Multiple Investors[39]

During 2012 the Ombudsman was contacted by a lawyer representing 143 investors complaining that they had not been properly informed by around 20 financial institutions when acquiring, through those institutions, shares in a listed company that had since been placed into court-ordered insolvency proceedings. These investors had lost their entire investment. That the company had been placed into insolvency proceedings did not, on its own, warrant the Ombudsman's involvement: the Ombudsman's role is not to exonerate shareholders from the risk of financial market uncertainties inherent in any investment in stocks and shares. Furthermore, mediation could not result in a solvent financial institution bearing the consequences of a potential breach by a company of its duty to provide information.

What was unique about this mass dispute was not only that the company was listed on the Alternext market, but that it had done so through a private placement. In light of applicable regulations, the Ombudsman considered that the financial institutions were required to inform their clients of this dual risk when they placed orders to buy the share in question; the risk was aggravated by the fact that investors did not have access to a prospectus approved by the AMF.

Since all the requests related to the same grievance, the Ombudsman shared her analysis of the situation with the claimants' lawyer. First, she had reviewed the information provided to clients on the risk associated with investing in companies listed on Alternext through private placement. Second, she recommended that the amount of any goodwill gesture be fairly adjusted in accordance with the degree to which each investor was seasoned and experienced, so that only claims made by inexperienced investors who were genuinely unable to understand the risks associated with the Alternext market and the particular method used to list the company on that market would be upheld.

The Ombudsman then contacted each of the institutions involved to share this analysis with them and ask them, for each of their clients, to provide her with information on the order in question or any warnings given when it was placed, as well as information about each client's profile as an investor. While the Ombudsman's analysis necessarily looked at the obligation upon all the institutions involved, the losses suffered could only be assessed on a case-by-case basis. After reviewing each investor's profile, as a matter of equity the Ombudsman in some cases recommended no compensation while in other cases proposed a gesture of goodwill in line with the degree to which the investor in question was seasoned and experimented.

This case highlights the benefits of mediation. First, mediation allows equity to be restored—something that no court can do. In this particular case, this was an argument to which the financial institutions involved were sensitive. From the claimants' perspective, the involvement of the Ombudsman enabled imbalances between them and the institutions in question to be corrected. Given the uncertainty and cost associated with court proceedings, these claims may never have been brought to court, and would thus have remained without redress. Finally, the analysis of these requests as a combined whole by an independent third party removed the risk of unequal treatment before the law by examining the obligation upon each of the financial institutions together. The Ombudsman's actions in connection with a mass dispute should not be seen as a substitute for the introduction of class actions in France, an issue currently under discussion. In France, the use of mediation is always based on a voluntary and confidential approach by the two parties. The confidentiality associated with mediation is a critical factor in negotiations with companies: mediation makes it possible for individual losses to be compensated quickly without damaging the company's reputation. Conversely, the key unique feature and major benefit of a class action is that, because the court's decision is made public, it addresses the issue of dissuasion

---

[39] Quoted from *AMF Ombudsman's Report 2012* (Autorité des Marchés Financiers, 2017) 4–5.

as well as that of compensation. As such, mediation is not a replacement for class actions; in reality, it should rather be seen as a helpful addition to a class action if the parties wish to avail themselves of it.

More generally, the mass dispute involving 143 claims received by the mediation unit in 2012 provided an opportunity for a number of account-keeping institutions to change the information they issue to their clients when the latter place orders in shares admitted to trading on the Alternext market via private placement. These institutions have included within their warning systems more detailed and specific information on the risks associated with this type of investment.

Financial Disclosure re a Foreign Company[40]

A case was brought before the Ombudsman's Office in 2016 comprising 102 individual cases, of which 97 were closed by the end of the year. It related to the financial disclosure by French account keepers to their clients, shareholders of a large foreign company, and to the tax consequences under French law of a spin-off voted for by said foreign company. As a result of the spin-off, the former shareholders were allocated proportional bonus shares in the newly created subsidiary. Under French tax law, the newly awarded shares are deemed to be a taxable dividend.

French shareholders awarded these bonus shares contacted the Ombudsman after noticing on their transaction advice slips an advance, non-fixed withholding tax in respect of dividends, sometimes pushing the shareholders' accounts into the red. In their view, their account keeper should have given them prior warning of this spin-off and its tax-related consequences. In the absence of such notice, they felt they were denied the opportunity to sell their shares before the transaction and thus avoid these consequences. Initially, the Ombudsman reminded the shareholders that case law consistently considers that an account keeper is obliged neither in usage, equity nor law to inform its clients of an event affecting an issuer.[41] However, Article 322-12 II of the AMF's General Regulation establishes two exceptions to this disclosure non-obligation:

> II.—The custody account-keeper shall send, as quickly as possible, to each holder of a securities account the following information:
>
> 1° Information relating to operations in financial securities which require a response from the account holder, which it receives individually from the issuers of financial securities;
>
> 2° Information relating to the other operations in financial securities which give rise to a modification to the assets recorded on the client's account, which it receives individually from the issuers of financial securities …

On reading this Article, it would appear that the second of these situations should apply in this particular case, given that the spin-off is an operation in financial securities giving rise to a modification to the assets recorded on the shareholder's account. However, the Ombudsman also noticed that the information sent by the foreign issuer to the account keepers contained no tax-related elements, which is perfectly understandable and normal in such a case.

---

[40] Edited from *AMF Ombudsman's Report 2016* (Autorité des Marchés Financiers, 2017) 27–28.
[41] Ruling of the Commercial Chamber of the French Court of Cassation no 88-17.291 of 9 January 1990; Ruling of the Commercial Chamber of the French Court of Cassation no 06-18.762 of 19 February 2008.

> Therefore, although complaints can be made against certain account keepers for not passing on information in their possession to their clients as quickly as possible, in respect of the Article quoted above, they cannot be criticised for not communicating the tax-related consequences of this operation in financial securities because they themselves had not received such information from the foreign issuer.
>
> Consequently, the Ombudsman issued a recommendation not in favour of the applicant in all these cases.

i. Compensation Schemes

Act no 51-1508 of 31 December 1951 is the starting point introducing compensation schemes into French Law.[42] This has also been described as the beginning of a 'socialisation of risks' (*socialisation du risque*) in France.[43] Scholars often consider that compensation schemes have contributed to replace the liability framework by a new framework based on solidarity in which wrongdoer's liability and harm suffered by individuals are ultimately disentangled.[44]

Act no 51-1508 created the so-called *Fonds de garantie automobile* (FGA) to compensate individuals who had accidents with land vehicles, and in particular to deal with situations where drivers at fault were unknown, insolvent or uninsured. Other compensation schemes have subsequently been created to deal with mass damage associated with (among other things) terrorism,[45] HIV and blood transfusion,[46] asbestos,[47] and others.

Nowadays, the development of compensation schemes appears twofold.[48] On the one hand, specialised funds dealing with specific risks have mushroomed in the last 30 years. On the other hand, this evolution has also been accompanied by an extension of the missions assigned to general funds, which are already operating at more general levels. This is the reason why various funds with different operating rules still coexist under French law.

Among the recently created specialised funds, the following may be highlighted:

— *Fonds de prévention des risques naturels majeurs* (fund for the prevention of major natural hazard);[49]
— *Fonds international d'indemnisation pour les dommages dus à la pollution par les hydrocarbures* (international fund for damage caused by oil pollution);[50]

---

[42] Act no 51-1508, 31 December 1951 (relative aux comptes spéciaux du Trésor pour l'année 1952).

[43] Responsabilité et socialisation du risque, in Rapport public du Conseil d'État, 2005, Documentation française.

[44] Y Lambert-Faivre, 'L'évolution de la responsabilité civile, d'une dette de responsabilité à une créance d'indemnisation' (1987) *RTD civ* 1, 19.

[45] Act no 86-1020, 9 September 1986 (relative à la lutte contre le terrorisme et aux atteintes à la sûreté de l'État).

[46] Fonds d'indemnisation des transfusés et des hémophiles—FITH created by Act no 91-1406, 31 December 1991 (portant diverses dispositions d'ordre social).

[47] Fonds d'indemnisation des victimes de l'amiante—FIVA created by art 53 of Act no 2000-1257, 23 December 2000 (de financement de la Sécurité sociale pour 2001).

[48] Responsabilité et socialisation du risque, in Rapport public du Conseil d'État, 2005, Documentation française, p 247 et seq.

[49] Act no 95-101, 2 February 1995 (relative au renforcement de la protection de l'environnement).

[50] Act no 2004-596, 24 June 2004 (autorisant l'approbation du protocole à la Convention du 27 novembre 1992 portant création de ce fonds).

—   *Fonds de garantie des risques liés à l'épandage agricole des boues d'épuration urbaines ou industrielles* (risk guarantee fund associated with the agricultural spreading of urban or industrial sewage sludge);[51]

—   *Fonds national de garantie des calamités agricoles* (fund for agricultural disasters).[52]

Among general funds, three of them may be highlighted:

—   Office National d'Indemnisation des Accidents Médicaux, des Affections Iatrogènes et des Infections Nosocomiales (ONIAM—national compensation fund for medical accidents), a general compensation scheme created in 2002;[53]

—   Fonds de garantie des assurances obligatoires de dommages (FGAO—fund for compulsory damage insurance) created in 2003[54] to compensate physical and material harms caused by road traffic accidents, hunting accidents, technological disaster, mining-related property damage;

—   Fonds de garantie des victimes d'actes de terrorisme et d'autres infractions (FGTI—fund for victims of terrorism and other offences) created in 1990.[55]

It is not possible to provide here a thorough description of the functioning of all compensation schemes due to their diversity and differences in operating rules. However, on a higher level, their framework may be described as follows. The proceedings usually start with the victim submitting an application to the fund to claim compensation. The fund may accept or dismiss the claim based on its review of the information and evidence submitted. If the individual does not agree with the fund's decision—whether it is positive or negative—he/she may bring his/her action to court.

Contrasted feedbacks and heterogeneity in guarantee funds make it very difficult to draw clear-cut conclusions on the functioning of compensation schemes in France. Some indicators tend to be positive. For instance, with regard to ONIAM, it seems that compensation rates have steadily increased over the past decade.[56] Individuals may however struggle to meet the compensation requirements fixed by ONIAM. Concerning FIVA (victims of asbestos), some observers have considered its effectiveness to be unique in Europe.[57] In its annual report for 2015, FIVA highlighted that its services had issued more than 20,000 compensation offers to applicants. Out of these 20,000 offers, only 6% were challenged before courts. Sums allocated varied depending on the diseases at stake. They usually amounted to 20,000 and 170,000 euros per individual. In 2015, FIVA paid a total amount of €438.4 million to compensate asbestos victims.[58]

---

[51] Act no 2006-1772, 30 December 2006 (sur l'eau et les milieux aquatiques).

[52] Act no 64-706, 10 July 1964, modified by Act no 2006-11, 5 January 2006 (d'orientation agricole).

[53] Act no 2002-303, 4 March 2002 (relative aux droits des malades et à la qualité du système de santé). Arts L 1142-1 et seq and L.1142-22 of the Code of Public Health.

[54] Act no 2003-706, 1 August 2003. Arts L. 421-1 et seq of the Insurance Code.

[55] Act no 90-589, 6 July 1990 (modifiant le Code de procédure pénale et le Code des assurances et relative aux victimes d'infractions). Arts 706-3 et seq of the Code of Criminal Procedure.

[56] ONIAM, Rapport annuel 2015, http://www.oniam.fr/indemnisation-accidents-medicaux/rapport-d-activite.

[57] Association Nationale de Défense des Victimes de l'Amiante (ANDEVA), *Le Bulletin de l'Andeva*, no 52 Numéro 52 (Sept 2016) https://www.andeva.fr/?12-1-Fonds-d-indemnisation-le.

[58] FIVA, Rapport annuel 2015, p 13 et seq, http://www.fiva.fr/documents/rapport-fiva-2015.pdf.

Regarding FGTI (victims of terrorism and criminal offences), a 2013 report from the Senate highlighted its positive results, and presented it as an essential mechanism to facilitate victims' compensation in France.[59] However, in the aftermath of the 2015 attacks in Paris, testimonies of victims indicated a less positive experience. They highlighted, for instance, the administrative burden and practical difficulties in obtaining compensation.[60]

Example: Rules before the Fund for acts of terrorism committed on the French territory (FGTI)

First phase: out-of-court resolution

First, the public prosecutor informs FGTI of an attack and specifies the identity of the victims. FGTI contacts the victims directly. Alternatively, the victims can also reach out FGTI directly if they have not been identified by the Public Prosecutor. The applicant needs to provide the following documents and information:

— compensation claim form;
— date and location of the attack;
— information on the police forces intervening during the attack;
— copy of the identity card/passport;
— medical certificate;
— payslips;
— tax notice.

FGTI must issue its decision within two months. If the applicant accepts the offer, the acknowledgment of agreement is transmitted to the President of the CIVI (see below) for approval. The agreement becomes then binding and the decision is notified to the applicant and FGTI. FGTI ultimately distributes the agreed sums.

Second phase: trial court procedure

In case of a dispute between FGTI and the applicant or if FGTI does not issue its decision within two months, the case is brought before a special court, known as Commission d'indemnisation des victimes d'infractions (CIVI). There is one CIVI in each High Court of First Instance (Tribunal de Grande Instance).[61] CIVI decides on the merits like a regular court. Parties may appeal the decision.

---

[59] Sénat, Rapport d'information fait au nom de la Commission des lois sur l'indemnisation des victimes, Par MM. Christophe Béchu et Philippe Kaltenbach, rapp no 107, 2013, 60 et seq, https://www.senat.fr/rap/r13-107/r13-1071.pdf.

[60] M Hajdenberg, 'Victimes du terrorisme: vers une indemnisation au rabais?' *Mediapart* Attentats du 13-novembre: notre dossier enquête, 25 April 2016, https://www.mediapart.fr/journal/france/250416/victimes-du-terrorisme-vers-une-indemnisation-au-rabais?page_article=1.

[61] There are currently 164 High Court of First Instance in France.

C. Italy

There are a number of established and well-functioning ADR entities in Italy. One example of these is the Arbitro Bancario Finanziario (ABF), which is the ADR scheme established by law for claims against banks.[62] The secretariat of the ABF is provided by the Banca d'Italia, and decisions in cases are made by a panel of independent members.[63] The outcomes of the ABF's proceedings make a significant contribution to the supervision on the banking system. The rules specify that the ABF's decisions 'become part of the broader pool of information at the Bank's disposal for its regulatory and control functions'. An example of how the decisions of the ABF have led to systemic action is in the case study below.

Loans secured against one-fifth of salary or pension

The most common type of dispute submitted to the ABF in recent years concerns disputes concerning loans secured by a pledge of one-fifth of salary or pension (71% of all disputes in 2016). A consumer is by law entitled to terminate a loan fully or partially at any time, but disputes often arise if the lender demands repayment of part of the costs incurred by the complainant in the event of early termination.

ABF's decisions have highlighted that in many cases the intermediaries:

— provide for unclear contract terms, which do not clarify if a cost is referred to the initial part of the contract ('upfront cost') or accrues over time ('recurring cost');
— in case of early termination, do not properly reduce the recurring costs of the loan.

ABF's case law on this matter has prompted various measures adopted by the Banca d'Italia in its supervisory and regulatory tasks, such as issuing general communications, communications to specific intermediaries, and Guidelines.

In two general communications (dated November 2009 and April 2011) the Banca d'Italia underlined the need to include in the contracts the clear indication of the various costs, highlighting in particular those that accrue over time (recurring costs) and therefore should be reimbursed to the client in case of early termination. Those general communications resulted in:

— an increase in the number of settlements, even before the dispute has been filed before the ABF;
— higher amounts awarded to the clients;
— a greater attention of the panels on the fairness and transparency of the contractual clauses concerning the costs of the loan (this also triggered some uncertainties among the Panels with respect to the exact interpretation of the various clauses).

In February 2016, the Bank of Italy sent a communication to 11 intermediaries who had been most involved in this type of loans reminding them that the ABF provisions require the complaints

---

[62] Consolidated Law on Banking (Legislative Decree no 385/1993), art 128-*bis*, introduced by Law 262/2005 (Investor Protection Law). See also *The Banking and Financial Ombudsman Annual Report: number 5* (Banca d'Italia, 2015).

[63] From 2017 there are seven regional panels across the country.

department of the intermediaries to keep up to date with the ABF's case law and assess customer complaints accordingly, and to resolve such disputes before a decision by the ABF's Panel.

In March 2016, a general communication of the Bank of Italy on complaints departments further underlined their duties. These communications were followed by a significant increase in the number of disputes settled by the 11 intermediaries. Since the number of disputes of this type of loan remains high, the Bank is to take further steps in 2018.

D. Sweden[64]

i. The Group Procedure for Consumer Disputes

The public out-of-court body, the National Board for Consumer Disputes (*Allmänna Reklamationsnämnden*) is assigned by law to safeguard consumers' interests by providing an out-of-court ADR mechanism for disputes between consumers and business operators. ADR is not mandatory for any party, and the National Board for Consumer Disputes only submits recommendations on how disputes should be resolved, which are not binding on the parties. The National Board for Consumer Disputes also provides mediation between the disputing parties.

The first legislation regarding group action ADR in Sweden was enacted as early as in 1991. Thereafter the Law (2015:671) on Alternative Dispute Resolution in Consumer Relations (lagen (2015:671) om alternativ tvistlösning i konsumentförhållanden) and Ordinance (2015:739) with Instructions for the National Board for Consumer Disputes (förordningen (2015:739) med instruktion för Allmänna reklamationsnämnden) was enacted on 12 November 2015 and came into force on 1 January 2016. This legislation was adopted in accordance with the Directive 2013/11/EU of the European Parliament and of the Council of 21 May 2013 on alternative dispute resolution for consumer disputes and amending Regulation (EC) No 2006/2004 and Directive 2009/22/EC, and the Regulation No 524/2013 of the European Parliament and of the Council of 21 May 2013 on online dispute resolution for consumer disputes and amending Regulation (EC) No 2006/2004 and Directive 2009/22/EC.

The scope of application is sectoral as it covers civil disputes between natural persons and business operators excluding the following types of disputes: disputes concerning health care; purchase of real estates; lease or transfer of tenant-ownership and leasehold; lease or rent of an apartment where the dispute concerns something else than monetary claims. Disputes shall also exceed a certain value and be filed within a year from when the business operator denied the consumers complaint in order to be assessed by the National Board for Consumer Disputes. A dispute will not be assessed by the Board if it is pending before or has already been resolved by a court or the Swedish Enforcement Authority.

The Consumer Ombudsman may initiate a group action and accordingly have standing at the National Board for Consumer Disputes if: (i) there are several consumers who are

---

[64] The author of this section is the law firm Hammarskiold & Co.

likely to have a claim against the business operator on essentially similar grounds; (ii) the disputes concern a situation that may be considered by the board; and (iii) the assessment is justified in view of the public interest. A group of consumers may file a group action if the Consumer Ombudsman has declined to initiate proceedings. The group action is based on an opt-out system, meaning that all consumers with claims on essentially similar grounds are covered by the recommendation even if they are not named or involved in the group action. There are no specific rules on case management depending on if the claim is raised by one person or a group. The process at the National Board for Consumer Disputes is only in written form. The National Board for Consumer Disputes offers the business operator to comment on the consumer's complaint within a reasonable time. The Consumer Ombudsman or the consumers in turn have an opportunity to comment on the business operator's response before a recommendation by the Board is given. Each party stands for its own costs. Costs for the National Board for Consumer Disputes and the Consumer Ombudsman are funded by the State.

ii. Case Studies

The National Board for Consumer Disputes has handled 23 dispute matters since 1991 until May 2016, as listed below.

No 1991-5771, The Consumer Ombudsman/Fordonia Förvaltning AB

The dispute concerned a leasing agreement. The case was because more detailed information was proved and the dispute was more clearly shown. The same dispute resulted in the below referred decision No 1992-0112.

No 1991-6099, The Consumer Ombudsman/Skandinaviska Dataskolan AB

The dispute concerned the cancellation of a purchase of a computer course because the consumers had cancelled the purchase because the course did not fulfil the consumers' expectations. The Consumer Ombudsman claimed that the National Board for Consumer Disputes should submit a recommendation on how disputes should be settled between Skandinaviska Dataskolan AB and consumers in general. The Consumer Ombudsman had received several hundred complaints against the company and therefore a group action was the most suitable option. The National Board for Consumer Disputes recommended the company to reimburse the consumers with the tuition fee for classes which the consumers did not attend, but with a deduction of 10%.

No 1992-0112, The Consumer Ombudsman/Fordonia Förvaltning AB

The dispute concerned clauses in a car leasing agreement between the company Fordonia Förvaltning AB and a number of consumers. The first clause gave the lessor a right to change the monthly rent of the car and the other gave the lessor the upper hand regarding the negotiations and arrangements following the consumer's return of the car. The National Board for Consumer Disputes considered that it was suitable for a group action in this case due to the number of consumers who were dissatisfied. The National Board for Consumer Disputes recommended the company to reimburse the monthly rent in accordance with the initially agreed fee since the clause was considered to be unreasonable. The second clause was considered to be invalid due to mandatory Swedish legislation.

No 1992-1761, The Consumer Ombudsman/Skandinaviska Dataskolan AB

A request for reconsideration of the above referred decision No 1991-6099. The request was dismissed since the claimant had not presented any new relevant information for the National Board for Consumer Disputes to reconsider its decision.

No 1993-0249, The Consumer Ombudsman/Pool Resor

The dispute concerned refund of the purchase of a trip on a cruise ship, but it was withdrawn due to the reason that the company already had compensated the consumers.

No 1993-1642, The Consumer Ombudsman/Skurups Kabel TV AB

The dispute concerned an increase of fees from a company to its consumers for cable television services from SEK 300 to SEK 1,200 a year. In the agreement between the company and the consumers there was a clause that allowed the company a possibility to change the fees if it was necessary due to external factors. The company argued that change of ownership was such a factor that gave the company that right. The Consumer Ombudsman disagreed and applied for an ADR group action because over 60 complaints had been reported from consumers. The National Board for Consumer Disputes concluded that the company had no right to charge the consumers the excess amount and recommended the company to reimburse the excess amount to the consumers.

No 1993-3381, The Consumer Ombudsman/Västindienspecialisten

The dispute concerned a company's right to increase agreed prices for trips due to currency fluctuations. The company's agreement with the consumers gave the company a right to increase the price if the currency fluctuations exceeded SEK 60 and was caused by an official decision regarding a devaluation of the Swedish currency. The Consumer Ombudsman claimed that the company should reimburse amounts charged due to devaluation. The Consumer Ombudsman claimed that a group action would be most suitable in the case since the dispute concerned many consumers and the fact that the company earlier had declared that it did not follow earlier recommendations by the National Board for Consumer Disputes regarding the same circumstances. The National Board for Consumer Disputes recommended the company to reimburse the consumers because the devaluation decision on which the company was basing its price increase was not considered to be such an official decision as the agreement referred to.

No 1993-3382, The Consumer Ombudsman/Plus World AB

The case involved the same circumstances and decision as the above referred decision No 1993-3381.

No 1993-3384, The Consumer Ombudsman/Places Travel Production AB

The case involved the same circumstances and decision as the above referred decisions No 1993-3381 and No 1993-3382.

No 1996-0519, The Consumer Ombudsman/Hyllinge Buss och Resetjänst AB

The dispute concerned reimbursement due to lack of air conditioning during a bus trip to Lloret de Mar in Spain, which had caused inconvenience for the passengers because of the heat in bus company's buses. The bus company had announced in its marketing that most of its buses were equipped with air conditioning, and the consumers had therefore a legitimate reason to believe that the bus was equipped with air conditioning, especially due to it being a trip to a warmer climate. The National Board for Consumer Disputes had earlier made decisions against the company in individual cases regarding the same trip. Due to the large amount of notifications and complaints, the Consumer Ombudsman decided to apply for a group action. It is unknown how the underlying facts were discovered. The National Board for Consumer Disputes recommended the company to reimburse the consumers with a discount by refunding 17% of the price for tickets on trips where there was no air conditioning in the buses (repay 600 SEK on a ticket costing SEK 3,500). The time from filing of the case until decision was 157 days. The company did not follow the recommendation by The National Board for Consumer Dispute but compensated the consumers in another way, on which information is not available.

No 1996-6109, The Consumer Ombudsman/Sydsvenska Dagbladet AB

The dispute concerned the admissibility of a surcharge. The company had, after the Swedish Parliament had adopted legislative changes to the VAT system, invoiced the consumers an additional fee corresponding to the increased VAT without having such a precondition in its existing agreement with the consumers. The Consumer Ombudsman claimed that the additional fee was not allowed and applied for an ADR group action since many consumers were affected by the additional fee. The National Board for Consumer Disputes recommended the company to withdraw its claims for additional charges corresponding to the increased VAT and to reimburse the affected consumers who had already paid.

No 1999-3902, The Consumer Ombudsman/Måleri & Byggentrepenad i Liljeholmen AB and Naso-National Air & Space Outlet Sweden

The dispute concerned termination of agreement regarding purchase of binoculars, and compensation due to expenses connected with the purchase. The National Board for Consumer Disputes concluded that the binoculars were considered useless and did not meet the requirements of what an average consumer in general could expect. Therefore, the National Board for Consumer Disputes recommended the company to reimburse the purchase price of SEK 229 to the consumers and compensate the consumers for the additional costs incurred from purchasing the product.

No 2000-0252, The Consumer Ombudsman/Telia Nära AB

The dispute concerned announcements of increased fees in accordance with an agreement between a telephone operator and the consumers. The increase was announced in a press release and on the operators' website. The National Board for Consumer Disputes did not considered this sufficient to be compliant with the terms in the agreement regarding how price changes should be announced. Therefore, the National Board for Consumer Disputes recommended the company to reimburse the affected consumers on a flat-rate basis with an amount of SEK 44 per month to the consumers from when the price increase was made until a correct announcement was made.

No 2000-1126, The Consumer Ombudsman/AB Stockholms Lokaltrafik

The dispute concerned compensation for travel passes. The application was withdrawn by the Consumer Ombudsman.

No 2000-2435, The Consumer Ombudsman/PFK Fondkommission AB

The dispute concerned refunds of custody fees. The National Board for Consumer Disputes rejected the application because the requirements for group action was not met since the consumers in the dispute did not have similar intention or knowledge, and they did not use their accounts at the company for the same, or similar, reasons.

No 2001-2785, The Consumer Ombudsman/Tele 2 AB

The dispute concerned a company's right to withhold an amount which the consumers had paid for its mobile subscription, and whether the company could still claim the subscription fee once the consumer unsubscribed. In accordance with the agreement the consumers had the right to use the subscription fee to make calls etc, but this was not the case if the consumer unsubscribed. The Consumer Ombudsman claimed that the agreement terms were unreasonable and therefore invalid. The National Board for Consumer Disputes dismissed the application and concluded that agreement terms were clear and on no ground unreasonable.

No 2003-6529, The Consumer Ombudsman/Kraftkommission AB

The dispute concerned damages due to a breach of contract when the company failed to supply electric power to the consumers. The breach of the contract caused the consumer additional costs when they had to enter a less favourable agreement with another company. The National Board for Consumer Disputes recommended the company to compensate the consumers for additional costs incurred by the company's breach of contract.

No 2010-4253, The Consumer Ombudsman/Hammarö Energi AB

The dispute concerned the company's right to charge the consumers for administrative costs, despite the fact that they had no such right according to the agreement with the consumers. The company argued that it would lead to an unreasonable result if they were not able to charge the consumers for increased administrative costs. The administrative cost was at first borne by the municipality, however in 2009 the company had to take over the responsibility, and therefore they urged that the changed circumstances gave them the right to charge the consumers for administrative costs. Due to complaints from consumers and the fact that approximately 200 consumers were affected by the company's decision, the Consumer Ombudsman decided to file a group action application. It is unknown how the underlying facts were discovered.

The National Board for Consumer Disputes recommended the company to repay the excess amount that was paid by the consumers and withdraw the new provisions. The National Board for Consumer Disputes stated that each contracting party shall bear the risk of changed conditions and the company had been able to predict the increased costs. Therefore there were no grounds for the company to adjust the agreement with the consumers. The process took 277 days. The company followed the recommendation and repaid the excess amount that was paid by the consumers. The media subsequently reported that the managing director of the company had to resign.

No 2010-6177, The Consumer Ombudsman/Viking Airlines AB, Res Nu i Stockholm AB etc

The dispute concerned 325 consumers' right to compensation when airline companies had denied some consumers boarding. Several airline companies were subject to the application but the National Board for Consumer Disputes dismissed the application against all companies except for one, Viking Airlines AB, since it was not proved that the other companies had any responsibility towards the consumers. The company argued that the tickets were invalid and that the tickets had been sold without permission. The National Board for Consumer Disputes deemed that the company was responsible towards the consumers but the matter was dismissed because a recommendation would have been meaningless since the company was declared bankrupt before any recommendation could be announced.

No 2013-07574, Anne Almquist et al/ Live Nation Sweden AB

The dispute concerned consumers' rights for compensation when a concert did not meet the consumers' expectations. The National Board for Consumer Disputes rejected the appeal on the grounds that the case required further investigation and could therefore not be handled by the National Board for Consumer Disputes.

> **No 2014-09369, The Consumer Ombudsman/Gotlandsbåten AB**
>
> The dispute concerned consumers' rights for compensation when their tickets for a ferry were cancelled. It was clear that the company had reimbursed the price for the ticket to the consumers, but according to the National Board for Consumer Disputes the company had not fulfilled its obligations because the company had not offered the passengers new tickets with similar conditions. Therefore the company was responsible to reimburse the consumers for their additional costs to arrange alternative transportation. The company was, according to the National Board for Consumer Disputes, not only responsible for direct costs, but also for indirect costs, due to its negligence.
>
> **No 2014-11304, Sveriges Aktiesparares Riksförbund/Swedbank Robur Fonder AB**
>
> The dispute concerned overcharging of management fees. The National Board for Consumer Disputes rejected the application and stated that the case required further investigation and could therefore not be considered by the National Board for Consumer Disputes.
>
> **No 2015-07942, Sveriges Aktiesparares Riksförbund/Swedbank Robur Fonder AB**
>
> Request for reconsideration of the above referred decision No 2014-11304, regarding overcharging of management fees. The request was refused since the applicant had not presented any new relevant information for the National Board for Consumer Disputes to reconsider its decision.
>
> According to the applicant's website, the association is planning to apply for a group action in the District Court against the company, Swedbank Robur Fonder AB, see above.

E. The Netherlands

The Netherlands has a well-established and effective national ADR system, in which the principal ADR bodies are a network of complaint boards (Geschillencommissie) and separate systems for financial services (KiFiD) and healthcare insurance (SKGZ).[65] These bodies are designed to process individual complaints, but can inherently identify issues that affect multiple individuals. In relation to traders in around 50 business sectors, the Geschillencommissie apply the standard terms and conditions that are agreed every three to five years between the relevant trade association(s) and the national or other consumer associations, in a formal review conducted under the auspices of the Social and Economic Council's Self-Regulation Coordination Group (SER CZ).[66]

Although the system is designed to process individual cases (and class actions are excluded in the procedural rules of Kifid[67] and SKGZ),[68] there are various features that

---

[65] See F Weber and C Hodges, 'The Netherlands' in Hodges, Benöhr and Creutzfeldt-Banda (n 25) ch 6; E Verhage, 'The Implementation of the Consumer ADR Directive in The Netherlands' in P Cortes (ed), *The New Regulatory Framework for Consumer Dispute Resolution* (Oxford, Oxford University Press, 2017) ch 11.

[66] Sociaal Economische Raad (SER), Coördinatiegroep Zelfreguleringsoverleg (CZ).

[67] Art 2.1 (e) Rules of Procedure Financial Complaint Committee (Kifid), Conciliation and (binding) advice (2017) (See: https://www.kifid.nl/fileupload/reglementen/Reglement%20Geschillencommissie%20def.pdf).

[68] Art 3(4) Rules of Procedure Healthcare Ombudsman SKGZ (2015), art 3 (6) Rules of Procedure Healthcare Complaint Committee SKGZ (2015). See: https://www.skgz.nl/wp-content/uploads/2016/04/reglement_ombudsman_2015.pdf and https://www.skgz.nl/wp-content/uploads/2016/09/reglement_geschillencie_2015.2.pdf.

address mass issues. One important mechanism is the fact that generic issues are raised in the regular review and amendment of the standard terms and conditions of many sectors. As a result, requirements may be clarified. The Dutch system is thought to emphasise the importance of the observance of the agreed terms and conditions, supported by a strong element of self-regulation, through the persuasive power of a trade association over its members in this system, and the effects of decisions of courts or of the Geschillencommissie on complaints, and the public regulatory authorities.

Second, with regard to consumer disputes the Geschillencommissie system is administered by a single body, Stichting Geschillencommissie (SGC), which runs a computerised management system that enables case management techniques to be applied to cases.[69] SGC will identify that a cohort of cases have the same subject matter, and can then list them all for a panel hearing on the same day, or select a small number as test cases, possibly notifying parties that their cases are 'on hold' pending a decision by the complaint board of a representative selection of similar cases. The parties will be notified of the outcome of the representative cases, and invited to settle their cases between themselves, without which their cases will proceed to decision by the board. This technique has been used successfully in various instances, notably multiple cases against airlines over delayed boarding or flights. It is notable that 43% of the cases processed in 2016 were settled (36% by the parties, 5% with the involvement of experts during the preparation of cases, and 2% during the hearing).[70] The average duration is three months (including a potential settlement).

Similarly, KiFiD uses case management in relation to financial services cases. The president and case handlers can, for example, decide whether to list cases together or to hold some back pending an authoritative decision by one of its panels (and the president of KiFiD decides how many members shall sit on a panel) or by a court. In the latter situation, the power to refer points of law to the Supreme Court of the Netherlands has proved useful.[71]

F. United Kingdom

i. The Landscape of Consumer Ombudsmen

Many sectors in the UK have operated ADR schemes, sometimes going back to the 1960s.[72] Some sectors rely on mediation-arbitration models attached to business codes of conduct, such as travel (ABTA), motor vehicles (Motor Codes), dentists and so on. Official standards and matrices have been applied for ADR systems by regulators, such as the OFT (now CMA) and OFCOM, which mandate and raise standards of practice. There is a close link between ADR bodies and public regulatory authorities, now required by article 17 of Directive 2013/11/EU. There is also a move towards transparency of complaints (naming types, numbers, traders), which improves trading standards.

---

[69] See Weber and Hodges (n 66) 148–49.
[70] https://www.degeschillencommissie.nl/over-ons/publicaties/.
[71] Code of Civil Procedure, Arts 392–94.
[72] This section is based on extensive research reported in Hodges, Benöhr and Creutzfeldt-Banda (n 25).

Another ADR model, what might be described as 'consumer ombudsman', has proved to be highly effective in delivering both individual and collective redress. The ombudsman model has increasingly been adopted for regulated industries, with ombudsmen in financial services, pensions, communications, energy, legal services, aspects of environment (Green Deal), property, furniture, and recently for any type of consumer dispute, and it is spreading. A sectoral consumer ombudsman is particularly effective where it operates together with the sectoral regulatory authority as an integral part of the market regulatory mechanism. This designed level of cooperation is far easier under an ombudsman model than a mediation/arbitration model of ADR. The sector that has the most experience in that respect is financial services, where the relationship between the Financial Services Ombudsman and the Financial Conduct Authority has proved to be highly effective, efficient and swift. Similar effects can be seen in relation to communications and energy.

The effectiveness of the consumer ombudsman model is based on various features. First, traders in some sectors are bound by decisions of the ombudsman, so must engage with the process. Two main models exist here: in several sectors, statute can provide that traders are bound by the ombudsman's decision if the consumer accepts it,[73] whilst in some sectors the adherence is indicated in advance by membership of a particular scheme.[74] Second, traders typically fund the ombudsman scheme in full, so it is free to consumers. Third, ombudsmen decide every individual case, but have developed internal processes to identify and coordinate groups of similar cases so that consistent and efficient outcomes are achieved. The mechanisms are similar to how an English or Welsh court would case manage similar cases, especially by identifying (through efficient monitoring and use of information technology) where cases involve similar issues and then deciding critical common issues. Fourth, the ombudsmen have the ability to feedback information on trends to traders, regulators and consumers through publishing general data, and this can affect market behaviour.

Many consumer ombudsmen are free to consumers, being funded by business, either through statutory levies or contact arrangements between businesses and ombudsmen. Nearly all of them publish statistics on numbers of cases and case-handling times, which show that usage is broadly increasing (apart from a reduction in financial services form a large spike in numbers caused by one or two large cases, notably PPI), and durations are swift. In contrast, the arbitration-style ADR schemes usually charge a fee to consumers (although some may be refunded if the consumer loses); they can also be swift, but do not intrinsically have the ability to handle mass cases.

ii. The Financial Ombudsman Service

The Financial Ombudsman Service (FOS) was established by legislation in 2001,[75] but has roots in previous voluntary ADR bodies that were established 20 years earlier for insurance and banking. The procedure will not be explained in detail here, but it involves stages that can be classified as triage, mediation and decision. Every individual contact received by the FOS is responded to.

Consumer Ombudsmen schemes typically receive more inquiries about possible complaints than they receive formal claims, as shown in table 6.9. In 2016/17 the FOS received

---

[73] This applies in legislation on financial services, pensions, legal services.
[74] This applies for communications and energy.
[75] The Financial Services and Markets Act 2000.

enquiries from consumers (around 5,000 each working day: 604,278 by phone and 790,101 letters and emails), which led to a more detailed investigation as a total of 321,283 new complaints.[76] The FOS covers 56,000 businesses, whilst half the total number of complaints dealt with involved just four banking groups, and 4,015 financial businesses accounted for just 3% of complaints, each with just 25 complaints. Over half (52.5%) were about PPI.[77] Excluding PPI cases, 83% of complaints were resolved within three months, and 38,619 binding decisions were made. The FOS' cost base was £259.9 million with 3,676 employees at the end of the year. The FOS publishes data on individual complaints against firms.[78]

Table 6.10: Financial Ombudsman Service statistics 2010–16

Year	Contacts[79]	Cases[80]
2010–11	1,012,371	206,121
2011–12	1,268,798	264,375
2012–13	2,161,439	508,881
2013–14	2,357,374	512,167
2014–15	1,786,973	329,509
2015–16	1,631,955	340,899
2016–17	1,394,379	321,283

The FOS is geared towards processing individual complaints. However, it is able to deliver 'individual "collective" redress'.[81] First, although individual decisions do not create legal precedent, the large body of ombudsman 'lore' is available on the FOS' website, which demonstrates what constitutes fairness in particular situations and outlines approaches which can then be applied to specific sets of facts in individual complaints. Second, there is a regulatory requirement on financial institutions to observe the Ombudsman's decisions:

> the ombudsman's experience means they have unparalleled insight into behaviours and trends across the whole of the financial services industry. That insight is shared through FOS publications and reports, for instance on age-related complaints or financial scams, and through liaison with the regulator, government, trade and consumer bodies and the press. The FCA requires businesses to take into account decisions they have received from the ombudsman so that systemic issues can be identified and addressed.[82]

---

[76] *Fairness in a changing world. Annual review 2016/2017* (Financial Ombudsman Service, 2017).

[77] Other major case types were loans and credit; car and motorbike insurance; packaged bank accounts, interbank transfers, electronic money and other banking services; current accounts; warranties, mobile phone cover, home emergency cover and other insurance; credit cards; mortgages; household insurance; mortgage endowments; other products; other problems and concerns that people didn't know where else to take (for example, debt related worries and confusion about how to sort out a problem).

[78] See http://www.ombudsman-complaints-data.org.uk/.

[79] These constitute initial enquiries and complaints.

[80] These are referred to adjudicators and ombudsmen for further ADR.

[81] C Mitchell, 'The ombudsman—individual "collective" redress', paper delivered at the Conference on Empirical Evidence on Collective Redress in Europe, Oxford, 12–13 December 2016. The following text draws on her paper.

[82] ibid.

Third, although the FOS has no specific collective claim mechanisms, it has developed a number of procedures to deal with multiple horizontal issues, notably a lead case process, a test case procedure (usually on a point of law, which may be referred to court),[83] and collaboration mechanism under the FCA/CMA/FOS Coordination Committee.[84] The last of these (called the Wider Implications procedure until 2012) applies where there is a new or emerging issue that raises significant implications for consumers in general, or for industry, or even for one business, and it may involve more than one of the FCA, FOS and OFT. Most issues have been identified by FSA or FOS; the consumers' association has raised one, and industry none.

Under the 'lead case' process, the FOS identifies if a common principle exists in a number of similar cases, and whether it would be appropriate to group the cases together and identify an individual 'clean case' for the group in which the common issue arises without other complications. The other cases would be put on hold pending resolution of the lead case, and the result of the lead case applied in the others, although, if the decision is against the provider, the FOS might 'lean on' the provider to settle the other cases voluntarily. If the consumer in the lead case loses, the FOS sends an anonymised copy of the decision to all group members, asking them to inform the FOS if they think that their cases are different and why. The 'lead case' procedure has significant similarities to how a court would approach case management under a Group Litigation Order. The common theme is simply efficient and effective case management.

The largest case has been claims against financial providers over sale of PPI policies, which is discussed further below as it demonstrates the important situation where the integrated actions of a regulator and an ombudsman can be highly effective. In responding to the huge increase in volume of cases relating to PPI, the FOS introduced an IT case management tool named 'Navigator', which

> helps to analyse the permutation of circumstances in each case, applies the ombudsman service 'jurisprudence' to that permutation, and *suggests* an appropriate response which the adjudicator can accept, reject or modify. Navigator has been absolutely essential in enabling the ombudsman service to reconcile the competing demands of volume, quality and consistency.[85]

In his 2016 independent review of how the FOS handled the PPI challenge, Richard Thomas CBE concluded: 'The ombudsman service's "methodology"—an informal, inquisitorial/investigatory approach with very few hearings—proved scalable and robust and it is difficult to see how such large volumes could have been resolved any other way'.[86]

The Parliamentary Public Accounts Committee's examination of PPI claims also concluded that it was 'straightforward and free' for consumers to claim compensation through the FOS, and strongly criticised the fact that too many complaints were made through the services of claims management companies,[87] which were intermediaries who ought to have

---

[83] The test case procedure has not been applied, although one insurance firm did seek to invoke the test case procedure over the impact of the Icelandic volcano on travel insurance claims, but the ombudsman said it was inappropriate in the circumstances of the particular case.

[84] These procedures are described at Hodges, Benöhr and Creutzfeldt-Banda (n 25) 278 ff.

[85] R Thomas, *The Impact of PPI Mis-selling on the Financial Ombudsman Service* (Financial Ombudsman Service, 2016).

[86] ibid.

[87] 'Financial Services Mis-selling: Regulation and Redress', House of Commons Committee of Public Accounts, Forty-first Report of Session 2015–16, HC 847.

been unnecessary and who could take too much of an award as fees. A separate review by the FCA into the financial advice market concluded that the FOS 'has a valuable role in its outreach work with firms, publicising its resources and guidance, and the data it collects'.[88] It recommended that the FOS should go further and consider undertaking regular 'Best Practice' roundtables with industry and trade bodies where both sides can discuss relevant issues such as the evidence used when considering historic sales and suitability requirements.[89]

The FOS publishes data that identifies the number and types of different problems, and the banks against whom claims have been brought.[90]

Cases

Wide scale impact[91]

Perhaps the most visible effect of the FOS's findings is the recent change to insurance law. Previously, all UK insurance law was based on the Marine Insurance Act of 1906 which required anyone proposing for insurance to demonstrate utmost good faith by disclosing anything the insurer may consider material to the risk. This may be fine for commercial shipping contracts where the parties are equal but the consequences of getting it wrong might be very serious for the retail consumer who could hardly second-guess what the insurer would want to know.

Over a number of years FOS developed an approach to misrepresentation, in line with the Association of British Insurers' Statements of Good Insurance Practice, which recognised that consumers wouldn't necessarily know what an insurer would think was material to the risk and required that the insurer should ask clear questions to get the information it needed. This approach was considered by the Law Commission and adopted in the Consumer Insurance (Disclosure and Representation) Act 2012 which came into effect in April 2013. So now an approach which the ombudsman applied to individual complaints is imposed across the industry so that all consumers forming insurance contracts have the benefit of it, and not just those who complain.

And, of course, mass claims like mortgage endowments and PPI have required the development of processes and handling in a way that has impacted on consumers generally with many complaints being settled without individual consideration.

Other influences

But there are many less immediately obvious examples of how the ombudsman's findings can help other consumers. FOS has a duty to tell the regulator what it sees and it has always shared insight and information to help the regulator (and its predecessor, the Financial Services Authority) carry out its regulatory role. The FCA's interventionist approach means that concerns about businesses or issues can be followed up through supervision, and enforcement action taken where appropriate. This has important, beneficial consequences for all consumers—but is, of course, extremely hard to measure.

By way of example, over a period of three years FOS raised a number of concerns with the FCA about a particular business and its PPI complaint-handling process. This resulted in a fine of over

---

[88] *Financial Advice Market Review Final report* (Financial Conduct Authority, 2016).
[89] ibid, Recommendation 22.
[90] See http://www.ombudsman-complaints-data.org.uk/.
[91] Mitchell (n 80).

£2 million and a remediation exercise meaning nearly 5,000 consumers received redress. Another business unfairly rejected complaints because it thought its sales processes were both compliant and robust. Sharing FOS experience and working with FCA meant a change of approach on the part of the business and the review of a very significant number of complaints.

Explaining its approach to issues through the newsletter *Ombudsman News*, material on the website, published decisions and outreach events means that FOS helps businesses understand exactly what fairness means in particular circumstances. Pointing bankers and insurance underwriters beyond the precise wording of their account terms or policies to consider what actually happened in a case benefits all their customers. Rigidly applying policy or account terms and conditions without regard to the customer as a person can, and does, cause unfairness.

Another area where the FOS has influence is with claims management companies (CMCs). These commercial organisations thrive in the mass complaints areas of mortgage endowments and PPI. They bring complaints on behalf of consumers and receive a proportion of any compensation paid. A consumer does not need a representative to bring a complaint to the ombudsman whose procedures are easy to follow—even for those with vulnerabilities. And the CMCs often bring speculative claims to businesses wasting time and money. FOS has worked closely with CMCs to ensure that only appropriate cases are brought and that the necessary information is provided. Ensuring they understand FOS' approach means that many issues can be resolved without the need for formal complaints. So, for instance, in 2014–15 80% of complaints about packaged bank accounts were brought by CMCs—that figure has now fallen to 40%.

FOS also works with the media to provide information about complaint trends and issues. As an example, publication of the insight report on financial scams attracted media attention to raise awareness of the tactics of fraudsters and help consumers avoid problems.

Although impact is hard to measure, there are some instances where it can be gauged quite accurately. In 2011 the ombudsman issued a final decision concluding that the cloud of volcanic ash that had impacted on travel leading to a surge of travel insurance claims for delay could amount to adverse weather conditions meaning that many claims would be paid. The decision reflected the fact that the majority of insurers had settled these claims where their policies did not specifically exclude this risk. The business in question brought proceedings for judicial review to challenge the ombudsman's decision but the court rejected this challenge. The business then agreed not to pursue its legal action and several hundred complaints were settled on the back of this single complaint.

In June 2012 the ombudsman issued a final decision in which he found that a business had not handled fairly its decision to withdraw from the pet insurance market. The approach the ombudsman took led to the business offering a completely new policy to the complainant and additionally to all those customers who had been adversely affected by its decision.

iii. Integrated Voluntary, Regulatory and Ombudsman Redress: PPI

This section illustrates how various techniques can be integrated into a holistic practical approach. The three elements are: first, voluntary complaint and redress procedures by businesses, where procedures are sometimes subject to regulatory requirements; second, redress powers of regulatory authorities to order redress (the specific powers vary between sectors); and third, the availability of a specialist ombudsmen service, to whom complaints that are not resolved direct between consumers and businesses may be referred, either on a 'normal' basis or under the rules of a specific redress scheme, such as one mandated by a regulatory authority.

The most prominent example of this integrated approach relates to claims over the mis-sale of Payment Protection Insurance (PPI) products in the financial services sector. PPI was

> a major retail market, with sales of over 5 million policies a year during 2000 to 2005, with premiums in the region of £7 billion a year. It was very profitable for firms. Often the underlying loan served as a loss leader on which to sell PPI. It was targeted at consumers taking on debt, many of whom were financially vulnerable, as their focus was typically on securing the loan with the insurance incidental to the transaction.[92]

The 2016 independent report found that:

> At least 45 million policies were sold,[93] possibly as many as 60 million. From these sales, well over 16.5 million[94] claims for compensation have already been brought forward by consumers—the vast majority stimulated by claims management companies (CMCs). At the top of the iceberg, 1.3 million[95] of these claims have converted into complaints brought to the ombudsman service. Over 1 million cases have been closed by the ombudsman service, with average 'uphold' rates as high as 89% in 2009, dropping to a 'mere' 62%[96] [in 2015].[97]

The core statistics were stated as at mid-2016 in a report by the National Audit Office (NAO),[98] supplemented by an independent report:

— £22.2 billion compensation was paid between April 2011 and November 2015 following mis-selling of payment protection insurance (PPI);

— 59% of customer complaints to financial services firms related to mis-selling (including PPI) in 2014, compared to 25% in 2010;

— £298 million fines issued by the Financial Conduct Authority for mis-selling activity since April 2013;

— £834 million total operating costs of the Financial Conduct Authority (£523 million), Financial Ombudsman Service (£240 million) and Financial Services Compensation Scheme (£71 million) in 2014–15;

— 62% of mis-selling complaints were upheld by the Financial Ombudsman Service since April 2013;

— 17% of payment protection insurance cases at the Financial Ombudsman Service have been waiting over two years to be resolved (39,300 complaints);

— £898 million amount of compensation received by consumers from the Financial Services Compensation Scheme related to mis-selling by defunct firms, between 2010–11 and 2014–15;

— In 2013, the value of goods and services produced in the UK financial and insurance sectors was over £120 billion, about 7% of gross domestic product.

[92] *The Financial Conduct Authority: Approach to Regulation* (Financial Services Authority, 2011) para 5.12.
[93] FCA August 2014—Thematic Review TR14/14—Redress for payment protection insurance (PPI) mis-sales.
[94] FCA November 2015—CP15/39 Rules and guidance on payment protection insurance complaints.
[95] Financial Ombudsman service 2014/15 Annual Review.
[96] FCATR14/14.
[97] Thomas (n 84).
[98] *Financial Services Mis-selling: Regulation and Redress* (National Audit Office, 2016) HC Paper No 851.

Sums set aside at early 2016 took the total potential compensation bill to almost £27 billion, and some have estimated that the compensation paid or provided for has now exceeded £30 billion, with some suggestions that this figure could rise further still.[99]

Several important points arise from this case study. First, the actions of businesses, regulator and ombudsman can clearly be seen to form an integrated model of delivering redress. A summit of representatives from all the major banks and credit card providers, regulators and the Financial Ombudsman Service in April 2012 agreed action to help make PPI claims easier and that claims could be resolved without a consumer needing to use a Claims Management Company.[100] As experience accumulated, improvements were made to the arrangements.

It should not be overlooked that many banks and financial providers operated voluntary redress mechanisms, which processed the majority of PPI claims without the direct involvement of external agencies. Consumer complaint mechanisms have been subject to increasingly specific regulation and supervision by the regulator: the Financial Services Authority was succeeded by a new regulator, the Financial Conduct Authority, from the end of 2012.[101] The existence of both regulatory scrutiny and of the ombudsman as a second stage dispute resolution mechanism creates incentives for businesses to resolve disputes directly with consumers. However, the general public impression has been that banks have been slow to respond well to rectify their selling of PPI and to paying redress.[102] During the 2000s, the FSA built a large part of its supervisory approach on the assumption that 'the vast majority of firms intend to treat their customers fairly'[103] but this was shown to have been wrong,[104] and major reforms to the regulatory system were introduced after the financial crash that commenced in 2008, including new legal power for supervisors to ban products.[105] The FSA set out a proposal for guidance on the fair assessment and redress of complaints related to sales of PPI, and rules requiring firms to re-assess complaints against the proposed new guidance,[106] in response to which the banks instituted judicial review proceedings, which the court rejected.[107] Final Guidance was issued in 2013, jointly by

---

[99] Thomas (n 84).

[100] Press release, *Commitment to Help Consumers Agreed at PPI Summit* (British Bankers Association, 23/04/2012), at http://www.bba.org.uk/media/article/commitment-to-help-consumers-agreed-at-ppi-summit.

[101] For the FCA's general approach see *The Financial Conduct Authority: Approach to Regulation* (Financial Services Authority, 2011).

[102] *The Cost of Redress: the Lessons to be Learned from the PPI Mis-selling Scandal* (Citizens Advice Bureau, March 2014).

[103] FSA, *Treating Customers Fairly—Towards Fair Outcomes* (2006) 7. Uphold rates differed between institutions. In cases handled by the FOS between 1 July and 31 December 2011 they ranged between 6% and 100%: *Complaints Data on Individual Financial Businesses* (FOS, February 2012). The average uphold rate in the 169,132 new cases against 221 businesses in the first half of 2016 was 48%—ranging from 3% to 92% across the individual businesses: *Ombudsman News—Issue 134* (FOS, July 2016).

[104] E Ferran, 'The New Mandate for the Supervision of Financial Services Conduct' (2012) *Current Legal Problems* 1–43.

[105] FS Act 2012, cl 22, inserting FSMA s137C.

[106] http://www.fsa.gov.uk/pages/Library/Corporate/Annual/ar09_10.shtml. See *Finalised guidance. Payment protection products. FSA/OFT joint guidance* (Office of Fair Trading and FSA, 2013).

[107] *R (on the application of the British Bankers Association) v Financial Services Authority* [2011] EWHC 999 (Admin); [2011] Bus LR 1531.

the FCA and Office of Fair Trading.[108] In 2016, the NAO concluded that 'Overall, banks' handling of complaints has been poor, requiring ongoing action from FCA and FOS'.[109]

The FCA issued guidance in 2012 on what a payment protection insurance customer contact letter should contain and how it should be presented.[110] The FCA has undertaken some interesting behavioural research aimed at how best to encourage consumers who may be due redress to respond to customer contact letters. While large redress exercises such as PPI receive considerable publicity, many instances where consumers are due redress understandably do not. In these cases, the firm alerts customers to a potential issue, often in the form of a letter that gives customers information, which they need to answer. The research (based on a real case in which a firm was voluntarily writing to almost 200,000 customers about a failing its sales process) found that a number of simple changes to the way that contact letters were written produced dramatic improvements in consumers' response rates, compatible with a simple model of busy people reviewing quickly the post that they receive.[111] The firm's original letter received a 1.5% response rate, which was particularly low compared with other redress exercises undertaken by the FSA, although understandable in this particular setting.[112] Use of salient bullet points had the largest single effect, increasing response rates over the control by 3.8 percentage points, just over 2.5 times compared to the original letter. Use of a simplified text and including a statement that the claims process would only take five minutes each increased response by 1.4 percentage points, almost doubling the response rate. Adding a message on the envelope to 'act quickly' had only a small positive effect and there was no impact of use of the FSA logo. Unexpectedly, there was a small but statistically significant decrease in response using the CEO's signature. Sending a reminder letter, which was a copy of the original letter, had much more effect if it had salient bullets, and improved response rates to almost 12%, which was equivalent to an additional 20,000 people responding to claim redress. Gender plays little role in response to the letter, whilst there were marked differences across age groups.[113] There were fewer marked differences across those people due different amounts of redress. With the control letter there was little change in response between those who were due £50 or more and those who were due less than £10. But with the best letter, there was a stronger relationship between response and redress due; however, this variation was still less than the variation in response with age. The fact that response rates to the control letter did not vary much with the size of redress suggested that the control letter failed to focus consumers' attention on the amount of redress owed.

---

[108] *Payment Protection Products. FSA/OFT Joint Guidance* (FCA and OFT, 2013).

[109] *Financial Services Mis-selling: Regulation and Redress* (National Audit Office, 2016) HC Paper No 851.

[110] *Payment Protection Insurance Customer Contact Letters (PPI CCLs)—Fairness, Clarity and Potential Consequences* (FSA, July 2012) FG12/17.

[111] *Encouraging Consumers to Claim Redress: Evidence from a Field Trial* (FCA, 2013).

[112] Several reasons were suggested. First, many consumers had already been provided with a refund from the firm on their own initiative. Second, a number may also have been happy with the sales process and not felt in need of redress. Third, the potential value of redress was low, the average redress due was only £21. Fourth, the relationship between the firm and the consumer had already ended, which may mean the firm has an out-of-date address or that the consumer is less likely to open the envelope.

[113] With the control letter the middle-aged responded the least and older age groups responded far more. But the pattern changed for the best letter: the young responded the least and response increased with age. So the treatments had the greatest relative effect on the middle-aged, who are arguably the busiest.

The FCA has audited firms' performance in the delivery of redress. It has found some redress processes to be inadequate, breaching requirements, in response to which it ordered rectification, and instituted sanctions against some. A 2013 review of 18 medium-sized firms found that six firms were handling PPI complaints as the FCA would expect but that for the remaining 12 firms there were still significant issues with their PPI complaint handling to be put right.[114] The FCA also carried out mystery shopping scrutiny of providers in 2013, which found problems in the quality of investment advice given by banks and building societies, following which the firms involved cooperated with the regulator and agreed to take immediate action.[115] Significant fines were imposed on some firms.[116]

The FOS took the strategic decision to process cases prioritising the proper handling of individual cases (considered to be a *sine qua non* of the ombudsman service) over an 'industrialised' approach. An independent review by Richard Thomas CBE strongly supported that decision.[117] He commended the achievement of resolving more than one million cases, with 800,000 alone closed in the three years to 2016, involving a major exercise in expanding, training and supervising staff (around 4,000 at the peak) without resorting to out-sourcing.

The FOS was found to have operated well.[118] The NAO concluded that 'The Ombudsman has continued to provide an effective service to complainants following a massive increase in complaints, but it has struggled with a backlog of older payment protection insurance cases.'[119] Consumer satisfaction rate has been very high, even if the huge scale of the tsunami of PPI cases presented a considerable challenge for the FOS, causing some processing delays.[120] However, delays in relation to resolving historical cases, often caused by the unavailability of reliable evidence, would almost certainly have been longer if cases

---

[114] *TR13/7—Payment Protection Insurance Complaints: Report on the Fairness of Medium-sized Firms' Decisions and Redress* (FCA, August 2013).

[115] *Assessing the Quality of Investment Advice in the Retail Banking Sector. A Mystery Shopping Review* (FSA, February 2013). Findings included that the adviser gave the customer unsuitable advice in 11% of cases and that the adviser did not gather enough information to make sure their advice was suitable, so it was not possible to assess whether the customer received good or poor advice, in 15% of cases.

[116] The FSA imposed a financial penalty of approximately £4.3 million on Lloyds TSB Bank, Lloyds TSB Scotland and Bank of Scotland for failure to pay redress promptly to PPI complainants between 5 May 2011 and 9 March 2012. The Final Notice contains detailed findings by the FSA of inadequacies in the implementation of the redress payments process. The Final Notice focused on failures in the planning of the redress payments process, a reliance on manual processes in the face of overwhelming numbers of complaints (which hampered the ability to track and check the processing of payments), a lack of quality control and inadequate resourcing of parts of the PPI redress process. The FSA highlighted that a full reconciliation process had been conducted to ensure that customers had not been disadvantaged as a result of the delays in payments being made. The FSA fined the Co-operative Bank plc £113,300 in January 2013 for its failure to handle a number of PPI complaints. The FCA fined Lloyds Banking Group £117 million for mishandling thousands of PPI complaints between March 2012 and May 2013, and extracted an agreement by the bank to review 1.2 million complaints, for which a further £710 million was added to the £12 billion already set aside to cover repayments. The FCA fined Clydesdale Bank £20,678,300 (after a 30% discount for early settlement) on 15 April 2015 for failures in processes for handling 126,000 PPI complaints between May 2011 and July 2013, in which 42,200 may have been rejected unfairly and 50,900 resulted in inadequate redress.

[117] Thomas (n 84).

[118] *Financial Services Mis-selling: Regulation and Redress: Forty-first Report of Session 2015-16* (HC Paper No 847: House of Commons Committee of Public Accounts, May 2016).

[119] *Financial Services Mis-selling: Regulation and Redress* (National Audit Office, 2016) HC Paper No 851.

[120] The NAO found that 'In 2014-15, 74% of complainants said it handled their complaints efficiently and professionally.' ibid, para 4.9.

had been processed in court, either individually or collectively. The independent report concluded:

> This report has also probed whether more could or should have been done to group cohorts of cases together and treat them all in identical or very similar fashion. However, given in particular the complexities of PPI complaints, there would have been significant risks from excessive standardisation in terms of unacceptable quality, inconsistency and poor customer service. It is not surprising that no obvious basis has been identified for aggregating cases more effectively or more efficiently than has been achieved by Navigator. The conclusion has to be that any wholesale attempt to group cases any further into cohorts has not been, and is unlikely to be, a viable option.[121]

There were no apparent attempts to establish aggregated consumer litigation, or calls for such a solution by any of the many commentators on the PPI sage, including Parliamentary, consumer or other.

The fact that this integrated system is new has still allowed a new breed of parasitic intermediary to be established, claims management companies (CMCs), which have caused significant extra and unnecessary transactional costs. Lawyers have played almost no role in advising or representing consumers on PPI claims, or similar low value consumer claims. The estimated amount of commission received by claims management companies on PPI claims between April 2011 and November 2015 was between £3.8 billion and £5 billion, representing up to 23% of total compensation paid in such cases.[122] CMCs were assumed to charge between 25% and 33% of redress received by customers.

A significant number of PPI claims brought by CMCs were unsubstantiated or fraudulent, necessitating regulatory action.[123] In a significant number of cases, CMCs have operated illegally and caused significant consumer detriment.[124] Regulatory pressure has been introduced to control CMCs, involving action by various regulators[125] and the FOS and the Legal Ombudsman. The Claims Management Regulator was given extra powers in December 2014 to fine CMCs for breaking the rules.[126] By mid-2016 it had issued four fines totalling £1.6 million. In January 2016, it revoked the licence of a company that made 40 million nuisance calls over a three-month period. As the availability of ombudsmen has spread across different trading sectors, so has consumer knowledge of the availability of ombudsmen instead of lawyers. The existence of a free ombudsman service should

---

[121] Thomas (n 84) para 1.7.

[122] *Financial Services Mis-selling: Regulation and Redress* (National Audit Office, 2016) HC Paper No 851.

[123] See recently *Claims Management Regulation. Proposals for Amendment to the Conduct of Authorised Persons Rules* (Ministry of Justice, August 2012); *CAB Evidence Briefing: The Claims Pests—CAB Evidence on PPI and Claims-management Companies* (Citizens Advice Bureau, November 2012); *Claims Management Regulation: Approach and Enforcement of the Referral Fee Ban* (Ministry of Justice, November 2012); Press release, 'Rogue PPI claim companies targeted by fines and toughened regulations' (Ministry of Justice, 21 November 2012). *Payday Lending Compliance Review. Interim Report* (OFT, November 2012), OFT1466; *The PPI Claims market: Dealing with malpractice* (Ministry of Justice, February 2013); *Rogue PPI Claim Companies Targeted by Fines and Toughened Regulations* (Ministry of Justice, 21 November 2013).

[124] *The Cost of Redress: the Lessons to be Learned from the PPI Mis-selling Scandal* (Citizens Advice Bureau, March 2014).

[125] The main offices were the Claims Management Regulator, the Financial Conduct Authority, the Information Commissioner, and local authorities' Trading Standards Departments. The number of CMCs peaked at 3,400 in 2011 and fell to 2,300 by November 2011: Press release: *Rogue PPI Claim Companies Targeted by Fines and Toughened Regulations* (Ministry of Justice, 21 November 2013).

[126] Financial Services (Banking Reform) Act 2013, s 139.

make the role of CMCs or other intermediaries redundant in consumer claims. The NAO concluded that 'Although complaining directly to FOS is straightforward and free, many consumers who have been mis-sold financial products fail to receive full compensation, because of lack of awareness or reliance on claims management companies.'[127]

The FCA consulted in late 2015 on introducing a deadline for PPI complaints, with the stated rationale that 'An FCA-led communications campaign may empower consumers and encourage more of them to complain directly to the firms concerned, rather than using CMCs or other paid advocates, and therefore benefit in full from the redress paid out.'[128] Proposals were made in 2016.[129] This took place against a background of widespread dissatisfaction over the activities of CMC, although the FCA was careful to take a balanced line.[130]

iv. Ombudsman Services: Energy, Communications, Property and Others

Ombudsman Services (OS) provides ombudsman schemes across a variety of regulated and non-regulated industries in the private sector. The two largest schemes provided are those in the energy and communications sectors.

Established in 2002, The Ombudsman Service Ltd, trading as Ombudsman Services, is a not for profit private limited company, and a fully independent organisation. While not created by statute, in most areas of its operation legislation requires that the services provided by OS are in place. OS was first approved by Ofcom, the UK communications regulator, as the Office of the Telecommunications Ombudsman, to provide redress under the terms of the Communications Act, 2003. In 2008, the Energy Ombudsman was approved by Ofgem to provide redress under the terms of the Consumers, Estate Agents and Redress Act, 2007. In 2015 OS launched a new service which accepts complaints across all consumer sectors, the Consumer Ombudsman. This service is approved by the Chartered Institute of Trading Standards under the Under the Alternative Dispute Resolution for Consumer Disputes (Competent Authorities and Information) Regulations 2015.

OS is impartial and independent of industry, consumers, regulators and government, although it works closely with all of these groups. OS's services are free to use for consumers, with the costs borne by business rather than the public purse.

OS has in the region of 10,000 participating companies, and last year received 220,111 initial contacts from complainants and resolved 71,765 complaints. OS saw a year on year increase in complaints of 118% between 2013 and 2014 and a further 35% increase between 2014 and 2015. In the energy industry alone OS has seen a 336% increase in complaint volumes between 2013 and 2015. The company currently employs more than 600 people in Warrington and has a turnover in excess of £27 million.

---

[127] *Financial Services Mis-selling: Regulation and Redress* (National Audit Office, 2016) HC Paper No 851.

[128] CP 15/39, para 2.5.

[129] *Rules and Guidance on Payment Protection Insurance Complaints: Feedback on CP15/39 and Further Consultation* (CP16/20: FCA, August 2016). The FCA also sought views on making rules and guidance on handling PPI complaints in light of the Supreme Court judgment in *Plevin v Paragon Personal Finance Ltd.* Comments by 11 October 2016.

[130] Para 2.18 of CP 16/20 noted that: 'We have always acknowledged that some consumers may reasonably prefer to pay for the assistance of a CMC in making their complaint. We also acknowledge that some CMCs have played an effective role in identifying and challenging some examples of poor complaint handling by firms, and that our own supervisory work has benefitted from the examples these CMCs have provided to us.'

OS is developing procedures to deal with collective claims along the same lines as the FOS. However, OS currently utilises its data and insights to spot systemic issues and identify broader trends. Where OS determines that a large number of consumers have experienced a similar problem, rather than waiting to receive individual complaints and then dealing with these retrospectively, OS takes a more proactive approach. First, it works with firms to clarify the decision-making principles that the ombudsman would apply to such cases, and also by publishing information for consumers on what they should expect from their supplier in relation to that particular issue. This helps to ensure that cases are resolved appropriately by firms at the first tier, and can prevent a mass redress situation from developing at ombudsman-level. This facilitates a smoother complaint-journey for consumers and, as a result, can also help firms with reputation and customer retention.

OS's preventative approach also involves horizon scanning to proactively tackle future high impact events. By anticipating where large-scale issues may arise for consumers and by working with industry to prepare for them, potential consumer detriment can be addressed more quickly and robustly. This broader perspective allows OS to work with government and regulators to identify where there are emerging issues that can be addressed. This systemic approach therefore allows OS to inform policy and regulatory interventions and industry-led solutions to common problems.

Case study: Large energy network

Following a period of severe weather, OS identified that a large energy network operator was likely to receive a high volume of complaints regarding loss of supply. Around 70,000 customers had lost supply, with 30,000 claims made to the network.

It was the network's intention to reject claims for compensation and send a deadlock letter with the first response. They suggested that OS should not take on these cases because the decision to refuse compensation was in line with industry standards.

OS confirmed that, as consumers must have the right to ADR, it would not make any blanket rejection. However, OS committed to work with the network to help it resolve complaints fairly at the first tier, delivering fair resolution to all parties but with a swifter and simpler process for consumers. The following steps were taken:

— OS set out the decision-making principles it would apply to cases on its website. The decision-making principles were not specific to the network operator but gave guidance on how OS would deal with complaints about loss of supply due to severe weather. That way, consumers could better judge whether their energy network had handled their complaint reasonably.

— OS also set out the best practice for an energy network during loss of supply due to severe weather, which it published on its website, so consumers had a better understanding of the standards and practices they could expect.

— OS also published scenarios to help consumers see whether their circumstances might warrant a guaranteed standards payment.

— OS liaised with Ofgem regarding its intentions, to ensure that the regulator was satisfied with OS's approach.

The network's proposed approach could have meant significant cost to the business and its customers. OS's proactive work with this network led to early resolution of many complaints and provided clarity for consumers.

Case study: Preparing for high impact events- smart meter roll-out

The smart meter roll-out provides an example of where OS is focussing on horizon scanning and tackling future high impact events. While smart metering is likely to reduce the complaints that OS receives on matters such as billing and switching, the roll-out process itself will generate consumer complaints.

OS is working closely with industry to identify any problems that may emerge during the roll-out of smart meters. By doing so, it will enable suppliers to anticipate and avoid problems in the first place, and to develop clear protocols so that complaints on common issues (eg the installation process, or final bills from old meters) can be dealt with quickly and satisfactorily.

7

Reassessing the Objectives

The empirical findings set out in the earlier chapters identify a shift in systems and intermediaries that can be attributed to two factors. First, the newer options are more attractive because they satisfy all of the performance criteria (ease of access, cost, speed, ability to deliver outcomes) more effectively than the litigation option. Second, the newer options deliver more functions than their antecedents.[1] In particular, the newer mechanisms deliver, directly or indirectly, more of the 'market regulatory' functions than the older mechanisms, and do so more efficiently.

This shift in intermediaries, together with consideration of functions, raises the question of reassessing the *objectives* that are sought.

I. The Primary Objectives

The two primary objectives of a legal mechanism that delivers a remedy based on damages are *delivering compensation* and *affecting future behaviour*. The main focus of this book is on monetary compensation, so we do not deal with other remedies aimed at stopping ongoing breaches of law (the prohibitory injunction).

Both of these objectives are, of course, social goods. However, in the context of the EU, at least, both of these objectives take on particular importance in the context of the *market*. Ensuring that the primary market actors—consumers and traders—have confidence that compensation will be delivered to those harmed by breaches of the rules of the market should support confidence in the market itself, and hence in the willingness of the actors to use the market. The same reasoning applies in relation to ensuring confidence that behaviour in the market will be fair and in accordance with the rules.

A. Subsidiary Process Objectives

There are also subsidiary process objectives of economy and efficiency. First, the mechanism should increase *access* of those directly affected to the mechanism. This is typically called the 'access to justice' objective. However, access to justice in the form of access to the mechanism does not guarantee access to, or delivery of, the primary objectives. It is delivery

---

[1] See the list of Objectives for Market Regulation set out at ch 1 above.

of the primary objectives, in other words the delivery of outcomes, rather than the mere possibility of access to them, that is more important.

Aggregation reduces cost in all of the collective mechanisms considered in this book. In the case of collective litigation, the means by which access is increased is through reducing the common costs of the process through aggregation (in most European civil procedure systems), or transferring those costs to a risk-taking intermediary (as typically in the US civil procedure system), which overcomes, or is said to assist in overcoming, the barrier to entry that such costs pose to individual claimants. In the case of regulatory redress and many European consumer ombudsmen, the costs to individual claimants are typically nil, and are borne by the state or the business sector that funds the regulatory or ombudsman system.[2] However, in most regulatory redress cases the costs of ordering or agreeing that redress should be paid appear to be notably low, as the case studies indicate that cases are resolved speedily.

The second subsidiary objective is to increase *process efficiency*. In other words, the collective redress process should be efficient. In collective litigation, this is often called the objective of 'judicial economy' but that term is too restrictive.[3] The real economy sought is that of the process as a whole, and thence reduction in the costs of the parties and intermediaries as well as the judge and judicial system. Again, aggregation reduces cost in all of the mechanisms considered.

II. Delivering Compensation

There is little controversial about the objective that a mechanism should be available that delivers compensation for harm caused as a result of harm caused in breach of legal rules. Well-established theories have been expounded to justify the need for delivery of compensation, as matters of social fairness and social solidarity, and of compensatory or corrective justice, and distributional justice. It may be helpful to give a short—necessarily incomplete—indication of some of these theories. The principal reason for doing so, however, is the conclusion that none of these theories demand a particular *mechanism* by which the compensation objective is delivered or achieved. As far as the people involved in the compensatory transaction are concerned, and as far as society generally is concerned, the compensatory objective is merely the functional one of providing *money*. That function can be satisfied by a number of possible mechanisms.

---

[2] See C Hodges, I Benöhr and N Creutzfeldt-Banda, *Consumer ADR in Europe* (Oxford, Hart Publishing, 2012); P Cortes (ed), *The Transformation of Consumer Dispute Resolution in the European Union: A Renewed Approach to Consumer Protection* (Oxford, Oxford University Press, 2016).

[3] R Bernstein, 'Judicial Economy and Class Actions' (1978) 7(2) *The Journal of Legal Studies* 349; S Issacharoff, 'Collective Action and Class Action' in C Piché (ed), *The Class Action Effect: From the Legislator's Imagination to Today's Uses and Practices* (Montreal, Éditions Yvon Blais, 2018).

A. Social Solidarity and Risk Spreading

When a member of society suffers harm caused by another, money is provided for the cost of care and support and to compensate for pain and suffering or moral damage. The individual is provided with care and money *by others*. The essential justification is social. It reflects the social humanitarian relationship that human beings have for one another when they live together in the community of a modern civil society.[4] Thus, members of society combine to give mutual support to those of their number who may suffer harm.

There are two rationales for this arrangement: one humanitarian (or religious) and the other economic (and involving a greater element of self-interest than the former). The existential fact is that an individual might encounter such a level of misfortune that he or she would not have the resources to cope or regain some form of prior normality. In response to this, the social rationale based on humanitarian *solidarity* is a belief that one is part of a group engaged in *mutual* living together for the benefit of all. A simple altruistic concern for other human beings motivates giving mutual support when it is needed. This may be making a one-off gesture of support or payment in response to an unexpected disaster, such as a tsunami or terrorist attack, or it may be more institutionalised and ongoing or permanent. As Cane notes, 'Losses that may be crushing if imposed on an individual can be borne easily when distributed amongst a large group of people; this is clearly in the interests of those at risk, as well as of society as a whole.'[5] The rationale is to support social harmony and cohesion. This may support self-interest in that arrangements to support others should support one's self in the event of misfortune, which can happen to anyone. There is also the prospect of enhancing society's collective economic benefits through supporting speedy rehabilitation so that those who are injured can swiftly return to becoming productive members of the socio-economic system.

However, both the principle and the extent of social support attract strongly divergent interpretations in different political systems. For example, in a communist or socialist state, equality is a fundamental value, so in theory every citizen should be equally looked after by the state. The reality may be somewhat different, as the history of communist regimes demonstrates. In contrast, in the USA, there is strong emphasis on individual freedom, and the notion of supporting one's fellow citizens is not as strong.[6] In post-war Europe, welfare state policies were introduced in order to ration limited resources but also based on socialist principles, widening social security and providing national health coverage.[7] Contemporary European states have evolved into market-based systems in which greater general

---

[4] J Finnis, *Natural Law and Natural Rights* (Oxford, Clarendon Press, 1980). For law as a social system see: DJ Galligan, *Law in Modern Society* (Oxford, Oxford University Press, 2007); J Habermas, *Between Facts and Norms* (Cambridge, MA, Harvard University Press, 1996); E Durkheim, *The Division of Labour in Society* WD Halls (tr) (Basingstoke, Macmillan, 1984) (organic solidarity); F Pirie, *The Anthropology of Law* (Oxford University Press, Clarendon Law Series, 2013).

[5] P Cane, *Atiyah's Accidents, Compensation and the Law* 8th edn (Cambridge, Cambridge University Press, 2013) 412.

[6] A striking recent manifestation of this can be seen in the Obama administration's attempts to introduce a universal healthcare system, and the strength of opposition to that system.

[7] T Judt, *Postwar: A History of Europe Since 1945* (New York, Vintage Books, 2010); F Fukuyama, *The Great Disruption* (New York, Simon & Schuster, 1999).

affluence permits citizens to provide their own self-insurance, but remaining inherently based on social solidarity principles.

Another perspective on the arrangement is that of *risk spreading*, akin to insurance. If a risk materialises in the form of a significant injury, the mechanism spreads the cost of dealing with the consequences of that injury. Thus, groups of individuals or businesses share risk amongst themselves in order to undertake risk spreading and sharing of the dealing with the consequences of the occurrence of damage. The groups may be, in the first instance, all those who have taken out first-party insurance with a particular commercial insurer, or all those who have third-party liability insurance with the insurer of the defendant who funds the claimant, or all taxpayers in a particular state. There may be some combination of these sources of funds, and funding may ultimately come from lower down chains of commerce, for example where part of the price paid by customers of companies is allocated to the seller's insurance cost. Further, all insurance mechanisms involve wider pools, since individual insurance companies invariably take out reinsurance contracts with reinsurance companies (and often different layers of cover with different reinsurers), which have the effect of sharing risk on a very wide basis. Insurance, therefore, acts as a mechanism for subdividing populations into comparatively homogeneous risk categories.[8]

At one level, those involved in particular activities—such as employing workers, driving cars, running fleets of commercial vehicles, flying aeroplanes, manufacturing medicines, running hospitals, working in particular medical specialisations—may in general pool risks, pay premiums that are roughly similar, and provide the capital from which claims are paid, but it is extremely difficult to view any one notional pool in isolation and as operating distinctly from any other, such that premiums and the availability of insurance is closely related to the individual risk of any one contributor. One way or another, the practical effect is that we are all perpetually insuring everyone else, and funding the cost of the consequences of others' misfortunes and accidents.[9]

Members of risk pooling groups need not, of course, all contribute the same financial contributions. Taxation is usually regressive, so that the rich pay more than those who have less. Individuals who pay for commercial insurance may be charged premiums related to the risk of the activity that is covered, or the risk of attracting liability claims, or the geographical area in which they operate (trading in the USA has a high liability risk because of the perceived high incidence of claims and their higher value than elsewhere), but may also depend on the state of health or competition of the insurance market.[10]

Despite political differences in the extent of social support, the idea of spreading the risk and cost of caring for and supporting those injured is fundamental in *all* of the socio-legal mechanisms of tort liability and first-party insurance, and not just of state funded systems.

---

[8] J Simon, 'Driving Governmentality: Automobile Accidents, Insurance and the Challenge to the Social Order in the Inter-war Years' (1998) 4 *Connecticut Insurance Law Journal* 521–88.

[9] Cane (n 5) 411 ('The effect of the tort system is not, in general, merely to shift a loss from one person to another; the loss is normally distributed over a large number of people, and over some period of time.').

[10] P O'Malley, 'Fines, Risks and Damages: Money Sanctions and Justice in Control Societies' (2010) *Sydney Law School Research Paper No 10/40*; G Wagner, 'Tort Law and Liability Insurance' (2006) 31 *The Geneva Papers* 277; T Baker, 'Insurance as Tort Regulation: Six Ways that Liability Insurance Shapes Tort Law' (2006) 12 *Connecticut Insurance Law Journal* 1; R Merkin and J Steele, *Insurance and the Law of Obligations* (Oxford, Oxford University Press, 2013); R Merkin, 'Tort, Insurance and Ideology: Further Thoughts' (2012) 75(3) *The Modern Law Review* 301.

But while risk sharing and social rationales explain the rationale for formalised compensation arrangements that respond to injuries, *they do not necessarily illuminate what sort of mechanism should be in place to achieve compensation, other than that it should be sufficiently effective in producing the outcome of adequate compensation for an adequate number of those injured, within a reasonable time after they suffer injury and incur losses as a result of the injury.* As Cane says, all sorts of permutations and combinations are possible.[11] The variations in mechanisms and the extent of the support offered that are found in different political systems are considerable. However, most analysis of compensation systems and rules focuses not on the basic political philosophies but on more restricted analysis of legal mechanisms, to which we now turn.

B. Justifications for Tort Liability

Providing compensation is assumed to be a central objective of liability law, as enforced through court and litigation systems, wider analyses of other options, such as social security and no-fault schemes, have been of minority interest. We will briefly examine some theoretical ideas here.

Compensatory or corrective justice—a responsibility to make good harm caused—has been asserted virtually universally, leading exponents being Aristotle,[12] Aquinas,[13] Grotius,[14] Pufendorf[15] and Beever.[16] Thus, corrective justice is supported by some as being the sole justification for private law, irrespective of any social policy.[17] A related theory adopts a rights-based analysis, based on basic values of inter-personal morality, fairness and justice.[18]

A further approach—civil recourse theory—rejects the argument of corrective justice that the state rectifies private wrongs, and asserts that a person who has been wronged by another is awarded by the state a private right of action and an enforcement mechanism as a proportionate response, to use if the person so chooses.[19] The focus is, therefore, on a

---

[11] Cane (n 5).

[12] *Nichomachean Ethics, Book V* (T Irwin tr, Indianapolis, Hackett Publishing, 1999) paras 1131b–1134a.

[13] T Aquinas, *Summa Theologica* (Fathers of English Dominican Province trs, New York, Benziger Bros, 1947), part 2(2) question 62 arts 1–3.

[14] H Grotius, *De Jure Belli ac Pacis Libri tres* (FW Kelsey tr, Oxford, Clarendon Press, 1925) book 2 ch 17 para I.

[15] S Pufendorf, *Of the Law of Nature and Nations* (HC Oldfather and WA Oldfather trs, Oxford, Clarendon Press, 1934) book 3 ch 1 § 2.

[16] A Beever, *Rediscovering the Law of Negligence* (Oxford, Hart Publishing, 2007); A Beever, 'Our Most Fundamental Rights' in D Nolan and A Robertson (eds), *Rights and Private Law* (Oxford, Hart Publishing, 2012) ch 3.

[17] EJ Weinrib, *The Idea of Private Law* (Cambridge, MA, Harvard University Press, 1995); EJ Weinrib, *Corrective Justice* (Oxford, Oxford University Press, 2012).

[18] R Stevens, *Torts and Rights* (Oxford, Oxford University Press, 2007); R Stevens, 'Rights and Other Things' Law' in Nolan and Robertson (n 16).

[19] B Zipursky, 'Rights, Wrongs, and Recourse' (1998) 51 *Vanderbilt Law Review* 1; B Zipursky, 'Philosophy of Private Law' in J Coleman and S Shiro (eds), *The Oxford Handbook of Jurisprudence and Philosophy of Law* (Oxford, Oxford University Press, 2002); B Zipursky, 'Civil Recourse, Not Corrective Justice' (2003) 91 *Georgetown Law Journal* 695; JCP Goldberg, 'The Constitutional Status of Tort Law: Due Process and the Right to a Law for the Redress of Wrongs' (2005) 115 *Yale Law Journal* 524 (suggesting a constitutional grounding for a right to redress); AJ Sebok, 'Punitive Damages: From Myth to Theory' (2007) 92 *Iowa Law Review* 957 (suggesting a recourse-based account of punitive damages); J Solomon, 'Equal Accountability Through Tort Law' (2009) 103 *Northwestern University Law Review* 1765; JCP Goldberg and BC Zipursky, 'Civil Recourse Revisited' (2011) 39 *Florida State University Law Review* 341; JCP Goldberg and BC Zipursky, 'Rights and Responsibility in the Law of Torts'

state controlled system of law, rather than on personal relationships or morality. One public function is to provide a more socially acceptable solution to disputes permitting individual freedom to exact retribution through taking the law into one's own hands.[20] It is no accident that civil recourse theory emanates from USA, which exhibits a legal culture dominated by litigation and in which public regulation is disfavoured. These theories contrast with analyses based on notions that there is purpose behind a social welfare or state policy of supporting the rule of law by enabling vindication of private rights between citizens.

Distributional justice concerns the *redistribution* of power and resources on the basis of what is just or equitable (and not, as discussed below, on grounds of what is economically efficient).[21] The essence of the idea is to redistribute resources from society, or those who have an abundance, to those who suffer harm, especially if the latter have limited resources and need assistance in order to restore them after misfortune—although such a description moves into the sphere of compensational and corrective considerations. The concept has been used to justify a system of private redress by preventing oppression, such as by incentivising the owner of a factory to take precautions to safeguard the health and safety of workers, or incentivising a manufacturer to market safe products to consumers. The risk of most accidents is not distributed equitably but tends to fall on those sections of the community least able to protect themselves. Since the activities that generate risks are typically socially beneficial, the argument is that those who benefit from them (society) should assume, or at least share, the burden of losses.[22] 'Enterprise liability in tort was influenced by the social welfare perspective of workers' compensation, but also reflected the striking growth in private liability insurance.'[23] An example of re-distribution can be seen where high levels of general damages (ie moral or pain and suffering) are paid in countries where a significant proportion of the population have no or limited access to healthcare (because it is primarily available as a purchased service), such as in the United States.

Against the above background, *negligence* liability developed as the primary approach under tort law, based on a desire to overcome difficulties that workers and bystanders faced in claiming under contract law against expanding business enterprises that were a century or more ago uncontrolled by public regulatory constraints. Hence, negligence liability was applied to dangerous activities or situations,[24] and later through a duty of care that encompassed bystanders (neighbours).[25] Under negligence liability, the basic standard is careless behaviour that causes injury to another to whom a duty of care is owed. This concept is easier to apply in relation to its original circumstances of inter-personal relationships between individuals than in relation to the consequences of complex industrial activities.

---

in Nolan and Robertson (n 16) ch 9; JCP Goldberg and BC Zipursky, 'Tort Law and Responsibility' in J Oberdiek (ed), *Philosophical Foundations of the Law of Torts* (Oxford, Oxford University Press, 2014).

[20] EL Sherwin, 'Interpreting Tort Law' (2011) 39(1) *Florida State University Law Review* 227 (civil recourse reflects the need for the not entirely laudable function of a peaceful alternative to private revenge).

[21] AI Ogus, *Regulation: Legal Form and Economic Theory* (Oxford, Clarendon Press, 1994) 46–51.

[22] Cane (n 5); A Ogus, 'Shifts in Governance for Compensation to Damage: A Framework for Analysis' in WH van Boom and M Faure (eds), *Shifts in Compensation between Private and Public Systems* (New York, Springer, 2007).

[23] RL Rabin, 'The John G Fleming Lecture: A Brief History of Accident Law—Tort and the Administrative State' (2012) 20 *Tort Law Review* 11.

[24] *Rylands v Fletcher* [1868] UKHL 1.

[25] *Donoghue v Stevenson* [1932] UKHL 100.

Cane's review of tort law concluded that its conceptual structure is disorganised and ramshackle.[26] General dissatisfaction with negligence, both in theory[27] and practice,[28] gave rise to a shift to *strict liability*, which is triggered where damage is caused by *creating a risk of injury* that then materialises.[29] Strict liability does not involve any judgement that the person should have behaved differently, in contrast to negligence liability, but is liability for the consequences of particular (usually commercial) activities. Accordingly, this approach adopts an 'enterprise liability' approach. It is important to note that both negligence and strict liability involve proof of causation. Since its high point around the 1960s, however, strict liability has waned, as can be illustrated in relation to the imposition of liability on the manufacturers of products (product liability). In the USA, product liability expanded its scope over several decades until reaching a robustly generic approach as confirmed in the 1965 Second Restatement of Torts. However, the scope subsequently waned, and, in the Third Restatement of 1998, negligence reappeared as the standard for design defects and failure to warn claims, leaving strict liability merely for manufacturing defects.

III. Affecting Future Behaviour

We strongly suggest that the true objective here is *to achieve real change in future behaviour*. Debates on both public and private enforcement have traditionally adopted a different—and more limited—objective, namely to provide 'deterrence'. We consider that that term and concept is inadequate and unhelpful for several reasons. First, the word 'deterrence' now has a number of different meanings, and the concept has become insufficiently clear and confusing. The principal conflicts are between the traditional legal meaning (fear of adverse consequences, arising out of a concept of individual responsibility for individual acts), and an economic meaning (a concept of rational cost-calculators).

Second, both those traditional concepts of deterrence (fear of adverse consequences and cost calculation) are subject to major problems. Both concepts of deterrence fall short in providing an adequate explanation of the mechanism of how behaviour is affected and changed in practice, and especially of how it is *effectively* achieved to an acceptable degree. The term deterrence lacks far too much specificity in explaining *how* future behaviour is affected and *how much*.

In contrast, a substantial and growing body of scientific and empirical evidence on human behaviour (in other words, scientific evidence, not theoretical assertion) provides convincing explanations as to how human behaviour is *in fact* affected, both in general and specifically, and in individual humans and where humans operate in groups (ie organisations). That scientific evidence both undermines (we think demolishes) the claims that private enforcement is particularly effective in affecting human behaviour and it also provides clear conclusions on what approaches are far more effective in doing so. The scientific

---

[26] Cane (n 5) 29.

[27] See discussion of economic theory below.

[28] The burden and cost of proving the existence of a duty of care, the standard of care in a given situation, and that the defendant's conduct failed to reach that standard, proved major hurdles for many accident victims.

[29] Cane (n 5) 477.

approach to affecting behaviour explains why advanced public regulatory authorities are increasingly moving away from deterrence as a primary (and certainly sole) enforcement policy in many different market contexts.

Overall, the concept of deterrence does not accurately identify the basic objective of *delivering* behavioural change. It is insufficiently ambitious in merely concentrating on achieving *some* undefined and unquantified influence on future behaviour. The extent to which such influence or change might *in fact* be delivered is rarely specified, quantified or studied. It is merely asserted that there must be some effect, and that is as far as the inquiry goes. The assumption that some effect results from an enforcement action is held to be sufficient to justify the entire mechanism of enforcement, without inquiring further whether it works, and to what extent.

Further, the concept of deterrence is accompanied by the implication that any deterrence achieved is and always will be theoretically perfect. In other words, deterrence will be completely effective. However, the evidence that is needed is, first, on how breaches of law are caused (root cause analysis, not just limited to the actions of any individual), second, on how different mechanisms can and do affect or prevent such breaches (mechanisms and quantifications) and, third, a comparison of the different options. Those steps have been taken by some public regulators but are largely absent from the world of private law enforcement.

Deterrence is inherently limited in its effectiveness because it is essentially about avoiding bad behaviour, as opposed to affecting future behaviour (eg doing the right thing). That contrast is between seeking to affect behaviour by negative and repressive means, as opposed to positive and supportive means. There is a related contrast between the essentially ex post action that is inherent in enforcement actions and the ex ante effect of principled voluntary behaviour and compliance and regulatory systems. The latter are predictably more effective than the former.

We will expand on these ideas a little further, although this is only a short summary given that the focus of this book is more on other issues. The inadequacy of the liability- and private-enforcement-based claims (and discourse) on deterrence stands in stark contrast to the far more developed understanding that has developed in public regulatory enforcement. Indeed, the two worlds are almost light years apart. The regulatory space is now engaging fully with the points lacking from the private enforcement space of *how* to support generally law-abiding people and businesses to maintain cultures of ethical behaviour and performance, that deliver outcomes of compliance with society's rules. An idea of these issues is given below.

A. Deterrence in Traditional Legal Theory of Individual Actions and Enforcement

Whilst tort law is primarily focused on achieving the compensation goal, it can, at least in a general sense, be argued to promote a particular standard of behaviour. Liability rules establish standards of conduct, and court judgments uphold such standards, expressing disapproval of undesirable activity,[30] and amplify the detailed requirements in particular

---

[30] P Cane, *The Anatomy of Tort Law* (Oxford, Hart Publishing, 1997) 119.

situations. That broad approach has been developed by some to argue that tort law provides a public regulatory function. But there are real difficulties here.

A traditional model of 'law enforcement' postulates the following steps. A law is made. There is general observance of the rules. Isolated individuals who breach the law are identified and subjected to punishment. That punishment achieves future compliance by the offender (specific deterrence) and everyone else (general deterrence). The *status quo ante* of general observance is restored. Compliance is achieved through the magic of deterrence.

The traditional approach is to divide regulation of behaviour into just two components: rules and enforcement (a binary model). The traditional purpose of both is to achieve compliance with rules. Classical theory holds that the purpose of enforcement is to achieve deterrence, and imposition of sanctions affects future behaviour through the mechanism of deterrence, by deterring all or an adequate volume of non-compliance. The key assumption is that people will avoid breaking a rule out of fear that undesirable force will be applied to them. However, the empirical evidence is that deterrence has little effect on future behaviour in many situations. Decisions are taken for many reasons, and the supposed fear of legal penalties may have very limited or no effect on behaviour.

Sanctions are always imposed after (ex post) an event, and determination that the event constitutes a breach, and that mechanism of affecting behaviour will always be less effective and more uncertain than preventing the action in the first place by ex ante means. Various theories try to support the idea that ex post sanctioning affects future behaviour, but all fail to engage with the reality of how decisions and actions are actually taken in the real world, especially if it is a complex world. Thus, as discussed below, classic economic theory of rational cost calculators, which suggests that imposing high fines deters future breaches of rules, has been significantly undermined by behavioural science (behavioural economics, nudge). Deterrence can be seen as an enforcement policy that equates to a regulatory system categorised as 'command and control': both involve authoritarianism and both are old-fashioned in being developed in earlier ages of social control. In modern democracies, dictators do not command or penalise subjects.

The traditional legal meaning of 'deterrence' rests on the assumption that the imposition of a sanction ex post commission of a breach will affect the future behaviour of the person sanctioned (specific deterrence) and of everyone else who becomes aware of the sanctioning event (general deterrence). However, a major lack of clarity arises because of a failure to address the quantification issue: *how much* is the future behaviour affected by a sanction, or knowledge that a sanctioning system exists? The implication is that the imposition of a sanction will not just reduce the incidence or severity of future identical or similar breaches of the law, but it will entirely prevent such breaches. The inability to explain or measure the extent of the deterrent effect in any given case of enforcement—ie the extent to which there is *complete* deterrence (no future breach) or *partial* deterrence (some reduced incidence or severity)—perhaps explains why use of the term 'deterrence' persists as a general concept. It may, in fact, be almost impossible to state with any convincing accuracy the *extent* to which future behaviour is affected by the imposition of any individual sanction, or series of sanctions.

It is plausible that the extent of such deterrent effect may vary depending on many *variables*, such as the type of harm, the incidence of similar types of harm, the severity of the penalty, the predisposition of the offender or any future offender, the extent to which a future offender believes he will escape detection, the culture of the society, the existence of other factors affecting behaviour, such as regulation or social pressures, and so on. The list is almost endless. Accordingly, it is important to consider the *specific context* in which different forces or incentives will affect behaviour. Context is fundamentally important in measuring whether, and to what extent, individual forces or incentives in fact affect behaviour. Proof of the success or extent of any deterrent effect could only rest on convincing empirical evidence, and not on mere assertion that the deterrent effect exists.

The problem with the idealistic theory is that it fails in too many instances in the real world to take account of what motivates human actions and how decisions are reached in complex organisations and markets. In the early twenty-first century, repeating an assertion that ordering an organisation to pay compensation *might* have *some* deterrent effect in *some* circumstances is lazy and grossly uninformed. It flies in the face of extensive scientific and evidence on how humans behave and how regulation works.

Some studies find that the existence of liability rules, and increases or decreases in the risk of litigation and in damages, affect conscious decisions.[31] That should be no surprise. The effect of large fines and/or damages may affect the availability of insurance and the commercial viability of an activity, which resulted in discontinuance of marketing products such as light aircraft, and vaccines. US studies show that manufacturers of vaccines were driven from the US market by the cost of liability and insurance.[32] Four manufacturers refused to produce swine flu vaccine for a mass vaccination programme until protection from liability was put in place.[33]

Large payments may induce production of lengthy product information and warnings, but might not result in an increase in *actual* safety of use. Liability risk has clearly led companies to increase the information they provide about products and activities. However, this had led to printed disclosures that are so lengthy or complex that people fail to understand what they are being told. One example amongst many is that progressively more detailed warnings that medicinal products including sodium valproate have teratogenic effect and can give rise to congenital abnormalities in babies have been included in product literature since 1983, accompanied by public information campaigns. However, a 2016 survey by the UK regulator indicated that one in five of the women taking valproate were unaware of the risks it posed in pregnancy, and less than one in five had seen any of the educational materials from the toolkit.[34]

Large payments may result in an increase in care in the delivery of services, but might induce an increase in spending on diagnostic tests and 'defensive medicine'.[35] Sloan and Chepke concluded that there is no statistical association between the sophistication of

---

[31] BT Fitzpatrick, 'Do Class Actions Deter Wrongdoing?' Vanderbilt Law Research Paper No 17-40.

[32] R Manning, 'Changing Rules in Tort Law and the Market for Childhood Vaccines' (1994) 37(1) *Journal of Law and Economics* 247; R Manning, 'Is the Insurance Aspect of Producer Liability Valued by Consumers? Liability Changes and Childhood Vaccine Consumption' (1996) 13 *Journal of Risk and Uncertainty* 37.

[33] The protection was the National Swine Flu Immunization Program of 1976, 42 USC 5 247b(G)-(1) (1976). An influential previous liability decision was *Reyes v Wyeth Laboratories* 498 F.2d 1264 (5th Cir 1974), *cert denied*, 419 US 1096 (1974); see AW Reitze Jr, 'Federal Compensation for Vaccination Induced Injuries' (1986) 13 *Boston College Environmental Affairs Law Review* 169.

[34] Alert number NHS/PSA/RE/2017/002 (MHRA, 6 April 2017), available at https://improvement.nhs.uk/uploads/documents/Patient_Safety_Alert_-_Resources_to_support_safe_use_of_valproate.pdf.

[35] D Kessler and M McClennan, 'Do Doctors Practice Defensive Medicine?' (1996) 111(2) *Quarterly Journal of Economics* 353; D Dewees, D Duff and M Trebilcock, *Exploring the Domain of Accident Law. Taking the Facts Seriously* (Oxford, Oxford University Press, 1996).

physicians' practices and the frequency of lawsuits against them.[36] They concluded: 'There is no convincing empirical evidence to indicate that the threat of a medical malpractice claim makes health care providers more careful. This lack of empirical support represents a serious indictment of medical malpractice as it currently exists.'[37] Spikes in liability insurance premiums occurred in the mid-1970s, mid-1980s and around 2000, however, there has been a long-term decline in the volume of medical malpractice litigation in USA.[38] A series of studies by Kessler and McClellan found no difference in mortality rates between those groups of states that had and had not introduced tort reforms, suggesting that liability-restrictive reform reduced defensive medicine (in this case, diagnostic and therapeutic procedures in excess of what is called for solely by professional judgement) without harm to patients.[39]

Not only does the evidence suggest that tort law has limited potential to deter,[40] but tort law also does not distribute the cost of accidents in the way general deterrence theory would require.[41] Merely asserting that private enforcement increases deterrence and affects behaviour does not engage more fundamental questions. The two main issues are, first, whether the behaviour and outcomes that result are desirable and, second, whether the desired behaviour and outcomes are better achieved by other means.

B. The Economic Theory of Deterrence

Since at least the mid-twentieth century, 'law and economics' theory has been the dominant model of how businesses operate, and how sanctions should be imposed. This is a theory of how efficient competitive *markets* should work. The idea is that all businesses in the market make decisions based on a rational and disinterested calculation of the total costs and benefits (utility maximisation assumption),[42] so that, in markets that operate in conditions of perfect competition, commercial costs accurately include all the costs of production *and*

---

[36] F Sloan and L Chepke, *Medical Malpractice* (Cambridge MA, The MIT Press, 2008). See MM Mello and TA Brennan, 'Deterrence of Medical Errors: Theory and Evidence for Malpractice Reform' (2002) 80 *Texas Law Review* 1595, 1598. See also J Arlen, 'Economic Analysis of Medical Malpractice Liability and Its Reform' NYU School of Law, Public Law Research Paper No 13-25 NYU Law and Economics Research Paper No 13-15; JM Gilmour, *Patient Safety, Medical Error and Tort Law: An International Comparison. Final Report* (Toronto, Osgoode Hall Law School, 2006).

[37] Sloan and Chepke, ibid, 80–81.

[38] DA Hyman and C Silver, 'Double, Double, Toil and Trouble: Justice-Talk and the Future of Medical Malpractice Litigation' (2014) 63 *DePaul Law Review* 547; M Paik, BS Black and DA Hyman, 'The Receding Tide of Medical Malpractice Litigation: Part 2—Effect of Damage Caps' (2013) 10(4) *Journal of Empirical Legal Studies* 639. The fall in claim rates was concentrated in claims with larger payouts, which might be expected to be most affected by a damages cap. Stricter caps have larger effects.

[39] Kessler and McClellan (n 35) 353; D Kessler and M McClellan, 'The Effects of Malpractice Pressure and Liability Reforms on Physicians' Perceptions of Medical Care' (1997) 60 *Law & Contemporary Problems* 81; D Kessler and M McClellan, 'How Liability Law Affects Medical Productivity' (2002) 21(6) *Journal of Health Economy* 931; D Kessler and M McClellan, 'Malpractice Law and Health Care Reform: Optimal Liability Policy in an Era of Managed Care' (2002) 84(6) *Journal of Health Economy* 175.

[40] This was questioned some time ago even in USA: GT Schwartz, 'Reality in Economic Analysis of Tort Law: Does Tort Law Really Deter?' (1994) 42 *UCLA Law Review* 377.

[41] G Calabresi, 'Does the Fault System Optimally Control Primary Accident Costs?' (1968) 33 *Law and Contemporary Problems* 429. The point is noted in Cane (n 5).

[42] M Allingham, *Rational Choice* (New York, NY, St Martin's Press Inc, 1999); MS Archer and JQ Tritter, *Rational Choice Theory: Resisting Colonization* (New York, NY, Routledge, 2001).

of liability compensation, which produces the result that the activity level of production of goods and services is optimal, in the sense that they inherently exhibit the optimally efficient levels of production, quality and safety, and accidents are reduced to the optimal level. In other words, commercial activities will be optimally safe—but not absolutely safe.

This theory, therefore, holds that transferring the costs of harm to those who cause them is the economically rational objective of a tort liability system. Thus, the objective of liability rules, and of the liability system, should be to induce efficient levels of activity, which will inherently supply adequate safety. The intention is that accident costs will be allocated to the actor who is best placed to avoid them, by undertaking a cost–benefit analysis that rationally incentivises action to reduce unnecessary costs. In default of the lowest cost avoider, or if costs are difficult to anticipate, liability should be transferred to the actor best placed to spread the risks. This will produce optimal efficiency, and hence optimal safety precautions.[43]

Further, allocating the cost of accidents to those that cause them will deter breaches of the liability rules by ensuring that firms' cost–benefit calculations take into account such costs, so that it is not economically rational to defy the law.[44] Since complying with the regulatory standards imposed by liability rules involves extra cost above the level that is commercially necessary just for production, firms will only pay that marginal extra price when they believe that non-compliance is likely to be detected and penalised, such that it is likely to be cheaper to comply than to infringe.[45] Accordingly, this theory is claimed to supply a 'public law' vision of tort,[46] under which tort is said to provide inherent general deterrence. As Cane points out, general deterrence is a theory about who should bear the costs of 'accidents'. It is not a theory about who should be paid compensation.[47] It leads to a *theoretical* assumption that deterrence, here with a specific meaning in an economic model, affects how players in a market make decisions and behave.

C. Criticisms of Economic Analysis of Liability Law

The classic theories of deterrence in legal philosophy and in economic analysis of law have been subjected to extremely strong criticism.[48] The economic model has been attacked on a series of grounds, including difficulties in extrapolating the general theory of markets to individual cost–benefit decisions that are notionally made by actors or after the event by judges and juries. Examples include difficulties in identifying all actors, or the actor

---

[43] G Calabresi, *The Costs of Accidents: A Legal and Economic Analysis* (New Haven, CT, Yale University Press, 1970); R Bowles, *Law and Economy* (Oxford, Oxford University Press, 1982) ch 7; AM Polinsky, *An Introduction to Law and Economics* 2nd edn (Boston, Little Brown & Co, 1989) chs 6 and 7; RA Posner, *Economic Analysis of Law* 8th edn (New York, Aspen, 2011) ch 6.

[44] G Becker, 'Crime and Punishment: An Economic Approach' (1968) 76 *Journal of Political Economy* 169.

[45] Becker, ibid 169; GJ Stigler, 'The Theory of Economic Regulation' (1971) 2 *Bell Journal of Economics and Management Science* 3; M Faure, A Ogus and N Philipsen, 'Curbing Consumer Financial Losses: the Economics of Regulatory Enforcement' (2009) 31 *Law & Policy* 161.

[46] Rabin (n 23).

[47] Cane (n 5) 435.

[48] See C Hodges, *Law and Corporate Behaviour: Integrating Theories of Regulation, Enforcement, Culture and Ethics* (Oxford, Hart Publishing, 2015) ch 5.

who is the cheapest cost-avoider or behavioural influencer;[49] in identifying and calculating all relevant costs;[50] in the extent to which the person on whom the externalised costs are imposed is sensitive to such increased costs,[51] and because of the diluting effect of insurance (the 'merely a cost of business' effect). Almost no empirical evidence is available on the *amount* of deterrence that is delivered in practice. The high transactional costs of liability law and private enforcement are another factor, leading some to argue that the possible deterrent effect is not worth the price paid.[52]

Further, evidence from cognitive psychology and behavioural sociology (sometimes referred to as behavioural economics, or nudge theory) has significantly undermined classical economic theory. We will refer to this science further below. The economic theory assumes that a rational cost–benefit calculation is undertaken in relation to *every* decision, and is the *only* basis on which any decision is taken. The science, however, indicates that economic factors and calculations, and a rational calculation of the economic costs and benefits, play at best a limited role in decisions made by individuals, groups and even commercial organisations.[53] Further, it has questioned the ability of organisations to control the behaviour of all of its employees, and hence undermined the theoretical assertion that all external costs can be internalised.

D. Adding the Time Dimension

Both the traditional legal and economic models of enforcement assume that the need is to address *individual* breaches of law made as a result of *individual decisions and isolated actions* and addressed by imposition of an *individual* sanction.[54] This conception ignores empirical evidence that many examples of harm in business involve multiple causes spread over time, that breaches may be ongoing or recidivist, and may involve multiple humans or systems, and that root causes can only be addressed by adopting a number of actions, possibly lasting over time, and by addressing ongoing issues of culture. The ongoing dimension of time has to be addressed in any effective response.

---

[49] Cane (n 5) 442; GC Keating, 'Is the Role of Tort to Repair Wrongful Losses?' in Nolan and Robertson (n 16) 378.

[50] Cane (n 5) 454.

[51] TG Ison, *The Forensic Lottery* (London, Staples Press, 1967); DW Elliott and H Street, *Road Accidents* (Harmondsworth, Penguin Books, 1968); PS Atiyah, *Accidents, Compensation and the Law* 1st edn (Cambridge, Cambridge University Press, 1970); Cane (n 5) 442; J Stapleton, *Disease and the Compensation Debate* (Oxford, Clarendon Press, 1986), 126-8; Cane (n 30) 116, 119, 207. A 1964 study on automobile accidents concluded that 'there are no adequate grounds for believing that the proper cost allocation would either reduce accidents or change the total amount of driving appreciably': AF Conard, JN Morgan, RW Pratt, Jr, CE Voltz and RL Bombaugh, *Automobile Accident Costs and Payment: Studies in the Economics of Injury Reparation* (Ann Arbor, MI, The University of Michigan Press, 1964) 127.

[52] Dewees, Duff and Trebilcock (n 35); Cane (n 30); Cane (n 5) 391, 477.

[53] Some leading sources are TR Tyler, *Why People Obey the Law* (New Haven, CT, Yale University Press, 2006); A Tversky and D Kahneman, 'Judgment under Uncertainty: Heuristics and Biases' (1974) 185(4157) *Science* 1124–31; D Kahneman and A Tversky (eds), *Choices, Values, and Frames* (Cambridge, Cambridge University Press, 2000). For an accessible summary see D Kahneman, *Thinking, Fast and Slow* (London, Allen Lane, 2011).

[54] Issacharoff (n 3).

Examples: Dieselgate and Financial Sector

The failure by Volkswagen to reveal its concealed defeat device for measuring noxious gas emissions when a vehicle was being tested was not a single infringement but an ongoing series of infringements over an extended period. The root cause has been attributed to the *culture* of the organisation, rather than to individual actions by individual humans.[55]

Similarly, all major reports into the causes of the financial crisis of 2008 have concluded that culture in financial services is the single essential causative factor, and the issue that it is essential to address in mitigating the next inevitable crisis.[56]

In addressing undesirable events, science has again made a far more profound and detailed contribution than traditional legal or economic theories. The scientific approach is to undertake 'root cause analysis',[57] resisting the urge to swiftly find someone to blame.[58] A corrective mechanism needs the ability to:

— address the root cause of the behaviour so that it is *effectively* prevented or the risk of it recurring is adequately diminished, and
— monitor that desired changes are in fact made, and assess whether any 'fine tuning' is necessary.

It is interesting that the USA has partly addressed these issues with the concept of imposing a 'monitor' on a corporation, who might require employees to attend lectures on ethics. However, the appointment of a senior judge to try to control all the actions of all employees in a large corporation is simply futile, as any serious study of behavioural psychology shows. Importantly, it fails to affect culture.

E. Regulators' Abandonment of Deterrence for Supportive Responsive Policies on Achieving Compliance

Hodges' extensive study of the enforcement policies of UK regulators has demonstrated that the overwhelming majority of them have abandoned 'deterrence' as a means of responding to non-compliance by genuine businesses. The primary objective of regulators

---

[55] J Ewing, *Faster, Higher, Farther. The Volkswagen Scandal* (New York, WW Norton & Company, 2017).

[56] *Report of the High-Level Group on Financial Supervision in the EU* (European Commission, 2009); *Toward Effective Governance of Financial Institutions* (Group of 30, 2012); *Investing in Integrity. The Lord Mayor's Conference on Trust and Values* (City Values Forum, 2012); *A New Paradigm. Financial Institution Boards and Supervisors* (Group of 30, 2013); *The FCA's Approach to Advancing its Objectives* (Financial Conduct Authority, 2013); *The Salz Review of Barclays' Business Practices report to the Board of Barclays PLC* (2013); *Report of the Collective Engagement Working Group* (Collective Engagement Working Group, 2013).

[57] For systemic application of root cause analysis by a regulator see *The Transformation to Performance-based Regulation* (Civil Aviation Authority, 2014).

[58] RL Helmreich, 'Building safety on the three cultures of aviation' in *Proceedings if the IATA Human Factors Seminar* (Bangkok, University of Texas at Austin Human Factors Research Project, 1999) 39–43; S Dekker, *Just Culture. Balancing Safety and Accountability* (Aldershot, Ashgate Publishing, 2007); D McCune, C Lewis and D Arendt, 'Safety Culture in Your Safety Management System' in AJ Stolzer, CD Halford and JJ Goglia (eds), *Implementing Safety Management Systems in Aviation* (Farnham, Ashgate, 2011).

in relation to genuine businesses is to encourage improvement in performance of compliance rather than to punish. Nevertheless, 'hard' enforcement sanctions are used— but are generally reserved—for those whose motivation is to deliberately break the law, ie criminals. (The concept of hard enforcement by criminal, regulatory and civil law sanctions thus remains essential in cases of serious breaches of law.) Some sophisticated regulators segment market actors based on motivations,[59] stretching from criminal to chancer, careless, confused, compliant and ultimately champion. The response to a criminal would be hard enforcement, whereas that to the champion would be recognition and rewards. In between, the responses would move through enforcement, education, enabling and engagement.

For example, the 2014 UK government Regulators' Code[60] stresses the need for regulators to adopt a positive and proactive approach towards ensuring compliance, requiring that:

(1)   Regulators should carry out their activities in a way that *supports those they regulate to comply and grow*; and
(2)   Regulators should ensure clear information, guidance and advice is available to *help those they regulate meet their responsibilities to comply.*[61]

An extensive body of academic research demonstrates that regulators adopt responsive regulation widely across the world and across different sectors.[62] Adoption of the more old fashioned deterrent approach is restricted to enforcers who are not regulators (and hence have no ongoing relationships with businesses, or ex ante systems that aim to affect behaviour directly) or sectors that are exposed to ill-informed media and political criticism (which drives pressure to ask 'Who's to blame?' in response to major scandals). Examples of the former are competition enforcers and of the latter are financial services or healthcare regulators.

At the international level, recent papers from the Organisation for Economic Co-operation and Development (OECD) have focused on risk-based and responsive regulatory approaches, and omit reference to deterrence.[63] In 2017 the OECD noted that

---

[59]   See the segmentation of offenders' spectrum of compliance of the Scottish Environmental Protection Agency.

[60]   *The Regulators' Code* 2014. First introduced as the *Regulators' Compliance Code: Statutory Code of Practice for Regulators* (Department for Business Enterprise and Regulatory Reform, 2007), made under the Legislative and Regulatory Reform Act 2006, s 22(1).

[61]   Regulators' Code, provisions 1 and 5 (emphasis added).

[62]   I Ayres and J Braithwaite, *Responsive Regulation: Transcending the Deregulation Debate* (Oxford, Oxford University Press, 1992); K Hawkins, *Environment and Enforcement: Regulation and the Social Definition of Pollution* (Oxford, Clarendon Press, 1984); J Braithwaite and P Grabosky, *Of Manners Gentle: Enforcement Strategies of Australian Business Regulatory Agencies* (Oxford, Oxford University Press, 1987); H Genn, 'Business Responses to the Regulation of Health and Safety in England' (1993) 15 *Law and Policy* 219; P Grabosky, 'Beyond the Regulatory State' (1994) 27(2) *Australian and New Zealand Journal of Criminology* 192; P Grabosky, 'Green Markets: Environmental Regulation by the Private Sector' (1994) 16(4) *Law and Policy* 419–48; BM Hutter, *Compliance: Regulation and Environment* (Oxford, Clarendon Press, 1997); N Gunningham and P Grabosky, *Smart Regulation. Designing Environmental Policy* (Oxford, Oxford University Press, 1998); F Haines, *Corporate Regulation: Beyond 'Punish or Persuade'* (Oxford, Clarendon Press, 1997); PJ May and S Winter, 'Regulatory Enforcement and Compliance: Examining Danish Agro-Environmental Policy' (1999) 18(4) *Journal of Policy Analysis and Management* 625; BM Hutter, *Regulation and Risk: Occupational Health and Safety on the Railways* (Oxford, Oxford University Press, 2001); K Hawkins, *Law as Last Resort* (Oxford University Press, 2002); F Haines, 'Regulatory Reform in Light of Regulatory Character: Assessing Industrial Safety Change in the Aftermath of the Kader Toy Factory Fire in Bangkok, Thailand' (2003) 12 *Social and Legal Studies* 461; BM Hutter and C Jones, 'From Government to Governance: External Influences on Business Risk Management' (2007) 1 *Regulation & Governance* 27; J Black and R Baldwin, 'Really Responsive Regulation' (2008) 71(1) *Modern Law Review* 59.

[63]   *Risk and Regulatory Policy: Improving the Governance of Risk* (OECD, 2010). A shift from deterrence to responsive regulation can be seen from *Consultation on Public Consultation Best Practice Principles for Improving*

'governments are searching for simple and effective regulatory solutions to promote more efficient outcomes without resorting to additional rules or sanctions'.[64]

F. Affecting Corporate Behaviour

The issue of how best to affect corporate behaviour—or rather, the behaviour of *people* in organisations—has been the subject of very extensive scrutiny. The principal focus is on how both directors and managers, and regulators, should act, primarily in ex ante situations. Those two internal and external groups face essentially the same issue. The approaches that they have found to be most effective are significantly more sophisticated and focused than the technique of ex post adversarialism.

Various general points illustrate why behavioural and regulatory techniques used by managers and regulators are more effective than litigation. First, managers and regulators are able to act ex ante rather than ex post an undesirable event occurring. Prevention is always going to be more effective than cure. Many operational, compliance and regulatory systems specify standard procedures, such as quality systems, that guide behaviour.[65] Both the timing of such interventions and their level of detail and practical application far exceed anything that an award of damages could create after—perhaps years after—an individual event.

Second, the state of the art in affecting the behaviour of organisations relies on creating and sustaining a permanent *culture* of performance and behaviour based firmly on ethical values.[66] In contrast, enforcement through a fine or award of damages is a 'single shot' that is unlikely to affect institutionalised behaviour or culture, and may have little impact on someone when they next act in a way that breaks the rule. Further, adversarial litigation creates a culture that is the opposite of the cooperative culture. Enforcers find that resorting to a prosecution is resented by the defendant organisation, and induces less cooperation and openness in future.[67]

G. Behavioural Science on How People Make Decisions

It is necessary to explain the *mechanism* that affects future behaviour. Behavioural science answers that question, and the theory of deterrence does not. The underlying theories of classical philosophy (individual accountability) and classical economics (rational actors, discussed below) have been displaced by the findings of behavioural science on human motivations. This is a paradigm shift as significant as the scientific evolutions of Copernicus, Galileo and Darwin.

---

on *Enforcement and Inspections* (OECD, 2013) to *OECD Best Practice Principles for Regulatory Policy: Regulatory Enforcement and Inspections* (OECD, 2014). See subsequently *OECD Best Practice Principles for the Governance of Regulators* (OECD, 2013); P Lunn, *Regulatory Policy and Behavioural Economics* (OECD, 2014).

[64] *Behavioural Insights and Public Policy. Lessons from Around the World* (OECD, 2017).

[65] Hodges (n 48).

[66] C Hodges and R Steinholtz, *Ethical Business Practice and Regulation: A Behavioural and Values-Based Approach to Compliance and Enforcement* (Oxford, Hart Publishing, 2017).

[67] Hawkins, *Environment and Enforcement* (n 62); Hawkins, *Law as Last resort* (n 62).

Behavioural science has established many reasons why human beings frequently fail to do the right thing, frequently act on 'gut feel' and try subsequently to rationalise actions so as to make themselves feel honourable, and can be affected by stress, pressure of time, and incentives and perceived cultural imperatives within the organisation in which they operate.[68] It is not the risk of imposition of a sanction that affects human behaviour, but the *perception* of an individual that an action will be identified (and perhaps sanctioned). In other words, normal human beings (excluding psychopaths and sociopaths) respond strongly to emotions of shame and adverse criticism that adversely affects their reputation.[69]

More positively, human beings can be motivated to do the right thing through strong ethical values, sustained within the group to which they belong. This strength of motivation is strongly supported where people see fair rules that are made and applied fairly. The existence of law (rules of society) can be displaced if people perceive that the norms of the workplace differ. Hence, organisational culture is a critical element. An ethical organisational culture is hardly affected by ex post sanctions on the organisation to which one belongs, so is highly unlikely to affect future decisions of the people in that organisation.

In looking at 'corporate behaviour', there is an elementary danger of anthropomorphising organisations, ie referring to 'a company' as if it is a single entity with a single brain, rather than a collection of human beings who make many decisions and take many actions. Case studies of business employees who become rogue traders or involved in a cartel show that they act alone or in small groups that are concealed from their colleagues and managers. Their activities are hidden from the company, and their actions are not adopted as formal company policy. It is trite that their actions can benefit the company, and the response to that should be for the company to disgorge any illicit profit made as a result, which can be done voluntarily or through regulatory or ombudsman schemes. Importantly, the motivations of the employees who break the law typically involve not thinking properly (perhaps because of stress or time constraints), reacting to a perceived imperative to 'meet the numbers' of sales or revenue targets and hence keep jobs, or qualify for bonuses, or to be seen as the best team, or an unrestrained macho or sociopathic element.

Such employees not only break the law but—crucially—also typically break the social code of conduct between co-employees and any professional ethical rules. Hence, such social sanctions are usually have very considerable force, clearly far more so than imposition of fines or damages on the company.

The science outlined briefly here shows clear evidence of how intelligent new regulatory and compliance mechanisms achieve behaviour change, supported by empirical evidence that such behaviour change can be achieved.[70]

---

[68] Accessible books are D Ariely, *Predictably Irrational: The Hidden Forces That Shape Our Decisions* (New York, HarperCollins, 2008); MH Banaji and AG Greenwald, *Blindspot: Hidden Biases of Good People* (New York, Bantam Books, 2016); R Barrett, *The Values-Driven Organization: Cultural Health and Employee Well-Being as a Pathway to Sustainable Performance* 2nd edn (London, Routledge, 2017); MH Bazerman and AE Tenbrunsel, *Blind Spots: Why We Fail to Do What's Right and What to Do about It* (Princeton, Princeton University Press, 2011); J Haidt, *The Righteous Mind. Why Good People are Divided by Politics and Religion* (London, Penguin Books, 2012); M Heffernan, *Wilful Blindness. Why we Ignore the Obvious at our Peril* (New York, Simon & Schuster, 2011); Kahneman (n 53).

[69] See LM Friedman, *Impact. How Law Affects Behaviour* (Cambridge, MA, Harvard University Press, 2016) chs 7 and 8.

[70] See Hodges and Steinholtz (n 66).

H. Conclusions on Deterrence

Deterrence is not a convincing rational objective for public or private enforcement systems. The theory that economic factors will influence *future* behaviour through 'deterrence' is unreliable,[71] has been significantly demolished by behavioural psychology, and is increasingly abandoned by enlightened public enforcers. Imposing monetary sanctions may indeed have some effects on behaviour, but not necessarily the ones desired, or to the extent desired, and is highly unlikely to result in the detailed behaviour that is desired. The economic idea of deterrence carries the implication that the deterrence can be theoretically perfect. There is no evidence for that proposition. As a policy for delivering effective regulation or changes in behaviour it is grossly unreliable.

Instead, the goal of *affecting future behaviour* is the real fundamental objective. The means of successfully affecting future behaviour lie overwhelmingly in social and public regulatory mechanisms rather than private enforcement mechanisms. The former act both ex ante and ex post, whereas the latter act directly only ex ante and only at best in a diffused fashion ex post. Economic theory of deterrence is merely a theory that has been shown to have little engagement with the real world of how people in organisations behave. Behavioural science has illuminated that real world, but its conclusions have not yet been applied in legal theory.

Private enforcement has at best little impact on *regulating* future corporate behaviour. It may affect it, but its effects are unfocused. Trying to 'regulate' people solely by rules, and imposing sanctions for breaches of rules, misses the point—it will never work well enough. It is always reactive (backward-looking, responding to historic behaviour) rather than engaging with how to affect future behaviour.

If this is so, the only surviving objective for private enforcement is that of transferring money to people who are harmed. If that compensatory mechanism is the sole goal, the empirical evidence in this book suggests that some mechanisms are far more effective, efficient and speedy than others.

IV. Empirical Evidence on the Failure of the US Class Action as a Regulatory Mechanism

In the light of the scientific and empirical evidence above, it should be no surprise that empirical analyses of class actions have significantly questioned their ability to deliver behaviour change. Two recent summaries have been published of the empirical literature on US class actions, almost simultaneously. Professor John C Coffee Jr of Columbia University published a masterly historical account showing how different types of class actions have risen and then fallen in popularity (or incidence) in a series of waves.[72] He shows how this happened successively in merger and acquisition actions, mass tort actions, consumer actions, securities actions, and antitrust actions.

---

[71] Dewees, Duff and Trebilcock (n 35) asking at 8: if tort liability is deterrent, why wait for a death before attempting to deter it?

[72] JC Coffee Jr, *Entrepreneurial Litigation: Its Rise, Fall, and Future* (Cambridge, MA, Harvard University Press, 2015).

Coffee summarises the well-known distinctive characteristics of private enforcement in the USA, based on dislike for regulation[73] and assertion of the superiority of private enforcement as a means of affecting behaviour through deterrence. The critical feature is the role of the intermediary, the plaintiff attorney, who both controls the litigation and finances it, often appearing to be hiring the client, rather than the client hiring the lawyer. Coffee states that 'because most class members typically never learn of the action's pendency, they have no realistic means by which to escape.'[74] The private attorney takes on a public role of law enforcement (a 'private attorney general')[75] and can be called a modern day 'bounty hunter'. The attorney is 'a private actor, wielding a degree of public power, but motivated by powerful economic incentives, and yet subject to only limited accountability.'[76] As a result of a series of Supreme Court decisions,

> a common denominator is the fear that, once a class is certified, the plaintiff's attorney will gain a degree of leverage that the Court's majority considers extortionate and that will compel defendants to settle, because defendants cannot gamble on the unpredictability of juries or safely await vindication on appeal.[77]

Coffee concludes that

> two axiomatic ideas are locked in mortal combat … On the one hand, small claimants often hold meritorious claims that they cannot afford to litigate. Such 'negative value' claims (meaning that they cost more to assert individually than the plaintiff would recover, even if victory were certain) will be abandoned … unless an attorney can aggregate these small claims into an efficient procedural vehicle for common litigation … The unique 'opt-out' class recognized by American procedure solves this problem by using as its default rule the inclusion of all putative class members unless they opt out … [It] both answers the plaintiff's key problem and creates the defendant's core dilemma.[78]

Hodges analysed the *empirical* evidence on how US class actions have operated.[79] He identified issues of selectivity of case types (especially securities cases brought by investors); high transactional costs and reductions in sums received by claimants; the risk that high economic factors distort the legal merits of settlements; the limited evidence on evaluating the legal merits of outcomes; forum shopping; and aspects of conflicts of interest that have been criticised by European politicians as abusive. He noted that these features are predictable consequences of the policy of encouraging widespread private enforcement of law by incentivising intermediaries and reducing risk to claimants.

---

[73] R Kagan, *Adversarial Legalism: The American Way of Law* (Cambridge, MA, Harvard University Press, 2001).

[74] Coffee (n 72) 2.

[75] SN Subrin and MYK Woo, *Litigating in America* (New York, Aspen Publishers, 2006). For critical responses see JC Coffee, Jr, 'Rescuing the Private Attorney General: Why the Model of the Lawyer as Bounty Hunter is not Working' (1983) 42 *Maryland Law Review* 215; JC Coffee, Jr, 'Understanding the Plaintiff's Attorney: The Implications of Economic Theory for Private Enforcement of Law Through Class and Derivative Actions' (1986) 86 *Columbia Law Review* 669; B Garth, IH Nagel and SJ Plager, 'The Institution of the Private Attorney General: Perspectives from an Empirical Study of Class Action Litigation' (1987–88) 61 *Southern California Law Review* 353; LM Grosberg, 'Class Actions and Client-Centered Decision-making' (1989) 40 *Syracuse Law Review* 709.

[76] Coffee (n 72) 2.

[77] ibid 2–3.

[78] ibid, 3.

[79] C Hodges, *US Class Actions: Theory and Reality* (EUI Florence working paper, 2015/36) (ERC ERPL 14) http://hdl.handle.net/1814/36536; in German at http://hdl.handle.net/1814/46464. An edited version is C Hodges, 'US Class Actions: Promise and Reality' in H-W Micklitz and A Wechsler (eds), *The Transformation of Enforcement* (Oxford, Hart Publishing, 2016).

Hodges commented that the US model of private enforcement 'contains one major assumption, namely that individual citizens can assert right by themselves. That assumption appears to be illusory. The reality is that the enforcement of law is overwhelmingly only achieved where intermediaries are involved.'[80] He continued:

> In accordance with this model, the system includes an absence of barriers to investigation, and incentives to litigate and to succeed in settlements. First, access to evidence is through wide powers of discovery, deposition of witnesses of fact and interrogatories. Second, there are liberal rules on pleading allegations (notice pleading) and on liability. Third, the financial incentives are: no requirement on plaintiffs to fund a case; funding by lawyers, which may be on a contingency (no win no fee) arrangement and on a percentage of the recovery; funding in class actions typically being awarded by the court based on a percentage of the damages; no risk to a plaintiff of having to pay costs in the event of failure (i.e. no cost shifting); requirements on defendants to pay costs under many statutes;[81] levels of damages that are intended to provide deterrence and to cover plaintiffs' healthcare costs; the potential for punitive or triple damages; and the ability to exert significant bargaining power through assembling mass claims. Fourth, there may be elements of public sanctioning: decisions on liability and penalties being made by juries, and the possibility of punitive damages …

> Despite the huge literature that asserts the doctrinal value of the US theory and practice of class actions, it is striking that the above issues are not more widely discussed, and there is a relatively limited quantity of reliable empirical research.[82] It should be stressed that the issues listed above are intentional features of the US policy on private enforcement of law. … However, European politicians have rejected the US model as abusive.[83] Farhang has noted[84] that many US scholars suggest that, compared to administrative regulation, private enforcement regimes (1) produce inconsistency and uncertainty (since policy emanates from a multitude of litigants and judges); (2) mobilize less policy expertise; (3) are needlessly adversarial, subverting cooperation and voluntary compliance; (4) are extremely costly; and (5) are painfully slow and cumbersome.[85,86]

---

[80]   Hodges (n 79) 3.

[81]   See S Farhang, *The Litigation State. Public Regulation and Private Lawsuits in the US* (Princeton, NJ, Princeton University Press, 2010).

[82]   A summary of the empirical research on various aspects of US class actions, including some aspects not covered below, was N Pace, 'Class Actions in the United States of America: An Overview of the Process and the Empirical Literature' (2007), available at http://globalclassactions.stanford.edu/sites/default/files/documents/USA__National_Report.pdf. He also noted a number of reasons why little data has been collected, and the limitations of existing data. The current compilation has reviewed all the original sources, cross-checked with Pace's summary, and added more recent studies.

[83]   Green Paper on Consumer Collective Redress, COM(2008) 794, 27.11.2008, para 48 (US-style class actions are unacceptable in the EU since they produce 'abuse' caused by a 'toxic cocktail' of causes that are not part of European legal traditions and should not be permitted in the EU); European Parliament resolution of 2 February 2012 on 'Towards a Coherent European Approach to Collective Redress' 2011/2089(INI), para 2 (noted 'efforts made by the US Supreme Court to limit frivolous litigation and abuse of the US class action system' and stressed that Europe 'must refrain from introducing a US-style class action system or any system which does not respect European legal traditions'); Communication from the Commission 'Towards a European Horizontal Framework for Collective Redress', COM(2013) 401/2, 11.6.2013 (collective actions 'must not attract abusive litigation or have effects detrimental to respondents regardless of the results of the proceedings. Examples of such adverse effects can be seen in particular in "class actions" as known in the United States. The European approach to collective redress must thus give proper thought to preventing these negative effects and devising adequate safeguards against them.')

[84]   S Farhang, 'Public Regulation and Private Lawsuits in the American Separation of Powers System' (2008) 52 *American Journal of Political Science* 821.

[85]   E Bardan and R Kagan, *Going by the Book* (Piscataway, NJ, Transaction Publishers, 2002); F Cross, 'Rethinking Environmental Citizen Suits' (1989) 8 *Temple Environmental Law & Technology Journal* 55, 67–69; Kagan (n 73); RB Stewart and CR Sunstein, 'Public Programs and Private Rights' (1981–82) 95 *Harvard Law Review* 1193.

[86]   Hodges (n 79) 3 and 6.

In relation to the critical issue of whether the US system produces meritorious settlements and deterrence, Hodges concluded:

> A key point is to be able to assess the merits of individual cases and thus conclude whether they are justified, or whether settlements have been reached at levels that were justifiable. There is almost no data that would establish whether cases or settlements have good or poor merits. So the extent to which the system provides just results or effective individual or general deterrence is unproven (and has been a highly contentious issue). Although courts approve settlements and fee proposals by plaintiff attorneys, it is extremely rare for courts to question the merits of settlements, or reject them.[87]

Is a litigation mechanism an effective force to induce defendants to pay all they owe? It is entirely understandable that the threat of having to pay large damages will affect the conscious behaviour of people in corporations—the consequence being to avoid or reduce the money paid. The rational response of a corporation that faces large litigation may simply be to use extensive resource to defend it, over several years, whilst reserving funds to pay a final settlement, which may be less than the full amount claimed. The risk may drive some companies out of a market, or may incentivise extensive statements aimed at limiting liability (contractual exclusion clauses or extensive product safety information). But that potential or actual liability is far from affecting all—or many—decisions by people working in companies *in ways that internalised values systems, internal corporate compliance systems or external regulatory systems would achieve*. Those systems are far more immediate, focused and effective than *ex post* systems aimed at corporate profits rather than the individual behaviour of humans. In order to understand these points, we need to answer *how* various incentives and forces affect decisions, culture and behaviour.

V. The Objectives Restated: Multi-functionalism

Both in public and private enforcement there has been a shift in Europe away from 'deterrence' to a more fundamental approach to 'affecting future behaviour', accompanied by a range of different techniques to achieve that objective. This shift is more marked in some states than others, but it is a direction of travel. It can be seen in public regulators' approach to 'enforcement' increasingly more as supporting the improved performance of honest companies, whilst punishing those who have criminal intent. In this new approach, redress is one of a number of regulatory objectives, rather than the sole mechanism by which future behaviour is influenced. Redress is merely one tool in regulators' toolbox.[88]

Hence, the contemporary purposes of enforcement generally are to provide compensation and to affect future behaviour. Both of these objectives may be achieved by different mechanisms, but some mechanisms are clearly more effective than others. Mechanisms are particularly efficient where they combine the two objectives. This is why regulators can be efficient in delivering compensation, as an adjunct of their focus on behaviour. But the

---

[87] Hodges (n 79) 28.
[88] In UK, all consumer enforcers are empowered to focus on information, behaviour and redress: Consumer Rights Act 2015.

converse (private enforcers delivering behaviour change as an adjunct to delivering compensation) is far less effective.

A major paradigm shift is currently occurring in many public regulators in *how* they affect future behaviour, drawing on the findings of behavioural science and empirical evidence (rather than theory). Such approaches continue to involve large sanctions where appropriate, but the new paradigm of enforcement policies ceases to rely on deterrence. The simple assertion that imposing damages will lead to change is an approach that is prehistoric in behavioural terms.

In chapter 1 we noted 11 functions needed for market surveillance and control. We note further in chapter 8 how well the main collective redress mechanisms achieve outcomes related to those functions. It is worth noting that the new public regulatory and compliance mechanisms rely on approaches that involve addressing issues that transcend the traditional 'individual breach-individual sanction' model, and focus in addition on wider and systemic market behaviour. Delivering all 11 of the functions may require new intermediaries (other than lawyers and courts) and/or new combinations of intermediaries (such as regulators and consumer ombudsmen). But if this study concludes that lawyers using collective litigation has little effect on future behaviour of defendants (ie little regulatory effect), then the remaining justification for such a mechanism rests almost exclusively on its ability to deliver compensation. Further, if the ability of the collective action to deliver mass compensation is not particularly impressive, and the mechanism is outperformed by other newer intermediaries and mechanisms, a serious question arises about the ongoing justification for the mechanism.

8

Conclusions

This chapter analyses and compares the various mechanisms recorded above. We first set out an overview of the empirical evidence on the four main mechanisms, illustrating each with some selected leading case studies, and giving a short assessment of each mechanism individually. We then evaluate the four mechanisms against the 11 criteria set out in chapter 1 (section IV), in summary narrative and generalised mathematical form. This leads to clear conclusions on the relative merits of the four mechanisms, which we note before examining the implications for policy on both selection of mechanisms for delivery of collective redress and the wider goals of affecting behaviour and ensuring effective markets. We end with recommendations for future policy.

I. Overview of the Mechanisms

A. Collective Actions

An increasing number of Member States have introduced domestic collective actions especially since 2005, and the rate has increased since the Commission's 2013 Recommendation. However, no two national models are the same. Hence, not one confirms to the Commission's blueprint in the Recommendation. The reason for this disparity is that the introduction of a collective action mechanism is controversial in every jurisdiction, with the result that each mechanism is the result of local political bargaining. The necessity for safeguards is agreed in all European states. However, the list of possible safeguards is extensive, as summarised in Table 8.1 from the analysis by Money-Kyrle and Hodges.[1]

Accordingly, the outcome of political debate produces a different recipe in every country. An impartial observer would have difficulty in arguing that any single national model is a better balance between the need to facilitate payment of redress where it is due and the need to avoid abuse by intermediaries. The arguments of those supporting the positions either of consumer rights or of business have not changed. They have merely reoccurred in every Member State's internal debate, and the outcomes have differed because of political expediency rather than rational objectivity.

In conclusion, the European collective action mechanisms all include a number of safeguards, even if it is impossible to say whether any given mix of safeguards does or will

---

[1] R Money-Kyrle and C Hodges, 'European Collective Action: Towards Coherence?' (2012) 19(4) *Maastricht Journal of International and Comparative Law* 477.

Table 8.1: Summary of Principal Safeguards in Collective Actions

Mode	Certification	Process	Financial	Settlement
Stand-alone instead of follow-on Opt-in instead of opt-out Restriction of standing to certified personnel Independent governance	Certification by Court Certification criteria Notice to class members Judge not jury	Identify common issue(s) Adequacy of representation Superiority of the collective procedure Prioritisation of other pathways Evaluation of merits	Loser pays No contingency fees No third party litigation funding Identical damages No punitive damages	Court approval of settlement Court approval of lawyers' fees

achieve a satisfactory balance of interests. Safeguards remain central to the European collective action model, and distinguish that model from the notably more liberal US class action model.

This diversity presents significant challenges to any empirical assessment of the advantages and disadvantages of any European model for collective actions, whether it be any particular national scheme or the notional Commission scheme. Scientifically, it is too early to undertake any such empirical comparison, since the number of cases in most regimes remains very low.

However, it is possible to conclude from the data in this study that *usage* of collective actions is low in the majority of Member States. The numbers of cases in chapter 3 are low in comparison with the number of total individual litigation cases in each country and with the number of cases involving regulatory redress and consumer ombudsman (in those cases where such mechanisms exist).

In many Member States, there has so far been a low number of such 'class actions', as shown in Table 8.2. Some jurisdictions have had such mechanisms in place since the early 2000s, but numbers remain low. There are two exceptions—Italy and Poland—which have had class action laws since 2010, and where a larger number of actions have been commenced (whether by consumer associations or lawyers) but where success in obtaining certification of the action has been disappointing (roughly half of all actions commenced). The other exception is England and Wales, where the Group Litigation Order (GLO) mechanism is technically not a 'class action' model, but a case management tool.

Table 8.2: Number of collective actions in the selected Member States

	total	certified	final decision	pending	settled	dismissed	withdrawn
Belgium (consumer class action) (Sept 14– Nov 17)	5	2	0	1	1	0	1

(continued)

Table 8.2: (*Continued*)

	total	certified	final decision	pending	settled	dismissed	withdrawn
England and Wales (CAT class action) (2015–Aug 17)	2	0	0	0	0	1	1
England and Wales (GLO cases 1999–2017)	101	–	–	–	–	–	–
Finland (2007–17)	0	0	0	0	0	0	0
France (*actions de groupe*) (Oct 14–Nov 17)	12	0	0	9	2	1	0
Germany (KapMuG) (2005–9/2009)	24 + 12[2]						
Italy (2005–17)	50–100[3] 49 'tracked'	22	6	1	1	19	0
Lithuania (1/2015–8/2017)	5	0	0	2	0	3	0
Poland (civil + commercial) (2010–6/2017)	227 + 7	0	60 + 0 (49 cases still pending)	74 + 2	0	93 + 5	0
Sweden (2003–17)	30–50						

It is interesting to look more closely at the three jurisdictions that have higher numbers than the others.

i. Italy

There appear to have been between 50 and 100 class actions started between October 2005 and 2017. Out of 49 tracked class actions, 19 were not certified and 22 were certified; the

[2] See ch 3 s VII.
[3] See ch 3 s VIII.

outcome of others is not known. The litigation system is notoriously slow in Italy, typically taking up to 10 years for an individual case, and the mere fact that a case is certified as a class action is unlikely to speed things up. In relation to final outcomes on the merits, six out of seven final decisions (of this cohort of 49) were favourable to the class, and in the seventh case the action was dropped because a settlement was reached.

ii. Poland

From 19 July 2010 to 30 June 2017, 227 class actions were brought (an average of around 32 cases per year) in civil cases, and seven in commercial cases. This compares with a far higher number of cases brought in the courts: in 2015 for example, 6.5 million claims were brought in civil courts. Of the 227 civil and seven commercial claims, around 153 and five respectively were completed; 40 civil claims and all five commercial suits were refused certification; and 53 civil suits were returned because of various formal inadequacies. Only 38% of the civil claims reached the phase of substantive adjudication. A large number of those claims are still in the system. Only around 11 have been concluded with final judicial decisions.

iii. England and Wales

Between 1999 and 2017 there have been 101 cases in which a GLO has been made, enabling the individual cases in a cohort to be case managed as a group. Outcomes are generally unknown, but cases typically take several years. Judges have extensive case management powers in relation to any litigation, and this means that they are capable of managing multi-party litigation without making use of the GLO procedure.

There is no evidence that collective damages actions are particularly successful in terms of outcomes on the merits. Some claims succeed, of course, but not in overwhelming numbers, and there are clear instances that some claims fail where there appear to be merits. Such failures include situations where claimants or their lawyers do not produce sufficient evidence of individual damage or causation, as well as the more obvious examples of failing to comply with other technical requirements.

The overall impression from looking at the cases is that consumer associations try to raise matters of wide concern to consumers for which the legal system fails to provide better mechanisms, and lawyers and litigation funders pursue cases in which their potential commercial advantage is substantial. Equally, the absence of effective mechanisms to control the behaviour of commercial enterprises and governments leads to adversarial combats that can be unnecessarily long and costly.

Almost without exception, class action mechanisms take time, involve cost (which can act as a significant barrier to claimants and those who wish to initiate an action), reduce sums paid to claimants through funders' costs, and deliver limited outcomes. In Poland since 2010, only 11 out of possibly 234 cases have yet reached a substantive decision. The German Deutsche Telekom case is notoriously slow (13 years so far).

The reasons for the existence of difficulties with collective litigation are not hard to find. EU-style collective actions that need to apply extensive safeguards against abuse suffer from an inherent 'catch 22' problem: the more safeguards that are required to control against abuse, the more constrained the mode of operation of the mechanism. A serious risk of abuse requires strong safeguards. The list of safeguards in the Commission's

Recommendation includes several controls. It is simply not possible to calibrate the safeguards, so as accurately to control against abuse. Inherently, therefore, a collective action will not be particularly effective in delivering collective redress. In contrast, the US class action model contains weak safeguards and positively encourages private litigation, which inherently produces abuse because of the uncontrolled financial forces that arise and overwhelm the inherent conflicts of interest of the private sector intermediaries (lawyers and funders).[4] In order to solve that problem, one needs to look 'outside the box' of litigation.

The barriers to class litigation are well-known, and need not be examined in detail here. The two central problems relate to complexities of procedure (certification, investigating evidence, processing common and then individual issues, and enforcement) but especially attorneys' fees. Access to funding for claimants, consumer associations or intermediaries who seek to pursue collective litigation, as well as costs rules and risk, present major challenges—and European policy rejects adoption of the liberalised rules (no cost shifting, contingency fees, third-party funding) that exist to promote private enforcement generally under the US class action paradigm.[5] Given the European Recommendation's emphasis on the need for safeguards to balance the risk of abuse, there will always remain a 'catch 22' between liberating access to justice and controlling abuse by private actors.[6] Some States have been able to overcome this inherent problem by restricting enforcement of *both* regulatory and redress issues to public officials, in contrast to the US, where the opposite applies. A hybrid that exists in some European States of restricting control of injunctive action to approved NGOs may work on the basis of responding to individual infringements but does not address ongoing systemic behavioural aspects, and is treated with extreme caution in relation to empowerment to deliver redress.

a. Examples of Cases

The effects of these factors were clearly illustrated in many case studies from different jurisdictions. We select a few of the leading cases here by way of illustration.

In Germany, the Deutsche Telekom case that led to the Capital Market Test Case Proceedings (KapMuG) has not been resolved after 13 years.

In France, the consumer association UFC Que Choisir? sued Foncia in October 2014 in the Nanterre High Court of First Instance, claiming that fees charged to 318,000 tenants for sending them monthly rent payment receipts for €2.30 per month were unfair. The estimated total loss is €27.60 per individual and €44 million in total. The case remains pending.

After the three main French mobile phone operators (Orange, SFR and Bouygues) were found by the Competition Authority to have been involved in a cartel over prices and market sharing, and fined €534 million, UFC-Que Choisir? initiated a lawsuit in

---

[4] C Hodges, 'Collective Redress: A Breakthrough or a Damp Sqibb?' (2014) 34 *Journal of Consumer Policy* 67–89; DOI 10.1007/s10603-013-9242-0.

[5] RA Kagan, *Adversarial Legalism: The American Way of Law* (Cambridge, MA, Harvard University Press, 2001); S Farhang, *The Litigation State: Public Regulation and Private Lawsuits in the US* (Princeton, NJ, Princeton University Press, 2010).

[6] R Money-Kyrle and C Hodges, 'European Collective Action: Towards Coherence?' (2012) 19(4) *Maastricht Journal of International and Comparative Law* 477.

2006 to obtain compensation of €1.2–1.6 million paid by their 20 million subscribers in overcharges of circa €60 each. 220,000 consumers registered on a website, but only 12,521 sent the documents required to join the action. In December 2007, the Paris Commercial Court held the action inadmissible as the procedure chosen was a disguised *action en representation conjointe*, under whose rules soliciting of consumers was not allowed. That result was upheld by the appeal court and the Court of Cassation in 2011.

In Lithuania, an investors' association claimed in 2013 against the auditor of an insolvent bank on behalf of shareholders who had bought shares in 2011. The court refused the class action as there was no commonality in the claims.

In Spain, court proceedings following an electricity outage took four years to reach the result that the case was dismissed because individual damages could not be proved and the court upheld a compensation package offered by the supplier three years earlier after the regulator had intervened. In a subsequent case, the company made a settlement offer that was accepted by 99% of customers.

The Netherlands has a different model from other Member States, in that the aim of its collective action procedure is to encourage and approve a settlement agreed between the parties.[7] All of its nine cases settled under its Collective Settlement Act (WCAM) procedure give effect to settlements already agreed. Indeed, the Netherlands is seeking to be the jurisdiction of choice for approving international settlements, especially those following settlement by a US court of claims in the US, where the Dutch court can purport to settle all non-US claims, irrespective of the stability of such an approval under other national conflict of laws rules.

b. Assessment

The case studies reveal an overwhelming number of instances in which collective litigation faces serious challenges concerning viability and the delivery of fair, timely, efficient and cost-effective redress. The evidence is that the collective action mechanism is, as the European Commission has itself said, 'too complex, costly and lengthy to fully reach its objectives'.[8] This is true both intrinsically and by comparison with better alternatives.

This conclusion should be no surprise given the well-known challenges with private enforcement mechanisms generally in Europe. The EU has harmonised class actions for injunctive relief, and some individual Member States have introduced them for damages, but national models all differ.

---

[7] F Weber and WH van Boom, 'Dutch Treat: The Dutch Collective Settlement of Mass Damage Act (WCAM 2005)' (2011) *Contratto e Impresa/Europa* 1, 69; XE Kramer, 'Enforcing Mass Settlements in the European Judicial Area: EU Policy and the Strange Case of Dutch Collective Settlements (WCAM)' in C Hodges and A Stadler (eds), *Resolving Mass Disputes. ADR and Settlement of Mass Claims* (Cheltenham, Edward Elgar, 2013); I Tzankova, 'Collective Redress in Vie d'Or: A Reflection on a European Cultural Phenomenon' in DR Hensler, C Hodges, and I Tzankova (eds), *Class Actions in Context: How Culture, Economics and Politics Shape Collective Litigation* (Cheltenham, Edward Elgar, 2016); DR Hensler, 'A Class Action "Mash-up": *In Re Royal Dutch/Shell Transport Securities Litigation*' in Hensler, Hodges, and Tzankova, ibid.

[8] Inception Impact Assessment, *A New Deal for Consumers—Revision of the Injunctions Directive* (European Commission, 31/10/2017) Ares(2017)5324969, citing Study supporting the assessment of the implementation of 2013 EC Recommendation on Collective redress.

B. *Partie Civile*

The *partie civile* mechanism, in which private parties may piggy-back on criminal prosecutions, is a logical development of the recognition that mass harm can involve consequences that have traditionally been separated legally into distinct categories of criminal and civil, but those two streams can be merged so as to provide process efficiency. Indeed, the piggy-back mechanism provides three particular advantages. First, duplication of evidence gathering and production of evidence in court can be avoided, saving time and cost. Second, the process involves no cost to individual claimants, since the State assumes the investigation and prosecution costs. Third, the fusion of criminal and civil aspects is a step towards providing outcomes that people want, namely redress and state responses. Individuals are not concerned with lawyers' division of rules and processes into categories of criminal, administrative and civil aspects. The important issue is to deliver a fair outcome for people speedily, and cheaply.

The piggy-back mechanism has proved somewhat effective, but some disadvantages remain. The success of the mechanism relies on three critical points. First, there must have been a breach of criminal law that public prosecutors take up and decide to pursue. Second, particular defendants must be convicted who have adequate funds to pay claimants (deep pockets). Third, the criminal judge must be required to process the private actions (as in Belgium) rather than (in most States) merely to have the discretion to process such claims.

i. *Examples of Cases*

In Belgium, 600 people joined a criminal action as *parties civiles*, and after some defendants were convicted, the court of appeal of Mons appointed two special masters to resolve the civil claims, who encouraged mediation, and the case was settled for around €10 million after two years.

ii. *Assessment*

The piggy-back technique is a significant and useful evolution in combining the two tracks of public and private consequences, and has various advantages, such as that the evidence is not taken twice, and the action required by claimants is initially minimal. Importantly, the key intermediary is independent and does not have a commercial conflict of interest in the outcome of the case but acts in the public interest. However, the two parts of the procedure remain *consecutive* rather than *contemporaneous*.

C. Regulatory Redress

Regulatory redress is delivered where a public body uses its authority to achieve redress by a trader for consumers or the environment. This mechanism is an evolution of the idea of fusion found in the piggy-back mechanism. The public body (typically a sectoral regulatory authority or consumer enforcement authority) usually possesses an express power to order or seek a court order for redress to be paid. However, the evidence is that such a power is rarely formally invoked (ie by instituting proceedings) and in many cases the issue is resolved between authority and trader by agreement. Indeed, some authorities may achieve redress without even possessing a formal redress power, although they usually do possess other persuasive enforcement powers, such as the power to remove a licence.

Undoubtedly, the fact that a regulator possesses a toolbox of enforcement powers adds weight to its request for redress to be made. The threat of imposition of criminal or administrative sanctions is a factor that assists agreement on redress as one of the elements necessary to conclude a case. Indeed, an enforcement policy may incentivise redress by stating that a sanction is likely to be reduced where redress is proposed, agreed and made voluntarily by a trader. Equally, a trader may value the opportunity to resolve all aspects of a case—criminal and civil—in one go, achieving 'global peace'.[9]

The most advanced authorities now approach enforcement by:

a.   identifying the root cause of the problem,
b.   agreeing actions to reduce the risk of reoccurrence of the problem,
c.   ensuring that such actions are implemented by the infringer and others,
d.   ensuring that redress/rectification is made, and
e.   imposing a proportionate supervisory sanction.

The leading examples of regulatory redress are in Denmark and the UK, but other examples are arising across Europe. The approach is essentially part of a wider approach to regulatory enforcement by public authorities who see their role as having expanded beyond mere prosecution of infringements. The wider approach encompasses addressing rectification of markets to a level competitive balance, having been unbalanced by an infringing trader. Rebalancing requires removal of illicit profits from the trader and payment of redress to those who have suffered loss. Such rectification also supports consumer and commercial confidence in the market, and encourages trading and thus a vibrant market. This wider vision of the role of a regulator appears to be spreading.

Delivery of regulatory redress therefore requires regulatory authorities to have the function, powers and willingness to use redress powers. When these features exist, the evidence indicates that they are extremely successful: faster and more economical in addressing systemic infringements of market rules than where redress claims are left to individuals or private intermediaries to pursue. Rather than increasing the effort, cost and time of investigations, authorities who have well-stocked toolboxes of enforcement powers, including an ability to order or seek a court order for redress, are able to resolve more cases more quickly, with most settling disputes without the need for court proceedings.

i. Examples of Cases

In Denmark, the Consumer Ombudsman (the national enforcement authority) has, since 2008 (and for antitrust since 2010), relied on the class action, which only the Ombudsman may use on an opt-out basis, as part of the toolbox of enforcement powers to reach a succession of agreed cases that include redress, without the need to bring an action. The redress power constantly influences discussions and assists businesses to reach holistic solutions.

---

[9] DR Hensler, B Dombey-Moore, B Giddens, J Gross, EK Moller and NM Pace, *Class Action Dilemmas. Pursuing Public Goals for Private Gain* (RAND Institute for Civil Justice, 2000) 110.

In the UK, a range of redress powers are relied on by sectoral regulators, such as for financial services and energy to deliver large sums in redress. Other authorities, such as those for water or gambling, achieve redress without having explicit powers. All enforcers of consumer protection law are empowered under the Consumer Rights Act 2015 to adopt 'Enhanced Consumer Measures' that give flexibility to include behavioural, redress and information outputs.[10] Between April 2014 and November 2015, the Financial Conduct Authority established 21 informal redress schemes, which it estimates provided £131 million in compensation to consumers. The energy regulator Ofgem has switched its practice, with fines imposed falling from around £15 million in 2010 to £5 million in 2015, whilst redress paid by firms over the same period has increased from virtually zero to over £70 million, coupled with extensive discussions and agreements with firms on actions that they will take to change behaviour. In 13 cases concluded by Ofgem in 2015/16, £43 million was paid out by licensees (£26 million to customers and £19 million to charities). In the first half of 2016, the Environment Agency agreed payments to environment charities by 10 firms that contacted it and seven firms that it contacted, totaling £403,000. In 2014, Ofwat (the water regulator) accepted an undertaking by Thames Water on a £79 million prices reduction, spending £7 million on customers, and a £1 fine.

Since 2012, the Bank of Italy has initiated four proceedings in which the regulated entity involved promptly refunded their customers, or provided the Bank of Italy with detailed information about their initiatives, to a total €692,345.67. In 2014, the Bank of Italy issued two redress orders concerning mistakes in the calculation of interest, for a total amount of €118,506,000. It is standard practice for the Bank of Italy to ask regulated entities to adopt initiatives in order to refund customers for sums unduly paid, even without initiating a proceeding. In 2015, refunds stemming from informal requests by the Bank of Italy totalled around €65,000,000.

ii. Assessment

The regulatory redress mechanism is highly efficient and effective. The outstanding feature is the ability to achieve a generic solution for all those affected, often without their need to take action in making a claim, ie on an opt-out basis. The critical point here is that this opt-out power is exercised by an independent public intermediary, rather than one who has a commercial conflict of interest in the outcome. Further, redress payments are not subject to deduction for intermediaries' costs.

Where achieving redress is simple, this can be undertaken by the trader spontaneously, such as by crediting customer's bills or making a payment to an independent environmental charity for clean-up costs. Where calculating individual redress payments is more complex, such as where individual reliance or causation or quantum elements need to be assessed, the arrangement can require that a scheme is operated. Such redress schemes can be established on an ad hoc basis, but it is particularly effective where they can be administered by existing ombudsman bodies. Regulators may oversee the correct formulation and operation of

---

[10] R Money-Kyrle, 'Collective Enforcement of Consumer Rights in the United Kingdom' in M Schmidt-Kessel, C Strünck and M Kramme (eds), *Im Namen der Verbraucher? Kollektive Rechtsdurchsetzung in Europa* (Jena, Schriften zu Verbraucherrecht und Verbraucherwissenschaften, Band 5 Jenaer Wissenschaftliche Verlagsgesellschaft, 2015).

a redress scheme, and may prosecute traders where this is done wrong, and require them to do it correctly.

D. Consumer Ombudsmen

Despite much interest in ADR mechanisms, especially consumer ADR, it is only *consumer ombudsmen* who are able to resolve individual *and* collective cases. Arbitration or mediation ADR models are designed to resolve individual cases, but not collective cases. The consumer ombudsman model, by contrast, does aggregate data, and typically processes multiple similar individual cases consistently. The aggregation mechanism exists as a matter of ad hoc practice, rarely written in a law, and occurs automatically in practice. The aggregation mechanism is in effect similar to the case management approach of an English court, such as specified in the Group Litigation Order. The ombudsman is required to process every individual case, and has the power to do this by applying a consistent approach to cases that are similar, such as involving similar facts or the same legal rules.[11]

A major innovation is that the ideal consumer ombudsman design is able to deliver a wider range of functions that just dispute resolution. The range of functions typically includes the following:

(i)   Providing consumer information and advice/Triage
(ii)   Dispute resolution: individual collective redress
(iii) Capture and aggregation of data on all cases and contacts received
(iv)   Identification of issues and trends
(v)   Feedback and publication of information to traders, regulators, consumers and markets
(vi)   Exerting pressure on improving market behaviour.

The leading examples of consumer ombudsmen are in the UK and Belgium, with some in Germany, France and Ireland. The initial model is for consumer ombudsmen who have jurisdiction in particular regulated sectors—such as financial services, energy, communications, utilities, transport and postal services. Since the 2013 Consumer ADR Directive raised the profile of ADR bodies generally, the more advanced model is where an integrated national architecture of consumer ombudsmen exists. The leading state with such a model is currently Belgium, where there is a single national Consumer Ombudsman Service website, and the principal sectoral Ombudsmen operate in a coordinated fashion. In the UK, functional coordination is emerging through the existence of a private website function that can transfer consumer complaints to many traders, and where they are not settled, can transfer the file immediately into the relevant ombudsman or other ADR scheme. This model has enabled creation of increasingly large databases by combining data from resolver, ombudsmen and participating traders.

The cases reported by consumer ombudsmen in this study show that redress is achieved swiftly. Ombudsmen systematically share their experience and knowledge with their

---

[11] Caroline Mitchell, Lead Ombudsman of the Financial Ombudsman Service, uses the term 'individual "collective" redress'.

sectoral regulator, the industry, and consumers. They have influenced behavioural change by businesses, policy by regulators, and legislation introduced by Parliaments.

i. Examples of Cases

Inquiries received by the UK Financial Ombudsman Service[12] have increased from 562,340 in 2003 to around 1.5 million in 2015/16 (peaking at 2.3 million in 2013/14), from which a total of 340,899 new complaints were processed in 2015/16.[13] The members of the European National Energy Ombudsman Network (NEON) comprising just six Member States, handled 103,835 energy-related disputes in 2016, 34% of which deal with invoicing and (e-)billing, metering issues (14%), commercial practices (12%), and provider change/switching (11%).[14]

In Belgium, the Consumer Mediation Service (the residual ADR entity) was able to settle 50% of the complaints received in 2016. In 37% of the cases a recommendation was issued.

ii. Assessment

The consumer ombudsman mechanism has a number of strengths and few weaknesses. First, the process operates as an automatic opt-in procedure for those claimants who contact it. Second, it applies the same approach to all similar cases. Third, it identifies generic issues, and notifies the fact to relevant traders, consumers and regulators. That identification can trigger generic resolution of all relevant cases in a class, either voluntarily by a trader or as a result of the intervention of a public authority. Fourth, the process is typically free for consumers. Fifth, redress payments are not subject to deduction for intermediaries' costs. Sixth, it is notably faster than courts, since the process contains a number of efficiencies, such as on the ability to gather evidence quickly, the availability of expertise in the ombudsman, avoiding the need to obtain external expert opinions, and a process that moves seamlessly through stages of triage, mediation and decision, without needing to switch between different external bodies or processes. Seventh, the ombudsman model does not bind the consumer to accept any outcome, unlike the arbitration ADR model, which is therefore less attractive to consumers.

II. Applying the Criteria

In chapter 1 we suggested a set of 11 criteria against which the various mechanisms would be evaluated.[15] The criteria are reproduced below, with short summaries of the conclusions from the conclusions on each mechanism noted above and from the case studies. An indicative scoring of the mechanisms against the criteria is given at the end of this section. Criteria 1, 2, 3, 4, 5, 6, 9 and 11 are functional criteria, and criteria 7, 8, 10 are performance criteria.

---

[12] See annual reports at http://www.financial-ombudsman.org.uk/.
[13] *Annual Report and Accounts for the Year Ended 31 March 2016* (Financial Ombudsman Service, 2016).
[14] *Annual Report* (NEON, 2017).
[15] See ch 1, s IV.

A. Criteria 1: Advice

To what extent does the mechanism enable consumers to access advice before or during the processing of their complaint? To what extent also does the system provide advice to traders, especially small traders who may not be familiar with the law or dispute resolution options or processes, so as to achieve swift, cost-effective and fair resolutions?

Lawyers and consumer ombudsmen typically give information and advice to consumers in response to a question about a legal problem. The difference lies in the fact that the lawyer is typically paid by the client for giving advice and has an inherent incentive to maximise the time taken. Certain payment regimes, where the lawyer is paid on a no-win-no-fee basis, disincentivise taking cases that have poor merits. However, funding and costs regimes of national civil procedure systems are complex and may contain a complex mixture of incentives and disincentives.[16] A consumer ombudsman, by contrast, should have no financial incentive in an individual case, and is regulated to maintain independence.

Public officials are not established to deliver detailed advice to consumers in individual cases, so the regulatory redress and piggy-back mechanisms do not score well on this criterion. Individual ADR schemes operate as independent arbitrators or mediators and do not provide advice functions.

B. Criteria 2: Identification of Infringement and Harm

How is it that a problem involving breach of law and/or damage has occurred is identified?

All of the mechanisms studied here function essentially to *process* claims rather than to *identify* them. They all tend to be invoked once a mass issue has been identified through some other stimulus and investigation mechanism. Raising an issue with a lawyer or regulator might provide this trigger, but it would normally need to be followed by investigation on whether an infringement has occurred and how extensive it is.

However, the consumer ombudsman model has the inherent advantage over the other processing mechanisms that it inherently identifies systemic infringements from aggregating data from individual consumer queries and complaints. Traders ought to be able to do this, but some might not then react responsibly. Some regulators receive or supervise complaint handling mechanisms, but the picture on scope and effectiveness is mixed across sectors and countries. The consumer ombudsman is well placed to identify a mass infringement from considering only a small number of individual cases. It can then inform the trader and the regulator. A regulator is very well placed to confirm whether an infringement has occurred through investigative powers.

National landscapes that have single websites providing advice and access to an ombudsman system have been shown to identify trends and systemic issues quickly because they attract a sufficiently large number of individual contacts, for which the subject matter can be electronically analysed swiftly. A good example is the unique portal/access point of the Belgian Consumer Mediation Service, or resolver.co.uk in the UK.

---

[16] C Hodges, S Vogenauer and M Tulibacka (eds), *The Costs and Funding of Civil Litigation: A Comparative Approach* (Oxford, Hart Publishing, 2010).

C. Criteria 3: Identification of People Harmed and Due Redress

Must individuals come forward, or can they be identified without coming forward?

The individual ADR scheme does not identify mass claimants, it merely responds to such of them as come forward. The piggy-back system also responds only to parties who opt-in.

The collective action mechanism only identifies the existence of a class of claimants after an issue has come to the attention of the lead lawyer/intermediary. It does not identify issues spontaneously. It then requires individuals either to opt-in or opt-out. Under either model, they need to receive information in order to exercise their option. Traders ought to have information enabling their customers to be identified, at least for some years. The cost of notification through individual communications and news media might be significant. Where liability rests on proof of individual issues such as reliance or causation, identification of the cohort can raise significant challenges.

The consumer ombudsman cannot identify all relevant individuals per se, but can do so with the cooperation of a trader. The most effective intermediary is a regulator who has powers to order a trader to identify all customers who are affected and the extent to which they ought to receive redress. It can oversee that process by the trader.

D. Criteria 4: Access

To what extent is the mechanism user-friendly for consumers or claimants to access?

Under regulatory redress, people do not need to opt-in for the regulator to order that they receive redress: it is intrinsically an inclusive opt-out mechanism. The typical situation is where a supplier knows the identity of all customers from computerised records, and can readily apply a refund to all accounts, or contact them to proceed to quantify with individual losses.

It is swift and simple for consumers to access a consumer ombudsman. Accessing an arbitration-style ADR ought to be simple (but usually carries a cost).

Accessing lawyers and courts may be simple, but issues of building funding may present difficulties and take time. An opt-in mechanism might not catch all in the class; an opt-out mechanism will catch all, but members may need to opt-in to collect distributions.

E. Criteria 5: Cost to Access

What cost must a person who claims to have suffered harm pay, and fund, in order to access the process? Or is access free?

There should be no cost to access a regulator or consumer ombudsman. Joining a piggy-back mechanism should be free, although some civil claimants choose for legal representation, especially when their claims are complicated, eg in case of personal injuries (although mostly this kind of representation is covered by a legal expenses insurer). An arbitration-style ADR usually carries a modest cost. A collective action will usually involve some cost to access and for ongoing representative work by the intermediaries.

F. Criteria 6: Triage

To what extent does the mechanism act as a triage to prevent unmeritorious cases or unnecessary cases proceeding further? This may include, at one extreme, preventing fraudulent claims being advanced and, at the other extreme, to swiftly resolving cases that should be resolved one way or the other?

At the start of a case, most of the mechanisms do not screen the merits of the case of individuals who join the group, or offer advice on the strength of an individual case. A lawyer may do this, but might not as it involves cost, and be more interested in building the perception of a large class, for whom a substantial overall settlement can be sought. A consumer ombudsman undertakes triage automatically on receiving an individual case.

G. Criteria 7: Duration

How long does the mechanism take from start to conclusion? How long does it take to resolve issues, from when they first arose (ie when damage occurred, before a claim was made) to final resolution?

The case studies show that regulatory redress and consumer ombudsmen are notably short processes, typically a few months or less. A collective action that settles might be relatively short, but still longer than the first two mechanisms. A collective action that is fought can take many years. The piggy-back can reduce overall duration of two procedures, but unless one or both parts settle, duration will still be some years. Simple ADR is not relevant for a collective case.

H. Criteria 8: Costs

How much are the gross transactional costs of a collective procedure, and the standing costs of a process? Who bears the costs, both initially, and finally?

Excluding defence costs, transactional costs of regulatory redress are low where cases settle, as they appear to do in the vast majority of instances. Many authorities can recover costs from defendants. Processes such as the piggy-back and the consumer ombudsman involve some cost. However, such costs are usually borne by companies. In adversarial procedures, such as a collective action and piggy-back mechanisms, there is inevitable duplication of costs that are avoided by the existence of non-adversarial intermediaries in regulatory and ombudsmen regimes. The costs of lawyers and funders in collective actions are notoriously high.

I. Criteria 9: Outcomes

What is achieved? Are the outcomes the ones desired by the parties, the law or society?

In theory, all of the mechanisms ought ultimately to deliver redress. They should all achieve fair and just outcomes. Issues of potential bias arise with any intermediary, however, and each regime raises different risks and calls for different responses.

It is unclear to what extent private enforcement mechanisms achieve skimming off illegally-made profits.

J. Criteria 10: Compensation for Loss: Making Whole

Is a person who has suffered harm fully recompensed? How much of an award is lost in transactional costs, eg of intermediaries? Are extra emotional or other costs incurred and recompensed?

The main issues here are entitlement and recovery. Although a person who makes an individual claim in an ADR scheme ought to be awarded full compensation, it is not possible for an individual to be involved in a collective arbitration-style ADR system. People who are subject to a regulatory redress order or a consumer ombudsman scheme should receive 100% of loss as compensation, with no deduction for transactional cost. In litigation, entitlement to compensation is subject, first, to negotiation (and hence usually less than 100% of a claim) and, second, to deduction of representative's costs. The evidence is that collective actions rarely provide full compensation: damages are reduced by transactional and intermediaries' costs, and sums can remain undistributed to those who have suffered losses.

K. Criteria 11: Changes in Behaviour

Does the mechanism directly produce changes in systemic behaviour that reduces the incidence or future risk of non-compliance with the law? To what extent does the mechanism, therefore, act as a regulatory mechanism?

As discussed in chapter 7, the two traditional goals of collective redress are compensation and deterrence, but we suggest that the correct goals are redress and behaviour change.

The evidence that collective actions deter future behaviour is extremely limited, and the evidence that exists does not indicate that effects on changes in a range of relevant corporate behaviour are strong. In fact, the evidence that public or private fines or damages delivered through enforcement adequately affect future behaviour *in an effective regulatory capacity* is highly unimpressive.[17]

If aim is to reduce the risk of future repetition of both the same infringement by the same trader and by other traders, as well as other related possible infringements, imposition of requirements to pay money for past behaviour have limited effect on the actions of the many people in large organisations whose behaviour and systems need to be affected. Far more detailed and systemic actions are needed to control the many 'moving parts' of an organisation. The deterrence model is far too simplistic. Regulators stand the best chance of engaging with an organisation and the people within it in specifying and agreeing what needs to change in practice, and the multiple sub-cultures that exist in an organisation. There is increasing and strong evidence that the most effective way to affect future behaviour of most businesses is through a supportive approach to achieving compliance, especially

---

[17] C Hodges, *Law and Corporate Behaviour: Integrating Theories of Regulation and Enforcement* (Oxford, Hart Publishing, 2015).

a relationship that is based on evidence supporting mutual trust and cooperation.[18] Leading consumer ombudsmen are currently moving into this behavioural space to work with companies in achieving behavioural and cultural change in response to the ongoing information produced by complaint systems.

L. Summary

A summary of above conclusions in numerical form is attached at Table 8.3. This is a somewhat impressionistic exercise, but does provide a general comparative indication of the mechanisms. The following scoring values have been applied: Good = 3; Fair = 2; Poor = 1; None = 0.

Table 8.3: Scoring of Mechanisms against the Criteria

Mechanism	Collective Action	Piggy-back	Regulatory Redress	Simple ADR	Consumer Ombudsman
1. Advice	2	1	1	0	3
2. Identification of infringement	0	0	1	0	3
3. Identification of people harmed	2	0	2	0	2
4. Access	2	3	3	2	3
5. Cost to access	1	3	3	2	3
6. Triage	1	0	0	0	3
7. Duration	1	2	3	–	3
8. Costs	1	2	3	–	2
9. Outcomes	3	3	3	–	3
10. Compensation	2	3	3	–	3
11. Behaviour change	1	1	3	0	3
Total	16	18	25	4	31

III. Empirical Conclusions on the Mechanisms

The evidence found in this study provides clear conclusions when the various models are evaluated against objective criteria. The regulatory and consumer ombudsman

---

[18] Some examples of this new approach are: *Supervision of Behaviour and Culture. Foundations, Practice & Future Developments* (DeNederlandscheBank, 2015); *Delivering better outcomes for consumers and businesses in Scotland* (Scottish Government, 2016); *Primary Authority Statutory Guidance* (Department for Business, Energy & Industrial Strategy, Regulatory Delivery, 2017), https://www.gov.uk/government/uploads/system/uploads/attachment_data/file/648597/primary-authority-statutory-guidance-2017.pdf.

mechanisms clearly outperform the piggy-back mechanism in delivering collective redress, which itself leaves the private collective action in last place. The first two mechanisms are not only outstandingly quick and cost-effective in delivering redress payments. They also provide far more of the wider 'market regulation' and behaviour control functions than the older mechanisms. Those two mechanisms simply outclass the collective action mechanism. Regulatory redress and consumer ombudsmen are especially effective when the two mechanisms operate together in as a combination. Collective litigation appears to be a dead end for delivering redress, and for affecting future behaviour in the detailed way that regulators and consumer ombudsmen can do.

We note here that safeguards are required for any mechanism, especially one in which significant power is exercised. It is outside the scope of the current work to analyse in full the mode of operation of regulators or consumer ombudsmen and what safeguards might be necessary for their satisfactory operation. That analysis would be extensive, and examine issues of resources, governance and transparency. Here, we merely note that those mechanisms appear to operate satisfactorily in some States, and they deliver significant amounts of redress, and responses to market behaviour and trends.

IV. Implications of the Findings

A. Changes in the Dispute Resolution Landscape: A Shift to New Technologies

Significant shifts have occurred in mechanisms. First, the EU rejected the US model of maximising private enforcement in favour of a more balanced (public–private) approach involving safeguards.

Second, there has been extensive experimentation by EU Member States in collective action models for damages. The current position would present a huge challenge for harmonisation. There is no coherence in national class action laws, none of which correspond to the European Commission's 2013 blueprint. Each national system is tailored to domestic need, often uninfluenced by the Commission's blueprint, and the overview is of piecemeal development, which is uncontrolled.

Third, there has been a shift in the techniques by which redress is delivered. It is well known that there has been a significant shift in individual consumer–trader disputes from courts to ADR mechanisms. The 'old technology' of private litigation has been superseded in some Member States by a highly effective 'new technology' involving regulators and ADR schemes. These techniques have been approved by UNCTAD,[19] and deserve to be widely adopted.

However, fourth, there has been an equal shift in the case of collective redress, but this is far less recognised. The 'new technologies' of collective redress are regulatory redress and consumer ombudsmen (in the UK sense, not the Nordic sense). This shift should

---

[19] *Manual on Consumer Protection* (UNCTAD, 2016) ch 11.

not be surprising. In the same way that EU policy has followed (and led) developments at national level away from courts to ADR and online techniques and mechanisms, evolution and innovation has occurred in relation to mechanisms for delivering collective redress. Contemporary consumers and markets call for better performance and outcomes than the older mechanisms can deliver. It would seem to be more productive to continue to search for better mechanisms than to try to defend the old ones.

The empirical evidence of this project, which is the first to examine comparatively all of the leading mechanisms that deliver collective redress and not just the collective litigation option, clearly shows that the redress and consumer ombudsman models—especially where those two are combined—score far more highly than the collective litigation model across the criteria. The piggy-back technique is a logical development that attempts to sequence public and private enforcement so as to achieve some efficiency of process. But that first step has been eclipsed in efficiency and effectiveness by the two other techniques. Regulatory redress fuses private enforcement entirely into public enforcement. ADR in its traditional forms of arbitration or mediation can only deliver individual redress, absent a Dutch-style ability for a court to approve ex post a collective settlement. Consumer ombudsmen are an evolution of ADR in which the intermediary is neither a lawyer not a judge but a new independent public or quasi-public officer, whose process is highly efficient and affords a seamless conveyor-belt for both sides (in the best models, fusing information, advice, assisted negotiation and decision).

Given the significant shifts that have taken place in the availability of new mechanisms, political policy and rhetoric now needs to move to reflect these developments. The empirical results of this study are so clear that they clearly indicate conclusions for policy in delivering collective redress. They challenge the rationality of a policy that relies on collective actions to deliver collective redress. Other models that exist have proved themselves to be effective and the preferred contemporary options. Those models should be adopted as front-line delivery mechanisms.

B. Redress as an Integral Function in Control of Markets

If we merely consider mechanisms for delivering redress, we miss a far larger and more significant change that has occurred, and which is a major factor in driving the development of the new technologies. Both the ombudsman model and the regulatory model, especially where they operate in a parallel coordinated fashion, deliver significantly more functions than just dispute resolution. They both play essential roles in supporting fair and competitive markets—in other words, regulatory roles. That regulatory function is obvious in relation to public regulatory authorities, but it is equally important in relation to consumer ombudsmen.

A major question that arises, therefore, is not the obvious one of 'what mechanism delivers collective redress?' but 'what combination of mechanisms delivers the totality of the functions that are necessary for adequate support of vibrant, competitive and fair markets?' In this context, it is highly relevant that the new technologies deliver the goals of affecting future behaviour, redress, and efficiency, which the old technology cannot perform.

This wider vision is illustrated by the highly significant change in terminology from 'class actions' to 'collective actions' to 'collective redress'. As noted in chapter 2, that change reflected the growing realisation that litigation-based procedures are not the only mechanism, and that the objective should not be confused with the mechanism.[20] Redress is an objective, whereas class actions or collective actions are only one possible mechanism for seeking that objective. But the change in terminology to 'redress' also reflects a different focus, based on wider objectives relating to the paramount importance of maintaining a satisfactory market.

C. The Objectives for Market Regulation

It follows from the above that redress is only one aspect of how markets should be safeguarded and regulated. Public policy has developed swiftly in some Member States in the past 10 years, such that the role of regulators and public enforcers has broadened to move away from merely achieving safety or well-structured and priced markets, to encompass an aspiration to ensure, first, that consumers and vulnerable businesses receive redress as an integral part of a relevelled playing field and, second, that behaviour is effectively changed. Accordingly, the objectives of the most effective regulatory systems runs in the following sequence:

1.   Establishing clear rules and their interpretation
2.   Identification of individual and systemic problems
3.   Decision on whether behaviour is illegal, unfair, or acceptable
4.   Cessation of illegality
5.   Identification of the root cause of the problem and why it occurs
6.   Identification of which actions are needed to prevent the reoccurrence of the problematic behaviour, or reduction of the risk
7.   Application of the actions (a) by identified actors (b) by other actors
8.   Dissemination of information to all (a) firms, (b) consumers, (c) other markets
9.   Redress
10. Sanctions
11. Ongoing monitoring, oversight, amendment of the rules

In considering what mechanisms of public and/or private enforcement, either alone or in combination, can deliver these objectives, it can be seen how litigation primarily addresses item 9 alone, whereas the integrated co- and public-regulatory systems and ombudsman systems in some countries are able to address all items.

D. A Shift in Intermediaries

These considerations help explain why the regulatory intermediaries—regulators and ombudsmen—have emerged and are preferable to lawyers and courts as effective intermediaries. The former intermediaries simply deliver more functions than the latter, as well

---

[20] C Hodges, *The Reform of Class and Representative Actions in European Legal Systems: A New Framework for Collective Redress in Europe* (Oxford, Hart Publishing, 2008).

as better performance. The former are all relatively new, and have developed as European markets have been subjected to regulation and harmonisation. In effect, they have been designed to perform a wider range of functions in order to support markets.

In contrast, lawyers and courts have lengthy histories and their models were formed before the new intermediaries appeared. In an earlier age, lawyers and courts were the primary and sometimes only intermediaries, and their tools—private enforcement—therefore had to serve as best they could to provide not only private inter-personal redress but also enforcement of public norms. In contrast, the new regulatory intermediaries have the ability not only to deliver more functions to ensure fair and competitive markets, but also the ability to include redress as one of their wider outputs. It is time to recognise and make full use of the outcomes of these new technologies.

The design of a system is critical. For example, although many ADR schemes process unitary claims well and swiftly, a scheme has to be designed with particular features to be able to process multiple similar claims, and to have significant consequential influence on traders' behaviour. The design of arbitration-style ADR systems emerged as a means of overcoming from the disadvantages of courts. However, the design of consumer ombudsmen had a significant origin in regulating markets.

As noted in chapter 2, there has been a revolution in the traditional categorisation of law into two broad types: one the one hand, public law (administrative, regulatory and criminal), in which the paradigm enforcement mechanism is prosecution and imposition of a fine or other penalty and, on the other hand, private law, in which the principal mechanism of enforcement is an action for damages. That binary categorisation had already started to crumble when private organisations (trade associations and consumer associations) were empowered to use an injunction power.[21]

The goals that have occupied theorists since at least the middle of the twentieth century, namely compensation and deterrence, are seriously questioned. That fact is visible from the change in terminology from compensation to redress, and from deterrence to affecting future behaviour. We do not seek to argue the issues around these shifts here, since our focus in this book is merely on *delivering* collective redress. However, we note arguments that both the justification and purpose of enforcement has changed from deterrence.

The mid-twentieth century argument from law and economics was that any financial penalty—fines or damages—has the same effect on corporate behaviour, through the economic theory of deterrence. It was thus argued that private enforcement has a public function because deterrence affects future behaviour as effectively as public enforcement. That theory is widely understood by European economists and some legal academics, but has never been adopted as part of the formal policy of the EU outside competition thinking.

Instead, EU mechanisms involving public and private enforcement have tended to be developed in parallel, with different rationales and functions. That piecemeal approach, noted in chapter 2, reflects the continuation in most Member States of the public–private split. Thus, the primary objective of public enforcement is to affect behaviour, and that of private enforcement is to deliver damages.

However, the new intermediaries have exploded the traditional binary categorisation. Public bodies are increasingly seeing the delivery of redress as an integral part of their

---

[21] In Germany in the late nineteenth century, and at EU level under the Injunctions Directive.

role in maintaining balanced markets, and private bodies like consumer ombudsmen have expanded out of delivering just redress into market supervisory roles. The significance of these evolutions has profound implications for the design of legal systems and bodies that operate in a modern market setting. Old thinking will no longer do.

E. Shifting from Old to New Technology

The reason why collective actions have been little used in some Member States can now clearly be seen. The principal reason is that they are not needed because other mechanisms already exist and work better.

This is clearly so in all of the Nordic states, where extensive Consumer Complaint Boards and administrative injury compensation schemes have operated well since the 1980s. It is also true in the Netherlands, where the consumer ADR system has grown since 1970 and covers all trading sectors. The occurrence of settlement class cases in the Netherlands is a red herring, as discussed above: that phenomenon is caused by imaginative national capture of a 'global settlement market'. In Belgium, the consumer ombudsman system has expanded strongly in the current decade. In the UK, consumer ADR—both arbitration schemes and the now extensive sectoral ombudsman system—has grown strongly since 2000, coupled with a striking growth in regulatory redress by all leading sectoral regulators, now codified under the Consumer Rights Act 2015. ADR schemes have grown in Germany since 2000. In Italy, ADR is stronger than widely realised, and regulators' use of their powers to deliver redress has not been recognised but has been quietly highly effective in some sectors, notably financial services and energy.

In the regulatory space, the EU's method of controlling market sectors, both vertically in sectors (eg financial services, post, energy, communications, aviation, medicines, transport and many others) and horizontally (eg corporations, accounting, competition, workplace safety, environment, data protection, consumers and so on) has been to create competent regulatory authorities. Most of these exist at Member State level and currently only a few at EU level. National authorities are endowed with remits and powers, but their mode of organisation and operation, and what powers they use in practice, is left to national decisions and cultures. Some national regulators have developed more quickly than others in seeing that part of their function is to ensure that redress is delivered to those who are harmed by infringements of market rules. Delivering redress ensures that illegal profits are skimmed off, and the market is returned to a level, fair playing field.[22]

The conclusion is that the introduction of a collective action mechanism in these States has not notably increased consumer redress because the mechanism is not needed, and is not preferable to other existing models.

However, the effective new technologies have been developed only in some States and have not yet been introduced in others. Hence, what is needed is that the new, effective mechanisms should be spread. There is a clear and strong case that the most urgent need for

---

[22] C Hodges, 'A Market-Based Competition Enforcement Policy' (2011) 22(3) *European Business Law Review* 261; C Hodges, 'European Competition Enforcement Policy: Integrating Restitution and Behaviour Control' (2011) 34(3) *World Competition* 383.

the EU is to introduce regulatory redress and consumer ombudsman mechanisms across the Member States.

Does it matter if collective actions are introduced but regulatory redress and consumer ombudsmen are not? What would be the effect at this stage of spreading the older technologies without the new ones? The result would presumably be that there would be no significant improvement in consumer redress (*or* improvement in consumer markets). The introduction of an old style collective action might give rise to a political claim of acting in the consumer interest without in fact doing so. The political claim would be hollow, and consumers would remain without redress in too many instances. Such a response would now be unforgivable in the face of the empirical evidence.

F. The Need for Independent Intermediaries

As noted in chapter 2 above, Commissioner Jourová of the European Commission has proposed to add a collective damages power onto the Injunctions Directive. The damages power would be similarly exercised by approved bodies.[23] We see two major difficulties with this model.

i.   *The right model (regulators and ombudsmen), not the wrong model (lawyers, funders and courts).* The first issue is the preference for a model of awarding mass damages that has been shown to be highly ineffective and worse than other possible models—and one that the Commission has explicitly seriously criticised in its own Initial Impact Assessment. The proposal appears to be that damages in mass cases would be awarded by a court process, as a second stage to a finding of breach. But the empirical evidence is that such a (court-based) process would not satisfy the criteria, and that other approaches—regulatory redress and consumer ombudsmen—would be ignored. That would not be rational policy.

ii. *The requirement for independence.* The second issue concerns the nature of the intermediaries. It is essential that the intermediaries who are involved can be trusted to act impartially. Some of the possible intermediaries can be trusted to act in the public interest, and consumers' interests, to stop ongoing infringements. However, not all of the bodies can be trusted to act in the public or consumers' interests in seeking collective redress.

---

[23] Speech of Commissioner Jourova at the release of the US Chamber Institute for Legal Reform's Consumer public opinion poll on European collective redress and third party litigation funding, entitled 'Are consumers in the EU equipped to defend their rights?', Brussels, 28 September 2017. The Commission may refer to a statement in the Executive Summary of an academic study ('42. In respect of collective redress, it appears advisable to clarify and strengthen the role of consumer protection associations when filing individual or collective claims. The relationship between individual and collective claims should also be clarified.'): *An evaluation study of national procedural laws and practices in terms of their impact on the free circulation of judgments and on the equivalence and effectiveness of the procedural protection of consumers under EU consumer law Report prepared by a Consortium of European universities led by the MPI Luxembourg for Procedural Law as commissioned by the European Commission JUST/2014/RCON/PR/CIVI/0082. Strand 2 Procedural Protection of Consumers* (Max Planck Institute, 2017), available at http://ec.europa.eu/newsroom/just/item-detail.cfm?item_id=612847.

Both the two mechanisms that are effective in delivering collective redress—regulatory redress and consumer ombudsmen—involve intermediaries that are *independent* of any parties, and subject to objective governance and transparency requirements that support their acting objectively in the public interest. Neither public regulators/enforcement authorities nor regulated not-for-profit ombudsmen (unlike other potential bodies) have commercial conflicts of interest in seeking damages or costs from infringers. Hence, they can be expected to independently, will only pursue meritorious cases and will not pursue or settle cases influenced by their own financial interest.

However, there are clear dangers in endowing non-independent bodies—such as consumer associations or trade associations—with collective damages powers because of the conflict of interest that arises through the commercial incentives inherent in large money claims and costs issues, and the risk of capture of such bodies by other commercial service providers (litigation funders and lawyers). The risk of abuse arising out of empowering such bodies is considerable, and there has already been evidence of it.[24] Both consumer associations and trade associations are effective in using injunction powers, but they should *not* be given damages powers.

We suggest that entities that may be appropriate for enforcing general consumer protection law backed by a power to seek an injunction are not, therefore, necessarily entities that should be permitted to exercise a power to seek damages. Introducing a major financial incentive into the outcome of an activity introduces a major financial incentive and conflict of interest, which has been clearly shown to be the cause of abuse in the US system.[25] There is a risk here that the Commission may be stepping into the very elephant trap that it had earlier affirmed to avoid.[26]

The issue of independence is ultimately one of guarantying that an intermediary who is necessary to achieve desired outcomes (here, redress) can be trusted. This requirement for trust is behind the success of the *public* bodies in Denmark, the UK and elsewhere in delivering collective redress. For example, in Denmark, *only* the Consumer Ombudsman is trusted to use an opt-out class action mechanism; all others can use an opt-in mechanism. There will need to be safeguards against abuse of strong powers by public officials, as with private actors, but the two lists of safeguards will differ.

Thus, there is a public policy relationship between choice of mechanisms, actors and safeguards. In this instance, there is a strong argument that if an opt-out mechanism is desired in certain circumstances, selecting the right actor (a public rather than a private official) is critical, as well as imposing suitable safeguards on that public official. Some countries seem to think that it is acceptable for lawyers to call for an opt-out collective

---

[24] We note a worrying number of instances in case studies above.

[25] JC Coffee Jr, *Entrepreneurial Litigation: Its Rise, Fall, and Future* (Cambridge MA, Harvard University Press, 2015); *US Class Actions: Theory and Reality* EUI Florence working paper 2015/36 (ERC ERPL 14) http://hdl.handle.net/1814/36536; in German at http://hdl.handle.net/1814/46464.

[26] Commission Recommendation of 11 June 2013 on common principles for injunctive and compensatory collective redress mechanisms in the Member States concerning violations of rights granted under Union Law (2013/396/EU), recital 15, referred expressly to the need to '*avoid the development of an abusive litigation culture* in mass harm situations', and recital 20 stated 'In order to *avoid an abuse of the system* and in the interest of the sound administration of justice, no judicial collective redress action should be permitted to proceed unless admissibility conditions set out by law are met.' (emphasis added).

action and then for a judge to choose between an opt-in and an opt-out mechanism in the instant case. We suggest that such an approach raises significant risk in some Member States. Judges act alone and, although they usually publish their decisions and reasoning, they do not defend their decisions before elected representatives and public or social media. Regulators, on the other hand, take decisions in accordance with their organisational procedures and are subject to external oversight and scrutiny. Under a regulatory redress model, a decision to impose an opt-out collective damages order may need to be scrutinised by *both* an enforcement official and a judge—unless the defendant agrees. Under a private opt-out class action, the US experience has demonstrated that defendants usually settle cases after a class has been certified, and the amount paid is influenced more by what can be negotiated rather than what is owed on the merits: external scrutiny of merits is rare. Accordingly, if the EU wishes to ensure trust in its legislative decision-making and its justice system, these issues of selecting the right intermediary and the right safeguards are critical.

It is interesting here to note the current political rhetoric. The Commission Report summarises this as:

> While consumer organisations make a strong case for EU-wide intervention in this field, business organisations generally focus their concerns in relation to EU action on the consumer area and refer to proportionality or subsidiarity concerns, urging the Commission to concentrate on public enforcement or on redress via ADR/ODR or the small claims procedure.[27]

A few years ago, businesses might have been expected to argue against any form of collective redress mechanism, and around five to 10 years ago there were calls for use of ADR. It seems highly significant that business is now calling not only for a collective redress mechanism, but also one that they can trust, primarily involving *public* bodies.

G. What Traditional Redress Systems Will Fail to Achieve

A significant motivation for the drive towards introducing a damages collective action in the EU appears to be frustration at the failure of cases like PiP, Volkswagen and Ryanair. The Commission's 2018 Report described the underlying problem in the 'dieselgate' case as about misleading information.[28] As mentioned in chapter 2, Volkswagen's refusal to compensate or retrofit cares fitted with 'defeat devices' aimed at producing fraudulent test results for noxious emissions, in contrast to its agreement to do so in the US when threatened with public enforcement powers and class actions there, and also its refusal to agree a pan-EU approach with the Commission, was a source of annoyance. Ryanair's cancellation of many flights just outside the period when it would be required to compensate customers, and its subsequent failure to provide adequate information or support to stranded customers, likewise annoyed authorities and politicians.

This frustration usually goes hand in hand with a loud cry for collective action mechanisms. However, we need to have clarity about the causes of such frustration, and hence

---

[27] *Report from the Commission to the European Parliament, the Council and the European Economic and Social Committee on the implementation of the Commission Recommendation of 11 June 2013 on common principles for injunctive and compensatory redress mechanisms in the Member States concerning violations of rights granted under Union law (2013/396/EU)*, COM(2018) 40 final, p 20.

[28] ibid, 2.

which mechanisms would respond to such problems and which would not. Most legal reforms seem to stem from the necessity to have a 'quick' tool to manage these high-profile mass cases. Generally, they are not the result of a well-thought policy addressing all the possible options and objectively weighing their advantages and disadvantages. Consequently, and to achieve a political win, most reforms are the result of a political compromise trying to reconcile the diverging interests of opponents and proponents. Achieving the most optimal and efficient device is usually not the primary goal.

H. The Need to Re-examine Mechanisms for Controlling Market Behaviour (Enforcement)

Deeper issues arise here than just comparing different mechanisms for delivering collective *redress*. It is illuminating to consider the *case types* that arise, and how well different methods of enforcement respond to them.

For example, examination of the case studies in chapter 3 on injunction and damages cases—especially those cases that are unsuccessful—illuminates the need to provide effective mechanisms that respond to instances of misleading information, unfair contract terms, unfair charges. However, countries differ in the mechanisms that they use to respond to those problems. In some countries, resort to a collective action to address such issues would seem to be a mediaeval approach—slow, costly and ineffective.

Underlying this is an issue of which public, private or other (hybrid or new) mechanisms are effective. That issue has received almost no scrutiny. Even raising that issue might provoke entrenched assumptions about the role of private enforcement or public enforcement. But the issue has to be faced, and illuminated with empirical evidence. What mechanisms—irrespective of how they may have been categorised, such as public or private enforcement—in fact respond most effectively and efficiently to different types of unfair market behaviour?

Private enforcement of unfair trading by a trade association and/or consumer associations, backed by powers to seek an injunction and to seek evidence (the German model) may have worked well. But might co-regulatory models (such as the Dutch trade association agreement on terms and conditions) be better? The German reliance on removal of profits (skimming-off) by private associations is well-known to be little used because of the financial disincentive that money recovered is paid to the Federal budget. Would a regulatory redress solution be better?

Are private claims for damages by investors effective in preventing managers' future behaviour in making misleading or wrongly-timed announcements? Do they merely deliver money to some shareholders at the disadvantage of others, and restrict the business' financial health?

Overall, it appears that judicial collective actions are only needed when better mechanisms do not exist. This conclusion is particularly striking when one looks for the evidence. Although England and Wales has had a certain number of GLO cases, the case types are those in which the highly effective regulatory redress and market ombudsman systems currently do not respond. The low number of collective actions in all Nordic states, and the types of cases brought, reflect the extensive use there of Consumer Complaint Boards and injury compensation schemes.

The British competition damages cases that have caused such difficulties in the Competition Appeal Tribunal (CAT) would not be necessary if the Competition and Markets Authority (CMA) had activated its power to approve voluntary 'regulatory redress' schemes—which it only introduced in 2017 (see page 60 above), some 15 years after the Financial Conduct Authority (FCA) started to use this approach with increasingly excellent results.[29]

Similarly, problems with rail or bus transport, or with delayed or cancelled flights, have largely been solved in Germany by the Transport Ombudsman (*Schlichtungsstelle für den öffentlichen Personenverkehr*). There is no longer any need for private court enforcement of such matters. In Italy, cases against banks, energy, communications companies and others, especially over unfair contract terms and charging issues, are increasingly handled by effective regulatory/ombudsman-type mechanisms that have developed there fairly recently. Collective action cases in Belgium do not duplicate the increasingly wide and effective national ombudsman system. In France, the ADR system is generally less advanced than in other leading European states, so collective actions are brought against unfair trading that would not exist in some other jurisdictions.

The conclusions here are as follows. First, serious research and policy evaluation needs to be devoted to examining, comparing and reforming mechanisms that respond to different types of market issues. Second, adoption of modernised systems and mechanisms is needed. This empirical re-evaluation should be objective, and not held back by traditional assumptions. Third, the mechanisms that work less well should not be allowed to prevent the spread or the use of those that work well. If collective actions remain, as necessary to respond to areas that are not covered by better mechanisms, they should be restricted to being mechanisms of last resort, so as not to impeded use of the better mechanisms.

I. Restatement of the Fundamental Goals of Redress Systems

We suggest that the fundamental objective of a redress system is not merely to deliver redress but to function as part of a wider market control system. The redress component should deliver at least the following functions:

1. To *identify* a mass problem;
2. To *deliver* appropriate redress or non-monetary compensation;
3. To provide *feedback*. Passing on information on the existence of a mass problem to independent authorities who do not have conflicts of interest for them to act in addressing the problem and obtaining collective redress. Hence, to contribute to *affecting the future behaviour* of a trader and of the market generally, and thereby ensure than an unbalanced market is rebalanced so as to be a level playing field;
4. To provide *standing mechanisms* to which consumers and traders can refer individual and collective issues to have them resolved efficiently and expeditiously. The traditional answer to that has been courts, but courts have proved to be far from ideal in

---

[29] *Guidance on the Approval of Voluntary Redress Schemes for Infringements of Competition Law* (Competition and Markets Authority, 2015). See also C Hodges, 'Ethical Business Regulation and Competition Enforcement: Challenging Orthodoxy' (2017) 5 *European Competition Law Review* 237.

handling both small value individual cases and aggregations of multiple cases. If that is so, alternative structures need to exist and to be readily and permanently accessible. The best structures are *consumer ombudsmen*, as outlined above.

5.   To achieve both of these goals in the most efficient manner, in terms of speed/duration, costs, and finality.

Let us amplify these ideas. One should consider *how* mass problems are identified. This usually occurs when *individual* consumers come forward, with individual claims, and scrutiny of the subject matter of all claims by an expert intermediary identifies ones that are similar, and that there is a systemic issue. The expert intermediary identifies that there is a *mass* problem, which gives rise to a number of similar individual claims. But with whom do consumers raise such problems, and how can this be done in a manner that is most efficient, that identifies a systemic problem as quickly as possible, and determines that the issue does give rise to breaches of law that give rise to the need for redress? Who should the intermediaries be?

Such intermediaries may in theory be public authorities, not-for-profit ombudsmen, ADR schemes, consumer advisers, ECC-NET offices, consumer associations, trade associations, the media and so on. But not all of them will perform with the same efficiency or effectiveness in identifying a systemic issue. Some of these bodies can be arranged in national landscapes so as to be more effective and efficient than others.

After a systemic issue has been identified, it has to be resolved through a structure and process that is *available* and that meets the criteria set out above. The available dispute resolution process has to be permanent in order to be available, trusted and reliable. If it is not rational that the collective damages process takes place within a court structure—because courts fail to satisfy the criteria—then the standing process has to be a pre-existing consumer ombudsmen scheme or, in the case of personal injuries, an effective administrative compensation scheme. Accordingly, consumer ombudsman schemes need to be available in every Member State so to administer mass claims, since they do this far more efficiently and swiftly than courts, as the data shows.

The objective of 'affecting future behaviour' has traditionally been stated as the theory of deterrence, but research by Hodges has shown that (a) the empirical evidence for deterrence as a means of regulating individual or corporate behaviour is limited, (b) the science of behavioural psychology offers far more effective insights into how to affect future behaviour, through adopting a range of approaches in which most people are supported to achieve performance, as opposed to punished for non-compliance, (c) many UK regulatory agencies have adopted supportive, responsive, and often no-fault regulatory policies rather than deterrence-based enforcement policies, and (d) the ideal model appears to be to encourage consistent systemic ethical behaviour, through various approaches that support relationships built on trust (and hence co-regulatory models).[30]

If the above approach has validity, it has fundamental implications for legal systems that are based on principles of fault and deterrence. Their ability to affect future behaviour can be significantly questioned. Equally, this demonstrates why effective regulatory and

---

[30] Hodges (n 17); C Hodges and R Steinholtz, *Ethical Business Practice and Regulation: A Behavioural and Values-Based Approach to Compliance and Enforcement* (Oxford, Hart, 2017).

ombudsmen systems are more effective in affecting behaviour than litigation-based systems. The idea that a single response to a single instance of non-compliance will result in ongoing or systemic change in behaviour, for example, as a result of the imposition of a single financial penalty, is not supported by behavioural or management science.

J. Facilitating Settlement: The Requirement for Structures to be Available

A familiar argument is that the existence of the compulsory powers of a civil court will encourage parties to settle cases. But it is not as easy as that in large cases, or where the merits of individual cases have to be assessed. The regulatory redress and consumer ombudsmen models can give rise to cases in which particular redress arrangements are needed in order to respond to particular circumstances, and such arrangements need to be processed through a suitable redress scheme. In some instances, ad hoc redress schemes have been created, but it would be preferable for such ad hoc arrangements to be operated through an existing mechanism,[31] such as a consumer ombudsman or administrative injury redress scheme. The existence of such a standing mechanism should itself facilitate speedy settlement.

There needs to be readily available an effective *mechanism* that the parties can use. A theory that defendants who are found to have infringed trading law would then typically avoid mass damages claims by settling them has not been established to be valid in practice. Indeed, there is empirical evidence that cases of this type have not been swiftly settled. Arguments on whether an infringement has occurred, and appeals, could be expected to rise in cases where the financial implications were high for defendants, leaving both parties (especially claimants) without resolution for some time. This is what typically happens at the initial certification stage in collective litigation. One of the main reasons why fighting rather than settling is the outcome here is that the primary process (here, the court procedure) does not *itself* include options of triage, *mediation* and decision, in that sequence. In other words, the parties have to agree to go into a different system and process if they wish to negotiate. The existence of a single integrated process is what makes the consumer ombudsman model distinctive from other ADR schemes, and particularly effective. Consumer ombudsmen can apply the rules of either the law or an ad hoc scheme, and they can triage multiple individual cases, assessing them against acceptance criteria, before facilitating a mediated negotiation.

Accordingly, various consequences would flow from access to a damages claim being as a second stage to the right to exercise an injunction power. First, this perpetuates a court-based system, rather than involving more efficient ombudsman bodies. It would tie both claimants and defendants into slow and costly court procedures. Second, injunctions are not a relevant first stage in every case (such as infringements that have already ceased, or infringements where the initial regulatory response is wider and more sophisticated than an order to stop).[32] So, would there be an increase in injunctions threats and actions by

---

[31] An example is where the UK FCA agrees or orders a redress scheme to be administered by the Financial Ombudsman Service.
[32] See Hodges and Steinholtz (n 30).

those seeking to claim damages? Third, a two-stage process (finding of infringement and calculation of damages) is inappropriate for some types of case, where individual issues predominate (such as reliance of statements, and personal injury causation), and has been shown to attract abusive 'legal blackmail' claims.[33]

K. The Requirement to Base Policy on an Examination of all the Options, and on Empirical Evidence

The European Commission has committed itself to basing policy and rule-making on evidence, and to reducing regulatory burdens.[34] It is a Better Regulation requirement that policy on collective redress should be based on an objective analysis of *all options*.[35] The European Commission seeks to concentrate on things that matter, rather than on details ('bigger and more ambitious on the big things, and smaller and more modest on small things').[36] It aims to simplify rather than complicate. Proposals must satisfy strict 'impact assessment' criteria, aimed at ensuring that EU legislation can only be proposed if it will make a significant impact on the market. While wishing to 'step up enforcement', the Commission notes that its aim here is 'to promote a more effective application, implementation and enforcement, in line with the Commission's political priorities'.[37] In December 2016, it said that it will adopt 'a more strategic approach to enforcement in terms of handling infringements', will develop 'an inventory of the mechanisms of redress available at national level to which citizens may turn to seek remedies in individual cases', and 'will ensure the full application of the EU legislation on mediation and alternative dispute resolution'.[38]

However, too often, assertions on collective redress assume that the only option is the court-based collective action mechanism. In the light of this study, a wider and profoundly more sophisticated analysis is required. New technologies are available that operate better than the old mechanisms and deliver more functions.

L. Summary of Implications for Policy on Collective Redress

We suggest that a significant body of evidence in relation to improving enforcement generally, and collective redress in particular, has been assembled in this project, which implies

---

[33] See C Hodges, *Multi-Party Actions* (Oxford, Oxford University Press, 2001).

[34] Communication from the Commission to the European Parliament, the Council, the European Economic and Social Committee and the Committee of the Regions, *Better Regulation for Better Results: An EU Agenda*, COM(2015) 215 final, 19.5.2015.

[35] Communication from the Commission to the European Parliament, the European Council and the Council, *Better Regulation: Delivering better results for a stronger Union* (European Commission, 2016), COM(2016) 615 final, 14.9.2016.

[36] *Political Guidelines for the Next European Commission* of 15 July 2014 and mission letters of 1 November 2014 from the President to Vice Presidents and Commissioners.

[37] Communication from the Commission to the European Parliament, the European Council and the Council, *Better Regulation: Delivering Better Results for a Stronger Union* (European Commission, 2016), COM(2016) 615 final, 14.9.2016.

[38] Communication from the Commission, *EU Law: Better Results through Better Application* COM(2016) 8600, 21.12.2016.

clear policy conclusions. The evidence suggests the following conclusions for future policy on collective redress for Europe:

1. Member States and the EU should establish a policy on a coherent, modernised approach to market behaviour and enforcement, which identifies how all of the 11 functions noted above are delivered.

2. Redress should not be considered on its own but as an integral part of contributing to strong and competitive markets. Hence, mechanisms that address the 11 market functions noted above need to be considered holistically. The goal should be to provide mechanisms that address all 11 functions and outputs in as economic a manner as possible, avoiding multiple mechanisms that only address individual functions.

3. The leading contenders for these tasks are the 'new technologies' of regulatory and ombudsmen mechanisms.

4. Sectoral and generic regulators should have redress powers as part of their enforcement toolboxes, subject to appropriate oversight mechanisms.

5. ADR mechanisms need to be modernised. Both sectoral legislation that requires ADR and the generic consumer ADR legislation[39] should specify that consumer ombudsmen models should be required, rather than other types of general ADR, at least in all major regulated sectors.

6. Analysis should be carried out on effective oversight mechanisms and barriers to the adoption regulatory and ombudsmen systems in those Member States that do not have them.

7. All entities that collect information on market activities should pool their data on problems in the market, so that systemic issues can be identified swiftly. In order to achieve this, the *national landscape* of consumer advice and consumer complaints (ie ADR entities) should be *rationalised and connected* with other formal market surveillance mechanisms. *A small number of integrated consumer ombudsmen* operating with a single national website should replace an ADR landscape that contains too many isolated ADR entities.

8. The power to seek damages—individually and collectively—should only be exercisable by approved independent entities that do not have any commercial conflict of interest, ie public authorities or not-for-profit approved ombudsmen.

9. Any entity that is authorised to use injunction powers should be required to inform the entities that are authorised to use damages powers of the existence of an infringement that has been established in circumstances where similar infringements may also have occurred.

10. A legal system may consider that it may need a collective mechanism as a long-stop for cases that involve disputes that do not fall within the remit of the new technologies. If so, there should be a clear prioritisation of the new technologies, and any cases that fall under their remit should only be able to default to the older mechanisms as a last resort.

---

[39] Directive 2013/11 of 21 May 2013 on Alternative Dispute Resolution for Consumer Disputes.

ANNEX: OXFORD CSLS-KU LEUVEN PROJECT ON EMPIRICAL EVIDENCE ON EU COLLECTIVE REDRESS: SUMMARIES OF COLLECTIVE CASES

I. Damages Cases

A. Collective Private Litigation

Country	Case
1.1 Austria	VKI represented 110 claimants made ill by a contaminated water supply system at a club, with a total of €170,000 in controversy, and reached a settlement for €130,000.
1.2	A real estate investment scam (WEB) led to the conviction of several bank managers. Several cases were brought by groups of individuals represented by lawyers. VKI brought a case representing 3200 claimants claiming compensation of €54 million. Legal fees to all sides ran at €400,000 a day and the case would have continued until 2011 if it had not been settled. It was not possible to obtain agreement to proceed on the basis of one or two test cases, which would have reduced costs, since the defendant did not agree to waive a limitation argument so all cases had to be pursued. The case was difficult to settle since VKI, the Ministry that finances VKI, the process financing company, and all represented consumers and their lawyers had to agree. Settlement was agreed after 1 year, at €19.7 million including costs. One consumer voted against the agreement, and it was concluded. Opting-out is not provided for under the law, that individual would have had to bring his own case if he had wished. The procedure would now be easier under the law Verbandsverantwortlichkeitsgesetz.
1.3 Belgium	Flight HQ 1509 of Thomas Cook Airlines Belgium was delayed on 23 March 2015 by 8 hours after a collision with an ambulance on the tarmac. Thomas Cook paid some money to at least some passengers. The Consumer Organization Test-Achats filed a class petition on 2 October 2015. Thomas Cook argued that all passengers had been fully compensated. The court ruled on 4 April 2016 that the criteria for admissibility of the class procedure were met, and decided that it should be an opt-in form since passengers would be aware of the action. The period to opt expired on 10 August 2016 and the procedure is currently in the negotiation phase.

Country	Case
1.4	After 8 strike days by different railway unions in 2015, Test-Achats gave the Belgian National Railway Company (NMBS-SNCB) a month to propose a settlement (*e.g.* simplification of a pre-existing compensation procedure and the payment of a compensation to the disrupted travelers), and then filed a class action petition on 23 November 2015. Approx. 44,000 people registered for the claim on Test-Achats' website. Some signals on settlement have been made; the case proceeds.
1.5	Test-Achats has created a website for people to register for claims against online concert ticket sellers who charge excessive prices: 3,000 have done so. The *juge d'instruction* of Brussels has ordered the Federal Computer Crime Unit to have those three websites blocked by the internet providers.
1.6	Test-Achats initiated a class action against Volkswagen for selling cars with software that cheats on emission levels. Nearly 9,000 consumers have registered. The case and negotiations proceed.
1.7 Czech Republic	In 2012, a young lawyer filed an application against his bank, Komerční banka, demanding the reimbursement of bank fees. Inspired by a successful German case, he argued that the clause establishing an account maintenance fee was null and void, as it did not specify which services were provided in return. He founded the website jdeto.de, soliciting thousands of clients willing to file similar applications. In February 2013, he teamed up with a well-known attorney, forming the company BSP Lawyer. BSP Lawyer solicited plaintiffs with the promise that clients would not bear legal fees in the event of a loss, but would instead receive a portion of the awarded legal costs in the event of a success. The duo then represented thousands of plaintiffs who filed actions against their respective banks. Therefore, this was not a single application, but rather thousands of individual applications lodged at different courts against different defendants, yet represented by the same two attorneys and very similar in content.
	The initiative gained significant media prominence in April 2016 after the District Court for Prague 4 declared an account maintenance fee null and void. As the value of the matter was merely CZK 4,200 (€ 155), neither side could lodge an appeal, since Czech law only allows appellate proceedings for matters exceeding the value of CZK 10,000 (€ 370). The decision was final and the bank returned the bank fees to the plaintiff.
	However, other district courts soon started issuing decisions to the contrary, upholding the account maintenance fees. Most of the matters were below the minimum value required for appellate proceedings and could not be challenged further. BSP Lawyer covered the legal fees in unsuccessful cases at this time. 190 clients represented by BSP Lawyer also filed complaints to the Constitutional Court, claiming a violation of their rights. In April 2014, the Constitutional Court rejected the complaints and a few weeks later, the Supreme Court confirmed that the maintenance fee was in accordance with Czech law.

Country	Case
	As the District Courts continued to rule in favour of the banks and order clients to remunerate the defendants' legal expenses, BSP Lawyer shied away from its initial promise of covering legal costs, the sum of which was then estimated at several million CZK. The remaining plaintiffs either withdrew their own applications, or, in closed cases, covered the opposing side's legal expenses from their own pockets.
	Although the applications themselves were, with a few exceptions, unsuccessful, they gathered significant media attention and were highly influential. Initially, most banks gave in to public pressure and lowered or removed their account maintenance fees. The media often referred to the cases as a 'group application', which led to suggestions of introducing a true class action suit into Czech law. As of 2016, the Ministry of Justice is yet again considering various options for implementing mass collective redress instruments.
1.8 Denmark	Minority shareholders in Bank Trelleborg complained over a share redemption scheme that was applied against a minority of shareholders in the bank, which—save for the minority shareholders' stock—was taken over by another bank due to financial difficulties. The minority shareholders alleged that the takeover bank was not entitled to apply the provision in the listed companies act on redemption of a minority stock. The leaders could not identify all 15,000 shareholders (they applied for disclosure from the bank but were refused by the court) so formed a single purpose association of all those they knew about, and declared that to be the 'class' (giving them 100% ability to identify class members), which the court approved. The Association (and the class members individually) were granted free legal aid. The High Court found in December 2010 that the statutory provisions on compulsory redemption schemes could not be used, the High Court did not concur, that the minority shareholders had incurred any loss. The High Court thus upheld the Associations declaratory claims but dismissed its pecuniary claims. The case was appealed to the Supreme Court, which ruled in January 2012 by 6-3 that the bank's redemption was illegal, but by 9-0 that no loss had been suffered. Costs were awarded to the defendants with DKK 2,000,000 to be paid by the state (due to the legal aid).
1.9 Finland	No cases where the class action has been used in proceedings.
1.10 France	Following successful criminal proceedings, yhe consumer association *UFC Que Choisir?* sued Foncia in October 2014 in the Nanterre High Court of First Instance claiming that fees charged to 318,000 tenants for sending them monthly rent payment receipts for €2.30 per month were unfair. The estimated total loss is €27.60 per individual and €44 million in total. The case remains pending.
1.11	The *Confédération Syndicale des Familles* (CSF) sued Paris Habitat-OPH in October 2014 in the Paris High Court of First Instance claiming that charges for the installation of remote monitoring systems were illegal. The case was settled with a total payment of €2 million divided between 100,000 individuals.

Country	Case
1.12	*UFC Que Choisir?* sued telecom company *Free* in 2014 in the Paris High Court of First Instance on behalf of 141,632 individuals over poor quality of 3G mobile services between 2012 and 2015. Under a settlement in 2017, claimants were to receive between €1 and €12, totalling c €1.7M.
1.13	The consumer association *Consommation, Logement et Cadre de Vie* (CLCV) sued Axa and AGIPI on behalf of 100,000 individuals in October 2014 in the Nanterre High Court of First Instance claiming that a life insurance contract that guaranteed a minimum return rate was illegal. The case remains pending. The defendants made a procedural challenge in 2016, which was rejected by the Court of Appeal of Versailles in November 2016.
1.14	The Confédération Nationale du Logement (CNL) sued the housing group Immobilière 3F on behalf of 480,000 individuals in January 2015 in the Paris High Court of First Instance claiming that clauses imposing a penalty of 2% for delayed payments were unfair. Judgment was given in January 2016 that the action was admissible but the claimants had failed to produce evidence to support the allegations. Court of Appeal declared class action inadmissible in November 2017, as housing cases are excluded.
1.15	*Association Familles Rurales* sued telecom company SFR on behalf of 1 to 2 million individuals in May 2015 in the Paris High Court of First Instance claiming that information about the geographical coverage of the 4G network was misleading. The case is pending.
1.16	*Association Familles Rurales* sued camping company Manoir de Ker An Poul on behalf of 12 families in August 2015 in the Vannes High Court of First Instance claiming that the practice of requiring clients to purchase a new product every 10 years in order to keep their plot was abusive. The case is pending.
1.17	Association *CLCV* sued BMW Motorrad France on behalf of 600 individuals in December 2015 in the Versailles High Court of First Instance claiming that motorcycles were defective. The case is pending.
1.18	Following a successful criminal prosecution in 2016, *UFC Que Choisir?* sued BNP Paribas on behalf of between 2,000 and 5,000 individuals in September 2016 in the Paris High Court of First Instance claiming that information on the product 'Garantie 3 Jet' was misleading. The estimated total loss is €27.8 million. The case is pending.
1.19	Following a successful criminal prosecution in 2015, *CLCV* sued BNP Paribas Personal Finance on behalf of 4,655 individuals in November 2016 in the Paris High Court alleging unfair commercial practices including misleading information re the 'Helvet Immob' mortgage loan product; case pending.
1.20	Patient association *APESAC* started an *action de groupe* on behalf of 2,000 to 4,000 people in May 2017 against Sanofi over the drug Depakine alleging that it caused malformation and developmental problems in babies and children, and alleging lack of vigilance. Preliminary hearing in 2017. Case proceeding.

Country	Case
1.21	Trade association *Confédération Générale du Travail (CGT)* sued *Safran Aircraft Engines* in May 2017 on behalf of 34 employees alleging discrimination. Pre-mediation proceedings; case pending.
1.22	After the three main French mobile phone operators (Orange, SFR and Bouygues) were found by the Competition Authority to have been involved in a cartel over prices and market sharing, and fined €534 million, *UFC-Que Choisir?* initiated a lawsuit in 2006 to obtain compensation of €1.2 to €1.6 million paid by their 20 million subscribers in overcharges of c €60 each. 220,000 consumers registered on a website but only 12,521 sent the documents required to join the action. In December 2007, the Paris Commercial Court held the action inadmissible as the procedure chosen was a disguised *action en representation conjointe*, under whose rules soliciting of consumers was not allowed. That result was upheld by the appeal court and the Court of Cassation in 2011.
1.23 Germany KapMuG	After settlement of a US class action for $120 million, 17,000 small investors individually sued Deutsche Telekom, Kreditanstalt für Wiederaufbau and several banks in 2003 and 2004 before the District Court in Frankfurt, alleging that the prospectus used for the third initial public offering in 2000 was not correct with respect to the accounting profit of €8.2 billion from an intracompany sale of the US subsidiary 'Sprint' and the validation of the value of real estate owned by Deutsche Telekom. The test case procedure under KapMuG was brought into effect in 2005 to assist processing of this case. In May 2012 the Frankfurt Court of Appeals held that the prospectus was correct with respect to all the allegations raised by the claimants. The test case plaintiff appealed and in October 2014 the Federal High Court remanded the case, holding that the prospectus was at least partially wrong and misleading. The case remains pending before the Frankfurt Court of Appeals. In November 2016, the Court of Appeals issued a new test case decision, completely in favour of the test case plaintiff. The defendants again appealed to the Federal High Court. Meanwhile the test case plaintiff died. A new decision of the Federal High Court can be expected in summer 2018.
1.24	In October 2008 investors in Conergy AG sued the company over breach of accounting rules and producing late information. The case remains pending.
1.25	Various actions were brought in 2006-2008 against Corralcredit Bank AG over alleged delay in announcing plans to sue board members who had engaged in derivative activities. In August 2014 the Frankfurt Court of Appeals confirmed the main issues in favour of the Plaintiffs. An appeal is pending.
1.26	After Hypo Real Estate Bank almost collapsed in 2008, investors sued it alleging failure to announce information. The Munich Court of Appeals confirmed in December 2014 that the bank had misled investors. An appeal is pending.
1.27	Investors sued VIP 4, an investment firm for film, media and entertainment, over alleged false and misleading information in a 2004 prospectus. The Munich Court of Appeals confirmed the allegations in part in 2011. The Federal High Court overturned the decision in part in July 2014. Some issues were therefore resolved, and others remain before the Munich Court of Appeals.

Country	Case
1.28	In October 2015 278 institutional investors sued Volkswagen AG claiming €3.25 billion over admitted use of illegal defeat devices in levels of environmental emissions. In August 2016 the District Court of Braunschweig referred a list of 193 issues of fact and law to the Court of Appeals Braunschweig for a decision in model case proceedings. That Court of Appeals selected a test case plaintiff in March 2017. Many plaintiffs face a possible limitation barrier.
1.29	Investors sued Daimler AG over 2005 failure to announce an impending resignation by the Chairman of the supervisory board. The company was fined by the Federal Financial Agency BaFin, but that was set aside by the Frankfurt Court of Appeals. In 2007 the Stuttgart Court of Appeals held that the company was not liable for damages. The Federal High Court overturned that decision, and on re-hearing the Stuttgart Court of Appeals again dismissed the allegations. In 2010 the Federal High Court made a reference to the European Court of Justice, and after that the Federal High Court again overturned the lower court's decision. The Stuttgart Court of Appeals suggested a settlement. The parties settled the case and all claims were withdrawn in December 2016. The terms of the settlement were not disclosed.
1.30 Germany Unfair Competition and skimming odd cases	1. Action re advertisement for mattresses: dismissed 2. Action for disclosure of information re advertising for charges for mobile ringtones. 3. Action for disclosure of information on advertisement for mattresses; subsequent suit for payment; settled with €25,000 to Federal budget. 4. Action re calculation of currency conversion on telecom contacts: dismissed as only actionable individually. 5. Action for disclosure of information to calculate profit on banned ingredients in a medicine: dismissed as ingredients were legal. 6. Action, following injunction on an online advent calendar, for disclosure of information to calculate profit: successful. 7. Action re 'subscription trap': successful. 8. Action for disclosure of information to calculate profits of failure to advertise that services were free: partly successful. 9. Action for an injunction against use of standard contract terms in telecom contacts (successful): further stage re disclosure of information re calculating profits. 10. Action for disclosure of information by a dentist for calculation of profits: dismissed. 11. Action for disclosure of information and accounting against a savings and loan association re handling fees charged: successful. 12. Case re advertising of search engine as 'today free of charge'; undertaking signed 2006. Conduct continued. Action for disclosure of information to calculate profit 2007: partly successful, appeals until 2010. Claim for €400,000 ended with payment of €12,300.

Country	Case
	13. Case re standard contracts of a mobile phone service provider, re deposit of €9.97 for the SIM card, and 'no-use-fee'. Action in 2011: injunction granted, confirmed on appeal. The provider changed the wording re SIM card: second action 2013: held unfair and order for disclosure. 'No-use-fee' was banned in 2011; upheld on appeals: 2013 action to disclose information: ordered, upheld on appeal 2015. No compensation paid to date; no action for disgorgement brought, negotiations ongoing re €430,000.
1.31 Greece	Consumers association EKPOIZO sued Citibank in 1998 over surcharges for accounts that had an average balance below GRD5,000 and other general terms and conditions. The Association of Greek Banks intervened. The case lasted until 2001 when the Supreme Court partly upheld the allegations. It awarded GRD 30 million as moral harm.
1.32	Consumers association EKPOIZO sued National Bank of Greece and Geniki Bank over misleading advertisements on the Annual Percentage Rate (APR) applicable to consumer loans. After a year, the courts upheld the claims, prohibited the advertisements and awarded €10,000 moral damages.
1.33	Five consumer associations sued the Public Power Corporation (PPC) in October 2011 over the fact that their electricity bills to customers included a property tax mandated under Law 4021/2011 and a Ministerial Decision. The tax related to the enhanced supervisory and reorganisation measures of credit institutions and the ratification of the Framework-Agreement with the European Financial Stability Facility. The Ministerial Decision permitted the PPC to cut-off power supply to people who did not pay, and many were cut-off. The first instance court upheld the complaint, prohibited PPC from including the tax in its bills and from cutting-off power in any case, and recognised the plaintiffs' right to compensation. PPC appealed but withdrew the appeal and the initial judgment became final. PPC and the Greek State filed a motion against enforcement, and in December 2012 the Supreme Court decided in favour of PPC. In December 2014, finalised in March 2016, the Supreme Court upheld the constitutionality of the tax but not the power cut-offs. Parallel proceedings were brought in the administrative courts in 2011 and appealed in the Council of State in 2012, which also upheld the constitutionality of the tax but not the power cut-offs.
1.34 Italy	Since 2010, 58 class actions commenced; 18 declared inadmissible, 40 still pending; 4 decided on the merits, apparently only one of which was in favour of the class. Many re breach of contract, some public services, and some unfair trading or competition. See text for details of 49 cases. Some examples: 1. Unione Nazionale Consumatori sued a tour operator over a vacation package to Zanzibar where people were accommodated initially in a different hotel to the one stated, and then transferred to it but it was still under construction and did not have the amenities stated. Some consumers opted-in and 12 were awarded €1,300 each. The case was not appealed as the defendant was bankrupt.

Country	Case
	2. Altroconsumo succeeded against bank Intesa San Paolo's application of more expensive commissions. Only 3 of the class of 104 were compensated (€200) as able to produce supporting documentation.
	3. Claim by Codacons against a hospital Policinicl Gemelli di Roma over 188 children who contracted tuberculosis whilst patients, caused by an infected nurse who carried on working. Class claim permitted, but pending. Parallel criminal proceedings in which liability established for breach of safety rules.
	4. Adoc's claim against a bus company for inferior quality of vehicles was rejected on the merits in 2012 as manifestly unfounded.
	5. Altroconsumo's claim against RAI TV for breach of a public service agreement to provide impartial information, with 55,000 consumers registered on a website requesting refund of €500 each, declared inadmissible as class members lacked legal capacity to sue.
	6. Claim by a committee of commuters against Trenitalia over repeated train delays declared inadmissible in 2012 on various technical grounds, including lack of communality.
	7. A citizen's claim against a Florence public service provider forbad management of streets after snowing was declared inadmissible in 2011 (the law at the time applied only to products and not services).
	8. Altroconsumo case against transport companies for excessive boat trip prices, associated with a Competition Authority decision not then issued, abandoned as competition claims were not permitted.
	9. Codacons' case angainst Voden Medical for misleading advertising on the reliability of Voden self-testing product. The Court of Appel of Milan ruled in favour of the plaintiff and ordered Voden to reimburse the purchase price to all the clients who opted-in; the success of the actions was anyway limited by the very low number of opt-ins.
1.35 Lithuania	An investors' association claimed in 2013 against the auditor of an insolvent bank on behalf of shareholders who had bought shares in 2011. The court refused the class action as there was no commonality in the claims.
1.36	A municipal authority claimed against heat energy supply firms for unjust enrichment through charging higher prices than they were committed to purchase by public tender. The court declined to certify the class claim: firstly, the procedure had been conducted incorrectly and the notification to the respondent was too abstract and unclear for respondent to identify the scope of the group and the amount of damages suffered by each claimant; secondly, the representative did not have the power to lodge compensatory claims on behalf of each group member; and thirdly, there was no commonality of claims because factual circumstances were not identical or similar as the claimants based their claims on different contracts with the defendant.
1.37	An investors' association claimed on behalf of 100 people for a declaration that (a) their contracts to buy bonds in a bank that became insolvent were null and void as concluded under undue influence of mistake or misleading and (b) money transferred to the bank was as deposits. The court dismissed the claim as there was no commonality of claims.

Country	Case
1.38 The Netherlands	Settlements under WCAM are: — DES: 34,000 DES victims plus future vs. drug manufacturers—$48,000,000 (see below) — Dexia: 300,000 investment product purchasers vs. bank—$1,370,000,000 (see below) — Vie d'Or: 11,000 insurance policyholders vs. regulatory authority, auditors, and actuaries—$62,000,000 — Shell Petroleum: 500,000 shareholders alleging securities fraud related to restatement of petroleum reserves by Royal Dutch Shell—$352,600,000 (see below) — Vedior: 2000 shareholders alleging securities fraud related to merger and acquisition—$5,770,000 — Converium: 13,000 shareholders alleging securities fraud related to failure to disclose accurately loss reserves—$58,400,000
1.39	**DES:** Between 1947 and 1976, many women took the medicinal product diethylstilboestrol (DES) during pregnancy to prevent premature birth and miscarriage. It was later found that the drug was associated with cervical cancer and other injuries. In 1986, six daughters of women who had taken the drug initiated proceedings against thirteen manufacturers. The plaintiffs could not establish which manufacturer's product was responsible for their individual harm, but the Dutch Supreme Court held in a controversial decision that a theory of alternative causation could apply. The decision also required that DES-users should register in order to preserve their rights. After publication of this decision a DES Centre was established. Within six weeks over 18,000 mothers, daughters and sons had registered. Some estimates were that 440, 000 people might have been affected. The pharmaceutical industry and its insurers initiated negotiations and seven years later, in 1999, a settlement was reached that a DES fund would be established of €35 million, funded almost equally by manufacturers and insurers, on condition that the settlement would be final. Under the pre-existing law on collective actions it was required that all defendants should opt-in, which the defendants believed was unworkable, so they persuaded the Ministry of Justice to propose urgently an Act that adopted an opt-out procedure (WCAM), which came into force on 27 July 2005 and enabled the litigation to be settled.
1.40	**Dexia:** A company offered various types of equity lease agreements to customers from 1992, which involved the investment of loans in shares. A total of 713,450 agreements were concluded with 395,000 customers. After the share index (AEX) fell from 700 to 270 points between September 2000 and May 2003, the loan debts significantly exceeded the share values. Various collective actions were commenced alleging that the sellers had not alerted customers of the risk that share values could go down as well as up. Dexia Bank Nederland had acquired the loan company without knowledge of the exposure, the company having been merged into Dexia rather bought as a subsidiary.

Country	Case
	A mediation in 2005 between Dexia and various representative associations led to agreement that consumers would be paid all or part of their residual claims at the end of their contracts' duration, and the bank wrote off €1 billion. The Amsterdam Court of Appeal approved the agreement in January 2007. The settlement was therefore binding an all borrowers except those who opted out: 90% of consumers accepted the terms but 23,000 opted out. At the time of writing, a number of these opt-out cases are being pursued individually and remain unresolved, but many, usually represented by claims management intermediaries working on a 'no cure no pay' fee basis, have as yet not initiated individual proceedings. The Court established a team of 30 people (including 10 judges) to deal with the individual claims of those who opted out. Discussions have proceeded between the Court and the lawyers for the Bank and the individuals about which of several options might be agreed for proceeding to resolve these individual opt-out claims.
1.41	**Shell:** On 9 January 2004, following an internal review Shell (Royal Dutch and Shell Transport, the two former parent companies of the Shell Group) announced that it would re-categorize c 3.9 billion barrels of oil equivalent (boe) out of its reported proved reserves. The re-categorizations were based on a determination that the reserves did not strictly comply with the definition of 'proved' reserves established by the U.S. Securities and Exchange Commission (the SEC). On 24 August 2004, the UK Financial Services Authority and the SEC announced final settlements of their investigations with respect to Shell. As a result of the settlement, Shell, without admitting or denying the SEC's findings or conclusions, entered into a consent agreement with the SEC and paid a civil penalty of $120 million.
	A number of putative class actions were filed in U.S.A. against Shell in relation to the re-categorization. One class action was commenced in the U.S. District Court for the District of New Jersey. A non-U.S. shareholder, Mr Peter M. Wood, was recruited into that action through an appeal on the website www.royaldutchshellplc.com. The U.S. District Court for New Jersey initially ruled that Mr Wood could represent all non-U.S. shareholders, but a new judge reversed the ruling on the issue of 'subject matter jurisdiction'.
	After the announcement of the re-categorizations, the price of Shell's shares fell. Shell made an offer to compensate certain non-U.S. shareholders for losses alleged as a result of the price fall, without any admission of wrongdoing, illegal conduct, or causation of loss. Shell entered into an agreement with a foundation (the Shell Reserves Compensation Foundation) and various associations that represent the interests of retail shareholders and the institutional investors, including the Dutch Equity Holders' Association and others, under which non-U.S. Shell shareholders would receive $352 million. The agreement called on the SEC to distribute $96 million of the $120 million fine to the non-U.S. investors, an amount that corresponded to their share of investor base. The non-U.S. arrangement would benefit both the shareholders who were parties to the agreement and other shareholders who fell within the definition of Participating Shareholders. That agreement was contingent on the U.S. District Court of New Jersey declining jurisdiction over the non-U.S. investors, which it did on 13 November 2007, and on approval by the Amsterdam Court of Appeal, which is expected to rule in early 2009. An agreement approved in this way would be expected to be enforceable throughout the EU.

Country	Case
	In March 2008 Shell announced settlement in principle of the U.S. shareholder class action claims for an additional $79.9 million plus $2.95 million, being proportional to the amounts payable under the proposed Dutch settlement, plus legal costs, subject to approval by the U.S. Court. The U.S. Court approved the agreement and awarded lead counsel $33 million in fees and expenses. U.S. lead counsel was also paid $27 million for the contribution to the settlement in the Netherlands. The Amsterdam Court of Appeals approved the $353.6 million WCAM settlement in May 2009.
1.42 Norway	From 2008 to November 2011, 38 class cases were registered. Some were withdrawn or rejected. There were 22 rulings, of which 13 were approved and 9 denied
1.43 Poland	Class actions brought: TABLE_BELOW Some examples below.
1.44	In April 2011, the Warsaw District Court refused to certify a class action of victims of the collapse of the Katowice International Trade Hall. In September 2011, the Warsaw Court of Appeal rejected the appeal, making it final. The District Court held that a class action is admissible only if class members have non-personal claims (not related to personal injury or death), and as only 5 out of 16 class members had such claims, it was not possible for the class to be certified. The Supreme Court refused to consider cassation in 2012.
1.45	Flood victims sued the public authorities whose duty it was to maintain flood defences in the Sandomierz area on 1st September 2010. The 17 class members' claims amounted initially to over 9 million PLN. The class was divided into sub-classes: one claiming 100.000 PLN, another 400.000 PLN, another 600.000 PLN, and yet another 1 million PLN. After the Court of Appeal in 2011 demanded that the quantification of damages and specification of sub-classes be more precise, the lawyers and the class representative changed the claim to a mere declaratory relief, as it was very difficult to quantify the claims and each victim's losses were different. The class was certified in September 2012, and the court set the time limit for opting in to be 6th March 2013. There were around 300 victims (physical and legal persons), yet in September 2013 when the district court of Krakow finalized the class, it consisted of 27 members, with claims valued at 17,3 million PLN. The class won the case.

The table embedded in row 1.43 Poland:

Year	Cases brought	Returned for irregularity	Certification rejected	Case denied	Cases remaining
2010	21	–	–	–	–
2011	37	11	4	-	20
2012	35	10	6	1	33
2013	22	5	5	6	29
2014	41	7	9	2	51
2015	32	7	9	2	52
Part 2016	15	5	3	1	57

Country	Case
1.46	19 small business owners sued ZUS (the Office for Social Insurance), claiming they had been initially informed that when they officially suspended business their obligation to pay social insurance contributions with respect to the business would be suspended too. ZUS later changed its interpretation of law and demanded back payments with interest.
1.47	Flood victims in the Płock region sued public authorities for neglect in management and supervision of flood defences.
1.48	The Regional Consumer Ombudsman for Warsaw sued BRE-Bank (now MBank) in December 2010, alleging an unfair clause in mortgage contracts that resulted in the class members overpaying the interest on their mortgages. The district court certified the action in May 2011, and an appeal was rejected in September 2011. The class was advertised in January 2012, and the court declared the class closed in September 2012. The district court of Lodz decided for the class on 3rd July 2013. It stated that the court procedure should facilitate individual actions of class members against the Bank to recover the amounts overpaid, as well as possibly enticing the parties to settle with no need for further litigation. An appeal was rejected in April 2014.
1.49	An investment company Amber Gold invested in gold and some other commodities and, promising returns exceeding 10%, attracted thousands of investors. It operated from 2009, and it seems that since mid-2010 the financial supervision authorities had some knowledge of dubious practices taking place within the company. In August 2012, the company announced its liquidation and offered no money back to investors. The decision followed press and television coverage of the suspected failure of the business and financial crimes of its owner. The owner and his wife were arrested and face many years in jail. Prosecutors received over 4000 complaints, and the law firm dealing with the class action was contacted by over 3000 investors within two weeks. In August 2012, the class action (700 people collectively claiming 41 million PLN, although with an estimated loss for all investors of 200 million PLN) was lodged in the Gdańsk District Court. The class was divided into more than 100 sub-classes, each claiming different amounts. The future of this litigation was uncertain as the company was declared insolvent. A new suit was brought against the state, alleging that public prosecutors failed to act in a timely manner in reaction to a public enquiry into the company's finances. In March 2016, the Court of Appeal certified this class action, involving over 170 people with losses exceeding 21 million PLN, again with claims being standardised. Class members can join until 14 December 2016. A criminal suit against the couple has also commenced, and criminal courts in Poland have the power to order perpetrators of crimes to compensate their victims. Commentators are speculating that the civil suit will be concluded faster, as the prosecutors are planning to examine testimony of 430 witnesses.
1.50 Portugal	Consumers' association DECO brought three actions in 1998 and 1999 alleging that Portugal Telecom had over-charged almost 2 million customers a total of c €120 million (an average of c €60 each). A settlement agreement covered various situations, including the following: (a) every consumer who had his or her telecom receipts for the relevant years could present them to Portugal Telecom and would be reimbursed of the total amount overpaid;

Country	Case
	(b) since most of consumers did not have their telecom receipts, they could be reimbursed by making free calls on 13 Sundays (beginning in March and ending in June) and on the World Consumer's Day.
1.51 Spain	**The Endessa case.** An electricity surge in local demand in September 2007 led to failure of supply to 40,000 consumers. One month later, the consumer association OCU filed a collective action claiming undetermined individual damages for those affected. The association submitted a complex calculation that claimed over € 450 per day. The national regulatory body intervened, as a result of which Endessa made a general offer, with compensation to be paid through a scheme, and amounts varying depending on the consequences for individuals, ranging from €122 to €300. The consumer association rejected the offer. The court proceedings took until November 2011 (4 years), when the Court of Appeal dismissed the claim on the basis that there had been failure to prove individual damages suffered, and it upheld the compensation package that had been offered in 2008 by Endessa. In March 2010, there was another electricity failure, affecting 10,000 people and businesses. This time, OCU did not file a collective action because of the previous experience. Endessa made a settlement offer, which 99% of customers accepted, and the Girona Chamber of Commerce agreed to resolve individual issues through providing arbitration facilities.
1.52	**The NGC bank case.** This involved the validity of swap agreements, under which customers ended up owing the bank. They alleged a flaw in consent. There were thousands of individual decisions, which went for or against customers/bank, depending on individual facts. In December 2010, the consumer association ADICAE decided to bring a collective claim on behalf of 16,000 customers. In the event, 1,216 people joined the action. The same lawyer represented all claimants, with many identically drafted powers of attorney. The relief claimed was reimbursement of the initial payment. The consumer association needed to establish that the damage was caused by the same sole act event. In December 2012, the court held that (1) there was a lack of procedural standing by ADICAE and (2) there was misjoiner of actions in relation to the 1,260 aggregated cases. It would have taken perhaps 20 years for the court to work through all individual circumstances.
1.53 Sweden	Some 30-50 class cases have been brought since 2008, many of which have not been publicised. Details of 18 cases are in the national report: 1. 500 passengers sued the owner of the airline after it went bankrupt and they were stranded. Case settled with payment of SEK 810,000. 2. An individual sued a security company for setting up an illegal database of 658 suspected graffiti vandals, claiming SEK 25,000 per person. The defendant refused to disclose the names and the case proceeded as an individual case. 3. An association sued a life insurance company on behalf of 15,000 members when the proceeds of sale of a subsidiary's asset management business were transferred to the parent company. The group action was withdrawn and the case was settled in arbitration. 4. Eight people sued when they could not participate in an online game because of data transmission problems. The court declined to certify the class action.

Country	Case
	5. 30 property owners sued over disputed ownership of an electric heating facility located on their property. The case was settled.
	6. An individual claimed a refund of the difference between the amount invoiced by a phone operator during a period and the agreed rate. The District Court dismissed the case because the plaintiff failed to define the members of the group. The defendant changed its practice to comply with the claim and the case was dropped.
	7. Damages were claimed on behalf of 41 children who had been removed from municipal orphanages and placed in foster care. The court declined to certify the case as a class claim.
	8. Seven people sued the Air Navigation Services of Sweden on behalf of 20,000 over aircraft noise. A settlement was agreed in which the authority agreed to fund research to reduce aviation noise.
	9. An individual sued a university for gender discrimination on behalf of 43 people. The court awarded payment of SEK 35,000 per person, which was affirmed on appeal.
	10. An individual sued a university for gender discrimination on behalf of 23 people. The court awarded payment of SEK 35,000 per person, which was affirmed on appeal.
	11. The claim sought damaged for negligence by a bank when an unauthorised person withdrew funds from an account. The case settled and the court approved payment of SEK 200,000 to the plaintiff and 10 other group members.
	12. The Consumer Ombudsman sued an electricity company on behalf of 7,000 customers whose supply had been affected. The court and appeal court permitted a group action even though damages would have to be calculated individually (between SEK 1,000 and SEK 10,000 per customer). The case was settled and the company paid SEK 3,342,542 to the Consumer Ombudsman for distribution amongst 1,881 group members. Before the court action, the claim had been raised in the National Board for Consumer Disputes, whose recommendation against the company was not followed.
	13. A claim on behalf of 33 real estate owners demanding performance of a contract by a builder of a marina, alleging diminution in value of properties c SEK 500,000 each, was certified as a group claim and then settled individually.
	14. A group was certified against the State on behalf of 97 persons who had privately purchased alcoholic beverages online to be delivered to Sweden from abroad. Individuals claimed between SEK 800 and SEK 10,000. The court held that it was not possible to award damages, which was upheld on appeal.
	15. Individual claims were brought by 194 people over purchase of bonds that lost value in the financial crisis. The individual cases were settled.
	16. An association claimed negligence against the auditor of an insolvent finance company, with total damages of SEK 63 million. The court refused to certify the class claim as individual cases could be pursued.

Country	Case
	17. An association claimed against the State for violation of the European Convention of Human Rights for failure to prevent defamation when names were published on a webpage alleging the identities of convicted criminals. The court dismissed the claim because a non-profit organisation did not have standing in a group action. 18. An association announced a claim on behalf of a million members alleging overcharges by an asset management company.
1.54 Ukraine	288 people sued the owner of land from whom they had leased plots for 5 years for various breaches (non-review of lease remuneration, deterioration of soil caused by misuse of crop rotation and lack of soil fertilisation). The court upheld the majority of the complaints in April 2012. The court of appeal rejected the defendant's appeal. The Supreme Court quashed the judgment and remitted the caser for reconsideration in 2012 (reasons not published). Later, the Supreme Court accepted a cassation by an individual plaintiff and ordered termination of his lease agreement, reversing in part its previous decision to remit the case.
1.55 UK: England and Wales	101 GLO cases have been brought since 2000, numerically most for child abuse, followed by health, medical and pharmacological cases, and then claims by prisoners. Many cases collapse or settle. See text for some major cases.
1.56 UK CAT	After JJB Sports was fined for involvement in a cartel involving replica football t-shirts in 2003, the company gave 16,000 people an exchange of a current England shirt and mug with retail value £25, irrespective of whether the shirts had been bought in its shops of from other retailers. The consumers' association *Which?* believed that c2 million consumers had purchased shirts and that prices had been inflated by £15-£20 per shirt. In March 2007 it instituted the first collective claim for damages under Schedule 4 of the Enterprise Act 2002 in the Competition Appeal Tribunal. A settlement was reached in January 2008 that JJB Sports plc would pay £20 per shirt bought to those consumers who signed up to the action and could produce their shirts or other proof of purchase, and sign a statement of truth. *Which?* had been contacted by c 600 people (involving c 1,000 shirts), although did not have full details for all of them. A major dispute over costs took some time to resolve.
1.57 UK CAT	After a determination of infringement by the Competition and Markets Authority in March 2014 involving resale price maintenance from February 2010 to February 2012, an official of the of the National Pensioners Convention brought an action in the Competition Appeal Tribunal for damages against Pride Mobility Scooters claiming to represent 27,000-32,000 people, and claiming damages between £2.7 and £3.2 million. The CAT issued a preliminary judgment in March 2017 that the case could only proceed if it were significantly reformulated as to the basis of calculation of damages of each claimant. The representative withdrew the claim in May 2017, saying 'the case was not worth enough money to proceed given the costs', and she agreed to pay Pride £309,000 in costs.

Country	Case
1.58 UK CAT	After a determination of infringement by the European Commission in 2007 that Mastercard had breached competition law over business-to-business charges for credit card transactions, a representative claim was issued in the CAT in 2016 on behalf of millions of consumers, claiming £14 billion damages. In July 2017, the CAT rejected the application for a CPO as an opt-out class action.
1.59	In 2017 Richard Lloyd brought a representative action (CPR rule 19.6) against Google on behalf of an estimated 5.4 million users of the iPhone alleging that between 1 June 2011 and 15 February 2012 Google had illegally harvested iPhone users browsing data by bypassing privacy settings on the Safari browser without consent. Pending.

B. Civil Piggy-back on Criminal

Country	Case
2.1 Belgium	Gellingen gas explosion on 30 July 2004 on the construction site of Husqvarna Belgium from gas pipes owned by Fluxys. In criminal proceedings, 23 (physical and legal) persons appeared as defendant before the *Raadkamer* of Tournai, and later 14 defendants were referred to the magistrates' court (*Correctionele Rechtbank*). Around 600 persons joined as *parties civile*. On appeal, Husqvarna Belgium and Fluxys were fined, while other defendants were either acquitted or got a suspension of the sentence. The court appointed—apart from the magistrate—two '*experts coordinateurs et conciliateurs*' to (a) coordinate the expert operations, (b) operate as intermediaries between the court and the experts and (c) to work towards global settlements. Fluxys (the deep-pocket defendant) reached a settlement with the victims, possibly paying up to € 10 million.
2.2 Italy	The Parmalat bankruptcy caused heavy losses, and claimants joined the criminal prosecution.
2.3 UK: England and Wales	Compensation Orders are routinely made by Criminal Courts against those convicted. Orders are also made for the confiscation and forfeiture of assets, including a 'civil recovery' order without a triggering conviction. Statistics are not available.
	An example of disgorgement of profits was against an individual who sold unlicensed medicines as 'Flabjab' with a claim that it would lead to slimming. Product worth over £10,000 was seized by the MHRA. On conviction, he and his company were fined a total of £10,000, ordered to pay £19,000 in court costs, and ordered to pay £800,000 as disgorgement of profits under s 243 of the Proceeds of Crime Act 2002.
	An example of removal of the proceeds of crime was after a man was jailed in July 2016 for defrauding the electrical waste recycling industry out of £2.2million, obtained by falsifying paperwork to illegitimately claim that his firm had collected and recycled more than 19,500 tonnes of household electrical waste during 2011 which had never been handled. He was disqualified from acting as a company director for 12 years, on the basis that that he was 'a risk to the public'. The Environment Agency instituted proceedings to remove £2.2million from him as proceeds of crime.

C. Regulatory Redress

Country	Case
3.1 Denmark	The Consumer Ombudsman (the national consumer protection enforcement officer) has agreed a significant number of settlements with companies involving cessation, behavioural change and redress, including over: 1. unlawful charge for 'extra entries' in a telephone directory where no contractual relationship existed: agreed that c 400 customers could claim in 2009. 2. misleading financial advice by a Jyske Bank's marketing of investment bonds and a unit trust: payment in 2012 to c. 1,100 customers amounting to 80% of the total invested. This followed a rare case in 2009 in which the bank refused to accept the finding against it by the Danish Complaint Board of Banking Services. 3. wrongful retroactive revocation by Sampension of average interest rate guarantees: a payment to each policyholder of 5% of their account balance, plus the ability for individuals to renounce the transfer within 4 weeks. 4. improper sales campaigns over the sale of shares in Roskilde Bank: compensation of 60% of customer's net loss.
3.2 Finland	At the beginning of 2016, the Consumer Ombudsman was flooded with questions by consumers, claiming that the price increases intended to enter into force on 1 March 2016 by electricity transmission company Caruna, which had a monopoly in an area, had been excessive. The Consumer Ombudsman monitors inter alia the contract terms between electricity transmission companies and consumers in order to guarantee consumer protection. At the end of February 2016 the Consumer Ombudsman and Caruna reached a negotiated agreement that Caruna would not implement the proposed price rises, but would reduce its fixed basic prices for electricity transmission by 25 per cent for all customers and both of its network companies for the next 12 months, and not raise prices in 2017. During the negotiations, the Consumer Ombudsman considered commencing a class action but it was not necessary. After the Caruna price increases and negotiations, the Consumer Disputes Board received hundreds of calls where consumers have notified that they are not satisfied with the increases or the negotiated solution. At the beginning of April the Consumer Disputes Board outlined the reasonableness of electricity transmission pricing in its plenum.
3.3 Finland	The Consumer Ombudsman brought a complaint in the Consumer Disputes Board in April 2011 on behalf of a group of 11 consumers who bought shares in a housing company who alleged misleading information on maintenance charges of new apartments. The Board held in April 2012 that the information had been an estimate and no compensation was owed.

Country	Case
3.4 Hungary	Around 154 cases in 2015.
	The Hungarian National Bank (HNB) sued two undisclosed banks over contract terms involving unfair exchange rate provisions that left many customers unable to pay when rates moved unexpectedly. The HNB lost at first instance, won on appeal, and largely won in the Supreme Court. The outcome was a declaration that the terms were null and void. Consumers were able to benefit from this indirectly. The banks [were supposed] to refund sums overcharged to debtors. [Did this occur?]
3.5 Italy: Banca d'Italia	Since 2012, the Bank of Italy has initiated 7 proceedings pursuant to art. 128-ter of the Italian Consolidated Banking Law, addressed to 7 different regulated entities.
	In 4 cases, the proceedings were filed before the issuance of an order to redress because the regulated entity involved promptly refunded their customers, or consented to provide the Bank of Italy with detailed information about their initiatives. In those cases customers were granted refunds for a total € 692,345.67.
	In 2014, the Bank of Italy issued 2 redress orders concerning mistakes in the calculation of interest, for a total amount of €118,506,000.
	When discharging its supervisory duties under the Italian Consolidated Banking Law, the Bank of Italy usually asks regulated entities to adopt initiatives in order to refund customers for sums unduly paid, even without initiating a proceeding pursuant to art. 128-ter of the Consolidated Banking Law. In 2015, refunds stemming from informal requests by the Bank of Italy totaled c €65,000,000.
3.6 Italy: Regulatory Authority for Electricity Gas and Water (AEEGSI)	In 2016, orders were made requiring businesses to make (a) 155,769 compensation payments for breach of the rules on continuity of electricity supply, (b) 54,238 for violation of commercial quality standards. Notable decisions in 2011 included: 1. ENI fined €700,000 and required to update and complete all required tariff adjustments, and to provide proof to AEEG. 2. 71 water providers required to refund €55 million to 11 million customers after unlawful cashing of amounts as return on capital for 5 months.
3.7	AEEGSI is empowered to accept undertakings including redress in order to settle infringement proceedings, eg in 2016: 1. In proceedings initiated for delayed billing against about 86,000 customers, in both the gas and the electricity sector, ENI S.p.A. undertook to (a) pay €25 to all customers involved in disruptions for whom, on December 31th 2013, there was a delay billing; another compensation of €10 to customers for whom, on December 31th 2014, there was a further delay billing; (b) for all cases of delay billing, automatic extension and interest free instalments (in a number of monthly payments equal to the not issued invoices) on the owed sum, in order to reduce the inconvenience caused to customers; (c) other matters on future behaviour.

Country	Case
	2. In proceedings initiated for no or late provision of automatic compensation for failure to comply with specific commercial quality standards against about 8,700 customers, Acea Energia S.p.A. gave commitments to: (a) pay €15 to customers affected; (b) pay €15 to a different class of customers.
3.8 Ireland	An enforcement investigation by the Central Bank of Ireland found significant failures by permanent tsb and its subsidiary Springboard Mortgages Limited associated with tracker mortgage options and rates (failure to inform of the consequences of decisions to break early from a fixed rate or discounted tracker period; or failure to inform of a right to be offered a tracker rate at the end of a fixed rate period). The firms agreed to implement a redress and compensation programme in July 2015 to address detriment suffered by 1,372 customers arising out of mortgage overpayments, mortgage arrears, legal proceedings and in some cases loss of ownership of properties and some homes. An interim measure was to apply a reduced interest rate to all impacted accounts.
3.9 UK: Financial Conduct Authority	*Single firm scheme (FSMA s404F(7): a series of cases* 1. Bank of Scotland agreed with the FCA that it would compensate some customers related to interest rate variation on Halifax tracker mortgages. 2. Welcome Financial Services Ltd agreed with the FCA and the Financial Services Compensation Scheme after mis-selling PPI. 3. Three arrangements were made with the manager and two depositaries in Arch Cru funds over payment of £54 mullion to customers. *Consumer redress scheme (FSMA s404):* — Intermediaries involve in Arch Cru funds. *Multiple arrangements agreed through undertakings by firms, or 'in the shadow of the rules', including:* 1. interest rate hedging products (IHRPs) sold by four banks. 2. ATM withdrawals. 3. a structured capital protection and a guaranteed minimum return product (Cliquet) sold by Credit Suisse International and Yorkshire Building Society (both fined) in which both companies agreed to contact customers who bought the product between 1 November 2009 and 17 June 2012 to offer them the chance to exit the product without penalty and with interest paid up to the date of exit. 4. A compensation scheme agreed voluntarily by Affinion International Limited and the FCA in relation to various card security products sold from 2005 at an average cost of £25 each was approved by shareholders and the High Court, resulting in payment of £108.2m compensation to 533,000 claimants, an average of £203 per claim. Between April 2014 and November 2015, the FCA established *21 informal redress schemes*, which it estimates provided £131 million in compensation to consumers.

Country	Case
	Notable cases in 2016 and 2017 of any type: — 16/01/16 Ariste Holding Limited, trading as Cash Genie, agreed to provide over £20 million redress to more than 92,000 customers for unfair practices. — 24/03/16 Credit card firm, NewDay, refunded over £4 million to over 180,000 customers after it was identified that, in a small number of circumstances, default fees and other charges triggered additional charges in a way they considered unfair. In addition, delays in posting transactions also meant some customers incurred additional charges NewDay felt were unfair. — 19/09/16 Payday firm, CFO Lending, entered into an agreement with the FCA to provide over £34 million of redress to more than 97,000 customers for unfair practices. The redress consists of £31.9 million written-off customers' outstanding balances and £2.9 million in cash payments to customers. — 2/11/16 Motormile Finance UK Ltd agreed with the FCA to pay £154,000 in cash to customers and write-off £414m of debt following failures in due diligence and debt collection. A new IT system and CEO were installed. — 15/11/16 Dollar Financial UK, trading as The Money Shop, Payday UK, Payday Express and Ladder Loans, agreed to provide £15.4 million redress to 147,000 customers for unfair practices. — 8/11/12 Bank RBS, after an independent investigation and discussions with the FCA, instigated an automatic refund for complex fees charged to SME customers in its Global Restructuring Group, estimated to amount to c £400 million, and established an independent complaints process overseen by a retired High Court judge — 28/03/17 Tesco agreed to pay redress to customers who bought shares or bonds after 29/08/14 when it made a misleading statement about the value of its publicly traded shares and bonds. The compensation was estimated at £85 million to purchasers of 320 million shares. A compensation scheme was established and run by KPMG, overseen by the FCA. — 20/01/17 HSBC voluntarily agreed to set up a redress scheme for customers who may have suffered detriment by paying an unreasonable debt collection charge imposed by HFC Bank Ltd and John Lewis Financial Services Limited between 2003 and 2009. The total payments were estimated at around £4 million. — 17/02/17 Express Gifts Ltd, a direct mail order and online business with permission to sell general insurance products, entered into an agreement with the FCA to provide £12.5m redress to approximately 330,000 customers who were sold insurance that offered little or no value. The firm agreed with the FCA that the insurance cover it had sold did not provide adequate value to customers because, although it covered all items purchased, these were predominantly items of clothing, which customers would not generally consider insuring.

Country	Case
	— 27/07/17 Lloyds Banking Group agreed to set up a redress scheme to refund all fees charged to mortgage customers for arrears management and broken payment arrangements from 1st January 2009 to January 2016. Lloyds will also offer payments for potential distress and inconvenience, and consequential loss that customers may have experienced as a result of not being able to keep up with unsustainable repayment plans. Lloyds estimated that approximately 590,000 customers would receive redress payments, totalling around £283 million. — 24/10/17 After working with the FCA since 2014, BrightHouse undertook to pay over £14.8 million (in the form of cash payments and balance adjustments) to 249,000 customers in respect of 384,000 agreements for lending which may not have been affordable and payments which should have been refunded.
3.11 UK: Ofcom	Ofcom imposed a reduced fine of £2 million on television channel GMTV Ltd over viewer competitions between August 2003 and February 2007 under an agreement that included an extensive programme of reparations and remedies, including offering refunds on a potential 25 million entries; holding 250 new free prize draws, each with a £10,000 prize, for all entrants on the refund database, at a total cost of £2.5 million; and making a £250,000 donation to the children's charity ChildLine, to take account of the data it had not been able to retrieve.
3.12 UK: Ofgem	In the 13 cases concluded in 2015/16, £43 million was or will be paid out by licensees, almost all as compensation to affected consumers, or voluntary redress payments to charitable organisations. *An example of agreed enforcement action:* Seven companies in the npower group agreed with Ofgem to implement operational actions, make consumer redress payments totalling £26 million, and pay regulatory penalties of £1 each, after mis-billing of consumers, and poor handling of subsequent complaints, after upgrading its computerised billing system. *An example of Alternative Action:* In October 2016, Co-Operative Energy agreed to pay £1.8 million to customers affected by issues relating to its implementation of a new IT system. Any compensation that could not be distributed to Co-Operative Energy customers would be allocated to the charity StepChange, to help energy consumers who are in financial difficulties.
3.13 UK: Ofwat	In 2014 Ofwat accepted an undertaking by Thames Water on a £79 million prices reduction, spending £7 million on customers, and a £1 fine.
3.14 UK: Gambling Commission	In 2016 the Gambling Commission agreed a regulatory settlement with Betfred in relation to failures by the company's anti-money laundering and social responsibility policies, including payment of £443,000 to victims of criminal activities, and £344,500 to socially responsible causes in lieu of a financial penalty.

Country	Case
3.15 UK: competition	Many of the private schools in the UK were found to have fixed prices. If the OFT were to have imposed its normal level of fine, it would have had to have been funded by parents who had not paid the inflated prices, and many schools might have been forced into bankruptcy. The negotiated solution was that the schools would pay comparatively modest amounts into a scholarship fund for the further education of those pupils whose parents had paid inflated fees.

D. Ombuds

Country	Case
4.1 Belgium	After resolving a case of late billing (a €5,200 bill for nearly four years, resolved through a discount and delayed payment agreement) the Energy Ombudsman proposes a change to the standard payment agreement which leads to amendment of national law that no supply later than fourteen months before the latest meter reading can be charged to the consumer.
4.2	After receiving many complaints in 2002 about the charging of premium SMS services, the Telecommunications Ombudsman drew attention to the issue, as a result of which the sector took the initiative of drawing up a code of conduct in 2004 that resolved most of the issues. The Telecommunications Ombudsman continued to monitor complaints and draw attention to ongoing issues and a rising trend, such that the sector amended its codes in 2008. As a result of the code and its amendments, and a Royal Decree laying down the Ethics Code for telecommunications as of February 2011, the number of complaints over premium SMS services fell significantly over the next 3 years.
	The Ombudsman also drew attention in 2013 to similar problems with 'third-party services' being charged denominated as 'M-commerce' or 'MPay', which prompted creation of a further code (the GOF Guidelines for 'Direct Operator Billing').
4.3	The Telecommunications Ombudsman drew attention to the recurring problem of unanswered primary complaints by different operators in its 2002 annual report. In the 2004 annual report attention was paid to the complaints evolution at the alternative operators (Scarlet, Tele2, Euphony and Versatel), who at that time were going through major changes regarding their offer and customer base. Although operators were obliged to provide end-users from 2005 with a 'service for support by telephone', details were unspecified and practice varied. Acting on the recommendation of the Ombudsman, the Act stipulated that operators were no longer allowed to impose expensive numbers to contact their support services. The Ombudsman continued to monitor operators' complaint services and ton highlight strong consumer dissatisfaction, which led to legislation and other initiatives in 2011, after which operators began to improve their customer support services. Complaints about this issue are at an all-time low in 2016.

Country	Case
4.4	The Telecommunications Ombudsman noted a new category of complaints in 2004, over TV games where viewers were invited to send the solution to the question by texting to an SMS short number or by calling to an 0905 number. However, giving the right answer was not enough to win a prize, and further selection was undertaken. The Ombudsman recommended all operators to credit the calls to 0905 numbers, since the games were illegal games of chance. The sector took drew up a code of conduct, which the Ombudsman considered to be unacceptable. Telenet decided to credit disputed 0905 calls to the account of all customers who had submitted a complaint to the Office of the Ombudsman. Other providers declined. Legislation was introduced in 2009 on games of chance, and in 2011 to regulate them.
4.5	The Telecommunications Ombudsman drew attention to extensive problems over termination of mobile or fixed telephony contracts, which peaked in 2012, particularly over operators giving unclear information about certain terms of the contract, especially the duration of the contract and the amount of cancellation fees. Clarifying national legislation on the provision of information was introduced in 2010, and based on new EU provisions in 2012.
4.6 France	
4.7 Sweden	Since 1991 consumer-trader disputes may be brought before the National Board for Consumer Disputes (*Allmänna Reklamationsnämnden*), which may issue a recommendation. The Consumer Ombudsman may initiate a group action before this Board. 23 such group cases have been heard since 1991. The main cases (some of which mirrored other similar cases) and recommended outcomes were: 1. A dispute over a car leasing agreement and rights to change the monthly rent and over rights on return. Recommendation that two clauses were invalid and monthly rent should be reimbursed if inconsistent with the initial fee. 2. Cancellation of purchase of a computer course that did not fulfil consumers' expectations. Recommendation to reimburse less 10%. 3. Refund of purchase of a cruise ship holiday; withdrawn as the company had compensated people. 4. A clause allowing a cable television company to change the fees was held to be illegal; 60 customers should be reimbursed. 5. After devaluation of the Swedish currency, a clause permitting a price increase if currency fluctuations exceeded SEK 60 ws held illegal and the company should reimburse. 6. Lack of air conditioning on buses: company should reimburse 17% of tickets on buses with no air conditioning. 7. After VAT was increased, a company invoiced existing customers for the increase, without contractual authority: cease and reimburse. 8. Binoculars found to be useless and not of the quality an average consumer would expect so consumers entitled to terminate the contract and company should reimburse purchase price of SEK 229 and compensate extra costs. 9. Compensation for travel passes: application withdrawn by the Consumer Ombudsman.

Country	Case
	10. Refund of custody fees: application rejected as similarity criteria for group certification not met. 11. Mobile telephone contact gave consumers the right to use the subscription fee to make calls etc, but not if the consumer unsubscribed: held term was reasonable. 12. Electricity company failed to supply and customers took out contracts with other suppliers: first company should compensate for additional costs incurred by the breach. 13. Company purporting to charge for increased administration costs outside the contractual right: should repay the excess paid, as company bore the risk of changed circumstances in agreeing terms. 14. Passengers denied boarding by airlines: dismissed against all but one airline that was deemed responsible. 15. Claim that a concert did not meet expectations dismissed. 16. Ferry tickets cancelled and reimbursed price: should reimburse extra costs. 17. Claim for overcharge of management costs rejected: needed further investigation.
4.8 UK: Financial Ombudsman Service	Payment Protection Insurance (PPI) was sold at a rate of over 5 million policies a year during 2000 to 2005, with premiums in the region of £7 billion a year. Between April 2011 and November 2015 banks paid £22.2bn compensation, often pursuant to internal reviews required by the FCA. Of the over 16.5 million claims for compensation made by consumers to 2016, over one million were made to the Financial Ombudsman Service, which adopted a consistent managed approach to processing individual claims.

II. Cases Involving Injunctions/Market Behaviour (Not Compensation)

Country	Case
B.1 UK-Belgium	A trader domiciled in Belgium, Duchesne S.A., sent unsolicited mail order catalogues to UK residents together with notification of a prize win, usually £10,000. The OFT instituted proceedings for an injunction in Belgium under national legislation implementing the Injunctions Directive. The Belgian court issued an order banning the practice as constituting a breach of the Misleading Advertising Directive, on the basis that consumers believed that they had only to make a purchase in order to secure a prize, whereas winners were pre-selected and few recipients would receive a prize. The company was reported to have received about 4,000 orders per day from its catalogues, and many consumers complained. On appeal the injunction was upheld, with a penalty of € 2,500 per mailing issued in breach up to a maximum of € 1 million. The first instance court and court of appeal in Belgium reached different conclusions as to whether Belgian or English law applied, but the activity would have been a breach of both.

Country	Case
B.2 Bulgaria	Decision № 86/17.08.2015 of the Supreme Court of Cassation under commercial case № 616/2015. The action was initially brought by the Commission for Protection of Consumers (CPC) against one of the major energy supply companies requesting (a) the court to declare the clauses in the general terms and conditions of contracts for supply of electricity unfair and void and (b) an injunction. The CPC's costs were reimbursed by the respondent. The case took two years to go through three judicial instances to the Supreme Court of Cassation. All courts held for the CPC.
B.3 Bulgaria	Decision № 131/10.09.2012 of the Supreme Court of Cassation under commercial case № 1036/2010. Brought by the CPC against another energy supply company for declaration of invalidity of clauses in general terms and conditions. The case took about three years to reach and be decided by the Supreme Court of Cassation, which confirmed the invalidity of the clauses.
B.4 Finland	The Consumer Ombudsman brings c 20 cases in the Market Court every year relating to unfair business practice, and c 2 cases on consumer protection. Processing times are c 5-6 months. Examples [in the National Report] include: prohibiting a tyre company from using a mark specifying the parameters of tyres; an unfair term on parking fees; misleading price comparisons and special offer prices by a sport and recreation equipment retailer; unclear marketing by a vehicle inspection company; unfair marketing at children by McDonalds.
B.5 German skimming-off cases	12-15 private actions since 2004. 1. 2005 Action re advertisement for 'very good' mattresses: dismissed as the plaintiff could not prove that the breach was intentional. 2. 2007 Action for disclosure of information re advertising for charges for mobile ringtones, which were not free but incurred a monthly charge of €4.99: dismissed as the plaintiff could not prove that the breach was intentional. 3. Action for disclosure of information on advertisement for mattresses; subsequent suit for payment: settled with €25,000 to Federal budget. 4. Action re calculation of currency conversion on telecom contacts: dismissed as only actionable individually. 5. Action for disclosure of information to calculate profit on banned ingredients in a medicine: dismissed as ingredients were legal. 6. Action, following injunction on an online advent calendar, for disclosure of information to calculate profit: successful. 7. Action re 'subscription trap': successful. 8. Action for disclosure of information to calculate profits of failure to advertise that services were free: partly successful. 9. Action for an injunction against use of standard contract terms in telecom contacts (successful): further stage re disclosure of information re calculating profits. 10. Action for disclosure of information by a dentist for calculation of profits: dismissed. 11. Action for disclosure of information and accounting against a savings and loan association re handling fees charged: successful.

Country	Case
	12. Case by vzby re advertising of search engine as 'today free of charge'; undertaking signed 2006. Conduct continued. Action for disclosure of information to calculate profit 2007: partly successful, appeals until 2010. Claim for €400,000 ended with payment of €12,300 to the federal budget. No compensation was paid to consumers. 13. Case re standard contracts of a mobile phone service provider, re deposit of €9.97 for the SIM card, and 'no-use-fee'. Action in 2011: injunction granted, confirmed on appeal. The provider changed the wording re SIM card: second action 2013: held unfair and order for disclosure. 'No-use-fee' was banned in 2011; upheld on appeals: 2013 action to disclose information: ordered, upheld on appeal 2015. No compensation paid to date; no action for disgorgement brought, negotiations ongoing re €430,000.
B.10 German test cases by consumer associations	The consumer association sued a major trader of electrical appliances over peeling of the enamel on an oven after 17 months. The trader gave the consumer a new oven but requested payment of €70 in respect of 17 months' use. The consumer paid under reserve and the vzbv sued for return of the money. The European Court of Justice held that the German legislation banning traders from imposing such a payment violated EU law.
B.11 Greece	Crete's Institute of Consumers, the General Association of Greece's Consumers and the Association of Consumers of Aetolia-Acarnania) sued Eurobank in 2015 over housing loans in 2007 based on Swiss Franc currency. The court held that consumers had been misled on repayment calculations, and prohibited the bank from further challenging the terms and conditions. There were thousands of associated injunction actions. Case resolved in 9 months.
B.12 Italy	Associazione Movimento Consumatori sued about 15 banks over cessation of alleged unlawful behaviour and removal of effects. No damages claim was brought, only injunctive relief. These No official data available, but ACM should have obtained 7 favourable interim decisions (order of immediate cease and desist). Cases pending on the merits.
B.13 Poland	In 2015 the President of the Competition and Consumer Protection Office conducted 232 proceedings concerning protection of collective consumer interests and 754 explanatory proceedings. It issued 144 decisions on the merits, including 40 decisions concerning practices abusing collective consumer interests, 24 decisions ordering to cease using such practices and 80 obligatory decisions; only 8 decisions involved a financial penalty.
B.14	The Municipal Consumer Ombudsman in Warsaw started group proceedings in December 2010 against mBank S.A. initially on behalf of 835 consumers for a declaration that the bank was liable for improper performance of mortgage credit agreements in Swiss Francs. The District Court in Łódź and the Court of Appeal in Łódź held that the action was admissible. After the deadline for people to join the group expired in March 2012, in October 2012 there were 1,247 members. The bank lost an application and appeal for security for costs. After the bank submitted a defence in January 2013 and the claimant replied in February, the court referred the case to mediation, to which the Municipal Consumer Ombudsman objected. The court gave judgment against the bank in July 2013. The bank lost an appeal, the Supreme Court on cassation remanded the case to the Court of Appeal in May 2015 and it has not been concluded.

Country	Case
B.15 Romania	The National Authority for Consumer Protection filed 43 claims in Tribunals between 2014 and 2016, mostly against banks on unfair contract terms. It has been successful in most claims, but a definitive judgment was only given in one case. Some cases await a decision by the Romanian Constitutional Court. In some cases, consumer protection associations apply to intervene. It has been held that CPA claims for damages are inadmissible, and can only be brought by individuals.
B.16 Ukraine	A consumers' association claim that evaporated milk did not comply with consumer protection laws and was flawed and falsified product that could pose a danger to consumers. It ordered cessation of production and marketing.
B.17 UK	Various public authorities have power to order the cessation of unfair or illegal behaviour, or to prosecute companies for this.

III. Cases Identified by BEUC and COJEF

From *Collective Redress. Where & how it works* (BEUC, 2012), http://www.beuc.eu/publications/2012-00308-01-e.pdf

Cases included above: Dexia 2007; DES; JJB Sports, plus the following:

C.1 Portugal	Failure to refund full ticket price on cancellation of singer at *Operama Carmen* performance 1999.
C.2 Portugal	Activation fee introduced by Portugal Telecom in 1999. DECO group action resulted in order to refund €120 million to 2 million customers.
C.3 Spain	Advance payment in advance required by an English language school. 50% of students used a credit provider approved by the school, which required full continuation of payments when school closed abruptly. OCU's group action led to court order of refund of €50,000 plus interest. DECO achieved similar result in Portugal.
C.4 Spain	Action by DECO against electricity providers over negligence in maintaining the network, involving a 2007 blackout affecting 300,000 consumers. An opt-out claim led to an automatic 10% bill discount and option for individual compensation.
C.5 Austria	1,200 investors in Riegerbank lost 96% when it was declared insolvent. VKI sued on behalf of 820, with average losses of €80,000 (total €95 million).
C.6 Sweden	Bankruptcy of Air Olympic left passengers stranded across Europe. An action in Sweden, obtaining names from a criminal action, achieved settlement totalling €70,000 for 500 opting-in, approved by court in 2007.

From *Enforcement of Consumer Rights: Recommendations and Strategies* (COJEF II, 2016), http://www.beuc.eu/publications/beuc-x-2016-051_cojef_ii-enforcement_of_consumer_rights.pdf

C.7 Italy	Altroconsumo started 2 class actions for *unfair commercial practices* against Fiat and Volkswagen for compensation for damage suffered by consumers from misleading information on fuel consumption, in the context of use an outdated test, the New European Driving Cycle (NEDC), which allows for manipulation and unrealistically low figures, instead of a new and more appropriate test procedure, the Worldwide harmonized Light vehicles Test Procedure (WLTP) has been developed and is expected to be introduced under EU law.
C.8 Austria	VKI sued Raiffeisenlandesbank for issuing *unfair and aggressive practice* in schools inciting children to open a bank account, and offering an inducement to do so. Case settle on basis that the bank agreed to stop the practice and to abstain in future.
C.9 Germany	BVV sued Gameforce for *unfair commercial practices* in offering on online game to children (Annex I, nr. 28) under the name 'Runes of Magic' with pricing for purchasing items that was not clear until subsequently. The court prohibited the practice.
C.10 Austria	VKI case against Disney Universe similar to Gameforce; the court found no 'direct exhortation'.
C.11 UK	Campaign on *unfair terms and practices* by Which? that mobile phone service providers should unlock the costs of the handset from calls, texts and data, so that consumers did not continue paying for the handset after the end of a contract and inadvertently continuing on the wrong contract. EE announced a change in practice; regulator Ofcom took some action. Belgium introduced legislation in 2012.
C.12 UK	Campaign on *unfair terms and practices* by Which? that mobile phone service providers should not introduce RPI-based price rises during the minimum term of the contract. Ofcom issued new rules.
C.13 UK	Complaint by Which? over a misleading advertisement on the price indication of mobile phone contracts by 02 upheld by the Advertising Standards Authority, after Ofcom took action.
C.14 Austria	VKI case that A1 Mobilkom Austria omitted the 'activation fee' of €49.90 from its marketed pricing information upheld by the court, which granted an injunction but was unable to award compensation.
C.15 Austria	VKI sued a mobile phone provider for *misleading practice* in advertising phones for free when concluding a certain tariff plan with a minimum duration of 24 months, although the same tariff plan without the phone was cheaper. Case settled with an undertaking to change pricing practice.
C.16 Austria	VKI sued T-Mobile for *misleading and aggressive practice* in sending an SMS to customers to opt out otherwise they would be charged for an optional package. The Supreme Court prohibited the practice.
C.17 Various	Complaints over unfair terms and data protection breaches by various online service providers. Outcomes unresolved.

C.18 Various	Altroconsumo complaint to the competition authority against Apple after US competition authorities fined it for misleading practices and information as to the guarantee on its hardware products. Settlements agreed in various countries.
C.19 Portugal	DECO case against BigBank over hiding a different borrowing rate in a second credit agreement with consumers. Mentored Latvia.
C.20 Slovenia	ZPS campaign over high telecommunications fees, mentored by UK.
C.21 Slovenia	German vxbv mentored ZPS over billing practices of mobile phone companies.

From *Guidelines for enforcement on consumer rights,* Consumer Justice Enforcement Forum, May 2013, available at http://www.cojef-project.eu/IMG/pdf/Conclusions_document_cases__FINAL_8_May.pdf

	Country	Case	Issue
C.22	Italy then 10 others	Apple	Unfair marketing of commercial guarantees
C.23	Various, coordination by consumer associations	airlines	Unfair contract terms in airline contracts
C.24	UK supercomplaint, then BEUC	airlines	Price transparency and payment surcharges in the air transport sector
C.25	Bulgaria	Telecom companies	Unfair commercial practices in the telecom sector
C.26	Italy	Ship sunk	Costa Concordia
C.27	Belgium	Promotional pyramid schemes	Herbalife
C.28	Latvia	Energy charges	Passing on of gas debts
C.29	Latvia	Financial services	Consumer mortgages
C.30	Malta	e.communications	Unfair practices in telecom market related to consumer inertia
C.31	Austria [France]	Medical devices	PIP breast implants

INDEX